INTRODUCTION
TO MASS
COMMUNICATIONS

SECOND EDITION

EDWIN EMERY

Professor of Journalism
University of Minnesota

PHILLIP H. AULT

Executive Editor
Associated Desert Newspapers
of California

WARREN K. AGEE

Dean of the William Allen White
School of Journalism
University of Kansas

New York · Toronto · 1965

INTRODUCTION TO MASS COMMUNICATIONS

Second Edition

DODD, MEAD & COMPANY, INC.

LIBRARY OF CONGRESS CATALOG CARD NUMBER: 65–15617
PRINTED IN THE UNITED STATES OF AMERICA

FOREWORD

The second edition of this book, like the first, is designed to give the reader a full description of the mass communications industries, to introduce him to all the areas of professional work in journalism and mass communications, and to illuminate for him the importance of the communicator in modern society. It thus seeks to give every reader a comprehensive picture of the mass media upon which he depends so heavily as a citizen, and for those who are considering careers in mass communications it offers current and detailed analyses of the communications agencies which seek their talents.

Part I, "The Role of Mass Communications," is an introductory essay which describes briefly and simply the communication process and the role of the mass media in developing the political, social, and economic fabrics of a modern democratic society. In it, and throughout the book, the authors' aim is to answer in a positive, yet realistic, way the question: Is journalism a desirable profession, important to society? One of the best replies to this question was given by the famous editor-publisher Joseph Pulitzer in 1904:

Our republic and its press will rise or fall together. An able, disinterested, public-spirited press, with trained intelligence to know the right and courage to do it, can preserve that public virtue without which popular government is a sham and a mockery. A cynical, mercenary, demagogic press will produce in time a people as base as itself. The power to mould the future of the republic will be in the hands of the journalists of future generations.

The story of how the mass media came to occupy such a crucial role is told in Part II, "The Historical Perspective." One chapter reviews the unending battle to win and preserve the rights to print, to criticize, and to report the news. Another describes the technological growth of printing and the fruits of man's inventive genius in broadcasting and film making which have added so greatly to the impact of the "press" in the six decades since Pulitzer defined its mission. A third offers a comprehensive synthesis of the history of the printed media, in terms of journalistic trends and the contributions of men who helped to shape the American newspaper. New to this edition is a chapter which traces in detail the relatively brief histories of radio, television, and film, focusing on the news and opinion roles of these essentially entertainment media. Part III, "Current Problems and Criticisms," reports on research findings concerning public acceptance of the mass media, reviews the major areas of criticism of their performance, discusses social and economic pressures which impinge upon the communicator, and summarizes internal and external efforts to improve the quality of his product.

The major section of the book is Part IV, "The Mass Communications Industries and Professions." Nine chapters describe in detail how the mass media and related agencies are organized, their current sizes and roles, and opportunities and qualifications for those contemplating professional careers in them. The authors' aim is to present in each chapter a unified picture of a major area of journalistic work, and to note the interrelationships between the various media and between editorial, advertising, and management functions.

Areas described are those of the newspaper, at the weekly, small daily, suburban daily, and metropolitan levels; the magazine, including general and specialized periodicals, industrial editing, and free-lance writing; television and radio, with emphasis upon news and public affairs broadcasting; book publishing; film making; press associations and feature syndicates; advertising, including the media, agency, and company department fields; public relations and information writing; and the growing field of mass communications research.

Part V, "Education for Mass Communications," describes the growth and present status of education for mass communications careers, including expanding interest in the broadcast media and in graduate training in communication research. It also discusses professional careers in teaching at the high school, junior college, and college and university levels. Evidence is presented of the current widespread industry support for training of young people who want to know: Is there a place for me in one of the mass media and an opportunity for growth and advancement?

Suggested study questions and projects appear after each chapter and at the end of the book a selected, annotated bibliography is offered those readers who wish to explore further some of the many facets of mass communications.

The book throughout represents a pooling of the professional media experience and scholarly interests of its authors, who wish to thank a number of individuals for their aid and interest in the project. Professor Jack B. Haskins of Indiana University, former senior research executive for the Curtis Publishing Company, wrote the chapter on "Mass Communications Research" in consultation with the authors, who wish to thank him for his interest in this subject and in the book itself. Professor Leslie G. Moeller, director of the University of Iowa School of Journalism, reviewed the entire manuscript for the first edition and made many valuable suggestions and criticisms; Professor Joseph A. Del Porto of Boston University read galley proofs and made helpful comments. Dean I. W. Cole of the Medill School of Journalism, Northwestern University, contributed to the planning of the book in its earliest stages. Professor John T. McNelly of Michigan State University and Dean Hugh E. Curtis of the Drake University School of Journalism supplied criticisms in preparation for the second edition.

Among professionals in the mass media with whom the authors consulted were James A. Byron, news director, WBAP and WBAP-TV, Fort Worth; Andrew Stewart, president, Denhard and Stewart, advertising agency, New York; David F. Barbour, copy chief, Batten, Barton, Durstine & Osborn, Inc., Pittsburgh office; Earl J. Johnson, vice president, and William C. Payette, Southwest Division Manager, United Press International, Dallas; K. P. Wood, assistant vice president, American Telephone & Telegraph Company; and William Oman, vice president, Dodd, Mead & Company, Inc.

Professors of journalism or communications who were helpful in reviewing chapters of the book were Milton E. Gross, University of Missouri; Max Wales and Warren C. Price, University of Oregon; William S. Baxter, Howard College; R. C. Norris, Texas Christian University; James R. Young and William Robert Summers, Jr., West Virginia University; Baskett Mosse, Northwestern University; Scott M. Cutlip, University of Wisconsin; Henry Ladd Smith, University of Washington; and Sam Kuczun, Robert Lindsay, Harold W. Wilson, and Roy E. Carter, Jr., University of Minnesota.

The authors wish to thank all of these individuals, and others who have expressed their interest in the book since it first appeared five years ago. They hope that the many changes they have incorporated in this completely revised edition will meet with the approval of all who read it.

EDWIN EMERY

PHILLIP H. AULT

WARREN K. AGEE

March, 1965

CONTENTS

CONTENTS

PART I

THE ROLE OF MASS COMMUNICATIONS

CHAPTER 1

COMMUNICATION
AND THE
MASS MEDIA

WHAT COMMUNICATION MEANS

Man has another fundamental need beyond the physical requirements of food and shelter: the need to communicate with his fellow human beings. This urge for communication is a primal one and, in our contemporary civilization, a necessity for survival.

Simply defined, communication is the art of transmitting information, ideas, and attitudes from one person to another.

Upon this foundation modern men have built intricate, many-faceted machinery for delivering their messages. The unfolding achievements of science are making this communication machinery more and more fantastic in its ability to conquer the physical barriers of our world. Our minds and our electronic devices are reaching into areas not considered even remotely possible by our grandfathers.

Men hurtling through space send back radio reports of what they experience. Cameras mounted on rockets give us closeup televised photographs of the moon's surface. Television programs are transmitted from one side of the world to another by bouncing their signals off a satellite in orbit. Each year brings additional wonders in the craft of communicating our messages. With computers and instantaneous transmission systems we are bending time and space to our will.

Yet all this costly structure is a meaningless toy unless its users have something significant to say. The study of communication thus involves

3

two aspects—a broad comprehension of the mechanical means and, more important, an understanding of how men use these tools in their daily round of informing, influencing, inspiring, convincing, frightening, and entertaining each other.

Each of us communicates with another individual by directing a message to one or more of his senses—sight, sound, touch, taste, or smell. When we smile, we communicate a desire for friendliness; the tone in which we say "good morning" can indicate feelings all the way from surliness to warm pleasure, and the words we choose in speaking or writing convey a message we want to "put across" to the other person. The more effectively we select and deliver those words, the better our communication with him.

Contemporary society is far too complex to function only through direct communication between one individual and another. Our important messages, to be effective, must reach many people at one time. A house-wife who is angry at high meat prices may talk to a half-dozen neighbors about organizing a boycott, but if the editor of the local newspaper pub-lishes a letter she writes, she communicates her idea to hundreds of women in a fraction of the time it would take her to visit them indi-vidually. The politician running for the Senate spends much of his cam-paign time visiting factories and meetings, shaking hands with the citizens in the hope of winning their votes. He knows, however, that he can reach only a small percentage of the voters this way, so he hires time on television and radio to deliver his message to thousands of voters simul-taneously. This is mass communication—delivering information, ideas, and attitudes to a sizable and diversified audience through use of the media developed for that purpose.

The art of mass communication is much more difficult than that of face-to-face discussion. The communicator who is addressing thousands of different personalities at the same time cannot adjust his appeal to meet their individual reactions. An approach that convinces part of his audience may alienate another group. The successful mass communicator is one who finds the right method of expression to establish empathy with the largest possible number of individuals in his audience. Although this audience may number in the millions, the contact fundamentally is between two individuals: the mind of the communicator must be in touch with the mind of each recipient. Successful mass communication is person-to-person contact, repeated thousands of times simultaneously.

The politician reaches many more individuals with a single television speech than he does through his handshaking tours, but his use of mass communication may be a failure if he is unable to project over the air the same feeling of sincerity and ability that he conveys through his handshake and smile.

Thus the mass communicator's task breaks down into two parts, knowing *what* he wants to communicate and knowing *how* he should deliver his message to give it the deepest penetration possible into the minds of his audience. A message of poor content, poorly told to millions of people, may have less total effective impact than a well-presented message placed before a small audience.

Every day each of us receives thousands of impressions. Many of these pass unnoticed or are quickly forgotten. The effectiveness of the impression is influenced in part by the individual's circumstances. A news story from Washington about plans by Congress to increase unemployment benefits raises hope in the mind of the reader who fears he is about to be laid off his job; the same dispatch may disturb the struggling small businessman who sees in it the possibility of higher taxes. The communicator's message has had differing effects upon these two members of the audience; it may have none at all upon another reader who is distracted by a television broadcast while he is scanning the newspaper.

Obviously the mass communicator cannot know the mental outlook and physical circumstances of everyone to whom his message goes. There are many principles and techniques he can use, however, to assure that his message has an effective impact upon the greatest possible number of individuals in the largest possible audience. Some of these he learns by mastering the basic techniques of journalistic communication (writing, editing, newscasting, graphic presentation, etc.); others he learns by studying the mass communication process and by examining the character of the mass media.

Research men call our attention to four aspects of the communication process: the *communicator,* the *message,* the *channel,* and the *audience.* (In research language, the communicator is also known as the *encoder;* the message—whether words, pictures, or signs—becomes *symbols;* the channel, in the case of mass communication, is one of the mass *media;* the person in the audience is known as the *decoder.*) A properly trained communicator understands the social importance of the role he has undertaken and also knows what he wants to communicate as his message. He understands the characteristics of the channels (media) to be used and studies the varying interest and understanding levels of groups of people who make up the total audience. He molds his message to the style requirements of each channel he uses and to the capabilities of the audiences he is trying to reach. He knows about the limitations and problems which communication researchers have studied.

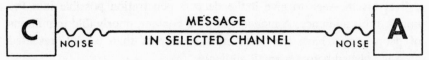

The communication process: Communicator (C) places his message in selected channel to reach audience (A) but is subject to "noise" interferences.

One of these is *channel noise,* a term used to describe anything which interferes with the fidelity of the physical transmission of the message (such as static on radio or type too small to be read easily); but broadly speaking, channel noise may be conceived of as including all distractions between source and audience. The professional communicator helps overcome its effects by attention-getting devices and by careful use of the principle of *redundancy* (repetition of the main idea of the message to make sure it gets through even if part of the message is lost).

A second kind of interference, called *semantic noise,* occurs when a message is misunderstood even though it is received exactly as it was

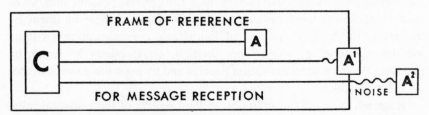

Communicator and audience member A have the same frame of reference; A[1] is only partially receptive; A[2] is unable to understand.

transmitted. The communicator, for example, might use words too difficult for an audience member to understand or names unknown to him (material outside his *frame of reference*). Or the words used may have one meaning for the communicator and another for the listener or reader (the common or dictionary meaning is called *denotative*, the emotional or evaluative meaning is called *connotative*—a word like "socialist" has widely differing connotations). Semantic noise can be reduced if the communicator will take pains to define his terms and adjust his vocabulary to the interests and needs of the audience he wishes to reach. Sometimes, difficult or strange words are understood by the reader because he grasps the *context* in which they appear, but it is also possible for a poorly defined word to be misunderstood this way. And if the material presented is too complex, the reader either will be forced to *regress* and restudy the message or, more likely, will turn to some other more rewarding and pleasant material.

Even if the communicator has surmounted all these hurdles, he still has other problems in message reception. The receiver interprets the message in terms of his frame of reference, we have said. Each person has a *stored experience,* consisting in part of his individual, ego-related beliefs and values and in part of the beliefs and values of the groups to which he belongs (family, job, social, and other groups). A message which challenges these beliefs and values may be rejected, distorted, or misinterpreted. Conversely, a person whose beliefs on a given subject are under pressure may go out of his way to seek messages bolstering his viewpoint. In cases where beliefs are firmly fixed, the communicator finds it is often more effective to try to redirect existing attitudes slightly than it is to meet them head on. Another audience problem is called *dissonance.* This occurs when a person takes an action which is inconsistent with what he knows or has previously believed, or else acts after considering two or more attractive alternatives. He is uncomfortable until he achieves some dissonance-reduction by seeking out messages which help adjust his beliefs to his action (a familiar example is the man who, having bought one make of car from among several attractive ones, continues to read advertisements for the car he bought—if he has switched makes, he needs even more reassurance).

The communicator is aided in his work by what are called *feedback effects.* These are reactions which take place along the communication process and which are transmitted backward: by the communicator (reporter) to his original news source; by another media worker (editor) to the reporter; by members of the audience to the editor, the reporter, or the news source; and by different persons in the audience to each other. Obviously there is much more discernible feedback in person-to-person communication than in mass media communication, and thus a better opportunity to deliver a convincing message face to face. But the communicator who has knowledge of feedback reactions in mass communication and who solicits them may enhance the acceptance of his messages.

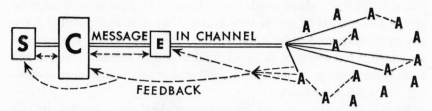

Mass communication for a given message at one moment in time is illustrated here: Source (S) has his message reported by communicator (C) in channel controlled by editor (E); some audience members (A) receive the message directly, others indirectly, but some are inattentive; feedback interactions may occur along the communication route.

All this is summed up in Professor Harold D. Lasswell's question: "Who, says what, in which channel, to whom, with what effect?" Chapter 17 on "Mass Communications Research" examines the different types of studies carried on by the mass media and by individual scholars to aid in more effective communication. The first steps for the would-be communicator, however, are to gain an understanding of the role of the communicator in our contemporary society and to examine the mass media through which audiences are reached. To take him through these steps is the purpose of this book.

WHAT ARE THE MASS MEDIA?

A message can be communicated to a mass audience by many means: hardly an American lives through a day without feeling the impact of at least one of the mass media. The oldest media are those of the printed word and picture which carry their message through the sense of sight: the weekly and daily newspapers, magazines, books, pamphlets, direct mail circulars, and billboards. Radio is the mass communications medium aimed at the sense of sound, whereas television and motion pictures appeal both to the visual and auditory senses.

The reader turns to his newspaper for news and opinion, entertainment, and the advertising it publishes. In the weekly the focus is upon the reader's own community; in the daily the focus is upon the nation and the world as well. Magazines give him background information, entertainment, opinion, and advertising; books offer a longer range and more detailed examination of subjects, as well as entertainment; pamphlets, direct mail pieces, and billboards bring the views of commercial and civic organizations. Films may inform and persuade as well as entertain. Television and radio offer entertainment, news and opinion, and advertising messages and can bring direct coverage of public events into the listener's home.

There are important agencies of communication which are adjuncts of the mass media. These are (1) the press associations, which collect and distribute news and pictures to the newspapers, television and radio stations, and news magazines; (2) the syndicates, which offer background news and pictures, commentary, and entertainment features to newspapers, television and radio, and magazines; (3) the advertising agencies, which serve their business clients, on the one hand, and the mass media, on the other; (4) the advertising departments of companies and institutions, which serve in merchandising roles, and the public relations departments, which serve in information roles; (5) the public relations counseling firms and publicity organizations, which offer information in behalf of their clients, and (6) research individuals and groups, who help gauge the impact of the message and guide mass communicators to more effective paths.

Who are the communicators who work for and with these mass media? We think of the core as being the reporters, writers, editors, announcers, and commentators for newspapers, news magazines, television and radio, press associations, and syndicates. But there are many others: news photographers; book and publications editors and creative personnel in the graphic arts industry; advertising personnel of all types; public relations practitioners and information writers; business management personnel for the mass media; radio-television script and continuity writers; film producers and writers; magazine writers and editors; trade and business paper publication writers and editors; industrial publication editors; technical writers in such fields as science, agriculture, and home economics; specialists in mass communications research; and teachers of journalism. Actors in television and motion pictures also are communicators in a special sense, adding emotional impact to the written script.

WHAT IS JOURNALISM?

A somewhat narrower definition is traditionally applied to the use of the mass media in order to identify the role of the journalist. In journalism there is an element of timeliness not usually present in the more leisurely types of writing, such as the writing of books. Journalism is a report of things as they appear at the moment of writing, not a definitive study of a situation. Historically the journalist has been identified by society as carrying out two main functions: reporting the news and offering interpretation and opinion based on news. A journalist may write an account that is entertaining as well as newsworthy; but a person who writes for sheer entertainment only, such as some television script writers, is not a journalist.

Periodical journalism constitutes the oldest and most widely identified area. Periodicals are printed at regular and stated intervals. To be considered newspapers, periodicals must appear at least weekly in recognized newspaper format and have general public interest and appeal. Commonly identified as "journalists" are the reporters, writers, editors, and columnists who work for newspapers, press associations and syndicates, news magazines, and other magazines devoted largely to public affairs, such as the *Reporter* or the *New Republic*. The print media they serve have been known collectively as "the press," although many newspapermen reserve that term for their medium.

News reporting and commentaries delivered by television and radio are equally a form of journalism, as are public affairs documentaries, direct broadcasts of news events, motion picture newsreels, and filmed documentaries. The reporters, writers, editors, and photographers in the television-radio-film area point out that the general descriptive term "the press" applies to them as well as to print media men when they are dealing with news and opinion. But they tend more often to identify themselves with the name of their medium than with the collective word "journalist." So do others in the list of communicators given above—photographers, book editors, advertising men, industrial editors, and so on.

The ephemeral nature of journalistic writing does not mean that it is poor and careless writing, as is sometimes assumed. Quite the contrary is true in many cases. Journalistic writing is a contemporary report of the changing scene, intended to inform readers of what is happening around them. The impact of journalism can and often does influence the course of events being reported, because it brings public opinion into focus and sometimes creates it. Thus the newspaper and broadcast reports of a president's stand on a foreign policy crisis can touch off heavy unfavorable reaction among the citizenry and force a shift in national policy.

The journalist deals in immediacy; he enjoys the stimulation of being close to events and the knowledge that his efforts can help shape the future. He is *communicating* the developments of the day to an audience whose lives are affected by the events he discusses. The sum total of articles printed in the continuing issues of a periodical constitutes a big slice of history as it is being made. Many of the facts reported in any issue soon are outdated by later developments; yet they are true at the moment of writing.

The television and radio journalist communicates news of contemporary events by means of electronic devices rather than with paper and ink. Although this makes the transitory nature of airwave journalism even more pronounced than that of the written word, it is not necessarily less effective and may sometimes be more so. Events with strong elements of sound or sight, such as a forest fire, a football game, or a political convention, are especially well communicated by television and radio.

Dramatic evidence of how electronic and newspaper reporting can dominate the life of the world during a great crisis is found in the reporting of the assassination of President Kennedy. The four days after the fatal shots were fired at Mr. Kennedy, including the subsequent murder of the alleged assassin, Lee Harvey Oswald, as millions watched in horror on television, and finally the somber grandeur of the Presidential funeral, were all splendidly reported by television, radio, and newspapers. They provided a massive portrayal of events and held the world tightly in the grip of intense emotion.

ALL MEDIA ARE INTERRELATED

Trying to separate the various mass media into tight compartments is a futile task, and pointless, too. They are closely interrelated, both in functions and in personnel. Employees shift from one medium to another with comparative ease. Certain details of technique are different and must be learned by the newcomer, no matter how much experience he may have in other fields, but the principles of mass communication among humans are remarkably similar in all media.

The newspaper reporter who happens to have a good voice may become a radio commentator. He must learn to write his copy in a more narrative style to please the ear rather than the eye, but the precepts of objectivity, fair play, and persistent digging for facts he learned on his newspaper beat still apply. Press associations supply the same daily budget of world and national news to radio and television stations as to newspapers, although the reports are prepared in slightly different form to meet the technical requirements of the various media. The broadcaster may desire to see his viewpoint preserved in more durable form, so he writes a magazine article or a book. An author whose novel becomes a best seller may soon find himself in a Hollywood studio writing screen plays at a salary that startles him.

A hard line of demarcation between motion pictures and television was maintained by the film industry during television's early years immediately after World War II. The film makers feared the commercial competition of TV. Inevitably this separation broke down because the two media are linked so closely in their appeal and techniques. Hollywood studios which once put clauses in their stars' contracts forbidding them to appear on television now film dozens of TV shows on their sound stages and outdoor sets. Numerous prominent motion picture actors "break in" on television, then move into films. Scripts first shown to the public as TV shows have been successfully expanded into feature-length motion pictures. Newspaper publishers also own about one-third of our television stations and one-tenth of our radio stations.

The mass media have a common need for men and women with creative minds, who can use words and pictures effectively to transmit information and ideas. This is true whether the communication is intended to enlarge the recipient's knowledge, entertain him, or convince him through advertising that he should purchase a commercial product or service.

Advertising is an essential part of the major media and constitutes an additional service to persons seeking that type of information. In newspapers and magazines, stories and advertisements appear side by side and are absorbed by the reader's mind almost simultaneously. On radio and television, presentation of the commercial has been developed into an intricate art, often closely integrated with the entertainment portion of the program which the advertiser also controls. At times, unfortunately, more ingenuity and effort go into the commercial than into the program itself. Large national advertisers conduct sales campaigns for their products in the press and on the air at the same time, spending huge sums to make certain that their messages reach a mass audience as frequently as possible. They are employing the proved technique of repetition. Without advertising revenue, newspapers and magazines could not be sold at their present prices and radio and TV programs could not be provided without charge.

Also, advertising has an important function in attracting an audience for the various media. The film studios, theatres, and television producers are heavy advertisers in newspapers and magazines, and newspapers take commercial time on radio and television to publicize their features in an effort to build circulation.

Thus it is evident that the mass media are heavily dependent upon each other. They turn to common sources for talent, for news, for ideas, and even for ownership. In the early days of radio, newspapers feared that the competition of this swift news-dispensing medium would ruin them; when television came along, newspapers, magazines, and motion pictures all were frightened of it at first. Gradually they learned that there is room and a need for all and that no medium need ruin another. The older media had to develop fresh techniques to meet the newcomer's challenge, and they improved themselves in doing so.

In the United States the mass media are commercial ventures, without government subsidy, and survive only if they make money. This is in the best tradition of the free enterprise system. They compete with each other for the audience's time and the advertiser's dollar. Yet all realize that basically they are serving the same purpose—to provide a transmission belt for the free flow of ideas.

SUMMARY

Communication is the art of transmitting information, ideas, and attitudes from one person to another. The mass communicator deals with a sizable and diversified audience, using the media developed for that purpose. His task involves both knowing *what* he wants to communicate and *how* he should deliver his message to gain the best possible effect upon the audience.

It is of primary importance that the communicator understand his role in our contemporary society and that he gain an understanding of the mass media through which audiences are reached. Then, by studying the communication process and by mastering the basic techniques of journalistic communication, he is able to do his job effectively.

The mass media include (1) those of the printed word and picture, which appeal to the sense of sight (weekly and daily newspapers, magazines, books, pamphlets, direct mail, and billboards); (2) radio, which is aimed at the sense of sound; and (3) television and motion pictures, which appeal both to the visual and auditory senses. Allied agencies of communication are the press associations, the syndicates, advertising agencies, advertising and public relations departments of companies and institutions, and research and teaching groups.

Among communicators of all types, the journalist traditionally has been identified as someone carrying out two main functions: reporting the news and offering interpretation and opinion based on news. One whose purpose is simply entertainment is not a journalist. Yet the functions of news, opinion, and entertainment are closely interrelated in the mass media, and the various media are heavily dependent upon each other, as succeeding chapters of this book will show.

STUDY QUESTION

What are the built-in problems of communicating on a mass scale?

PROJECTS

1. Clip a newspaper or magazine article and point out examples of "semantic noise." See if you can rewrite the faulty passages in order to clarify the meaning.

2. Write out your own definitions of (a) mass communication, (b) journalism.

3. Assume you have just been named editor of your hometown newspaper or manager of a hometown broadcast station. In 500 words or so, describe what changes, if any, you would seek to make in them, and explain why.

CONTINUING PROJECT

In order that you may become familiar with the literature of journalism and mass communications, and also gain insights into the very latest developments in the field, read *each week* an article in one of the trade or professional publications serving the various mass media and found in your school library. Insofar as possible read a *different* periodical each week. Turn in typewritten, single-spaced reports on 4″ x 6″ file cards, inserted horizontally and typed with almost no margin. Both sides may be needed. Place your name, date, and number of course in upper right-hand corner; title of article, name of periodical, and date of issue in upper lefthand corner; summary of content and author's treatment of subject in next paragraph, brief but adequate to indicate comprehension; and, finally, a paragraph briefly giving your evaluation and criticism of what you read.

A chapter from a book may be substituted from time to time. In addition, *Readers' Guide to Periodical Literature,* at the library, may be used to find suitable articles about journalism and mass communications in general interest magazines, such as *Saturday Review* and *Harper's.*

CHAPTER 2

THE SOCIAL
IMPORTANCE OF
COMMUNICATORS

COMMUNICATION, PUBLIC OPINION, AND DEMOCRACY

The mass media of communication play vital roles in our contemporary society. Those who work in these media hold positions of social responsibility, far more so than their friends in many other fields. Frequently their judgment is tested under pressure in matters of taste, social restraint, and fairness, with few absolute rules to guide them.

The jobs they perform make possible the general diffusion of knowledge about life in today's world and, more than that, influence many aspects of our social, political, and economic patterns. The communicator is a transmission channel for information. Also, by the way he selects and presents that information he helps in a small, sometimes unintentional, way to shape our society and contribute to its well-being.

Our mass media illuminate the social fabric of the nation. They are essential to the continued development of the economic fabric in a modern industrial state. And they continue to fulfill their historic role in protecting and improving the political fabric of a democracy. Among the many opportunities enjoyed by the communicator, none is more important than the opportunity to help shape public opinion.

In a democracy public opinion is the engine that keeps the wheels turning. Although we elect officials to conduct our government's business and give them power to make decisions which affect our pocketbooks,

16

our manner of living, and even our very survival, these men cannot exercise arbitrary power as is done in a dictatorship. They are restrained by the influence of public opinion—the very instrument that put them into office. If they stray too far from the desires of the mass of the people, counterforces begin to work. The most potent and obvious of these is the threat of defeat in the next election, a factor always near the surface of a professional officeholder's mind. More subtle forms of pressure can also be applied by adverse public opinion, such as moves to restrict the offender's responsibilities, damage his prestige, or discredit him in public.

Sometimes an excessive amount of time is required to correct a flagrant misuse of governmental authority, but ultimately it is almost always accomplished. In the long run, a democracy gets the kind of government that the majority of its people desires. To be successful, a political leader must convince the voters (1) that he represents the viewpoint of the majority or (2) that his policies are wise and should be endorsed by the voters.

How is public opinion brought to bear in political affairs, above and beyond the impact of events themselves? This is a complicated process insofar as arrival at a decision on an issue or an election contest is concerned. The average person is likely to be affected more strongly by social pressures, group associations, and the attitudes of "opinion leaders" he knows than by direct use of the mass media. These interpersonal communications act as channels to bring information and opinions to voters at the same time that the voters are exposed to the mass media directly. Since the social group and the opinion leader also reflect information and opinions gained from the mass media, there is a close interrelationship among the three—the mass media, opinion leaders, and the social group —in the decision-making process. Recent research indicates that a given decision is not influenced solely by what the voter learns directly from the mass media or by what he learns through the "two-step flow" of interpersonal communication (from the media to the group or opinion leader and then to the voter) but also by different types of communications at different stages of decision making.

But whatever other forces come into action, it is clear that the mass media of communication play a key role in the building of the political fabric of a democracy. They are the widely available channels through which political leaders express their views and seek to rally public backing for their policies. The President of the United States makes a statement in a press conference, and within minutes the news is sped around the world by the press associations. The American people read detailed accounts of his statement in their newspapers, hear summaries of it on radio broadcasts, and perhaps watch the President deliver his message on the television screens in their homes. President Franklin D. Roosevelt found his famous "fireside chats" on radio to be one of the most effective tools in winning support for his economic reforms and later in alerting the American people to the dangers of Fascist aggression. Development of television gave subsequent presidents even greater access to the public mind. President Kennedy used live televised news conferences with exceptionally good effect because of his easy delivery and quick wit. Many political observers believe that his performance in the televised campaign debates with Richard Nixon, his opponent, was the decisive factor in his election to the presidency. President Johnson chose to make less use of televised news conferences. Officials of federal, state, and local governments make use of the press conference, the radio interview, the television panel discussion, the magazine article, and even the book to reach the voters.

The media also work in the reverse direction to bring the officials news of what the people think and desire. Newspapers publish stories reporting the viewpoints of political opponents and the actions taken in public meetings concerning government policy; on their editorial pages they express their own reactions to developments and make suggestions; frequently newspapers publish the interpretative comments of well-known columnists. In the columns of letters to the editor the readers express their views. Still another form of expression appearing in the press is the public opinion poll, such as the Gallup poll or the Roper survey, in which carefully selected samples of the population are invited to give their views on timely issues.

Television and radio help to publicize this interplay of opinion through news reports similar to those appearing in the newspapers, interviews, and panel discussions. An especially effective television technique is found in programs such as "Meet the Press," in which a public official submits to intensive and sometimes belligerent questioning by a group of newsmen.

Weekly news magazines have become a significant factor in the two-way transmission of political policy and reaction. With more leisurely deadlines than the daily newspapers have, these periodicals provide background for the news developments and seek to put them into context. Magazines of opinion such as the *New Republic* or *Reporter* examine the news critically and express their views on its meaning, much as newspaper editorials do; whereas scholarly periodicals published at intervals of a month or longer delve more deeply into specialized aspects of the contemporary scene.

Books, particularly the heavy-selling paperbacks, convey facts and opinion about public candidates and officeholders. In many respects the paperback, often heavily subsidized and promoted by political factions, has replaced the political tract, such as Thomas Paine's *Common Sense* (1776), which was widely circulated in an effort to influence public opinion.

The political education role of the mass media reaches into the local scene, as well. If, for example, a municipal government decides to put into effect a new system of one-way streets, it turns to the newspapers, television, and radio for help in publicizing the plan. The newspapers publish charts of the new traffic routing and explanations of the streets along which cars are to move. The mayor broadcasts an explanation of the changes, and the stations repeat the instructions in their newscasts. TV viewers are shown pictures of the new routes, perhaps with cartoon figures being depicted following them. By the day the traffic plan goes into effect, a large majority of the motorists who customarily drive in the area are aware of the enforced change in their motoring habits. Without such publicity, there would have been a chaotic traffic tieup of bewildered, angry motorists.

The publicity process is of tremendous importance to public officials. Many of them owe their success in winning office to well-organized and cleverly conducted publicity campaigns. Some officials try to control the opinions of the citizens by manipulating and restricting the release of government information, with the hope that they can create a carefully calculated public image of a problem. If this image can be made to appear authentic, their own political solutions for the problem will seem more desirable; but if all the facts are made available to the voters, quite a different solution may seem best. Too many public officials are special pleaders for their own causes.

If political leaders attempt this approach, and many of them do, how does the public obtain the rest of the essential facts? It must depend largely upon the investigative work of the news media, which should be—

and usually are—dedicated to the cause of putting the complete story before the public.

The fight for free access to the news, from the national level in Washington down to the city hall in a small municipality, has become a major concern of the mass media. They are aware of the tendency among officials to make themselves "look good" by releasing and emphasizing facts favorable to their cause—the paper curtain of official mimeographed handouts which often stands between the public and the entire story. Diligent editors and commentators work on the principle that the public is entitled to all the facts in a political situation and that, on the basis of these facts, it can make its own decisions.

The news media have also the vital role of "watchdog" over the government, searching out instances of malfunctioning and corruption. In fact, if it were not for the searching eyes and probing questions of reporters, the public would have far less control over the affairs of city, state, and national governments than it does. Many of the most significant congressional investigations have been started as the result of revelations in the press. High government officials have been forced to resign because a reporter has uncovered evidence of unethical and sometimes illegal conduct by them.

Once a bad situation is exposed, public opinion can quickly be brought to bear for reform; but without the watchful eyes of newsmen to disclose the misbehavior, the situation might remain uncorrected indefinitely. Generally, the news media have been less zealous in observing the misdeeds of shady business enterprises, even when these have affected the general public welfare, than they have been in watching over the government.

Plainly, then, in a democracy the press is the "market place" of political thought. The policies and aims of government are made known through the channels of the press and are examined exhaustively by opposition political figures, and by commentators, editors, and the public at large. Stories from the newspapers and newscasts are used as the basis for discussions in classroom and clubs. When a high government official wants to test the public reaction to a policy idea, he often sends up a "trial balloon" in the form of a guarded newspaper interview suggesting the possible advantages of such a step, or he has a friendly columnist discuss the advisability of the move. Other editors and commentators pick up the proposal and examine it in print or on the air. Soon millions of Americans are aware of the tentative plan and are expressing either favorable or negative opinions. The official and his staff keep close watch on this reaction. If the plan encounters heavy opposition, perhaps stirred up by an antagonistic pressure group, the official quietly abandons it; but if it receives popular support, he takes positive steps to put it into operation, either by legislation or executive order. It is in such ways that public opinion shapes governmental policy in a democracy. Note the contrast in a dictatorship, where the ruling clique issues decrees arbitrarily and enforces them regardless of the public's feelings.

COMMUNICATIONS AND THE ECONOMIC FABRIC

Without an extensive and swift system of mass communications, the economic life of a major industrial country cannot function properly.

When we think how large the continental United States is—more than 3000 miles in width and covering many kinds of terrain, population, and living conditions—the degree of economic cohesion is remarkably high. People in the deserts of Arizona drive the same kinds of automobiles, wear the same makes of shoes, and eat the same brands of breakfast food as their fellow Americans in chilly New England. They are able to do so because of two major factors in contemporary American life—good transportation for moving the goods from the factory and a highly developed system of advertising and marketing.

Students of mass communications should be very conscious of the role and influence of advertising. Earlier we stated that three functions of the communication process are to inform, influence, and convince the public. Advertising performs these same functions. It informs readers and listeners about the products the manufacturer and merchant offer for sale; it influences them by stimulating their desire for those commodities; and, if it is successful, it convinces them that they should purchase the goods as soon as possible or as soon as they are needed.

Ever since this country was founded, Americans have lived in an expanding economy, except for a few temporary periods of depression. As the population grew and pushed westward, it automatically created a need for goods and services. But population growth itself would not be sufficient to keep the nation's industrial plants growing and its economy expanding, if Americans had not learned to want the products of those factories. Their desire for new products and their demonstrated willingness to purchase them encourage producers to develop attractive new commodities. With few exceptions, companies which spend money to advertise their goods become larger and more profitable than their competitors who do not. This lesson has been driven home so firmly that modern business practice leads most successful companies to expend fixed percentages of their income upon advertising. The advertising budget has become as essential in a company's financial operations as money designated for salaries, factory operating expenses, and distribution of the products.

It is no exaggerated claim for advertising to state that it has played a major role in the steady rise of the American standard of living, which has now risen to the highest point of any country in history. The existence of a free enterprise economy such as ours without advertising is inconceivable.

From the consumer's standpoint, the rival advertising of competing companies increases his range of choice and actually saves him time and money. From reading or viewing the advertising for new automobiles, he learns what new features each line of cars offers and sees photographs in color of the body designs. If his personal inclinations and the influences of his social group have given him a casual, indefinite idea of trading in his old car for a new one this year, the advertising brings him into action. He visits the showrooms of the cars which attract him most, and the chances are good that he will come home with a purchase contract in his pocket.

On a smaller scale, the dollars-and-cents importance of advertising in everyday living is evident if we watch a housewife read the grocery ads in her newspaper. She builds her week-end shopping list from these announcements. One market offers a special price on soap, another nearby market lists a bargain on pork roast. She decides to shop first at the market offering the pork roast, but may also visit the store featuring a special price on soap. Without advertising the housewife might have found these bargains by a prolonged search among the shelves, if she had the time. Or she might have missed them and paid full price for the roast at still another market. By checking the advertisements, she can shop more rapidly and effectively, and with an actual saving of money.

How does the food store benefit if it spends money on advertising to attract a shopper who buys goods at special low prices, thus reducing the shop's profit margin on those items? The answer to that question contains the secret of price advertising. The housewife saves money on the advertised items but having been attracted to the store by them, she is beguiled by point-of-purchase displays of additional items she hadn't realized she desired, and she buys these, too. The advertisement creates foot traffic in the market, and it is an axiom of merchandising that the more traffic that goes through a store, the more goods are sold. These additional purchases beyond actual realized needs help build our expanding economy.

Advertising in the United States is divided into two broad categories, national and local. National advertising is used by manufacturers to inform a nationwide audience, or perhaps a large regional one, about the advantages of their products. Sometimes a company devotes its advertising space to creating an image of itself in the public mind, emphasizing its reliability, friendliness, or public service, rather than concentrating upon a direct selling message for its products. This is institutional advertising, whose results cannot be measured directly upon a sales chart. Large corporations also use institutional advertising to influence public opinion on matters of national economic policy which are important to them. National advertisers use television, magazines, newspapers, and radio for the bulk of their advertising. Placement of the advertising campaigns is done through large advertising agencies, many of which have their head offices along Madison Avenue in New York City; these agencies earn their money principally by receiving a percentage of the price charged by the media for their space and time.

Local advertising is placed by merchants in their community newspapers and on their television and radio stations. It is directed to a well-defined, easily comprehended audience. Rarely does local advertising appear in magazines, because few periodicals have sufficient circulation concentrated in a single community. Chain-store merchandisers also use direct mail to distribute hundreds of thousands of advertising pieces called "mailers" at bulk rates. Sometimes these multiple-page advertisements are published simultaneously in newspapers. Whereas the main function of national advertising is to present products to a huge audience and to stimulate buying interest in them, local advertising is largely concerned with direct sales, making the cash register ring. Emphasis upon price is much greater in local advertising copy, because an attractive price is often the stimulus that converts the potential customer from intention to action.

The automobile manufacturer introduces his new models in the autumn with an elaborate national network television program featuring famous entertainment personalities and glamorous shots of the automobiles surrounded by beautiful girls. That is the national approach. A few days later the community auto dealer purchases time on his home-town television station. He appears on the screen, fondly patting the fender of a new model, and tells each viewer, "You can have this beautiful car for only $500 down. Come in and see it tonight; we are open until 9 p.m." That is the local follow-up.

A department store may take a half-page advertisement in a local newspaper just to publicize a bargain price for nylon hose. It knows that the expenditure will be profitable if the advertisement is attractive enough to draw a throng of women into the store. The item chosen is a low-cost one, regarded by most women as a necessity, with a frequent replacement need. Thus almost automatically thousands of feminine readers are potential customers for such a sale, if it is attractive enough.

At the end of the day the department manager can tell exactly how many pairs of stockings have been sold and compare this with a normal day's total. Thus he can measure the pulling power of his advertisement. However, the item may have been priced so low that, with the cost of the advertising added, the store may have lost money on the nylon hose sale. The venture would still be regarded as highly successful, however, if a large percentage of the sale shoppers bought additional unadvertised merchandise while they were in the store.

The mass media, then, play key roles in the business life of the country, at both the national and local levels of production and sales, by providing channels for advertising messages. They also help in other ways to shape the economic fabric of the country. They bring people, from industrial leaders to laborers, the necessary information upon which their business and personal decisions are based. They help the public to crystallize its attitudes on matters of national economic policy. They serve as sounding boards of public opinion for business, labor, agriculture, and other segments of society. Deprived of rapid and effective mass communications, a country whose sections and people have become as closely interdependent as ours would quickly tumble into economic and social chaos.

THE MASS MEDIA AS SOCIAL INSTRUMENTS

So far we have examined the mass communications industry in two of its major roles: (1) as the machinery for informing people and creating and reflecting public opinion in a democracy and (2) as an instrument for expanding our national economy through the power of advertising. A third important function is illuminating the social fabric and, in fact, influencing the shape of its patterns. The mass media serve the same purpose in transmitting the facets of our culture from the Atlantic to the Pacific as they do in binding the country together economically.

Virtually no aspect of our habits, desires, and relationships, both as individuals and as groups, escapes examination in our public media. Getting along with the neighbors, personal problems, our taste in popular music, racial tensions, athletics, interior decorating, teen-age dating, the role of organized labor, trends in fashion, the work and beliefs of religious groups—this melange of topics and a hundred others pertaining to the way human beings behave are constantly reported and discussed in the press, in books, and on television and radio programs. The methods of presentation vary widely. The treatment may be frivolous or soberly academic; the facts may be laid out starkly or clothed in the softer garb of fiction, depending upon the medium involved.

Our curiosity about each other as individuals is intense. We want to know how the other man lives. We chuckle at the ludicrous positions in which fellow humans entangle themselves and we read with sympathy of their tragedies. No matter how sternly he may deny it, every person has a little of the back-fence gossip in his soul; he likes to peek into the lives of others, whether merely to satisfy his curiosity or for the higher purposes of social research. Our books, newspapers, magazines, television, radio broadcasts, and films provide us with an abundance of such material. As we absorb our daily quota of such stories we are, without fully realizing it, receiving a multicolored picture of the contemporary social scene. The news media today are the recorders of day-to-day history on a broader scale than ever before. What historians who try to reconstruct the life of prenewspaper centuries would give to have similar material available about those days!

Any reader of the daily newspaper can, with a little thought, find a dozen ways in which its contents help to increase our social understanding.

Here is an example. Most people, even members of the Roman Catholic faith, have only the skimpiest knowledge of the lives of nuns. In their long flowing robes they seem to live in a world apart. Thus when Kathryn Hulme wrote a sympathetic, revealing, and true account of a particular nun's life, devotional duties, and psychological problems, her book, *The*

Nun's Story, was a national best seller. Hundreds of thousands of readers found it both an answer to their curiosity and an incentive to re-examine their own faith. Later millions of moviegoers around the world saw *The Nun's Story* as a film.

To read this book required several evenings; the film ran about two hours. Yet one of the book's main messages—that nuns are much like other people, despite their strict discipline and dark garb—was told later in a newspaper photograph which demanded only a few seconds of the reader's time. This showed a group of nuns in their black habits throwing bowling balls down a line of alleys, one nun biting her tongue in determination. Such is the communicative power of a picture.

A striking new style of dress worn by a famous actress in a motion picture can start a national fad. The weekly magazines and newspapers publish pictures of it; the television comedians joke about it. The fact of its existence is known quickly to millions of women, and soon many of them are purchasing mass-produced dresses in the same style. On a far more significant level, news stories of racial violence in the South when that region sought to adapt itself into an integrated society under pressure from federal courts and Congress undoubtedly influenced the subsequent outbreak of racial disturbances in Northern cities.

Editors are faced constantly with a problem concerning the type of material they should select for printing and broadcasting. At what level of education and interest should they aim the material they deliver to the public? Should they, for example, give prominence to the romance of two film stars on a European tour? Their dilemma lies in the fact that although the film stars' romance has no direct significance in the lives of the readers, most of them will read about it. In fact, readership studies indicate that stories of this type may attract far more readers than do reports of congressional debates, diplomatic maneuvering, and civic affairs which may surround them in print.

Should the editor in his wisdom dismiss the film star story as glamorous but trivial and omit it from his publication? Should he be teacher and literary censor for his readers or only the agent for bringing them what they will enjoy? Put still another way, how much should our mass media be used for entertainment purposes and how much for education? Should a radio station play only symphonic music when listener polls show a preference for jazz? Or only jazz when a substantial minority of listeners abhor it?

These questions have been argued for years without definitive results. Some contend that almost every story carries a moral or educational value, if the recipient wants to apply it. For example, a young actress with a famous name wrote a book about her dissolute life, full of sordid detail, which became a national best seller. Many readers were scandalized by her revelations but absorbed them avidly. Was this book sheer commercial sensationalism or did it, as those connected with its publication contend, illuminate a tragic life and serve as a warning about what is happening in contemporary society?

The old chicken-and-the-egg argument about which came first arises here. Do published stories and motion pictures about juvenile gang warfare and loose morals cause moral revulsion against such behavior, or do they incite others to similar misconduct? Arguments can be made in both directions.

Every person working in the editorial side of mass communications ultimately faces this problem in some form. The answers he reaches depend upon his tastes and the purposes of his particular publication. When a publication aims at a specialized audience, or at a cohesive group with known tastes, interests, and educational level, its directors can work out satisfactory ground rules on such matters. If the group to which the publisher appeals is too limited, however, his business fails and he has no audience at all.

In the case of the European film star romance, the New York *Times*, which has a reputation as the country's prime paper of record, might not have carried the dispatch at all, or at most it would have carried only a few paragraphs on an inside page. The New York *Daily News*, with a circulation that is greater than that of the *Times*, probably would have given the story a large headline. The tabloid *Daily News* is edited for quick reading by workers on the way to their jobs, crowded together in subways. The educational level of its audience is lower than that of *Times* subscribers, their reading time is less, and their desire for vicarious romance and adventure is higher. Both papers have skillful editorial direction; their treatment of news differs because they serve different kinds of audiences.

The problem of finding a suitable educational level is even greater for the largest and most costly of mass media, motion pictures and television. So many millions of persons see a feature film or a network television show that most sponsors and producers believe that they must seek a low common denominator in audience intelligence, for fear of boring a large portion of their viewers. As a result their shows are too often clever, slick, and empty. Also, in their fear of offending organized social, religious, and economic groups, they too often avoid dealing with major social problems. They set up a long list of tabooed subjects. Again, the effect is to rob their technically superior products of intellectual vitality. Happily, there are some courageous and mentally stimulating film and television productions which rise well above the general level, frequently dealing with mature, controversial subjects.

It is useless for extremists to argue that all mass media should be written and produced at a level suitable for a graduate school seminar, even though that may be what they desire for themselves. This would be unrealistic economically. Moreover, it would fail to serve the interests and needs of the mass public, unprepared to digest material at this specialized level. The sins of our mass media, however, are far greater in the other direction, of aiming their appeal too low. Wise editors and writers have found that even the most complex subjects can be presented in such a way that they can be understood by a mass audience and that such presentations find a ready public. The American public is able to absorb information and entertainment at a higher level than many policy makers in our mass media realize. Some of these policy makers have an ill-founded disdain for the public intelligence. This is one of the tragic misconceptions of our times.

There is need for the frothy episode, the titillating reports of romance and personal conflict, the crime story, the account of sports events; these are part of our social pattern and should be reported. Everyone wants some entertainment in life. The learned Supreme Court justice reads mystery stories for relaxation, and the corporation president pauses at breakfast to see if his favorite comic strip hero has extricated himself from his latest plight. But such aspects of mass communication should be kept in proportion and not be allowed to give the impression that our society is predominantly concerned with inconsequential affairs. A press that lionizes a gangster, emphasizes murder, and consistently gives the divorce antics of a popular singer preferential treatment over the significant news of the day undoubtedly has an adverse effect upon mass behavior, taste, and customs. Fortunately only a small number of individual units among the mass media are chronically guilty of this malpractice.

By and large, the mass media and those who work for them make an effort to record and influence the behavior of individuals and groups in the society of which the media are themselves a part. If they fall short, it is because this job is the most difficult of those undertaken by the media in their role of helping to shape the political, economic, and social fabric. There is room in the mass media for more men and women who are devoted to the improvement of our social pattern and who will seek to bring intelligent analyses of our problems to a public which equally is interested in social progress.

The responsibility of our mass media does not end with the factual reporting of news developments. Interpretation is also needed. What is the significance of this story? How is it related to events of the past and how will it affect the future? What interplay of forces brought it about? Unless such questions are examined in print and over the air, the deluge of news and pseudonews which engulfs the American public is only a chaotic jumble of names, actions, partial truths, and misconceptions. Our peril lies not in the lack of news and information, for no nation ever has had such an abundance at its command, but in the difficulty of sifting the significant from the inconsequential, digesting it, and comprehending the direction in which our society is moving.

The newspaper editorial is the oldest form of interpretation in the mass media. Having presented the facts of a situation in his news columns, the editor takes space on the editorial page to discuss the meaning of these facts, offer his comments about them, and perhaps propose actions to be taken.

Recent years have seen the rise of the newspaper columnist, who offers a highly personalized view of the news. Washington is the home base for most of the famous national columnists, whose work is distributed to hundreds of newspapers by the feature syndicates. Although some of these men and women present fresh factual material, most of them devote their space to an interpretation of national and international developments. To some degree the signed syndicated columnist has usurped the role of the editorial writers of the newspaper. However, a newspaper often publishes the columns of conflicting columnists to give its readers several viewpoints and then reaches its own editorial conclusions with little regard to the views of these men.

A third approach to the problem in newspapers is the interpretative news dispatch. Without offering an opinion, a skillful and experienced reporter tries to put the news into perspective by adding background information and showing cause-and-effect relationships. He doesn't say what should be done, as the editorial writer does, but reports what might happen on the basis of the information he has been able to gather. This type of dispatch, frequently called a "situationer," requires much skill in the writing lest it fall into the trap of editorializing in the news columns.

Radio's main interpretative work has been done by the commentator, who functions on the air much as the syndicated columnist does in the newspaper—a semiautonomous interpreter to whom the radio station allots time (usually paid for by a sponsor) but whose views are not regarded as those of the station management. For many years radio stations as institutions avoided taking editorial positions. Recently, however, this attitude has been changing, and radio is playing a stronger editorial role than ever before. Some stations broadcast clearly labeled editorials on local and national topics, repeating them several times a day to reach different segments of their ever-changing audience.

The television networks have developed reporter-commentators such as Walter Cronkite who present background studies of news situations in pictures and words, offering interpretation along with the information. These network personalities are supported by large staffs of cameramen, writers, and research teams to collect the information. Because of its strong visual impact, television is especially well adapted to the news interpretation role. A third of all television stations have editorialized fairly regularly since the late 1950's, frequently on local situations. Motion pictures generally have avoided editorial comment on news situations, except for production of some "message" pictures dealing in a general manner with such problems as racial discrimination and capital punishment. Some magazines conduct editorial pages, much like newspapers, whereas others leave the interpretative function to the writers of the articles they publish.

RESPONSIBILITY VERSUS PERFORMANCE

Like all other institutions of society, our press is imperfect. The greatest strength of our press lies in the fact that it operates as a competitive private enterprise—legally free to say what it wants—and yet it is from this freedom that its problems and shortcomings also arise. The Constitution of the United States guarantees the freedom of the press but does not define the responsibility of the press which should accompany the freedom. Interpretation of this responsibility is left largely to the integrity and the ethical and moral sensibilities of the men who write, publish, and speak. By misusing its power the press can easily inflame opinion and stir emotions in situations of social conflict so that great harm can result.

Our publications and broadcasts vary as greatly as the men who produce them. Some communicators bow too readily to the pressures of business and social groups and fail to exercise their press freedom fully for the common good. Other men, more concerned with profit than ethics, resort to sensationalism and intentional twisting of the truth in print; they are abusing the freedom given by the Constitution.

But where does sensationalism begin? One sincere man's definition may vary greatly from another's. At what point does the presentation of a political viewpoint become intentional distortion? Similarly, what one person wishes to read and hear is much different from the information of interest to his neighbor. There are few finites in the realm of public information.

The rapid breakdown during the 1960's on taboos against the showing of nudity and the increasingly open public discussion of intimate personal affairs has caused a major shift in the type of material shown on the motion-picture screen. Several Supreme Court decisions have greatly broadened the scope of sexual and social material that can be shown to the public without violating the law. In some quarters these developments are hailed as a victory for freedom of expression, in others as a trend harmful to the country's morals.

Television has reflected this trend in the choice of subject matter, but to a much lesser degree than motion pictures, because of its home audience. Newspapers have been even more cautious in liberalizing their treatment of moral material because of their family readership. A few magazines have pushed their photographic and written material seemingly to the limits of the laws governing pornography. Even so, there have been instances when the language in book excerpts reprinted in magazines has been toned down because the magazine editors were worried about postal regulations.

In general the trend is toward less and less legal restriction on what can be printed and spoken, from a moral standpoint. This increased freedom adds to the social responsibility of the communicator. He must keep asking himself, "Is this material I am offering the public a justifiable exercise of free expression, or cheap sensationalism merely for the sake of quick dollars?"

Our mass media serve many purposes and many tastes; therefore individual units differ widely in appearance, content, and manner of presentation. In this richness of variety there are abundant targets for the critics of the press, and the press would do well to listen to these critics more carefully than it does. However, the other alternative, a government-subsidized or government-controlled press, would be highly undesirable in a free country. The result would be dullness, stifled reportorial initiative, and, inevitably, a perverted presentation of the news. Despite its excesses and limitations, our press system is vastly preferable to any method of governmental control.

Another handicap under which the daily press, television, and radio operate is the need for speed. The daily television newscast is an intricate assembly line operation and cannot wait for the editors and writers to determine the ultimate truth in situations being reported. The same is true of newspapers. They must present the information available at deadline and leave to the more leisurely books and magazines much of the task of putting events into perspective. Thus the functions of the various media are interdependent. No significant news trend, and few insignificant ones, go unrecorded in at least part of our mass media.

Now we will see in historical perspective how the theory and reality of mass communications jibe, and then we will examine current criticisms of the media.

SUMMARY

The press is a fundamental institution of society, fulfilling a role that grows in importance as men are thrown more closely together and have an increasing need to communicate with each other. Collectively, the communicators who use the mass media thereby play key roles in shaping the political, economic, and social fabric. For individuals, the agencies of mass communication offer an opportunity to perform services of positive value to society.

Through the mass media, information and ideas are circulated to the population at large, and in turn the media reflect the opinions and attitudes of the public and of organized groups within the general public. In a free society the printed and spoken word are not merely devices for handing down decisions and carefully censored half-truths from on high;

they are the market place of public opinion from which political action can emerge. Skillful leaders can use the press to further their own policies, but if they get too far out of step with the public will, the press can become the instrument to defeat them.

The media, through the advertising function, are the means for bringing together the producer and purchaser of goods and services. Advertising is a part of the highly developed system of marketing upon which the economic life of a major industrial country depends. National and local advertising play related roles in the development of the economic fabric.

The media also are the means for recording and influencing the social behavior of individuals and groups. They illuminate the social pattern and transmit the facets of our culture from one ocean to another, just as they bind the country together economically. There are faults in the ways the media influence social action, just as there are faults in the social fabric itself. The press has yet to achieve its potential in such areas as interpretation of the news, and its very freedom makes for imperfections and misuse of power. But that same freedom offers the opportunity for the mass media and the people who work in them to perform more capably in the future.

STUDY QUESTIONS

1. Why is mass communication an essential part of our society?
2. What is the role of mass communications in linking the people and the federal government?
3. What factors determine the content of our mass media?

PROJECTS

1. Using books and periodicals available in your library, write a 500-word essay concerning the role of the mass media in influencing voting decisions. (See the bibliography at the end of this book for suggested references.)
2. Clip from your local newspaper two stories and an advertisement which you believe illustrate the role of mass communications in bulwarking the economy. Explain why in each case.

PART II

THE HISTORICAL
PERSPECTIVE

CHAPTER 3

THEORIES AND
REALITIES OF
PRESS FREEDOM

SOCIETY'S CRUCIAL FREEDOMS

The history of journalism and of the development of the mass media begins with the story of man's long struggle for personal liberty and political freedom, upon which the freedom to write and speak depends. It includes the record of technological progress in the use of the printing press, the film, and the airwaves for mass communication. The stories of how, over five centuries, the mass media developed their news, opinion, and entertainment functions are three of the main currents of this history. Finally, there is the relating of our journalistic tradition to the political, economic, and social progress of the people. The chapters which follow will complete this historical perspective; this one focuses on the story of men's unremitting battles for the right to communicate freely with fellow men.

Five centuries ago the printing press began to revolutionize man's ability to communicate information and ideas. But almost from the moment Johann Gutenberg introduced movable type to the western world, around 1440 in Germany, barriers were erected against its use to influence public opinion through the free flow of news and opinion. In the English-speaking world printers and writers struggled until 1700 to win the mere right to print. They fought for another century to protect that liberty and to win a second basic right: the right to criticize. Addition of a third right—the right to report—came equally slowly and with less success. Today's journalist knows that there remains a constant challenge to the freedoms to print, to criticize, and to report and that therefore the people's right to know is in constant challenge. This is true in the democratic western world where freedom of the press is a recognized tenet as well as in the larger portion of the world where it is denied. And it is true of the twentieth-century additions to the printing press: film, radio, and television.

Freedom of the press is intertwined with other basic freedoms. These are freedom of speech, freedom of assembly, and freedom of petition. Upon these freedoms rest freedom of religious expression, freedom of political thought and action, and freedom of intellectual growth and communication of information and ideas. A society possessing and using these freedoms will advance and change as it exercises democratic processes. Very naturally, then, these freedoms will come under attack from those opposed to any change which might diminish their own power or position in society—today as in past eras. The press, occupying a key role in the battle for these basic freedoms, is a particular target. To the closed mind, the press always has been a dangerous weapon to be kept as far as possible under the control of adherents of the status quo; to the inquiring mind, it has been a means of arousing interest and emotion among the public in order to effect change.

The social and political environments of the past five centuries have produced two basic theories of the press. The older we call the Authoritarian theory. The controlled society of the Renaissance era, into which the printing press was introduced, functioned from the top down; a small and presumably wise ruling class decided what all of society should know and believe. This authoritarian concept of the relationship between man and the state could brook no challenge from those who thought the rulers were reflecting error, not truth. Publishing therefore existed under a license from those in power to selected printers who supported the rulers and the existing social and political structure. The authoritarian press theory still exists today in those parts of the world where similar controlled societies are dominated by small ruling classes. A variant of this theory, called the Soviet Communist theory of the press by the authors of *Four Theories of the Press* (Fred S. Siebert, Theodore Peterson, and Wilbur Schramm; University of Illinois Press, 1956), arose with the twentieth-century dictatorship. Whether fascist or communist, it exalts the state at the expense of individuals and its government-owned and party-directed press is dedicated to furthering the dictatorship and its social system.

As the western world advanced through the Renaissance and Reformation into the democratic modern era, the second basic theory of the press developed. This we call the Libertarian theory. Its roots extend back into the seventeenth century but it did not become dominant in the English-speaking world until the nineteenth century. In libertarian theory, the press is not an instrument of government nor a spokesman for an elite ruling class. The mass of people are presumed able themselves to discern between truth and falsehood, and having been exposed to a press operating as a "free market place" of ideas and information, will themselves help determine public policy. It is essential that minorities as well as majorities, the weak as well as the strong, have free access to public expression in the press of a libertarian society.

In the battle against authoritarianism, the printer gradually became an ally of thinkers and writers who struggled for religious, political, and intellectual freedom and of the rising commercially based middle class which demanded economic freedom and political power in its contest with feudalism. Slowly the journalist evolved as one with dual functions to exercise: the opinion function and the news function. His media were the printed broadside and the pamphlet before he developed regularly issued newspapers in an established format. These appeared on the European continent before 1600, in England after 1622, and in the American colonies after 1704. In the eighteenth century they were joined by the early magazines. By our standards early newspapers were poorly printed, haphazard in content, and limited in circulation. But their influence can be measured by the amount of effort expended by those in authority to erect barriers against them and the stimuli to thought and action they contained. The traditions of freedom their printers and editors won by breaking down the barriers in the seventeenth and eighteenth centuries are the heritage of the modern newspapers and magazines developed in the nineteenth and twentieth centuries and of the film and electronic media of our times.

It was John Milton in his *Areopagitica* of 1644 who argued against repression of freedom of expression by advocating reliance upon truth: "Let her and Falsehood grapple: who ever knew Truth put to the worse in a free and open encounter?" Those who are afraid of truth will of course seek to prevent its entrance into a "free market place of thought," but those who believe in the public liberty should realize that its existence depends upon liberty of the press. Thomas Jefferson put it well in a letter to his friend, Carrington, in 1787:

I am persuaded that the good sense of the people will always be found to be the best army. They may be led astray for a moment, but will soon correct themselves. The people are the only censors of their governors; and even their errors will tend to keep these to the true principles of their institution. To punish these errors too severely would be to suppress the only safeguard of the public liberty. The way to prevent these irregular interpositions of the people, is to give them full information of their affairs through the channel of the public papers, and to contrive that those papers should penetrate to the whole mass of the people. The basis of our government being the opinion of the people, the very first object should be to keep that right; and were it left to me to decide whether we should have a government without newspapers, or newspapers without a government, I should not hesitate a moment to prefer the latter.

Jefferson qualified his final statement, however, by adding: "But I should mean that every man should receive those papers, and be capable of reading them." Jefferson used the word "reading" because the problem of absolute illiteracy still was a major one in his day; he meant also "understanding" in the sense of intellectual literacy. In these words of Milton and Jefferson are found the libertarian arguments for freedom of printing and other forms of communication, for freedom to criticize, and for freedom to report. They also argue for public support of the kind of mass media which carry out their responsibilities to provide free flow of news and opinion and to speak for the people as "censors of their governors." The ability of journalists to discharge their responsibilities to society is conditioned, as Jefferson warned, by the level of public education and understanding; there is a public responsibility in this regard implied in this philosophic statement of the role of press liberty in supporting all of society's crucial freedoms.

There is also a public responsibility, and a journalistic one, to maintain the libertarian theory that everyone can be freely heard in the press, through a variant concept called the Social Responsibility theory of the press. Today it is no longer economically feasible for anyone so minded to start printing or airing his views. Concentration of much of the mass media in the hands of a relatively few owners imposes an obligation on them to be socially responsible, to see that all sides of social and political issues are fairly and fully presented so that the public may decide. The social responsibility theory contends that should the mass media fail in this respect, it may be necessary for some other agency of the public to enforce the "market place of ideas" concept.

THE RIGHT TO PRINT

William Caxton set up the first press in England in 1476. It was more than 200 years later, in 1694, before freedom to print without prior restraint became a recognized liberty of the English people and their printer-journalists.

Prior restraint means licensing or censorship before a printer has a chance to roll his press. Unauthorized printing in itself becomes a crime. Under our modern concept anyone is free to have his say, although he stands subject to punishment if what he prints offends society (obscenity, sedition) or harms another individual (libel). Authoritarian government does not care to grant this much freedom; it wishes to control communication from the start and to select the communicators.

Caxton printed the first books in the English language and otherwise aided in bringing the culture of the Continent to England. He enjoyed royal support and needed subsidizing by the ruling class since his market was so limited by illiteracy. He and his successors improved the quality and volume of printing during the next half-century, which saw the rise of the Tudor dynasty. Henry VIII, in his efforts to grasp absolute power, issued a proclamation in 1534 requiring printers to have royal permission before setting up their shops. This was a licensing measure, imposing prior restraint. Except for short periods, the theory of prior restraint remained in effect in England until 1694.

Henry VIII took other measures to control the press, including banning foreign books, issuing lists of forbidden books, and punishing ballad printers who offended Henry and his powerful Privy Council. But neither he nor Queen Elizabeth I was able to frighten all the printers and writers into compliance. After 1557 the Stationers Company, an organization of the licensed publishers and dealers, was given power to regulate printing and to search out bootleg jobs which had not been registered with it. Severe penalties for unauthorized printing were imposed in 1566 and 1586, in the latter year by the authority of the infamous Court of the

Star Chamber. But despite arrests and smashing of presses of unlucky printers, some defiance always remained.

The struggle between the rising commercial class and the crown, which broke out into revolution in 1640 and brought the establishment of the Commonwealth in 1649 by Oliver Cromwell, gave printers some temporary freedom. James I and succeeding Stuart kings found that Puritan opposition was increasingly difficult to contain, and the journalists were more alert to their opportunities. Public interest in the Thirty Years' War on the Continent and in other political and economic affairs inevitably brought increased publication. Nathaniel Butter, Thomas Archer, and Nicholas Bourne produced the first regularly issued news book in 1621, on a weekly basis. Containing translated news from European news sheets, it was called a coranto. Diurnals, or reports of domestic events, appeared first as handwritten newsletters and later, after the Long Parliament raised the crown's ban on printing in 1641, in print.

But freedom was short-lived. By 1644 Milton was protesting against new licensing laws. After the execution of Charles I in 1649, Cromwell and his Puritan regime permitted only a few administration publications, censored by none other than Milton. The return of the Stuarts under Charles II in 1660 merely brought a switch in the licenser and censor to the royal party and more strict repression of unauthorized printing. Noteworthy, however, was the founding of the court newspaper, the London *Gazette,* in 1665. It remains today the oldest English newspaper.

The decline of the Stuarts, preceding the Revolution of 1688 which brought William and Mary to the throne, restored freedom to printers. Parliament allowed the licensing act to lapse in 1679. It was revived temporarily but finally died in 1694. Though severe seditious libel laws remained, and taxes on print paper and advertising were to be instituted beginning in 1712, the theory of prior restraint was dead. Newspapers by the score appeared in London, among them the first daily, the *Daily Courant*, in 1702. The early eighteenth century saw a flowering of newspapers and popular "essay" papers, edited by such figures as Daniel Defoe, Richard Steele and Joseph Addison, and Samuel Johnson.

Licensing and the theory of prior restraint did not die immediately in the American colonies. The Puritans imported the first press to New England in 1638 to print materials for their schools and Harvard College. Commercial presses followed, and some news broadsides and pamphlets appeared. In 1690 a refugee editor from London, Benjamin Harris, issued the first number of a Boston newspaper, *Publick Occurrences*, but his frank reporting nettled the colonial governor and council, which promptly ruled him out for not having a license. When the postmaster, John Campbell, brought out the first regular weekly paper, the Boston *News-Letter*, in 1704, he voluntarily trotted to the authorities for advance censorship and put "Published by Authority" at the top of his columns. It was not until 1721, when James Franklin began publishing his famed *New England Courant*, that a colonial editor printed in defiance of authority.

Freedom to print became an accepted principle in America; nine colonies had already provided such constitutional protection by 1787, when the Constitutional Convention met in Philadelphia. Many felt it was a state matter, but when the Bill of Rights was added to the Constitution, the First Amendment included freedom of the press among the basic liberties which Congress could not violate. Under British Common Law and American judicial interpretation, prior restraint violates press freedom. Suppression of publications in anticipation of wrongful printing, or licensing measures to control those who would publish, cannot be authorized by the Congress. In 1931 the Supreme Court for the first time applied the press guarantees of the First Amendment to the states, through the due process clause of the Fourteenth Amendment. The ruling came on an appeal against suppression of a Minneapolis news sheet under the Minnesota "gag law" of 1925 permitting suppression of malicious and scandalous publications. The court held the Minnesota law unconstitutional because it permitted prior restraint and said that those damaged by the newspaper had proper recourse through libel action.

Censorship is another form of prior restraint. In many countries today newspapermen's copy is subject to precensorship. This has never been true in the United States except for dispatches sent from battlefronts during wartime when censorship is exercised under military authority and in cases of outgoing dispatches in wartime which might aid the enemy. Since the Civil War, American newsmen have operated within the United States under voluntary censorship codes during wartime in publishing and broadcasting news. They have done so with admirable restraint.

The Post Office Department, with its power to exclude publications from the mails under certain conditions, has given publishers the most censorship troubles. Matters came to a head in 1946 after the department sought to withdraw use of the second-class mailing rate from *Esquire* magazine on the grounds that the rate was a privilege intended only for those making a "special contribution to the public welfare." *Esquire*, faced with an additional half-million dollars a year postal bill, appealed to the Supreme Court, which ruled in its favor. The court commented, "But to withdraw the second-class rate from this publication today because its contents seemed to one official not good for the public would sanction withdrawal of the second-class rate tomorrow from another periodical whose social or economic views seemed harmful to another official." The decision put the Post Office back to judging specific issues on the basis of obscenity or inclusion of illegal news of lotteries.

The motion picture industry has instituted its own regulatory code, as a form of self-censorship, through the Motion Picture Association of America. In addition, state and city censorship boards have exercised precensorship functions (increasingly challenged as unconstitutional by the courts), and pressures have been brought by such unofficial groups as the Legion of Decency. The same has been true of book publication; in addition, book publishers run the risk of having specific copies barred from the mails as obscene. Recent court decisions have tended to clip the powers of those seeking to restrict films and books, by drawing a line between material merely objectionable and that violating the courts' test for obscenity, but the issue has not been clearly resolved and the American Civil Liberties Union has been kept busy defending the right to print and the right to show films.

Radio and television, like the printed media, are not subject to precensorship. But more charges of "censorship" are raised in their cases, with the objection being to self-censorship or control of content in anticipation of adverse reaction. The broadcast media are more sensitive on this score because their managers realize that violations of what is considered to be "good taste" might cause difficulties for an individual station with the Federal Communications Commission under broadcasting's licensing provisions.

If history has proved licensing to be a dangerous practice inimical to press freedom, why did the American public agree to licensing of radio and television stations? The answer is that by common consent we have recognized that broadcast channels are in the public domain. Congress in 1912 first legislated that the Department of Commerce should issue licenses to private broadcasters and assign them wave lengths so that they would not interfere with government wave lengths. During World War I all wireless operations were put under government control, but by 1919 private broadcasters were again experimenting. Numbers of stations increased rapidly and chaos developed on the air waves. The radio industry, the National Association of Broadcasters, the American Newspaper Publishers Association, and other groups petitioned the government for relief.

This came from Congress through the Radio Act of 1927 which established a five-man commission to regulate all forms of radio communication. The government retained control of all channels, granting three-year licenses to broadcasters "in the public interest, convenience, or necessity" to provide "fair, efficient, and equitable service" throughout the country. Federal authority was broadened in 1934, with establishment of the seven-man Federal Communications Commission to exercise jurisdiction over all telecommunications. The responsibility of the license holder to operate his station in the public interest was more clearly spelled out. The commission was given the power to refuse renewal of a license in cases of flagrant disregard of broadcasting responsibility, but the FCC rarely has used this power. The law forbids any attempt at censorship by the commission; no station can be directed to put a particular program on or off the air. But the FCC undeniably is able to exercise indirect pressure upon license holders, who are understandably wary of its ultimate powers. FCC insistence upon stations building some record for broadcasting in the public interest has led to attention to news and public affairs programs; on the other hand, the licensing problem has led to broadcasters dragging their feet in airing controversial issues.

American radio and television are as free as American newspapers and magazines to provide whatever news their news editors see fit. Radio and television have also widely broadcast the opinion programs of individual commentators. But they have been reluctant until recently to broadcast opinion as that of the station itself. The FCC in 1941 issued a ruling that "the broadcaster cannot be advocate"; then in 1949 the commission decided that stations could "editorialize with fairness" and urged them to do so. Many broadcasters felt they did not have the trained manpower to do effective editorializing or did not wish to identify the station management as an advocate in controversial situations, and 15 years later only one-third of the stations were broadcasting editorial opinions (see Chapter 10).

THE RIGHT TO CRITICIZE

Winning the liberty to print without prior restraint did not free the press from the heavy hand of government. In eighteenth-century England, and in the American colonies, the laws of seditious libel ran counter to the philosophical theory that the press should act as "censor of the government." To the authoritarian mind, the mere act of criticism of officials was in itself a crime, and "the greater the truth, the greater the libel" was an established tenet. This meant that publishing a story about a corrupt official was all the more seditious if the official indeed was corrupt.

The journalist's problem was to establish the principle of truth as a defense against charges of sedition or criminal libel. Mere fact of publication then would not be sufficient to determine guilt, and the accused printer or editor would be able to present his case in open court, preferably before a jury. Once the principle of truth as a defense could be won, governments would be less likely to press sedition charges, and laws defining what constitutes sedition could be revised.

The landmark case in what is now the United States was that of John Peter Zenger, who was tried in New York colony in 1735 for seditious libel. Zenger was an immigrant printer who lent the columns of his weekly paper, the *Journal*, to the cause of a political faction opposed to the royal governor. Some of the leading citizens of the colony were aligned with Zenger in the struggle against the governor, whom they accused of various arbitrary actions in the *Journal's* columns. Zenger was jailed and brought to trial in a hostile court. At this juncture a remarkable 80-year-old lawyer from Philadelphia, Andrew Hamilton, entered the case as Zenger's attorney.

The crown prosecutor reviewed the laws of seditious libel and argued that since Zenger had admitted publishing the newspaper issues in question, the trial was as good as over. His aged opponent skillfully tilted with the presiding justice and the prosecutor and insisted that truth should be permitted to be offered as a defense, with the jury to decide upon the truth of Zenger's publications. These arguments were denied by the court, but Hamilton ignored the ruling and delivered a stirring oration to the jury. He ended with a plea for the jury to take matters into its own hands; "The question before the court . . . is not just the cause of the poor printer. . . . No! It may in its consequence affect every freeman . . . on the main of America. It is the best cause; it is the cause of Liberty . . .

the liberty both of exposing and opposing arbitrary power . . . by speaking and writing Truth."

Zenger was acquitted, and the court did not challenge the jury's verdict, even though it ignored existing law. A similar court victory on the issue of admission of truth as evidence was not won in England itself until the 1770's. The threat of trials for seditious libel remained until the end of the century, although in the colonies no further court trials of editors were held. Some editors were harassed by governors and their privy councils, but in general the colonial press was free to criticize the English authorities and to promote the cause of American independence (the reverse was not true, however, and Tory editors were suppressed by colonial radicals). By the early 1770's such papers as the Boston *Gazette* were openly seditious in their attacks upon constituted authority, but they continued to appear and to fan the fires of revolution.

Other editors besides Zenger contributed to the tradition of criticism as one role of the press. James Franklin, elder brother of the more famous Ben, proved a gadfly for both civil and religious authorities in Boston in the 1720's with his *New England Courant*. Benjamin Franklin was a cautious critic in his *Pennsylvania Gazette*. Colonial editors were vehement in their opposition to the stamp tax when it was applied to print paper in the colonies as it was in England. Isaiah Thomas, publisher of the *Massachusetts Spy,* and Samuel Adams, who used the columns of the Boston *Gazette* so effectively in his propaganda duel with the Tory Governor Hutchinson, led the patriot editors of the revolutionary period. Readers looked to their newspapers for opinion and partisan criticism.

Once the revolution was won, there was sharp cleavage along political and economic lines in the new nation. The newspapers continued to take pronounced partisan stands, accompanied by abuse and vituperation. The two political factions, the Federalists headed by Alexander Hamilton and the Republicans headed by Thomas Jefferson, split on many domestic issues and particularly over the country's emotional reaction to the French Revolution. Most of the weeklies and the few dailies which had started after 1783 were published in seaboard towns for the commercial classes and tended to be Federalist in sympathy. Hamilton sponsored some party organs in addition: John Fenno's *Gazette of the United States,* Noah Webster's *American Minerva,* and William Coleman's New York *Evening Post*. Topping the Federalist editors in partisan criticism was William Cobbett with his *Porcupine's Gazette*.

Jefferson countered with Philip Freneau's *National Gazette* and also had other Republican supporters, including William Duane and Benjamin Franklin Bache at the *Aurora*. The impulsive Bache, grandson of Benjamin Franklin, more than matched Cobbett in vituperative criticism. When it appeared that war with France was imminent in 1798, the Federalists decided to crack down on their tormentors.

The Alien and Sedition Acts they passed in 1798 were aimed at deportation of undesirable aliens and at curbing criticism of the government. Undesirable aliens in Federalist eyes were those who supported Vice President Jefferson; some were deported and others were harassed. The Sedition Act by its terms restricted prosecutions to those who "write, utter, or publish . . . false, scandalous and malicious writing" against the federal government, its officials and legislators, or its laws (including the Sedition Act itself). It provided for admission of truth as a defense. In theory, only false criticism was to be punished; but in practice, Federalist politicians and judges set out to punish anti-Federalist editors. One, for example, was jailed and fined for printing a letter to the editor which accused President John Adams of "ridiculous pomp, foolish adulation, and selfish avarice."

Vice President Jefferson, fearful for his own safety, retired to Monticello, where he and his supporters drafted the Virginia and Kentucky Resolutions, advocating the theory of nullification by the states of unconstitutional acts of the Congress. But the issue did not need to be joined; Federalist excesses in administering the Alien and Sedition Acts contributed to a popular revulsion and to Jefferson's election as President in 1800. The dangerous Alien and Sedition Acts expired the same year. Jefferson insisted that his administration permit partisan journalism, "to demonstrate the falsehood of the pretext that freedom of the press is incompatible with orderly government." He urged that individuals protect themselves against journalistic excesses by filing civil suits for libel. The calm course Jefferson took was vindicated when his party retained control of the government for a generation. Party newspapers, with one-sided news and fiercely partisan opinion, continued to flourish, but after the great crisis of 1798 no federal administration attempted to repress criticism. Soon after 1800 the libertarian theory of the press had eclipsed the authoritarian theory by common consent.

During wartime, national safety requirements and emotional feelings bring some restriction of criticism. The Civil War saw suppression of a few newspapers in the North, but considering the violence of many editors' criticisms, retaliation by Lincoln and his generals was almost negligible. During World War I, the Espionage Act of 1917 widened the authority of the Post Office Department to bar periodicals from the mails, and the Sedition Act of 1918 made it a crime to write or publish "any disloyal, profane, scurrilous or abusive language" about the federal government. The axe fell heavily upon German-language newspapers, in many cases unfairly. It also fell upon Socialist magazines and newspapers, because they opposed the war, and upon pacifist publications. Max Eastman's brilliant magazine, *The Masses*, was barred from the mails, as were two leading Socialist dailies, the New York *Call* and the Milwaukee *Leader*. Socialist party leader Eugene Debs went to prison for criticizing America's allies as "out for plunder." Clearly the theory of liberty to criticize was disregarded in these violations of minority opinion rights. During World War II only a few pro-Nazi and Fascist publications were banned—and they had few friends to plead their cause.

The right to criticize needs constant protection, as was demonstrated when Louisiana political boss Huey Long attempted to punish newspaper opponents through taxation. Long and his political machine imposed a special tax on the advertising income of larger Louisiana dailies, virtually all opposed to him. The Supreme Court held the punitive tax unconstitutional in 1936. In the early 1950's courageous newspapers and magazines which spoke out against Senator Joseph McCarthy of Wisconsin, and what became known as McCarthyism, were harassed and denounced. But neither McCarthy nor his followers could bring about actual legislation restricting criticism, much as they might have liked to do so.

Contempt-of-court citations bring about another kind of clash over the right to criticize. A series of Supreme Court decisions in the 1940's widened the freedom of newspapers to comment upon pending court cases and actions of judges. This was done by applying the "clear and present danger" theory to a judge's contention that administration of justice was being impeded by newspaper comment. But judges have great power in contempt-of-court matters and editors remain wary of criticizing their acts without pressing need to do so.

THE RIGHT TO REPORT

The right to report is not nearly as much a right safeguarded by law and legal precedent as the right to print and the right to criticize. Rather, it is based on a philosophical argument. What would be gained through the right to print and to criticize if no news were forthcoming? What good would a free press be for the reader if editors and reporters had no way to find out what government was going? Denial of the right of access to news is a denial of the people's right to know, the journalist maintains.

Yet, no person can be compelled to talk to a reporter; no government official need grant an interview or hold a press conference; courts and legislatures admit the press through historical tradition and have the power to eject the press (unless specific statutes have been passed requiring open legislative sessions). There is another side to the coin: no news medium can be compelled to print or broadcast any material it does not wish to use, including paid advertising.

While the laws of seditious libel were in vogue, no right to report was recognized. The mere reporting of a government official's action, or of a debate in Parliament, was likely to be construed as seditious (unfavorable) by some person in authority. William Bradford in Pennsylvania, James Franklin in Massachusetts, and other colonial editors were haled before authorities for reporting a disputed action of government. In England, reporting of the proceedings of Parliament was banned until 1771, when the satirical writings of Dr. Samuel Johnson and the open defiance of newspaper publisher John Wilkes crumpled the opposition.

The House of Representatives of the American Congress opened its doors to reporters in 1789, two days after it was organized as a legislative body. The Senate, however, excluded reporters until 1795. Congress came to depend upon newsmen, particularly the editors of the Jeffersonian party organ, the *National Intelligencer*, to publish a record of debates and proceedings. Not until 1834 did the government publish its own records.

Today there is little likelihood that the Washington correspondents will be denied access to the congressional press galleries, except when the legislators are meeting in emergency executive session (a rare event). But reporters are admitted to sessions of legislative committees only upon the willingness of the committee chairman and members. Some 40 per cent of congressional committee sessions were closed to the press in the 1960's. The situation in state capitals is similar. Television and radio reporters and photographers have won access to legislative sessions only by persistent effort, and their ability to use all their equipment is often circumscribed.

Reporters similarly are admitted to court sessions only by the agreement of the presiding judge. They may be excluded, with other members of the public, if the court deems it necessary. Juvenile courts, for example, operate without reportorial coverage in most cases. Ordinarily reporters are free to attend court sessions, since public trials are the rule, but they have no automatic right of attendance. Photographers and TV-radio men have had only spotty success in covering trials with cameras and microphones, due to restrictions applied to them by Section 35 of the Canons of Judicial Ethics of the American Bar Association. A long campaign by the National Press Photographers Association, the Radio-Television News Directors Association, and the American Society of Newspaper Editors to persuade the bar association to revise its Canon 35 failed when that group reaffirmed its stand in 1963. The objections were still to the increased coverage by picture and microphone as imperiling the dignity of the courts and over-exposing persons involved to publicity. The media groups then reverted to efforts to win local approval of courtroom photos and broadcasts, which is permissible under bar rules.

An important doctrine which has grown up is the doctrine of qualified privilege. This provides that a news medium in reporting the actions of a legislative body or a court is free of the threat of libel suits provided its report is accurate and fair. This doctrine carries with it the implication that the media have an obligation to report legislative and judicial sessions so that the public may know what government and courts are doing. Defamatory statements affecting the reputations of individuals made in legislative sessions and courts may therefore be reported without fear of damage suits.

The right to report is denied more often at the "grass roots" level of government than at the national level, insofar as legislative bodies are concerned. Boards of education, water commissions, city councils, county boards, and other similar groups often seek to meet in private and conduct the public's business in virtual secrecy. Newsmen wage an unending battle against this practice, without much avail, unless the public demands its right to know. Some newsmen accept the practice and forfeit their right to report the news firsthand, thereby forfeiting their most important right as journalists. Passage of "open meetings" laws in an increasing number of states during the 1950's, at the insistence of various news groups, somewhat improved the access to news at the local level. These laws provide that actions taken in closed sessions are invalid; but they do not force a reluctant legislative group to open the doors wide. By 1964 there were 29 states with "open meetings" laws and 37 with laws guaranteeing opening of public records to reporters needing access to them.

Perhaps the most publicized denial of access to news has been in the national executive departments. This increasing trend—stemming from the necessity for secrecy in limited areas of the national defense establishment and atomic energy research—has alarmed responsible editors and newsmen. Editors like Herbert Brucker of the Hartford *Courant* and J. Russell Wiggins of the Washington *Post and Times Herald* have spoken out vigorously against the drying up of news sources in executive departments. The American Society of Newspaper Editors and the professional journalistic society, Sigma Delta Chi, have well-organized campaigns demanding free access to news so that the people may know the facts necessary to make intelligent decisions.

Appointment of a House subcommittee headed by Representative John Moss of California, in 1955, to study the information policies of the government brought some relief. The Moss committee has acted as the champion of the people's right to know and the reporter's right of access to news. By publicizing executive department refusals to make information available on public matters, the Moss committee has forced some reforms. But Washington correspondents say they are fighting a losing battle against administrative orders which forbid federal employees from talking to newsmen and employ other devices to keep an executive department's actions secret unless the administrator deems it desirable to make them public. Bitter battles broke out between newsmen and the Pentagon at the time of the 1961 Cuban crisis and charges of "news management" continued to be heard against the Kennedy administration throughout its tenure of office, despite the President's attempts to clarify his concept of how far access to crucial information could be tolerated.

In this battle, as in others involving the right to report, the newsman's best weapon is the power of the press, which is in turn based on the pressure of public opinion. Reporters who are determined to find out the facts can usually prevail over reluctant public officials.

SUMMARY

Almost from the time Europeans began to use the printing press, five centuries ago, barriers have been erected against the free flow of information and ideas by those subscribing to an authoritarian theory of the press rather than a libertarian one. Printers and writers struggled until

1694 in England to win the right to print without prior restraint and to bring to an end the licensing laws first imposed by Henry VIII in 1534 and extended by other rulers and the Parliament. Freedom to print without prior restraint in the United States is guaranteed by the Constitution and by judicial decisions, both at the federal and state levels. Censorship, either by public agencies or by self-regulation, is another form of prior restraint which has affected all the mass media to some degree. Television and radio, although licensed in the public necessity under the Federal Communications Act, are not subject to any form of direct censorship.

The right to criticize—under which the press acts as "the censor of the government"—was not won until nearly 1800. The landmark case was that of John Peter Zenger, acquitted in 1735 in New York colony of charges of seditious libel. But not until the followers of Thomas Jefferson had repulsed the dangerous Alien and Sedition Acts of 1798 was the right to criticize firmly established. It still is challenged, particularly during wartime and periods of political reaction, and by the courts through contempt-of-court citations.

A third right, the right to report and to have free access to news, has been much less effectively established, even though the public values of the first two rights are dependent upon the third. Newsmen do not have guaranteed access to legislative or court sessions; they are excluded most often at the local "grass roots" level of government. The most alarming recent trend has been toward denial of access to news in the national executive departments, which newsmen and the Moss committee of the Congress have opposed.

Freedom of the press is intertwined with other freedoms—freedom of speech, of assembly, of petition. Freedom of religious expression, of political thought and action, and of intellectual growth depend upon society's defense of these basic freedoms. Unless the mass media can bring information to the public, and unless there is a free "market place of thought" in which clashing opinions may be aired, democratic processes cannot operate. For, as Thomas Jefferson said, "the people are the censors of their governors," and their representatives in this process are the men and women of the press.

STUDY QUESTION

How do the mass media act to preserve the individual liberties guaranteed to us by the Bill of Rights?

PROJECTS

1. Read John Milton's *Areopagitica: A Defence of the Liberty of Unlicensed Printing.* (See Mott and Casey, *Interpretations of Journalism,* cited in bibliography, or other source.) Is Milton's concept of the victory of truth in any open competition still valid in a huge, complicated society under the existing structure of mass communications? Discuss in writing the reasons for the answer you give.

2. Clip a newspaper article in which the reporter makes it apparent he was unable to attend a closed governmental meeting, but had to obtain information about it from those who attended or other sources. What do you feel has been left untold?

CHAPTER 4

TECHNOLOGICAL GROWTH

THE PRINT MEDIA

In the five centuries since Johann Gutenberg printed the Bible on his wooden hand press, technological advances in the graphic arts have been made in answer to society's needs for better communication. New machines and printing processes made possible the growth of the mass media. Newspapers, magazines, and books were turned out in sufficient quantities and at low enough costs to match the potential demand and were printed attractively enough to stimulate a greater demand. Advances in the art of printing were as necessary as production improvements if the printed mass media were to retain their positions in the swirl and flash of a modern society which also has the film and electronic media at its disposal.

The printing press is one of society's most important machines. Gutenberg's press resembled the wine press of his time, the 1440's and 1450's. The form containing type was placed on a flat bed and inked. A sheet of rough paper was placed over the type. Pressure was applied downward by a screw-and-lever arrangement that brought down a second wooden surface, called the platen. Perhaps 600 impressions could be made in a long day of hard work. This form of printing is called the letterpress process.

Gutenberg's greatest contribution was the introduction of movable type. Until his time, books had been hand-lettered, principally by the monks or slaves, on vellum or parchment. Beautifully illuminated with colored initials and borders, and richly bound, these books were works of art, treasured and few in number. Printing for more popular consumption had also been done from wooden blocks on which words or illustrations had been carved. The invention of movable type meant that the same carved letters or, better yet, letters cast from metal could be used over and over again. And many impressions could be made from the same form of type. Gutenberg and his associates learned to cast metal type from a mold and they produced a suitable printing ink. They also had a usable paper, cheaper than parchment, which originally had been developed by the Chinese and Egyptians.

Books appeared rapidly. It is estimated that 40,000 editions were printed before 1500, averaging 500 copies per edition for a total of 20,000,000 books (the incunabula, or "cradle books," of our museums). Many were cheap popular printings which disappeared; some, done in imitation of the finely printed, hand-lettered books, still survive today. Other forms of printing—broadsides, pamphlets, and finally the first crude news books and newspapers—followed. About 1620 a press was invented with a movable type bed which could be rolled in and out under the platen, simplifying the work. Letterpress printers used essentially the same methods and equipment throughout the seventeenth and eighteenth centuries. William Caslon and other typographers developed more attractive typefaces and expert printers like Benjamin Franklin contributed to the artistry of their craft, but the quality and quantity of printed materials remained limited. Newspaper pages were only about 10 by 15 inches in dimension, the capacity of the wooden press; type wore out quickly from the uneven pressure of the wooden platen; and the work was slow.

The iron press, first developed in 1798, was an important development. This gave a more even and a greater pressure and permitted use of larger forms. Another improvement was the substitution of a lever for the screw. The Washington Hand Press, adopting these and other improvements, appeared in 1827 and made it possible to make as many as 250 impressions an hour. This machine was used by frontier printer-editors as they crossed the American continent in the nineteenth century.

The hand-operated press was clearly inadequate, however, for larger newspaper, magazine, and book publishing operations. If steam power could be used, the number of impressions per hour could be greatly increased. But a better method of applying pressure to the print paper and type form would have to be found. Friedrich Koenig, a German, produced a cylinder press in 1811 which could be run by steam. The inked type form was carried on the flat bed underneath an impression cylinder which held the sheet of paper. By using two cylinders, and a long flat bed holding type forms at either end, Koenig could print both sides of a sheet in one operation. In 1814 the London *Times* produced the then amazing number of 1100 copies an hour.

These flat-bed cylinder presses, improved by David Napier in England and by R. Hoe & Company in the United States, sufficed for a time. Indeed, modern versions which can print and fold complete newspapers in one operation, using a continuous role of newsprint, serve many smaller newspapers and magazines today, delivering up to 6000 copies an hour. But in the mid-nineteenth century, the demands of the newspapers with larger circulations led to further improvements. The solution was complete adoption of the rotary principle.

The type-revolving press was introduced by R. Hoe & Company in 1846. The type was locked into forms placed on a slightly curved central cylinder, against which revolved several impression cylinders. But this press could not use a continuous roll of paper and it could not accommodate multiple-column headlines, illustrations, or advertisements in the locking up of the type.

Stereotyping was the answer to that problem. Impressions were made from the type form on papier-mâché matrices. Curved solid printing plates were then made by pouring molten metal against the matrice, under great pressure. The curved plates could be firmly attached to a rotary cylinder on a press. Any sort of make-up of the type could now be employed, and an additional advantage was that the type itself was not subjected to the pressure of the press and did not wear out as quickly.

All that now remained was the perfection of a printing process in which a continuous roll of newsprint would flow between an impression cylinder and a type cylinder. Automatic cutting and folding attachments were also needed. R. Hoe & Company and other press manufacturers supplied the needs and developed by the early 1870's presses that could print 18,000 copies an hour. As circulations of mass-read newspapers mounted, additional banks of cylinders could be added, either using duplicate stereotypes of the same pages or producing additional sections of a newspaper. By the end of the century, a New York paper could print 96,000 copies of a 12-page edition in an hour. Electric power had by this time superseded steam power in the printing process.

Cheaper newsprint was needed to feed into these monstrous presses.

This came through the invention of the Fourdrinier papermaking machine. This process of making low-cost newsprint from wood pulp, introduced into America from Germany in 1867, was a basic factor in the growth of the daily newspaper. It also permitted the manufacture of higher grade magazine and book paper in the quantities needed by a modern society. Print paper made by hand from rag stock was expensive and limited in supply. The new process, using water power to grind spruce logs into wood pulp, provided a suitable paper when the ground wood was strengthened with a small amount of rag pulp or sulphite pulp. Newsprint prices tumbled from $246 a ton in 1870 to $42 a ton in 1899, as demand brought increased production at a declining cost.

Typesetting machines were also developed during this period when many hand labor operations were mechanized. There were many experimenters, but it was Ottmar Mergenthaler's Linotype machine which was first successfully used by newspapers in 1886. Mergenthaler's first Linotype was basically the same as the Linotype or Intertype machines used today. Operated by a keyboard, it cast a slug from a line of matrices, which were then redistributed automatically. Its output at the start was three times that of a hand compositor. Use of the slugs also speeded up the work of the men making up the page forms. Other slug-casting machines used today set headlines, cast type and rules in quantities, and cast slugs from handset matrices for use in composing advertisements. Improvement of the matrix-casting process also brought the "dry mat," reproduced in quantity from one master type form and shipped out by advertisers and feature syndicates for reproduction throughout the country. Introduction of electrotypes made it possible to obtain widespread reproduction of illustrated advertising copy.

Color printing on rotary presses became practicable in the 1890's. Color inserts printed separately had been used earlier in newspapers, and women's magazines had offered their readers hand-colored illustrations before the Civil War. The biggest metropolitan papers of the 1890's could print both pictures and headlines in color by using additional ink fountains and impression cylinders. They developed Sunday feature sections carrying color and the Sunday comic section in five colors.

Illustrations had appeared in the earliest newspapers; more often than not they were small woodcuts used for decorating advertisements. Woodcut illustrations of news events were comparatively rare until *Frank Leslie's Illustrated Newspaper* and *Harper's Weekly* appeared in the

1850's. The two periodicals vied in running woodcut reproductions of drawings made on Civil War battlefields. Their circulation successes spurred newspapers on, but one large woodcut might take several days to complete, a bad time lag for a daily.

The reader-pulling power of illustrations was apparent to many publishers, and various advances were made during the post-Civil War period. The magazines did highly artistic work with woodcuts and engraved steel plates and ran cartoons and drawings in color by the 1870's. Zincographs, which were line cuts produced by etching on zinc plates with acid, began to appear at the same time. Sketches of prominent citizens, drawn by artists, proved popular in the newspapers of the 1880's. The remaining problem was to find a way of reproducing photographs on high-speed presses.

Louis Daguerre's invention in Paris in 1839 of the "daguerreotype," a photograph on metal, was the initial step toward modern photojournalism. The first famous American photographer, Mathew Brady, used both Daguerre's process and a faster "wet plate" process developed in Scotland in 1855 to make portraits of leading Americans and some 3500 Civil War battle scenes. But no one could reproduce his pictures directly in newspapers or magazines. Then Frederic E. Ives, head of the photography laboratory at Cornell University, produced a photoengraving of a pen drawing for the Cornell student paper in 1877. The next year he made his first halftone engraving by laying out a pattern of tiny points on a plate which would transfer the ink to paper point by point. If the points were close together, they would reproduce the dark mass of a photograph; the more widely they were spaced, the lighter the mass would become. In 1880 Stephen H. Horgan, art editor of the New York *Daily Graphic,* published a halftone of good quality in that pioneer illustrated newspaper. But it was not until 1897 that pressmen learned how to run halftones on rotary presses; as soon as they did, photographers began to carry cameras and flashlight powder out on regular assignments.

By 1900, then, electric-driven rotary presses, typesetting machines, stereotyping, color printing, photoengraving, and dry mats and electrotyping were part of the pattern of publishing. This century has primarily been one of improvements and refinements in that pattern. The tubular press permitted smaller-sized dailies to use the rotary principle at a reduced cost, printing some 35,000 copies an hour. Four-color printing, much more complicated than the earlier color printing process, became practicable for large newspapers in the 1940's. Run-of-paper (ROP) color printing gained headway in both advertisements and news columns, and by 1965 some color was appearing in dailies representing 90 per cent of total circulation.

Typesetting machines have become speedier and more versatile. Since the 1940's they can be run automatically by tapes punched on a tele-typesetter machine, and one operator can tend several Linotype or Inter-type machines. Headline type faces have been greatly improved, begin-ning with Cheltenham and Bodoni types soon after 1900 and extending to the sans-serif types. Larger and more readable body types also have come on the market. Automatic news printers, called teletypes, came into use in 1913, replacing Morse operators in newsrooms and press association offices. Transmission of photographs by wire began in the 1930's and was followed by the introduction of facsimile machines print-ing the photos directly in the newsroom. The Fairchild engraving ma-chine, producing plastic printing plates simply and cheaply from photo-graphs, opened the door to wider use of illustrations by smaller publica-tions in the 1940's.

Two other printing processes have been developed, in addition to the letterpress process so far described. One is rotogravure, developed in Germany and introduced in the United States just before World War I. In rotogravure, printing is done from plates on which the image to be reproduced is engraved or etched below the surface—the opposite of letterpress. The plate is covered with ink, then scraped clean so that ink remains only in the sunken areas, which vary in depth. When paper is pressed against the plate, it sucks the ink out of the crevices. The resulting image is not made up of dots, as in letterpress, but rather is an ink film of wide variations in depth and, consequently, in tone. Rotogravure gives photographs a richer, artistic quality and is used for Sunday newspaper sections and magazines.

Offset printing, the other new development, is based on lithography, an older process in which printing was done from the smooth flat sur-faces of stones. This is surface printing, in which the image is placed on the stone by using a greasy substance which has an affinity for ink. The nonprinting surface is covered with a thin film of water that repels the ink. Thus only the image is printed on the paper when pressure is applied. The same principles are used on the offset printing press. The image is transferred from the printing plate cylinder to a rubber blanket attached to a second cylinder. It is then printed on the paper which is carried on a third impression cylinder. The printing plates are made by photographing paste-ups of the newspaper or magazine page—printed matter, advertisements, drawings, and photographs. Type may be set by typewriter or cut from other publications. Engravings of line drawings or photographs need not be made (although the photographs must be "screened" separately in the plate-making process). Offset printing thus has cost advantages for smaller publications, particularly those using many pictures, and has been adopted by several hundred weeklies and small dailies. However, its principal use has been in long-run commercial work, such as label printing, and in magazines.

Later sections of this book will examine the impact of these technological advances upon the newspaper, magazine, and book publishing industries and upon the world of advertising. Certainly the print media have historically accomplished improvements in the graphic arts processes. But leaders in all the industries agree that the costs of these processes are higher than they should be if the print media are to continue to serve that part of the mass public which can buy only at low prices. Penny newspapers, nickel magazines, and low-priced, hard-cover books long since have disappeared; 10-cent newspapers, 50-cent magazines, and $10 books suffer in cost competition. The technological advances, however they improved the products, had their price. To this were added increase costs of supplies (newsprint prices have increased from $41 to $135 a ton since 1933) and higher labor costs. Another major "breakthrough" is needed in printing processes if the printed media are to remain truly mass in character. The major hope lies in further application of photography to the printing process, which would make some of the gigantic machinery costs no longer necessary. Researchers hoped to advance the commercial practicability of the "cold type" process begun in the 1950's with the introduction of such machines as the Fotosetter, Linofilm, and Photon. These produce words on film and transfer them directly to a printing plate. Already widely used in advertisement composition, they promised in the 1960's to make further inroads on "hot metal" typesetting, provided an economically feasible method of engraving photocomposed news copy could be developed and the photocomposition process could be speeded up by use of electronic computers. Some large dailies began in 1963 to use computers to prepare tapes for their typesetting machines, achieving tape production at a high speed and at a savings in cost because the computer could automatically perform the time-consuming tasks of adjusting spaces between words and type line lengths. The computer must be programmed to do this because it is only capable of performing such tasks as it is instructed to do.

FILM, RADIO, AND TELEVISION

Film, radio, and television have an interrelated history as the audio-visual mass media. These twentieth-century additions to the printed mass media primarily offer entertainment to their audiences (akin to the fiction area of magazines and books), but they too carry information and ideas to viewers and listeners.

Film was the first to emerge as a medium. Louis Daguerre's early photographs spurred interest in achieving the illusions of depth and movement by projecting pictures on screens—experiments which were achieved in the 1860's and 1870's. The genius inventor Thomas A. Edison used some of George Eastman's earliest Kodak film in inventing the Kinetoscope in 1889, but Edison was more interested in his phonograph and let the motion picture project lag. One of his assistants projected the highly popular *The Great Train Robbery* for the Nickelodeon era viewers of 1903, the first motion picture to tell a story. The first great milestone in motion picture art was David Wark Griffith's *The Birth of a Nation*, completed during 1914–1915.

Early motion pictures had to depend upon sight and occasional printed titles; the arrival of the sound motion picture in 1926 put the industry on its modern basis. The electronic sound recording and reproduction process, developed by Warner Brothers, was a by-product of telephone and radio technology. The first synchronized music was heard in *Don Juan* in 1926; the first dialogue, in *The Jazz Singer* in 1927. Technicolor was the next step forward in making motion pictures; the first three-color feature appeared in 1935. Cinerama, hailed as the most important development since the introduction of sound in 1926, ushered in the wide-screen vogue in 1952. Magnetic sound arrived with Cinemascope in 1953; magnetic strippings were used to put the sound on the same film with the pictures. The wide-screen development was exploited by the motion picture industry to help offset the inroads of television on its audiences.

Films of news events were among the first shown, beginning with the

Corbett-Fitzsimmons prize fight of 1897. These were combined in the newsreel, which became a standard portion of a motion picture theater program by the 1920's. Interpretative newsreels, like *The March of Time* issued by Time Inc., were also filmed, together with short subjects and travelogues of an educational nature. The documentary film, focusing on a social problem or economic issue, achieved maturity in the 1930's with such notable opinion-forming documentaries as *The River*. By the time of the arrival of commercial television in the late 1940's the technological processes and artistic techniques of film making were well established.

Radio's story begins with the work of Guglielmo Marconi, the Italian scientist who between the years 1895 and 1900 devised a practical system of sending telegraphic messages through space by means of electro-magnetic waves. This was "wireless" telegraphy, for which Marconi obtained the basic patents and formed the first commercial wireless company in 1897. The jump from transmission of dots and dashes to transmitting the sounds of the human voice was made in 1906, when Dr. Lee De Forest invented an improved vacuum tube, and both he and Reginald A. Fessenden made successful voice transmissions. De Forest made the first newscast, which was of the 1916 presidential election returns, but the potential of radio as a medium for mass listening was not seriously considered until 1919.

That year a Westinghouse Company engineer, Dr. Frank Conrad, used music to test the signals of his experimental station in Pittsburgh. Hundreds of radio amateurs listened in; a store advertised crystal sets to hear "Dr. Conrad's popular broadcasts," and the giant radio manufacturing and broadcasting industries thus were born. Two other great companies, General Electric and American Telephone & Telegraph, shared in the early development of radio with Westinghouse. The three created the Radio Corporation of America in 1919, which under David Sarnoff's leadership was to dominate the field.

Firsts came fast with the licensing of commercial stations beginning in 1920. That year KDKA, Pittsburgh, the Westinghouse station, and WWJ, the Detroit *News* station, began regularly scheduled broadcasting (newspapers were among the early owners of radio stations). In 1922 the AT&T station, WEAF in New York City, set up an experimental circuit using telephone lines to relay programs between eastern cities. Two rival chains developed, sponsored by AT&T and RCA; when AT&T withdrew from the broadcasting end of the business in 1926, the stations were merged as the National Broadcasting Company, an RCA subsidiary. The next year coast-to-coast network broadcasting was a reality, operated by the NBC Red and Blue networks (the Blue becoming American Broadcasting Company when it was sold by government order in 1943) and the newly established Columbia Broadcasting System. The Mutual Broadcasting System followed in 1934. Important regional networks also developed.

The federal government's power to control the airwaves and to license stations was used by the Federal Radio Commission in 1927 to establish a group of "clear channels" on which only one station could operate at night, so that rural areas could obtain unimpeded reception of powerful metropolitan stations. By 1947, 55 of 57 powerful clear channel stations —the lucrative prizes of radio—were owned by, or affiliated with, the networks. Although the Federal Communications Commission, established in 1934, restricted the number of stations networks could own, their influence remained dominant until television brought a decline in radio network programming.

FM radio and facsimile broadcasting made bids against the normal AM (amplitude modulation) radio during the 1930's. Frequency modulation radio was looked upon as the means of providing smaller towns with thousands of radio stations, since FM covers a smaller area with better reception. But only a few hundred FM stations survived, primarily as "better listening" stations, because cheap radio sets produced by mass methods did not have FM reception. An "FM boom" in the 1960's, based on improved FM programming, doubled the number of stations on the air in one decade, however. Facsimile broadcasting, begun on a daily basis by KSD, St. Louis, in 1938, was viewed as a possible way of delivering printed newspapers into the home, but this potential threat to the printing press likewise failed to reach mass-use status.

Television was the successful competitor, combining the appeals and techniques of film and radio. As early as 1923, a picture was televised between New York and Philadelphia, and WGY, the General Electric station in Schenectady, was televising regularly in 1928. By 1937 there were 17 experimental stations, and commercial broadcasting was just under way in 1941 when World War II intervened. The postwar spread of the coaxial cable and the microwave relay made possible network television (like FM and facsimile broadcasting, television is restricted to limited areas of reception), and the first coast-to-coast telecast was made in 1951 from the Japanese peace treaty conference in San Francisco. The

FCC replanned and allocated television channels during 1949–1952, hoping to achieve the licensing of many smaller local stations and educational stations, as well as of major stations, but growth of the television networks (CBS, NBC, and ABC became the leaders in TV as well as in radio) again became the pattern. Color broadcasting, using the RCA compatible system which permits either color or black-and-white sets to receive the same broadcast, was authorized by the FCC in 1953. Although prices of regular television sets had dropped rapidly with increased production and simplified construction, color television sets remained fairly expensive and complicated into the 1960's. In the 1950's radio broadcasting received a new stimulus with the introduction of the transistor principle in radio manufacture, which by the 1960's had brought the price of a set to a few dollars.

Radio and television also have international and space extensions. Radiotelephony began in 1900 and the first voice went overseas in 1915. Commercial transatlantic telephone service—by radio—began in 1927 and in the 1930's radio could broadcast news reports direct from Europe to U.S. audiences. Europe was first linked to America by submarine telephone cable in 1956. The first successful transmission of live television programs between Europe and America via the space satellite Telstar in July, 1962, ushered in a space communications revolution which by 1964 brought promise of worldwide telecasting through the use of satellites put in fully synchronous orbit (an orbit and speed that keep the craft directly over one point on earth). Syncom III, built by Howard Hughes, was successfully put in synchronous orbit in 1964. The Communications Satellite Corporation, formed by Congress in 1962 to unify the U.S. effort, expected to launch in 1965 a satellite named Early Bird which would permit regularly scheduled telecasts between America and Europe. The satellites also were to carry telephone messages, in far greater numbers than underseas cables.

SUMMARY

Technological growth of the mass media has kept step with society's increasing needs for better communications. The printing press, crude at first, was revolutionized by the perfection of the rotary principle when mass production demanded it in the late nineteenth century. Steam power and electric power replaced hand power in the printing process, and typesetting machines replaced hand compositors in the 1880's. Stereotyping, color printing, photoengraving, and dry mats and electrotyping were a part of the pattern of publishing by 1900. The Fourdrinier papermaking machine, introduced to America in 1867, permitted the making of low-cost newsprint from wood pulp. Among the important inventions are those of Johann Gutenberg, movable type; Friedrich Koenig, the steam press; Ottmar Mergenthaler, the typesetting machine; and Frederic E. Ives, photoengraving.

During the twentieth century the traditional letterpress printing process was improved and refined, and rotogravure and offset printing were introduced. Production costs of the print media are higher than they should be, however, if the print media are to continue to serve that part of the mass public which can buy only at low prices. A new "break-through" in printing technology, probably further extending the application of photography to printing, is needed.

Film, radio, and television are interrelated developments of the present century. Experiments with motion pictures were conducted in the 1860's and 1870's, and the Nickelodeon era arrived at the turn of the century. Standards for motion picture art were established by David Wark Griffith's *The Birth of a Nation* in 1914–1915. Other milestones have been the arrival of sound in 1926, Technicolor in 1935, and the wide-screen processes of Cinerama and Cinemascope in the early 1950's.

Radio broadcasting is based upon the telegraphy inventions of Guglielmo Marconi, made at the close of the nineteenth century, and the invention of Dr. Lee De Forest, whose improvement of the vacuum tube in 1906 permitted voice transmission. Commercial broadcasting began immediately after World War I, and coast-to-coast network broadcasting began in 1927. Facsimile broadcasting and FM radio were hopes of the 1930's but failed of widespread use despite the superior reception qualities of FM radio in contrast to conventional AM radio. Television, experimented with successfully as early as 1923, became a commercial enterprise after World War II. Coast-to-coast network telecasting was made possible by 1951 through the spread of the coaxial cable and the microwave relay. Color television dates from 1953. Telstar carried the first live transatlantic telecast in 1962.

STUDY QUESTION

What were the successive impacts of the industrial revolution on mass communications during the periods from about (a) 1810 to 1840, (b) 1865 to 1900, and (c) 1920 to the present?

PROJECTS

1. Write a 300-word essay on one of the following subjects: (a) letter-press printing, (b) offset printing, (c) FM broadcasting, (d) communications satellites.

2. Clip from magazines three examples of stories or advertisements which you think exhibit superior technical work in the use of type and illustrations. Write brief statements defending your choices.

CHAPTER 5

GROWTH OF THE PRINT MEDIA

THE BASIC EDITORIAL FUNCTIONS

Newspapers, despite their impact on society, have a relatively brief historical tradition. Two hundred and fifty years ago there was but one struggling weekly in the colonial outpost of Europe which was to become the United States. It was only about 125 years ago, in the 1830's and 1840's, that the "penny press" dailies ushered in America's first era of popular journalism, made famous by James Gordon Bennett and his New York *Herald,* Horace Greeley and his New York *Tribune,* and Henry J. Raymond and his New York *Times.* Bennett taught others how to search out and report the news; Greeley fashioned an editorial page; Raymond put his emphasis upon news interpretation. With their contemporaries and successors they laid the foundations for present-day American journalism.

The basic journalistic principles thus espoused were further advanced before the nineteenth century had ended by such noted publishers as Joseph Pulitzer, Edward Wyllis Scripps, and Adolph S. Ochs. The goals were two in number. The primary goal was ever-increasing concentration of effort on impartial gathering and reporting of the news and its comprehensive display. The other was demonstration of responsible opinion leadership, provided both through an intelligently written editorial page and integrity and zealousness in telling the news.

As even the colonial editor knew, however, there is a third editorial function of the press and that is to entertain the reader, as well as to inform and instruct him. What is called "human interest" news—stories with appeal based on writing skill rather than necessarily upon news value—has always been in great reader demand. Sensational news—stories involving the human passions, crime, and violence and spicy accounts of the doings of the famous—is likewise age-old in its appeal. The newspaper has also always contained a budget of nonnews material: short stories and other literary content (more prevalent a century ago than today), comics and Sunday feature sections (favorites since the 1890's), advice to the lovelorn (highly popular for early eighteenth-century readers), and a host of varying entertainment items.

The responsibility of any of the mass media has been to strike a balance among the functions of informing, instructing, and entertaining. The newspaper, as it reached out for mass circulation, sought to fulfill the first two functions in more popularized ways: a more readable writing style, skillful use of human interest elements in news, better make-up and headline display, effective pictures, color. Such popularizing, in the interests of appealing to the entertainment desire, need not detract from the newspaper's social usefulness. There is no reason why the "hard news" of political and economic importance should not be presented as interestingly as possible and in company with other less important, but more attractive, ingredients. But there is a line to be drawn. Over-emphasis on sensationalism at the expense of news and a lavish dressing up of purely entertainment features is merely cheapening, not popularizing.

How well American newspapers have responded to these basic principles over the decades is a matter of judgment. One thing is certain; they responded differently, for there is no such thing as a "typical newspaper" to analyze any more than there is a typical magazine, television or radio station, or book publishing house. What can be measured is the response made by the leaders in different historical periods, as they reshaped their journalistic products to fit the demands of their times and the desires of their audiences. As the sociologist Robert E. Park put it: "The newspaper has a history; but it has, likewise, a natural history. The press, as it exists, is not, as our moralists sometimes seem to assume, the willful product of any little group of living men. On the contrary, it is the outcome of a historic process in which many individuals participated without foreseeing what the ultimate product of their labors was to be. The newspaper, like the modern city, is not wholly a rational product. . . . it has continued to grow and change in its own incalculable ways."

THE COLONIAL PRESS

Early concepts of news. Reporting, as defined today, means gathering information of interest to other people and presenting it to them accurately in a way which makes them understand and remember it. This definition is broad enough to fit all media of information and comprehensive enough to provide a measuring stick for present and past performance.

The first newspaper publishers were primarily printers, not editors. The majority had a sense of what interested people, but only a few had real reportorial instincts. Only a few, too, were good enough writers to tell their stories in an interesting way. Since their access to news was severely limited, and inadequate transportation and communication facilities made the collecting of news a very haphazard business, they scarcely could be expected to be either complete or accurate in their reports. But even so, very few made any move to go out and find the news; they ran what came over their doorsteps or what could be gleaned from other newspapers and periodicals, particularly those coming from London. None had local news reporters as we know them today. Nevertheless, what meager news and entertainment they offered was eagerly devoured by their readers, who had little other choice.

James and Benjamin Franklin were early publisher-printers who were also journalists. James, in his *New England Courant*, gave Boston readers of the 1720's the first readable and exciting American newspaper. He printed news, despite the opposition of Puritan political and religious authorities, and covered local issues in a dramatic and crusading fashion. He and his contributors, including his younger brother Ben, wrote well and the paper had high literary qualities, modeled on the successful "essay" papers of Joseph Addison and Richard Steele in England. Personality sketches, feature stories, and human interest material lightened the pages. Benjamin Franklin carried on the traditions in his *Pennsylvania Gazette,* editing his meager scraps of news more cleverly than did his rivals and offering more substance.

During the Revolutionary War period, publishers such as Benjamin Franklin and Isaiah Thomas of the *Massachusetts Spy* were alert to forward the patriot cause, but even as well-to-do a publisher as Thomas did not attempt to have his own correspondent with Washington's army. The paper nearest to the scene of an event covered it; other papers copied the report or relied upon official announcements, messages sent to their local authorities from military and governmental headquarters, and reports of travelers.

The political pamphleteers. In their exercise of the opinion function, the editors of colonial newspapers were more political pamphleteers than newspapermen. Indeed, until the 1790's, the pamphleteer was more important than the editor. His product appeared in pamphlet form, like Tom Paine's *Common Sense,* or as successive installments in the weeklies, like the writings of John Dickinson. Even after the brief incisive editorial appeared at the turn of the century, the newspaper editor conducted his column in the partisan manner of the pamphleteer rather than in the responsible manner of the editorial writer whose comment does not knowingly depart from the truth.

James Franklin was the first American editor to raise his voice in criticism of authority and the first to use the crusading technique in his paper, the *New England Courant.* John Peter Zenger and his editorial advisers similarly nettled authority in the New York colony, and Andrew Bradford and Benjamin Franklin raised their heads on occasion in Pennsylvania. But the colonial press was most effective when it played the pamphleteering role. Republication of the famous "Cato Letters" of the 1720's and the "Letters of Junius" of the 1760's brought two English expressions on theories of liberty and representative government before the colonial public (the pamphleteer, for safety's sake, often used a pseudonym).

The colonists themselves developed a pamphleteering skill in the years preceding the Revolution. John Dickinson of Pennsylvania, an articulate spokesman of the colonial Whigs, wrote his series of "Letters from a Farmer in Pennsylvania" for the *Pennsylvania Chronicle* of 1767–1768. Dickinson was opposed to revolution and was actually a spokesman for the business class and its Whig philosophy rather than for the agrarian class. But he and the colonial Whigs could not afford to let the British Whigs impose commercial restrictions that were harmful to American interests. The mercantile system, preventing development of colonial industry and trade, and taxation measures imposed by a Parliament in which the colonial Whigs were not directly represented were threats which Dickinson could not ignore. His forceful arguments for home rule helped swing Americans of his economic group to the revolutionary cause after it became apparent that compromise was no longer possible.

Samuel Adams, the great propagandist of the Revolution, belonged to the Radical party. Only briefly an editor himself, he worked with the group of Boston Patriots assembled in the office of the Boston *Gazette* including the publishers, Benjamin Edes and John Gill, and the engraver, Paul Revere. Sam Adams was called the "master of the puppets" and the "assassin of reputations" by his enemies, and undoubtedly he was both. He wrote tirelessly for the columns of the *Gazette*, twisting every possible incident or administrative action of the British into an argument for revolution. When the news was dull and the fires of dissatisfaction needed fanning, he "blew up" minor scrapes into events of seemingly major import. When a crisis arose, such as the passage of the Stamp Act or the imposition of the tax on tea, Adams worked with others to fire up resistance throughout the colonies. His Committees of Correspondence, organized in 1772, kept the word moving among Patriot editors. When British rifles fired in Boston to restrain a street crowd, the *Gazette* called the affair the Boston Massacre. But a year later the *Gazette* was reporting on a memorial service held for the massacre victims, consisting of a propagandistic display in the windows of Paul Revere's house. Such touches as this were the work of Sam Adams, who knew how to stir the popular emotions.

Tom Paine, the political philosopher, arrived in the colonies from England in time to make two great pamphleteering contributions to the Patriot cause. His *Common Sense,* which sold 120,000 copies in three months in the spring of 1776, was a hard-headed, down-to-earth argument for independence that the common man could understand. That December, when Washington's discouraged army was camped on the Delaware river across from Trenton, Paine was drafted to write the first of his *Crisis* papers: "These are the times that try men's souls. The summer soldier and the sunshine patriot will, in this crisis, shrink from the service of their country; but he that stands it NOW, deserves the love and thanks of man and woman. Tyranny, like hell, is not easily conquered; yet we have this consolation with us, that the harder the conflict the more glorious the triumph. What we obtain too cheap, we esteem too lightly; it is dearness only that gives every thing its value. Heaven knows how to put a proper price upon its goods; and it would be strange indeed if so celestial an article as *FREEDOM* should not be highly rated." Paine's words lived to be broadcast to occupied Europe during World War II; at the time they helped to spur the first American victory of the war.

PRESS OF THE NEW REPUBLIC

In the early years of the new nation, two types of newspapers were developing. One was the mercantile paper, published in the seaboard towns, primarily for the trading and shipping classes interested in commercial and political news. Its well-filled advertising columns reflected the essentially business interest of its limited clientele of subscribers—2000 was a good number. The other type was the political paper, partisan in its appeal, and relying for reader support on acceptance of its views, rather than upon the quality and completeness of its news. Most editors of the period put views first and news second; the political paper deliberately shaped the news to fit its views. In the struggle over the adoption of the Constitution and the establishment of the new federal government, these party papers played a key role.

The *Federalist Papers*, written for the newspapers of New York state and reprinted throughout the country, were largely the work of Alexander Hamilton, brilliant leader of the pro-Constitution party which received its name from the series of 85 articles. Written for mass consumption, they still rank as one of the best expositions of political doctrine ever conceived. When Hamilton's party assumed control of the new federal government, Hamilton directed the editorial opinion of three Federalist party papers he helped to establish: John Fenno's *Gazette of the United States,* Noah Webster's *Minerva,* and William Coleman's New York *Evening Post* (begun in 1801 when the Federalists had become the party out of power). He dictated his ideas to his editors, who, with their Jeffersonian opponents, developed a briefer, one-argument form of editorial writing.

Ranged on the anti-Federalist side with Thomas Jefferson were his personally sponsored poet-editor, Philip Freneau of the *National Gazette,* and other masters of partisanship like William Duane and Benjamin Franklin Bache of the *Aurora*. Editors on both sides attacked each other with biting sarcasm and bitter invective. Their political sponsors were also viciously treated; the climax came when Bache accused Washington of being a "front man" for the Federalists and said, "If ever a nation was debauched by a man, the American nation has been debauched by Washington." William Cobbett, most fiery of the Federalist editors, retaliated in his *Porcupine's Gazette* with a classical character sketch of Bache in which the kindest word was "liar."

The American press survived the excesses of the 1790's and the dangerous effort at repression of press freedom through the Alien and Sedition Acts. But the traditions of partisan journalism lived on in the political party press of the nineteenth century. Particularly was this true of the frontier papers which supported Andrew Jackson and the Democratic party. The *Argus of Western America* of Frankfort, Kentucky, was one of these grubby but virile sheets which helped to spark the Jacksonian revolution. Amos Kendall and Francis P. Blair, two of its editors, graduated to Jackson's "kitchen cabinet," where Kendall served as Postmaster General and journalistic adviser to the President and Blair as editor of the hard-hitting administration paper, the Washington *Globe*. The tradition of an administration organ in Washington had begun with the *National Intelligencer* of Jefferson's day; but none was edited with more singledminded driving purpose than Blair's *Globe*. "Give it to Bla-ar," Jackson would say, and Blair would pass the word along to the party faithful. The Whigs had their strong editors, too, like Thurlow Weed of the Albany *Evening Journal*. The attitude of the political paper was well expressed by the pro-Jackson New York *Evening Post,* which advised its readers to buy a Whig paper if they wanted the other side of the argument of the moment. This was the spirit of the pamphleteer rather than that of the true journalist.

The political papers were much more important in the story of the development of the opinion function. The mercantile papers, however, played a role in the development of the news function concept. Even though their primary interest was in shipping news and digests of foreign news taken from European newspapers arriving by boat in the American ports, the leading mercantile papers took pride in excelling in their specialties. And as the struggle between the Federalists and the Republicans for control of the national government intensified, news of Hamilton's fiscal policies and Jefferson's moves became important to the business community. Competition was tough, too; in 1800 there were six dailies in Philadelphia (twice as many as in 1960) and five in New York. The weekly publishers had been forced into the daily field to meet the competition of the coffee houses, where the London papers were filed as soon as ships arrived with the latest issues and where news was freely exchanged.

So the individual papers began to go out after the news. Correspondents covered sessions of the Congress in Washington as early as 1808 and were well established by the late 1820's. Seaport dailies hired boats to meet the incoming ships out in the harbor so their editors would have a headstart on digesting the foreign news. The leading New York mercantile papers, the *Courier and Enquirer* and the *Journal of Commerce,* set up rival pony express services between Washington and New York to get presidential messages and congressional news faster.

What the mercantile papers did not do, however, was widen the appeal of their news columns to satisfy the demands of a new reading audience which was emerging from what is now called the Jacksonian revolution. More widespread education, extension of the right to vote, increased interest in politics by a growing laboring class, and other socioeconomic factors were operating to pave the way for a more popular and responsive journalism which was destined to overwhelm the older types of newspapers.

THE PENNY PRESS

Between 1833 and 1837 the publishers of a new "penny press" proved that a low-priced paper, edited to interest ordinary people, could win what amounted to a mass circulation for the times and thereby attract an advertising volume which would make it independent. These were papers for the "common man" and were not tied to the interests of the business community, like the mercantile press, or dependent for financial support upon political party allegiance. It did not necessarily follow that all the penny papers would be superior in their handling of the news and opinion functions. But the door was open for some to make important journalistic advances.

The first offerings of a penny paper tended to be highly sensational; human interest news overshadowed important news, and crime and sex stories were written in full detail. But as the penny paper attracted readers from various social and economic brackets, its sensationalism was modified. The "common man" reader came to want a better product, too. Popularized style of writing and presentation of news remained, but the penny paper became a respectable publication, offering significant information and editorial leadership. Once the first of the successful penny papers had shown the way, later ventures could enter the competition at the higher level of journalistic responsibility the pioneering papers had reached.

This was the pattern of American newspapers in the years following the founding of the New York *Sun* in 1833. The *Sun,* published by Benjamin Day, entered the lists against 11 other dailies. It was tiny in comparison, but it was bright and readable and it preferred human interest features to important but dull political speech reports. It had a police reporter writing squibs of crime news in the style already proven successful by London papers. And, most important, it sold for a penny whereas its competitors sold for six cents. By 1837 the *Sun* was printing 30,000 copies a day, which was more than the total of all 11 New York daily newspapers combined on the day the *Sun* first appeared.

Bennett and news enterprise. In those same four years, James Gordon Bennett brought out his New York *Herald* (1835) and a trio of New York printers who were imitating Day's success founded the Philadelphia *Public Ledger* (1836) and the Baltimore *Sun* (1837). The four penny papers became highly successful leaders, surviving into the twentieth century when mergers changed the names of all except the Baltimore *Sun.*

James Gordon Bennett can serve as the symbol of the penny press news enterprisers. He had been a Washington correspondent, reporter, and editor for other dailies before he launched the *Herald* in 1835. Disillusioned by a previous venture with a political paper, he kept the *Herald* relatively free of political ties. He more than matched the *Sun* with sensational coverage of crime and court news, on the one hand, and challenged the more sober journals with detailed coverage of Wall Street affairs, political campaigns, and foreign news, on the other. As profits from his big circulation and extensive advertising piled up, he spent money on news coverage. He matched his rivals in establishing pony express services to carry the news from Washington and other points. One *Herald* courier service stretched all the way from Newfoundland, carrying European news by pony rider, boat, and train to the first telegraph point. Bennett was among the first to use each of the new means of communication as they burst upon the scene in the 1830's and 1840's, hiring locomotives to race presidential messages from Washington and utilizing the telegraph as soon as Samuel F. B. Morse's invention proved itself in 1844 and wires were strung from city to city. He personally toured the country with presidential candidates and sailed to London on the newest steamship to arrange for better coverage of foreign news. By the 1850's he had made the *Herald* the leading newsgathering paper and the richest in advertising.

Bennett's competitors were not being left in the dust. The New York

Sun, Philadelphia *Public Ledger,* and Baltimore *Sun* were all in the race for news. So were such older New York papers as the *Courier and Enquirer, Journal of Commerce,* and *Evening Post.* So were two new competitors, Horace Greeley's New York *Tribune,* founded in 1841, and Henry J. Raymond's New York *Times,* founded in 1851. Greeley shunned the sensationalism which had helped the *Sun* and *Herald* to their initial circulation successes and concentrated instead on building up an editorial page and offering news interpretation, but he also covered the running news. His managing editor, Charles A. Dana, directed a reportorial staff of high quality, although perhaps not as slambang as the *Herald's* growing group of newsmen. By the time Raymond entered the New York field with the *Times,* the lines of staff organization were fairly well defined. The owner might still be editor-in-chief, but he had a news executive and a business manager operating the day-to-day business. Raymond concentrated on the *Times'* foreign coverage and editorial policy, seeking to give his reports more depth and meaning in the pattern of the *Times* of London.

The coming of the telegraph speeded the gathering of news, but it also increased the cost. In 1848 six New York morning papers formed the Associated Press of New York, forerunner of the modern press association of the same name. They did so to share the costs of telegraphing digests of foreign news from Boston and of routine news from Washington. Soon other papers asked to share in this common news report and the New York papers began selling it. Papers in the interior of the country could now, with the telegraph, get the news as rapidly as their eastern metropolitan competitors. The excitement of the Mexican War and of the political crises leading up to the Civil War spurred attention to the need for better mass communications.

The Civil War called for great efforts in news enterprise. The *Herald* sent its own small army of correspondents into the field; other leading papers followed suit. The printing advances of the previous two decades —the flat-bed cylinder press, the type-revolving press, and stereotyping— were needed to handle increased circulations. Sunday editions of daily papers came into being. The illustrated periodicals, *Harper's Weekly* and *Frank Leslie's Illustrated Newspaper,* led the way in using woodcut illustrations and maps, and newspapers followed suit as best they could. By the time the guns finally ceased firing, the traditions of news enterprise and emphasis upon the news function had been well established.

Greeley and the editorial page. Horace Greeley is recognized as one of the most influential editors in the history of American journalism. His New York *Tribune,* which he founded in 1841, was the first American newspaper to develop an editorial page which was the product of the thinking of a group of individuals. Not that it was a well-tailored, coherently organized page, such as many newspapers publish today. Orderly departmentalization had not yet come to newspapers in Greeley's day, and in any event methodicalness and consistency were not part of the Greeley temperament. But what the *Tribune* printed represented a dramatic change from the tradition of the pamphleteer.

Greeley was deeply conscious of his responsibility to the reader. He knew the *Tribune* had to be enterprising in reporting the news if it were to compete successfully for readers. But he felt it his responsibility to be just as enterprising in seeking to influence public opinion by devoting much space to serious discussion, editorial argument, and interpretation of events. The *Tribune* examined issues and debated ideas; it did not follow a set party line or insist that there was only one solution to a problem. True, it advocated some of its opinions as vehemently as did the pamphleteer, but in sum total it illuminated the social and economic issues of the day, from differing viewpoints, far more than any other paper had.

Unlike Bennett's *Herald,* which minimized the opinion function while concentrating on news enterprise, Greeley's *Tribune* made the opinion function the key to its popular acceptance. And popular it was. His weekly edition, in which the best of the daily news and opinion was reprinted for mail circulation (a practice of some bigger papers of the period), had the largest circulation of any contemporary publication. It was called the "Bible of the Middlewest," where many of the 200,000 copies went. "Uncle Horace," as Greeley was called, was as well known as any American of his time—only Lincoln, of the men of the period, has had more books written about him. Greeley lived through a period of momentous events and of great social change and, like Lincoln, was able to give expression to the aspirations and hopes of less articulate countrymen.

To many, the activities of Greeley and the *Tribune* must have appeared strangely inconsistent. The editor was greatly concerned with the impact of the industrial revolution upon society and the social ills which unrestricted capitalism produced. He was willing to examine and debate any seemingly reasonable experimentation in social reform or economic theory, in the hope that it would give workers and farmers a more equitable share in the accumulating wealth. So the *Tribune,* ostensibly a Whig newspaper, advocated a form of collective living called "associationism" and ran many columns of material written by the Socialist Albert Brisbane and the Communist Karl Marx. Few of Greeley's readers were won over to socialism, but they enjoyed the debate. Greeley's fight for free land in the West to which people in the slums could emigrate was more popular—but that stand was inconsistent with Whig political principles. Eventually his stand on the slavery issue led him into the Republican party, and he ended his career by running unsuccessfully for the presidency in 1872 as the candidate of the Liberal Republicans and the Democrats against General Grant, candidate of the Whig-minded Republicans.

Greeley was not always the great editor; he pressed his demands for immediate emancipation of the slaves upon Lincoln with such emotionalism that Lincoln was hard-pressed not to abandon his carefully worked-out strategy for keeping the northern and border states united in the common purpose of preserving the Union. But over a generation's time Greeley won the right to be known as the "Yankee radical"; he was responsive to the problems of his times and a purveyor of stimulating ideas. He brought together an admirable staff, including Charles A. Dana as his chief assistant and such thinking writers as Margaret Fuller, George Ripley, and Solon Robinson, to help produce the editorial page for which the *Tribune* was noted. They did much to teach others a fuller concept of the newspaper's opinion function.

The personal editors. Greeley belonged to the group of editors of the middle nineteenth century called the "personal editors," men who were as well known to their readers as were their newspapers, in contrast to the much more anonymous editors of modern corporate journalism. Some of Greeley's farmer readers were surprised to keep getting the *Tribune* after his death; they assumed the paper would quit publishing, so much did he seem to be the newspaper itself.

William Cullen Bryant, who joined the New York *Post* staff in 1825 and remained to edit it for a half-century, also fell into this category of the personal editor. His journalism was much more reserved than Greeley's and his thinking more logical, but through Bryant's personal editorial opinion, the *Post* exercised considerable influence. He supported

Jacksonian democracy and, like Greeley, he showed sympathy for the workingman. During the Civil War, he was one of the most effective interpreters of Lincoln's policies. Henry J. Raymond, founder of the New York *Times,* played a personal role outside the newspaper office, as a leader in the Republican party, although he tried to make the *Times'* editorial columns calmly interpretative in character.

There were editors outside New York City who made their influence felt during the Civil War period. One was Samuel Bowles III, publisher of the Springfield *Republican* in Massachusetts, a daily of just 6000 circulation. Bowles' editorial ability was so great that his weekly edition of 12,000 copies rivaled Greeley's 200,000-circulation in reputation and did much to unify the North and Middlewest in the pre-Civil War years. Another was Joseph Medill, builder of the Chicago *Tribune,* who was one of Lincoln's firmest supporters. The abolitionist editors, William Lloyd Garrison of the *Liberator* and the martyred Elijah Lovejoy, should be noted too, although they were agitator-pamphleteers.

In the post-Civil War years, the names of Edwin Lawrence Godkin and Henry Watterson stand out. They were editorial opposites; Godkin was a snobbish intellectual who exerted great influence on other intellectuals through his coldly logical reasoning, whereas Watterson, called "Marse Henry" by his many admirers, was a flamboyant exponent of the personal journalism school.

Godkin founded the *Nation* magazine in 1865 and succeeded Bryant as the driving force of the New York *Post* in 1881. British-born, Godkin decided the United States needed a high-grade weekly journal of opinion and literary criticism, similar to those in England. His distinctive style of writing and skill in ironic analysis made the *Nation* a favorite of other intellectuals. William James, the philosopher, said of him: "To my generation his was certainly the towering influence in all thought concerning public affairs, and indirectly his influence has assuredly been more pervasive than that of any other writer of the generation, for he influenced other writers who never quoted him, and determined the whole current of discussion." This was high accomplishment for the editor of a weekly magazine with no more than 10,000 circulation.

Like other mid-Victorian English liberals, Godkin did not believe the government should intervene in economic affairs. But he was in the forefront of those advocating political and social reforms: reconciliation with the South, civil service reform, extension of public education, Negro rights, women's suffrage. In both the *Nation* and the *Evening Post* he fought relentlessly against corruption in government, whether in the Republican Grant administration or in Democratic Tammany Hall. Godkin was a leader of the "mugwump" group of editors who broke with Grant and who helped to elect Grover Cleveland as President over the "tainted" Republican, James G. Blaine, in 1884. Such demonstrations of editorial independence from political pressures helped advance the status of the newspaper as an organ of opinion.

Henry Watterson served as editor of the Louisville *Courier-Journal* from 1868 to 1919, a half-century during which he became, according to Arthur Krock, "the last of those editors who wrote with the power of ownership." This was not entirely true, for Watterson was less an owner than the present editor of the *Courier-Journal,* Barry Bingham. What Krock meant was that Watterson was among the last editors of major papers to write exactly as he pleased, without concern for the newspaper's institutional character. He gaily exchanged fire with other leading editors, making picturesque and powerful comments in the field of politics. Perhaps his most important role was in helping to bring about a reconciliation between North and South in the post-Civil War years; his skillful representations to both sides did much to gain him a reputation, shared with Henry W. Grady of the Atlanta *Constitution,* as a spokesman for the new South. His role as "Marse Henry" also kept him as a spokesman for the old South.

THE "NEW JOURNALISM" ERA

Between 1865 and 1900 the dynamic capitalism of an expanding America, utilizing vast natural resources and the new machines of the industrial revolution, transformed the national economy. Industrialization, mechanization, and urbanization brought extensive social, cultural, and political changes: the "rise of the city," improved transportation and communication, educational advances, political unrest, and the rise of an extensive labor movement. The mass media could not fail to go through great changes along with the society they served. In the world of newspapers, the era is known as that of the "New Journalism," a designation used by the men who lived through that time to describe the activities of the master editor of the period, Joseph Pulitzer.

In the 35 years between the close of the Civil War and the turn of the century the population of the country doubled, the national wealth quadrupled, and manufacturing production increased sevenfold. It was the period of the coming of the age of steel, the harnessing of electricity for light and power, and the mechanizing of production processes. National growth and increased wealth meant cultural progress in literature, science, and the social sciences; a great stirring in scholarship and a rapid rise in the universities; and sharp increases in public school attendance and adult interest in popularized knowledge. Growing social and economic interdependence could be measured by two statistics for the year 1900: a third of the population was urban and 62 per cent of the labor force was engaged in non-agricultural work.

Communication facilities expanded in this period of the nationalization of the United States. Telegraph lines and railroad tracks reached near-saturation points; the telephone, coming into use in the 1870's, provided direct communication through intercity lines which covered the country by 1900. The federal postal service greatly extended free carrier service in the cities and instituted free rural delivery in 1897. The low postal rate for newspapers and magazines of 1885 opened the way for cheap delivery of publications. By 1900 there were 3500 magazines with a combined circulation of 65,000,000 an issue. Weekly newspapers tripled in number between 1870 and 1900, reaching a total of more than 12,000. During the same 30 years the number of daily newspapers quadrupled and their total circulation increased almost sixfold; the figures for 1900 were 1967 general circulation dailies, selling nearly 15,000,000 copies each day. It was this tremendous increase in the circulation of the printed mass media which was the impetus for inventions such as the rotary press, the typesetting machine, photoengraving, color printing, and processes for reproduction of advertising matter.

Obviously a "New Journalism" would emerge for this new society. Again, as in the penny press period, there was a new audience: More people were interested in reading; the labor class increased rapidly; and there was a heavy concentration of immigrant population in the rapidly growing eastern cities (New York City residents, who increased 50 per cent between 1880 and 1890, were 80 per cent foreign-born or of foreign parentage). Such readers, stirred by political and social unrest in a period when reform movements sought to readjust the economic balance to bring relief to the worker and farmer, looked for aggressive editorial leadership and opinion-forming crusading in their newspapers and magazines. But they also wanted impartial and thorough coverage of the news. The newspaper which appealed to them was also low-priced, easily read, popularized in content, and bright in appearance. Particularly in the big cities, the entertainment ingredient had to be high, and for the really new readers a new cycle of sensationalism was the major attraction.

Pulitzer and the news. Joseph Pulitzer serves as the symbol of the New Journalism era. An immigrant himself, he served his apprenticeship as a reporter before founding the St. Louis *Post-Dispatch* in 1878. In the next five years, Pulitzer built it into the city's leading paper by giving his readers what they wanted. He developed a liberal, aggressive editorial page and gave both the editorial and news columns a fierce crusading spirit. He insisted on accuracy, digging deep for facts, thoroughness of local news coverage, and good writing. One of his famous commands to his staff was "Accuracy! Accuracy!! Accuracy!!!" Another was "Terseness! Intelligent, not stupid, condensation." Still another showed his concern for the lighter side of the news; he reminded reporters to look for both the significant news and the "original, distinctive, dramatic, romantic, thrilling, unique, curious, quaint, humorous, odd, apt to be talked about" news.

In 1883 Pulitzer left the *Post-Dispatch* as his monument in St. Louis and invaded New York City by buying the run-down *World*. Within four years the paper had reached a record-breaking 250,000 circulation, had eclipsed the *Herald* as the leader in advertising volume, and had become the country's most talked-about newspaper.

Pulitzer's success lay in the fact that he had not forgotten the basic news function while he was wooing new readers with entertaining and sensational material. He gave his audience its money's worth in the equality and extent of significant news coverage and presented it in an enlivened style. He plowed money into the building of a competent staff of newsmen and he kept pace with mechanical innovations which permitted them to fashion a better product. He combined a popular editorial aggressiveness and crusading spirit with a great promotional skill to make the mass of readers feel the *World* was their friend. To attract them to its solid news stories and editorial column, the *World* offered big headlines, human interest stories, illustrations, and other sensationalized approaches. With the advent of color printing in the early 1890's, the *World* added popular Sunday supplements and the comic strip.

Some of Pulitzer's competitors did not sense the total character of his journalistic product and mistakenly assumed that sensationalism alone had made the *World* successful. One of these was William Randolph Hearst, who took over the San Francisco *Examiner* in 1887 and then invaded New York in 1895 by buying the *Journal.* The circulation war between Pulitzer's *World* and Hearst's *Journal* brought the cycle of sensationalism to a new height. Critics who eyed one of the comic strip characters of the times, the "Yellow Kid," dubbed the papers "yellow journals." The yellow journal prided itself on being the crusading friend of the "common man," but it underestimated his interest in significant news and overestimated his capacity for absorbing gaudy, oversensationalized news. The result was a degrading of the news function, which reached its climax during the period of the Spanish-American War. After a few years the *World* and other serious-minded papers withdrew from the competition, leaving the techniques of yellow journalism to Hearst and his imitators. While the yellow journals cannot be held solely responsible for causing the war, their news policies certainly contributed to the war fever of 1898.

There were other notable leaders in the New Journalism era. The master teacher of the art of human interest writing was Charles A. Dana's New York *Sun,* which developed many a great reporter or editor for other papers. Dana, however, resisted change and the *Sun* set its face against the general trend of the times. Edward Wyllis Scripps began developing his group of papers, headed by the Cleveland *Press.* They were low-priced, small in size, well-written and tightly edited, and hard-hitting in both news and editorial columns. Melville Stone's Chicago *Daily News* and William Rockhill Nelson's Kansas City *Star* were two more distinctive new papers fashioned in the New Journalism pattern. In the South, Henry W. Grady became known as a master news executive for his work with the Atlanta *Constitution,* and because of his own reporting skill.

It was Nelson who said the reporter "is the big toad in the puddle." It was in this period that the reporter came into his own. Men like Will Irwin, Lincoln Steffens, Jacob Riis, Julian Ralph, and Richard Harding Davis became widely known for their reportorial skill and exploits. Behind them were the news executives, like John A. Cockerill of the *World,* Amos J. Cummings of the *Sun,* and Arthur Brisbane of the *Journal.* By now metropolitan dailies had further developed their staffs. Below the editor-in-chief and managing editor were the city editor, who was in charge of local reporters; the night editor and telegraph editor, who superintended the flow of news dispatches; a sports staff; and the financial editor, literary editor, drama critic, and editorial writers. Rewrite men appeared to handle telephone calls from the beat reporters; desk men took over the chores of editing copy and writing headlines; a women's news staff developed; and the special Sunday edition staff of writers, cartoonists, and artists emerged. Men and women vied for positions on newspaper staffs, and the "romance of reporting" never seemed more attractive than it did to these eager, if largely untrained, newsmen and newswomen.

The people's champions. The rise of the architects of the New Journalism, in the 1870's and 1880's, brought a heightening of attention to the exercise of the opinion function. Joseph Pulitzer, the leading exponent of the New Journalism, has been named by his colleagues of this century as the leading American editor of modern times. A memo written by Pulitzer to an editor of his St. Louis *Post-Dispatch* summarizes his idealistic goal for the editorial page:

. . . every issue of the paper presents an opportunity and a duty to say something courageous and true; to rise above the mediocre and conventional; to say something that will command the respect of the intelligent, the educated, the independent part of the community; to rise above fear of partisanship and fear of popular prejudice.

No finer statement of the responsibility imposed upon those who exercise the newspaper's opinion function has ever been written. Those who even occasionally can meet such a challenge win the respect of both the newspaper craft and their readers.

Pulitzer and his contemporaries of the New Journalism era developed a growing independence of editorial opinion from partisan pressures. They did not hesitate to support political candidates, but they did not do this automatically as part of a political machine, as did the political press. Most of the leaders were champions of the "common man"—people's champions, doing battle against the trusts and monopolies that characterized big business, the crooked politicians who were "the shame of the cities," the money lenders and the speculators, and the opponents of reform. The majority supported the political leaders of the Democratic party—Grover Cleveland, William Jennings Bryan, Woodrow Wilson—

but they also gave aid to such progressive Republicans as Theodore Roosevelt and Robert M. La Follette. Pulitzer himself believed that the Democratic party best carried out the principles he espoused, but he bolted from the radical Bryan candidacy and gave aid and comfort to such New York Republicans as Charles Evans Hughes in their battles with Tammany Hall. His great editor, Frank I. Cobb, who carried on the traditions of the New York *World* after Pulitzer's death in 1911, was a close adviser to Woodrow Wilson and his solid champion. Cobb, however, insisted that it was part of his job to criticize the administration as well as to defend it. This is part of what is meant by "independence of editorial opinion from partisan pressures."

A distinctive feature of the New Journalism paper was its eagerness to crusade in behalf of the community welfare. Pulitzer developed the coordinated crusade, using both the news and editorial columns, at the *Post-Dispatch* and that paper remained famous for its tenacious attacks on wrongdoers in public or business life. These words written by Pulitzer in 1907, which became the *Post-Dispatch* editorial platform, sum up the crusading spirit:

> I know that my retirement will make no difference in its cardinal principles; that it will always fight for progress and reform, never tolerate injustice or corruption, always fight demagogues of all parties, never belong to any party, always oppose privileged classes and public plunderers, never lack sympathy with the poor, always remain devoted to the public welfare, never be satisfied with merely printing news, always be drastically independent, never be afraid to attack wrong, whether by predatory plutocracy or predatory poverty.

William Randolph Hearst, in his New York *Journal* and other newspapers, likewise was a crusading champion of the people. His editorial platform at the turn of the century called for nationalization of the coal mines, railroads, and telegraph lines; public ownership of public franchises; the "destruction of the criminal trusts"; a graduated income tax; election of United States senators by popular vote rather than by state legislatures which could be influenced by big business; and extensive new financial support for the public schools. To this he added an active support of labor unions that made them regard his papers as their champions.

One would suppose the liberals of the time would have clasped Hearst to their bosoms. But they did not. They distrusted Hearst's own political ambitions, which extended to the White House; they disliked the bitterness of his editorial attacks upon his opponents; repelled by the sensationalism and near-cynicism of his news policies, they rejected his editorial page as shallow and insincere. But undoubtedly Hearst had great influence upon the "common man" reader of the pre-World War I generation. By the 1920's, however, the Hearst papers were much less progressive in outlook, and by the 1930's their position was almost reversed from the one they had held in 1900. Always strongly nationalistic, in contrast to Pulitzer's support of international cooperation, the Hearst papers became bitterly isolationist by the time of World War I, and remained so even past their founder's death in 1951.

Edward Wyllis Scripps was the third of the great "people's champions" of the New Journalism era. Scripps set his circulation sights on the working people of the smaller but growing industrial cities of the country, as he developed his chain of newspapers from his headquarters at the Cleveland *Press*. His social goal was to improve the position of the mass of people through better education, labor union organization and collective bargaining, and a resulting reasonable redistribution of wealth. In this way, he reasoned, a peaceful and productive pattern of society could emerge in an industrialized America.

Scripps viewed himself as the only real friend of the "poor and ill-informed." He said his newspapers were the only schoolroom the workingman had; the public school system did not serve him adequately and other newspapers were either capitalistic in outlook or too intellectual in their appeal. He pictured himself as a "damned old crank" who was instinctively rebellious against the status quo in any field of human activity. He made a point of running small, tightly edited papers which could assert their independence of the business community and resist any attempted influence by advertisers. But he was businessman enough to make a profit on his journalistic ventures, and his employees found him to be cautious in wage policies. Politically, the Scripps papers were strongly liberal; they supported the third party candidacies of Theodore Roosevelt in 1912 and Robert M. La Follette in 1924, Woodrow Wilson's "New Freedom," the right of workers to organize, and public ownership. This liberal pattern continued after Scripps' death in 1926 and until the late 1930's when, under the influence of the late Roy W. Howard, the Scripps-Howard papers became substantially more conservative.

THE OPINION MAGAZINES

Highly important among the "people's champions" of the reform era at the opening of the twentieth century were the magazines. Dismayed by the bitterness of some of their attacks, Theodore Roosevelt called their work "muckraking," comparing the more sensational writers to the Man with the Muckrake in *Pilgrim's Progress*, who did not look up to see the celestial crown but continued to rake the filth. The magazine men and women, however, considered the appellation as a badge of honor.

Magazines had exercised the opinion function from colonial times, when Tom Paine wrote for Robert Aitken's *Pennsylvania Magazine*. Other early magazines of note had included Mathew Carey's *American Museum* and Hezekiah Niles' famous *Niles' Weekly Register,* a combination news magazine and documentary source founded in 1811. The following noted magazines were still being published in 1900: The *North American Review,* which began its long career in 1815; *Harper's Monthly,* which appeared in 1850; and the *Atlantic Monthly,* which began in 1857. These highly literary periodicals were joined by the *Century* in 1881 and *Scribner's* in 1886.

More influential in public affairs were *Harper's Weekly,* edited by George William Curtis and famous for the political cartoons of Thomas Nast; Godkin's *Nation;* the *Independent,* founded in 1848; and the following new arrivals of the 1880's and 1890's: Albert Shaw's *Review of Reviews,* Lyman Abbott's *Outlook,* the *Literary Digest,* the *Forum,* and Benjamin Flower's *Arena,* identified by magazine historians as the forerunner of the muckrakers. Three new magazines of the same period which depended upon humor, cartoon, and satire were *Puck, Judge,* and *Life* (the original *Life* featuring the famed Gibson girl drawings).

Entered in the mass circulation field during the 1880's and 1890's were Cyrus H. K. Curtis' *Ladies' Home Journal* and *Saturday Evening Post,* Robert J. Collier's *Collier's,* Frank Munsey's *Munsey's,* S. S. McClure's *McClure's,* and *Cosmopolitan,* which became a Hearst property. Low-priced and popular in appeal, they carried both fiction and nonfiction.

This was an impressive battery of magazines to turn loose during the reform era of the Theodore Roosevelt administrations (all of the public affairs and mass circulation magazines except *Munsey's* and the *Saturday Evening Post* joined in the chase). *McClure's* touched off the major muckraking movement in late 1902 when it offered almost simultaneously Ida M. Tarbell's "History of the Standard Oil Company" and Lincoln Steffens' "Shame of the Cities" series. Circulation shot up as citizens read about the unfair business practices of John D. Rockefeller and about crime and corruption in St. Louis, Minneapolis, Pittsburgh, Philadelphia, Chicago, and New York. Other *McClure's* writers were Ray Stannard Baker, Burton J. Hendrick, William Allen White, and Will Irwin.

Cosmopolitan countered with "Treason in the Senate," an attack upon conservative spokesmen of "the interests" written by David Graham Phillips, a Pulitzer editorial writer. *Everybody's,* a newcomer to the fray, shot into circulation prominence with Thomas W. Lawson's "Frenzied Finance," an inside exposé of Wall Street. *Pearson's, Hampton's,* and *La Follette's Weekly* were additional late starters. The farm machine industry, the beef trust, the New York life insurance companies, the patent medicine trade, corrupt political machines, and businesses generally were among the victims. Samuel Hopkins Adams and Mark Sullivan exposed the patent medicines in *Collier's.*

The cream of the writers moved to John S. Phillips' *American Magazine* in 1906, after a break with McClure. In the crowd were Miss Tarbell, Steffens, Baker, Finley Peter Dunne ("Mr. Dooley"), and a somewhat gingerly progressive named William Allen White, who achieved primary fame as the highly personal editor of the Emporia *Gazette* in Kansas. They continued to lead the muckraking movement until it dwindled away by the time of World War I.

Coming on the scene in 1914 was the *New Republic,* featuring the writing of Herbert Croly and Walter Lippmann. Shocking American complacency in the 1920's was H. L. Mencken's *American Mercury.* But by and large American interest in magazines of opinion has declined. Of all the magazines listed in this account only the *Nation, New Republic,* and *La Follette's* survived as magazines of dissent, to be joined by the *Reporter* in 1949. *Harper's* and *Atlantic* were the only survivors among the public affairs and literary periodicals listed; joining them in the quality magazine field which plays a role in opinion formulation were the *New Yorker* and *Saturday Review.* Among all the more general magazines mentioned, only the *Saturday Evening Post, Ladies' Home Journal,* and *Cosmopolitan* are still published. The *Post* continues its interest in public affairs, as do other current leaders in the general magazine field, among which are the picture magazines *Life* and *Look* and the *Reader's Digest.* The news magazines—*Time, Newsweek,* and *U.S. News & World Report*—also exercise the opinion function.

TWENTIETH-CENTURY NEWS TRENDS

Impartial gathering and reporting of the news was generally recognized to be the basic obligation of newspapers by the early 1900's. Some did the job in a much more comprehensive and intelligent fashion than others. But the editor who put views ahead of news, and who tied his newspaper to a political machine, had pretty well gone out of style. Slanting of news to fit the prejudices or political preferences of a publisher was also recognized as a detriment, although some newspapers continued to persist in the practice. The "Canons of Journalism" adopted by the American Society of Newspaper Editors in 1923 contain these two paragraphs which summarize the aspirations of modern journalistic leaders:

The right of a newspaper to attract and hold readers is restricted by nothing but considerations of public welfare. The use a newspaper makes of the share of public attention it gains serves to determine its sense of responsibility, which it shares with every member of its staff. A journalist who uses his power for any selfish or otherwise unworthy purpose is faithless to a high trust.

Partisanship, in editorial comment which knowingly departs from the truth, does violence to the best spirit of American journalism; in the news columns it is subversive of a fundamental principle of the profession.

No matter how impartial and well intentioned a newspaper's editors might be, they had to expend an increasing effort on comprehensive coverage and display of the news, and its intelligent interpretation, if they were to meet their full responsibilities. Great events of this century made the business of reporting the news far more complex, decade by decade. In the first decade, the story was one of economic and political reform in the United States. In the second decade, it was World War I. In the third decade, it was the world's effort at postwar readjustment. The fourth decade brought the Great Depression and a collapse of world order. The fifth and sixth brought World War II, the atomic era, and the cold war.

The mass media made a reasonable effort to fulfill their increased responsibilities for interpreting the news of events which all but overwhelmed the world. Professional standards had to be raised to meet the challenge. Better trained and more knowledgeable men and women came to occupy key reportorial assignments and news desk posts. The range of subject matter with which a Washington correspondent had to be familiar in the 1920's was narrow indeed compared to the complexities of Washington news in the 1960's. And since all news tended to become "local" in its impact with the narrowing of geographical barriers in the atomic age, every general assignment reporter had to know far more about such areas as international affairs, science, and economic trends than did his predecessors. The modern press associations, particularly, were put under heavy pressures. Newspapers were stimulated by the appearance of new competitors: radio, television, and the news magazine. Radio and television challenged the newspaper both in providing spot news coverage and in news analysis. The news magazines competed with the newspapers by giving the reader background information and point-of-view interpretation. Together, the print and electronic media offered a persistent reader-listener-viewer a sizable amount of information about the swirl of events which virtually engulfed even the most conscientious citizen.

Ochs and the Times. The editors of the New York *Times* built what is generally conceded to be the greatest single news machine of this century, publishing what was called by its admiring competitors a "newspaper of record." The story of the growth of the *Times* since Adolph S. Ochs rescued it from bankruptcy in 1896 illustrates the trend in acceptance of the news function responsibility, even though it is the story of a nontypical journalistic leader. For what the *Times* did in its methodical completeness was done at least in part, and in some respects as successfully, by other responsible newspapers.

Ochs told his readers in 1896: "It will be my aim . . . to give the news impartially, without fear or favor . . ." He also promised them all the news, in concise and attractive form, and a paper which would be "a forum for the consideration of all questions of public importance, and to that end to invite intelligent discussion from all shades of opinion." He made no attempt to match the sensationalism of the yellow journals of the time, and he shunned many of the popularized entertainment features of most newspapers, including the comic strip. His Sunday magazine featured articles of current news significance and became, with its more than 1,000,000 circulation of today, an important fixture in the magazine world. His book review section became the best known in the country. His coverage of financial and business news soon matched that of any older competitor. His editorial page, if quieter and more cautious than that of Pulitzer, was intelligently directed.

What made the *Times* great, however, was not so much these accomplishments as its persistence in gathering and printing the news in all its varied aspects. One of the great managing editors, Carr V. Van Anda, was given control of the *Times* newsroom in 1904 with the understanding that he should do whatever it took to do a comprehensive job with the news. Ochs was willing to spend money to get the news; Van Anda was willing to do the spending, and he knew how to get the news. It was an ideal association for a quarter of a century, during which time the *Times* rose to its position of news leadership. Van Anda rode the news, . 12 hours a day, seven days a week, giving as much attention to the entire flow of the news as to the major story breaks. He loved to match his wits against a deadline, to exploit an undeveloped but important story, and to beat his competitors on such a colorful story as the sinking of the "Titanic" or such a significant story as the first announcement of the Einstein theory of relativity. With the coming of wireless communication, the *Times* began to present two or three pages of wireless news from Europe each Sunday, and it eventually built its own trans-Atlantic wireless receiving station, which in turn gave way to a radio facility.

World War I gave Van Anda an opportunity to show his full ability. Using the cables and wireless almost with abandon, the *Times* added the reports of its own correspondents to those of the press associations and syndicates. It reported in detail not only on military operations but on political and economic developments in the European capitals. War pictures were carried in a rotogravure section added in 1914. Most importantly, the paper began to publish the texts of documents and speeches, beginning with the British White Paper of August, 1914, which covered six full pages, and including the Treaty of Versailles, which filled eight pages—more than any other American paper was willing to give that important document. This policy, combined with the publication of the annual *New York Times Index,* made the *Times* the leading newspaper for librarians, scholars, government officials, and other newspaper editors.

If there was any complaint to be registered against the *Times* of the Van Anda period, it was that the paper presented a voluminous amount of news without sufficient interpretation or screening for the average reader. The "dead pan" objective fashion of reporting was considered the best, if impartiality was to be achieved, as late as the 1920's. But Van Anda did a goodly share of interpreting the news, and the editors who followed him did more. The Washington and foreign staffs built by the paper ranked with the best, and during the following decades they came to offer interpretative analysis along with factual reporting. The *Times* developed experts in the fields of science reporting and labor news in the early 1920's, far ahead of the general trend toward specialized reporting. It followed with authoritative reporters in virtually every field of news activity. Its Sunday news in review section, offering a week-end analysis of major news events, became outstanding. No institution is perfect, and the *Times* suffers from some faults—perhaps because it became almost unwieldy in staff size and in the number of pages it printed —but it continues to stand as a shining example of a newspaper dedicated to carrying out the news function as completely as a group of men can manage to do.

One more wave of sensationalism was to precede the "era of interpretation," however. The 1920's were known as the "Jazz Age," and the papers which catered to a new group of readers won the dubious honor of being identified as "Jazz Journalism." The leaders were three new New York City papers which found upward of 2,000,000 readers without immediately disturbing the circulation balance of the existing dailies. Their sensationalism was accompanied by the two identifying techniques of the period: the tabloid format and great emphasis upon photography.

Leading the sensational tabloids was the New York *Illustrated Daily News,* founded in 1919 by Joseph Medill Patterson, cousin of Robert R. McCormick and partner with him in the publishing of the Chicago *Tribune.* Patterson, unlike his ultraconservative Chicago cousin, was unconventional in his socioeconomic beliefs—socialistic, his wealthy friends said. He wanted to reach and influence the lowest literate class of Americans and was attracted to the tabloid format by the success Lord Northcliffe was enjoying with it in England. The *Daily News* appeared with a photograph spread across its front half-page and was well stuffed with pictures, human interest stories, and entertaining features. By 1924 it had the largest circulation of any newspaper in the country, a position it continued to hold by a wide margin from that time on.

Prohibition, rum runners, gangsters, glamorous and sexy Hollywood stars, the glorified celebrities of sports and politics, and the usual quota of crime and murder all were grist for the tabloid's mill. Hearst entered the competition in 1924 with his *Daily Mirror,* followed by Bernarr Macfadden's *Daily Graphic,* which scarcely bothered to cover serious news at all. As in any cycle of sensationalism, other papers took on an excessive tinge, but the New York trio stood almost apart. One, however, was more sensitive to audience needs; when the Great Depression arrived, the *Daily News* swung into a modified course which made it a more serious (if still wise-cracking) medium, whereas the *Mirror* floundered along until 1963 and the *Graphic* slipped away into oblivion.

The tabloid format, it should be noted, did not have to be equated with sensationalism. It was used by other papers that were similar to the dailies of conventional size in all respects save that of the half-fold style. Among them were the Chicago *Sun-Times,* the New York *Post,* and the Scripps-Howard *Daily News* in Washington and *Rocky Mountain News* in Denver. Nor did photojournalism have to be lurid; the New York *Daily News* developed great enterprise in news photography and Patterson was instrumental in the establishment of Associated Press Wirephoto.

Interpretative reporting was not unknown before the 1930's, just as uncritical and sensationalized treatment of the news did not die out after that time. But the socioeconomic revolution known politically as the New Deal, coupled with the impact of international crises, forced editors to emphasize "why" along with "who did what." Old-style objectivity, which called for the reporter to stick to a factual account of what had been said or done, did not give the reader the full meaning of the news. The new concept of objectivity was based upon the premise that the reader needed to have a given event placed in its proper perspective if truth really was to be served. Older assumptions that such subjects as science and economics could not be made interesting to a mass readership were also discarded. Reporter-specialists who could talk both to their news subjects and to a popular reading audience appeared to cover politics, business, foreign affairs, science, labor, agriculture, and social work.

There was a sheer problem of just getting the significant news into the paper and read, even for the most conscientious editors, as the news flow mounted. Readership studies show that only one-fourth of the stories are read by 30 per cent or more of the potential audience, and one-fourth have 4 per cent or less readership. Content studies show a distressingly small percentage of stories about such important areas as foreign affairs and science are offered to the reader by the average American newspaper.

THE COLUMNISTS

The decline of the personal editor, and the rise of a more impersonal (but sometimes more effective) corporate newspaper journalism, left room for new actors on the opinion-making stage. These were the newspaper columnists. Their personal followings have been large, since syndicates gave them nationwide circulation. Readers who no longer knew, perhaps, anything of a personal character about the local newspaper publisher or editor, and who referred to the opinions they read as those of the newspaper rather than of any individual on its staff, looked to the columnists for the "personal touch."

The political column began in the 1920's with the work of David Lawrence of the *United States News,* Mark Sullivan of the New York *Herald Tribune,* and Frank R. Kent of the Baltimore *Sun.* Walter Lippmann joined the *Herald Tribune* syndicate in 1931 when the New York *World* closed its doors. United Feature Syndicate, owned by Scripps-Howard, contributed three outstanding columnists during the New Deal era, when the impact of social and economic change widened the horizons of columnists beyond the political level; meeting the challenge were Raymond Clapper, Thomas L. Stokes, and Heywood Broun. Their successors at United Features have been Marquis Childs and William S. White. Roscoe Drummond of the *Herald Tribune* syndicate and Peter Edson of Newspaper Enterprise Association also became leading Washington columnists, and Dorothy Thompson and Doris Fleeson became the best known of the women political columnists. At the right in their political outlooks were George Sokolsky and Westbrook Pegler of Hearst's King Features. Edgar Ansel Mowrer and Joseph and Stewart Alsop joined Lippmann as specialists in comment on international affairs. The gossip columnists were dominated by Drew Pearson and Robert S. Allen, whose "Washington Merry-Go-Round" began in 1931. An endless number of changing by-lines appeared on the country's editorial pages as the columnist continued to hold his position as an interpreter and opinion oracle, although the reaction of some newspapers to the "columnist movement" was the application of renewed vigor in their own editorial writing and interpretative articles and the minimizing of syndicated material.

THE NEWS MAGAZINES

The news magazines offered a relatively small segment of the population another means of keeping abreast of events. The biggest, *Time,* has built a 3,000,000 circulation; *Newsweek* and *U.S. News & World Report* have circulations of about half that number. Although some issues go to subscribers who use them to bulwark inadequate news coverage by small local newspapers, many go to relatively well-informed citizens who read one or more daily newspapers, listen to television and radio news, subscribe to public affairs magazines, read books, and take one to three news magazines.

Henry R. Luce's formula for *Time* was to organize and departmentalize the news of the week in a style "written as if by one man for one man," whom *Time* described as too busy to spend all the time necessary to peruse the other media. Coverage of national affairs, foreign affairs, science, religion, education, business, and other areas was to be written for this "busy man," not for experts in each of the fields. The magazine developed a big research and library staff, as well as its own good-sized newsgathering organization, to supplement press association services. Begun in 1923, *Time* helped to drive the older *Literary Digest* out of business with this approach. *Newsweek* appeared in 1933, with an almost identical format. *U.S. News & World Report* grew out of a combination of two of David Lawrence's publications in Washington, hitting its stride in the late 1940's. Two picture news magazines, Luce's *Life* (1936) and Gardner Cowles' *Look* (1937), offered additional news coverage and interpretative articles.

It should be noted that the news magazines offered both news and opinion to their readers. *Time* made no attempt to distinguish between the two functions, intermingling opinion and editorial hypotheses with the straight news. Its use of narrative and human interest techniques, and overuse of adjectives, added to its editorial bias. *Time* said it wanted to be "fair," not objective or even impartial. The trouble was, some readers mistook *Time*'s "fairness" (opinion-giving) for factual reporting. *Newsweek* injected less opinion into its columns and offered separate editorial opinions written by commentators.

THE PRESS ASSOCIATIONS

The major job of newsgathering beyond the local level is done not by the mass media themselves, but by the two big associations, Associated Press and United Press International. Newspapers, of course, cover their own local communities (although sometimes they even use press association reports about events taking place in their own cities). Some newspapers maintain area or state coverage through strings of correspondents who filter in news to a state desk; this practice varies from one part of the country to another, and many a large paper depends on the press associations for news of events as close as 50 miles from the city room, staffing only major news developments in its area. Only a small percentage of American dailies have their own Washington coverage, and the bulk of this is directed toward stories of regional or local interest, rather than the major news stories of the day. And only a handful of newspapers have their own correspondents abroad. The situation is much the same in television and radio, where the press associations supply virtually all the news for smaller stations, all but local news for many larger stations, and even the bulk of the news for the network-affiliated stations. The news magazines, too, use the press association reports for the basis of their work.

Cooperative newsgathering in this country began, as we have seen, in 1848 with the Associated Press of New York. The telegraph enabled the New York papers which controlled this early AP to sell its news to a gradually expanding group of papers. Opening of the Atlantic cable in 1866 gave the agency better access to European news, which it obtained under exchange agreements with Reuters of Great Britain, Havas of France, and other press services. Regional AP groups formed, the most powerful of which was the Western Associated Press. The dailies outside New York City resented the tight-fisted control of the AP by the New York morning dailies which had founded it; the new evening dailies of the Midwest felt they were being ignored in the supplying of news on the two differing time cycles for morning and evening publication.

A bitter battle broke out among the newspapers in the 1880's. A rival group to the AP took the name United Press (no relation to the present agency) and built up a sizable membership, as well as a first-rate foreign news service. The New York leaders of the AP attempted to absorb the new UP, and failing, deserted their own organization to join it. Control of the AP fell to the Western AP members, headed by Melville E. Stone, founder of the Chicago *Daily News*. Stone drafted exclusive news exchange contracts with the European agencies, cutting off the New York papers from their traditional supply of foreign news, and broke his rivals by 1897. An adverse court ruling in Illinois threatened the membership status of the AP at this same moment, so its headquarters were returned to New York in 1900.

The basis of the AP was its cooperative exchange of news. The members found it necessary to finance a larger and larger staff, however, which took over direction of the flow of news and eventually much of the newsgathering. Its organizational structure was not entirely democratic; the older and larger newspaper members kept control of the board of directors by giving themselves extra voting rights during the 1900 reorganization. Until an adverse Supreme Court decision in 1945, an AP member could prevent the entry of a direct competitor into the group by exercising a protest right which could be overridden only by a four-fifths vote of the entire membership.

Newspapers which could not gain entry to the AP, or which disliked its control by the older morning papers of the East, needed press association service from another source. Edward Wyllis Scripps, possessing both a string of evening dailies and an individualistic temperament which made him dislike monopoly, founded the United Press Associations in 1907 from earlier regional agencies. William Randolph Hearst, whose newly founded papers were denied AP memberships, started the International News Service in 1909. Other agencies came and went, but the AP, UP, and INS survived until 1958, when the Hearst interests liquidated a losing business by merging the INS into the UP to form the United Press International.

The strong men in the AP over the years were Stone, the first general manager, and Kent Cooper, general manager from 1925 to 1948. Builders of the UP were Roy W. Howard, who later became a partner in the Scripps-Howard newspaper group, and presidents Karl A. Bickel and Hugh Baillie. Since 1962 Wes Gallagher has been general manager of AP and Mims Thomason president of UPI. At the INS, Barry Faris was editor-in-chief and sparkplug from 1916 to the agency's end.

Unlike the AP plan of organization, the UP and INS had a service to sell to clients. Howard set out to do this job for the young and struggling UP by building up a foreign service, first in Latin America and then in

Europe. He embarrassed his agency by sending a premature flash announcing the end of World War I, but both Howard and the UP survived the incident. The enthusiasm and aggressiveness of the "shoestring" UP operation brought it into competitive position with the AP by the 1930's. In 1934 Kent Cooper brought an end to the restrictive news exchange agreements between the AP and foreign news agencies, and the AP joined in the foreign service race more determinedly. The AP also capitulated in supplying news to radio stations, five years after UP and INS entered that field in 1935, and made the radio and television stations associate members, without voting rights. The INS, smallest of the three agencies, did not attempt to supply news at the state level except in a few states; it concentrated instead on out-reporting and out-writing the other two on major news breaks and features. The UP-INS merger put the United Press International in a position of competitive equality with its older rival and assured the mass media that there would be intense rivalry between two well-managed and financially strong press associations which serve both in this country and abroad.

SOME CURRENT NEWSPAPER LEADERS

Opinions differ about the quality of individual newspapers; any "list of ten" compiled by one authority would differ to some degree from the listing made by a second competent observer. But newsmen generally agree that a top-flight newspaper must offer both impartial and comprehensive coverage of the news, as a first prerequisite for national recognition. The second prerequisite for recognition by the craft is a superior demonstration of responsibility in providing community opinion leadership and of integrity and zealousness in protecting basic human liberties. The second prerequisite is much harder to judge than the first.

The United States, unlike many other countries, has no truly national newspapers. It has two dailies without "home communities," however, which have won widespread respect and which circulate nationally with their regionally edited editions. These are the *Christian Science Monitor* and the *Wall Street Journal* (neither of which carries a nameplate which seems to indicate the general-interest character of the paper). The *Monitor,* founded in 1908 by the Church of Christ, Scientist, built a high reputation for its Washington and foreign correspondence and its interpretative articles. Edited by Erwin D. Canham since 1945, it serves more than 175,000 readers across the country from its offices in Boston. The *Wall Street Journal's* staff, led by Bernard Kilgore since 1941, has seen its readership jump from 30,000 to 800,000 since that time, to make the paper one of the country's top ten in size. The paper is produced in eight printing plants across the country, connected by electric typesetting devices to its New York office. It won its position on the basis of its excellent writing, clear-cut reporting of important news, and its specialized business and financial information. The firm in 1962 established an affiliated national weekly newspaper of more general appeal, the *National Observer*, edited in Washington.

The New York *Times*, generally recognized as the country's leading daily and "newspaper of record," also has a sizable national circulation, particularly for its Sunday edition. It clearly has been the leader over a period of time in developing its own Washington and foreign staffs, whose stories are also sold to other papers. Publisher-owner Arthur Hays Sulzberger ably carried on the duties of his father-in-law, Adolph S. Ochs, after Ochs' death in 1935 and maintained a remarkable news institution to which many staff members—editors and reporters—contributed leadership. The *Times* editorial page has been quietly effective.

When one turns to newspapers which have won top recognition for their editorial leadership and for their aggressiveness in defense of basic liberal principles of a progressive democracy, the names of four are readily apparent: the St. Louis *Post-Dispatch,* the Washington *Post and Times Herald,* the Milwaukee *Journal,* and the Louisville *Courier-Journal.*

The St. Louis *Post-Dispatch,* published by a third generation of the Pulitzer family, continued to offer American journalism a highest type of example in the exercise of the opinion function—excelling the standard set by Joseph Pulitzer's New York *World,* which ceased publishing in 1931. A talented *Post-Dispatch* editorial page staff, writing superbly and with a depth of understanding on a wide variety of subjects, made the editorial columns outstanding; other opinion features, including the cartoons of Daniel R. Fitzpatrick and Bill Mauldin, measured up. The paper continued to win recognition for its crusading zeal and its outstanding Washington bureau.

Rising to prominence since the 1930's has been the editorial page of the Washington *Post* (the editorial page itself did not add the "and Times Herald" following the 1954 merger of Washington's morning papers).

Financier Eugene Meyer and his son-in-law, Philip L. Graham, the paper's publishers, had as their major aim the molding of a vigorous, intelligent, and informative editorial page for capital readers. This they accomplished, with the help of an able staff who could tap Washington news sources for background and interpretation and the provocative cartoons of Herbert L. Block. The *Post* joined with the Los Angeles *Times* in the 1960's to create a syndicated foreign and Washington news report.

Known as "Milwaukee's Dutch Uncle," the staff-owned Milwaukee *Journal* has demonstrated editorial page excellence since the days of founder Lucius W. Nieman. The *Journal* has paid close attention to city and state affairs (with "On Milwaukee" and "Wisconsin" page-one editorials) and has cultivated both good writing and a wide grasp of political and human affairs on the part of its good-sized group of editorial writers. The same characteristics have been exhibited by the Louisville *Courier-Journal,* owned and edited by Barry Bingham. Both these papers exhibited local and regional news reporting of excellent quality.

Historical rivals of the New York *Times* in organizing and maintaining sizable news services whose Washington and foreign dispatches are syndicated to other newspapers have been the New York *Herald Tribune,* the Chicago *Daily News,* and the Chicago *Tribune.* The *Herald Tribune,* founded in a 1924 merger of two of America's famous early dailies, was owned by the Ogden Reid family until its sale in 1958 to John Hay Whitney, who sought to maintain its position of rivalry with the *Times* in New York as a major newspaper of character. The Chicago *Daily News,* long a leader in interpretative foreign correspondence, passed into a combined ownership with the *Sun-Times* when Marshall Field, Jr., purchased it in 1959. Although both the *Herald Tribune* and the *Daily News* rank among the top dozen American newspapers, few in the craft would accord the same high position to the late Robert R. McCormick's Chicago *Tribune* in light of the historical record of controversy aroused by its handling of the news (the same criticism applies to the Hearst newspapers).

Among other newspapers of highest quality, the Baltimore *Sun* and the Minneapolis *Star* and *Tribune* maintain both strong Washington bureaus and limited foreign staffs (the Minneapolis effort is part of one made by John and Gardner Cowles, owners also of the Des Moines *Register* and *Tribune,* and *Look*). Respected for their news play are such other leading papers as the Kansas City *Star,* Cleveland *Press,* Toledo *Blade,* and Chicago *Sun-Times* in the Midwest; the Washington *Star,* Providence *Journal,* and Hartford *Courant* in the East; the Miami *Herald,* Atlanta *Constitution,* and Raleigh *News and Observer* in the South; and the Denver *Post* and the Los Angeles *Times* in the West. Another dozen could be named with almost equal justice to such a list of current leaders in exercising the news function.

While all these newspapers have capable editorial pages, some have won particular attention. Examples of effective conservative opinion are found in the editorial columns of the New York *Herald Tribune,* the *Christian Science Monitor,* and the *Wall Street Journal.* Rising in quality and in aggressive independent opinion have been the pages of the Minneapolis *Tribune* and Toledo *Blade.* The Baltimore *Sun,* Chicago *Daily News,* and Providence *Journal* constitute another trio whose editorial pages have won substantial respect over a period of time. At the liberal left, the New York *Post* has admirers of its opinion pages (particularly of its columnists) and of the intellectual level of its political discussion (a level not matched, however, in its general news play). A paper of smaller circulation which has won attention for its vigorous editorial comment on political affairs and independent-mindedness is the McClatchy family's Sacramento *Bee* in California.

As Gerald Johnson once said, "The greatest newspaper is as difficult to identify as the greatest man—it all depends upon what you require." Certainly an intelligent, honest, and public-spirited editorial page is as much an essential of an effective newspaper as is comprehensive and honest reporting and display of the news.

SUMMARY

Impartial and comprehensive reporting and display of the news is the primary function of the newspaper; its other basic obligation is to provide responsible opinion leadership. A third function is that of entertaining the reader.

Our present-day concepts of gathering and reporting the news developed slowly. Many of the first newspaper publishers were primarily printers; James and Benjamin Franklin are examples of colonial American publishers who also were editors. Colonial newspapers were of two types: (1) the mercantile paper reflecting the interests of the business and shipping classes and (2) the political paper of frankly partisan appeal.

Editors of colonial papers and early political papers were more political pamphleteers than newspapermen in their exercise of the opinion function. Among the pamphleteers who used the newspaper's columns were John Dickinson, spokesman for the colonial Whigs; Samuel Adams, brilliant propagandist of the Revolution; Tom Paine, the political philosopher who produced the *Crisis* papers and *Common Sense;* and Alexander Hamilton and the other authors of the *Federalist Papers.*

What we call the "penny press"—newspapers of general interest written and edited for mass circulation—appeared between 1833 and 1837 to revolutionize American journalism. The first of these popularized dailies was Benjamin Day's New York *Sun.* James Gordon Bennett, founder of the New York *Herald* in 1835, serves as the symbol of the news enterpriser; he used ponies, steamships, railroads, and the telegraph in the "race for news." Henry J. Raymond's New York *Times* of 1851 represents the maturing of this popular press.

Horace Greeley, recognized as one of the most influential American editors, developed an editorial page for his New York *Tribune* (1841) which was the product of the thinking of a group of individuals. Greeley's contribution was enterprise in opinion leadership; the *Tribune* examined issues, explored ideas, and concerned itself with the social and economic issues of the day. He and his noted staff did much to teach others a fuller concept of the newspaper's opinion function.

Greeley was one of the "personal editors" of the nineteenth century. Others were William Cullen Bryant of the New York *Evening Post,* Samuel Bowles III of the Springfield *Republican* in Massachusetts, Joseph Medill of the Chicago *Tribune,* Henry Watterson of the Louisville *Courier-Journal,* and perhaps the most brilliant of the group, Edwin Lawrence Godkin, founder of the *Nation* and editor of the New York *Evening Post.*

A "New Journalism" arose in the 1870's and 1880's in response to vast social, economic, and political changes in the decades following the Civil War. Joseph Pulitzer was the leader in this new advance, with his St. Louis *Post-Dispatch* and New York *World.* Edward Wyllis Scripps, William Randolph Hearst, William Rockhill Nelson, and Melville Stone were among others who contributed to the emergence of the modern American daily. The rise of the "New Journalism" brought a group which used their editorial pages to champion the people's causes—notable among this group were Pulitzer, Scripps, and Hearst. They and the editors of the "muckraking" magazines helped to spark the reforms of the early 1900's.

The twentieth century has seen a growing acceptance of responsibility in fulfilling the news function, the rise in interpretative reporting, and the development of specialization in reporting. Sensationalism, as exemplified by the "Jazz Journalism" of the 1920's, still remained one characteristic of daily newspapers, however. The New York *Times* of the Adolph S. Ochs era serves as an example of better journalistic practices. The news magazines—*Time, Newsweek,* and *U.S. News & World Report*—have been important since the 1930's.

The major job of newsgathering beyond the local level is done by the press associations, Associated Press and United Press International. Cooperative newsgathering in the United States dates from 1848; the modern press associations date from the turn of the century.

Among current newspaper leaders, the *Wall Street Journal* and *Christian Science Monitor* have won national circulations as publications of a specialized character. The New York *Times,* recognized as the country's "newspaper of record," is one of a group of papers maintaining strong Washington and foreign news staffs; others ranking high in quality in this respect are the New York *Herald Tribune* and the Chicago *Daily News*. Recognized for their leadership in editorial page quality are the St. Louis *Post-Dispatch,* Washington *Post and Times Herald,* Milwaukee *Journal,* and Louisville *Courier-Journal*.

STUDY QUESTION

What are the principal changes which have taken place in American newspapers since colonial days?

PROJECTS

1. Clip a news magazine article and a newspaper story about the same subject in either the field of science or the field of international affairs. In a brief essay compare the treatment accorded each.

2. Write a 500-word essay concerning the journalistic contributions of one of the following: (a) Horace Greeley, (b) James Gordon Bennett, (c) Joseph Pulitzer, (d) E. W. Scripps, (e) William Randolph Hearst, (f) Adolph S. Ochs.

CHAPTER 6

RADIO,
TELEVISION,
AND FILM

NEWS TAKES TO THE AIR

Public interest in news made it natural for men to use any new medium of communication—the telegraph, the telephone, the underseas cable, the wireless, the motion picture film, radio broadcasting, telecasting, and the communications satellite—to hurry the news to waiting eyes and ears, or to bring news events directly to distant audiences.

The telegraph, the telephone, the cable, and the wireless were nineteenth-century inventions that could speed the transmission of messages to waiting newspaper editors and printing presses. The motion picture film became a competitor that could bring to audiences in theaters a visual portrayal of such an exciting event as the Corbett-Fitzsimmons heavyweight prize fight of 1897—the first news event so shown. Soon excerpts of films of news events were put together into newsreels, which were a part of the standard fare of the movie palace of the 1920's. But the time lag before a newsreel could be shown kept it from being more than an incidental competitor for the newspaper. Interpretative films like Time Inc.'s *The March of Time* of the 1930's and the development in that decade of the techniques of the documentary film—*The Plow that Broke the Plain* and *The River* were notable examples—foreshadowed the impact film would have on other news media once it had the direct way to reach the public that television provided. In the meantime news took to the air through the magic of radio.

The first news broadcast in the United States is generally credited to Dr. Lee De Forest, the man who in 1906 invented the vacuum tube that made voice broadcasting possible as the next step beyond Marconi's wireless telegraphy of the 1890's. On November 7, 1916, the New York *American* ran a wire to De Forest's experimental station at High Bridge, New York, so that the "father of radio" could broadcast to a few amateur radio enthusiasts the returns from the Wilson-Hughes presidential election. Like the *American* and other newspapers misled by the early returns from that closely contested election, De Forest signed off with the statement that "Charles Evans Hughes will be the next president of the United States."

The inventive and engineering resources of wireless and radio were needed for military purposes during World War I, and private broadcasting was banned until 1919. Even then few saw the possibilities of mass radio listening. One who did was David Sarnoff, son of a Russian immigrant family who got his start as a Marconi wireless operator. When three big companies of the communications and electric manufacturing industries—Westinghouse, General Electric, and American Telephone & Telegraph—pooled their patent rights interests in 1919 and formed the Radio Corporation of America, Sarnoff became RCA's sparkplug and the eventual head of both it and its subsidiary, the National Broadcasting Company.

It was a Westinghouse engineer, Dr. Frank Conrad, who offered the first proof of Sarnoff's contentions that people would listen to radio. His broadcasts of music in Pittsburgh in 1919 stimulated sales of crystal sets and led Westinghouse to open KDKA on November 2, 1920, as the first fully licensed commercial broadcasting station. The featured program consisted of returns from the Harding-Cox presidential election, one whose outcome was more easily predictable. The station got its vote results from the obliging Pittsburgh *Post*.

Other newspapers were more directly involved in broadcasting. One, the Detroit *News*, broadcast news regularly beginning August 31, 1920, over an experimental station that was to become a regular commercial station in 1921, WWJ. Others quick to establish stations were the Kansas City *Star*, Milwaukee *Journal*, Chicago *Tribune*, Los Angeles *Times*, Louisville *Courier-Journal*, Atlanta *Journal*, Fort Worth *Star-Telegram*, Dallas *News*, and Chicago *Daily News*. By 1927 there were 48 newspaper-owned stations, and 97 papers presented news over the air. The publishers thought radio newscasts stimulated sales of newspapers—and subsequent events proved them correct.

But despite these evidences of concern for news, radio's pioneers were more intent on capturing the public's interest by entertaining it than by informing it. Dramatic news events and on-the-spot sports coverage combined both objectives. News summaries themselves remained infrequent in the 1920's because they excited little advertiser interest, because radio itself did not collect news, and because news merely read from the newspaper sounded awkward and dull on the air. Meanwhile, KDKA broadcast accounts of prize fights and major league baseball games in 1921. The next year American Telephone & Telegraph's New York station, WEAF (now WNBC), used phone lines to bring its listeners the Chicago-Princeton football game from Stagg Field. By 1924 an estimated 10,000,000 Americans heard presidential election returns; there were 3,000,000 sets that year and the number of stations had grown from 30 in 1921 to 530. Twenty-one stations from New York to California joined in a March, 1925, hook-up to broadcast President Coolidge's inauguration.

Development of networks was vital for radio news progress. In early 1924 the Eveready Battery Company bought time on a dozen stations for its Eveready Hour performers—the first use of national radio advertising. By 1925 AT&T had organized a chain headed by WEAF with 26 outlets stretching as far west as Kansas City. RCA, Westinghouse, and General Electric had a competitive chain led by WJZ, New York, and WGY, Schenectady. In 1926 the big companies reached an agreement under which AT&T would retire from the broadcasting business in favor of RCA, and in return would control all forms of network relays. RCA, Westinghouse, and General Electric bought WEAF for $1,000,000. They then formed the National Broadcasting Company as an RCA subsidiary. The station chain organized by AT&T and headed by WEAF became the NBC Red network at the start of 1927, while the chain headed by WJZ became the NBC Blue network. Regular coast-to-coast network operations began that year. Sarnoff emerged in full control of RCA and NBC in 1930 when Westinghouse and General Electric withdrew under pressure of an antitrust suit.

Only 7 per cent of the 733 stations operating in early 1927 were affiliated with NBC. Some rivals organized a network service with the support of the Columbia Phonograph Record Company in 1927; financially reorganized the next year under the control of William S. Paley, it became the Columbia Broadcasting System. CBS bought WABC (now WCBS) in New York as its key station and by 1929 was showing a profit. In 1934 it had 97 station affiliates compared to 65 for NBC Red and 62 for NBC Blue.

Passage of the Radio Act of 1927 strengthened the two big networks, since the number of stations on the air was reduced by the new Federal Radio Commission to avoid interference in receiving stations' programs, and a group of some 50 powerful "clear channel" stations was authorized. By 1938 all but two of the clear channel stations were either network-owned or affiliated. And while only 40 per cent of the 660 stations then in operation were network-affiliated, they included virtually all of those licensed for nighttime broadcasting. The two independent clear channel stations, the Chicago *Tribune's* WGN, and WOR, New York, formed the loosely organized Mutual Broadcasting System in 1934 but found competition difficult. Mutual's complaints to the Federal Communications Commission (the regulatory body was renamed in the Communications Act of 1934) brought about the sale by NBC in 1943 of its weaker Blue network to Edward J. Noble, who renamed it the American Broadcasting Company in 1945.

The growth of the networks after 1927, and their success in winning advertising revenues, made radio a more disturbing challenger to the newspaper industry. So did radio's increasing interest in broadcasting news and public affairs. In 1928, Republican Herbert Hoover and Democrat Alfred E. Smith took to the air, spending a million dollars on campaign talks over NBC and CBS networks reaching many of the nation's 8,000,000 receiving sets. That year the press associations—Associated Press, United Press, and International News Service—supplied complete election returns to the 677 radio stations. Radio's success in covering that bitter presidential election whetted listeners' appetites for more news broadcasts. In December, KFAB in Lincoln, Nebraska, responded by hiring the city editor of the Lincoln *Star* to put on two broadcasts daily of what it called a "radio newspaper." Other stations developed similar programs, and as the great depression deepened after October, 1929, the public became even more interested in news. By 1930, KMPC in Beverly Hills, California, had put 10 reporters on the Los Angeles news runs.

A bitter war now broke out between radio and newspapers over broadcasting of news. Newspaper advertising revenues were sharply contracting as the depression years proceeded toward the 1933 national crisis. Radio, however, as a new medium was winning an increasing, if yet small, advertising investment. Why let radio attract with news broadcasts listeners who will become the audience for advertisers' commercials, asked some publishers. This argument gave more weight to public interest in news than it deserved, considering the demonstrated public interest in listening to such entertainers as Amos 'n Andy, Jack Benny, Walter Winchell, the Boswell sisters, Rudy Vallee, Kate Smith, and the stars of the radio dramas. But after both 1932 political conventions were aired on coast-to-coast networks, and after the Associated Press furnished 1932 election returns to the networks to forestall the sale of United Press returns, the American Newspaper Publishers Association cracked down. The press associations should stop furnishing news to radio; broadcasting of news should be confined to brief bulletins which would stimulate newspaper reading; radio program logs should be treated as paid advertising. There were dissenters to this approach, but after a majority of AP members voted in 1933 for such restrictions, all three press associations stopped selling news to stations. Radio now had to gather its own news.

Columbia Broadcasting System set up the leading network news service with former newspaperman Paul White as director. He opened bureaus in leading U.S. cities and in London and developed a string of correspondents. Hans Von Kaltenborn and Boake Carter, already CBS commentators, did daily news broadcasts. Kaltenborn, a former Brooklyn *Eagle* managing editor, had started broadcasting in 1922 and had joined CBS in 1930 to become the first of a long line of radio commentators. NBC organized a less extensive news service. Local stations got their news from the early editions of newspapers, despite AP court suits to stop the practice.

A compromise was soon proposed. This was the Press-Radio Bureau, which would present two five-minute newscasts daily on the networks from news supplied by the press associations. Bulletin coverage of extraordinary events also would be provided. In return, the networks would stop gathering news. The bureau began operating in March, 1934, but was doomed to quick failure. Stations wanting more news bought it from five new agencies which jumped into the field, led by Transradio Press Service. A year later UP and INS obtained releases from the Press-Radio Bureau agreement and began selling full news reports to stations. UP began a wire report written especially for radio delivery, which AP matched when it began to sell radio news in 1940. The Press-Radio Bureau suspended in 1940; Transradio succumbed in 1951.

Radio meantime was developing a blend of entertainment and news. The trial of Bruno Hauptmann in 1934 for the kidnap-murder of the Lindbergh baby attracted more than 300 reporters, including many with microphones. Listeners were bombarded with more than 2000 Press-Radio Bureau bulletins. President Roosevelt's famed "fireside chats" and the presidential nominating conventions and campaigns were major events. In December, 1936, the entire world listened by shortwave broadcast as Edward VIII explained why he was giving up the British throne for "the woman I love." H. V. Kaltenborn hid a CBS portable transmitter in a haystack between the loyalist and rebel lines in Spain to give his American audience an eyewitness account of the Spanish Civil War. Kaltenborn, Boake Carter, Lowell Thomas, Edwin C. Hill, and Gabriel Heatter were the public's favorite news commentators. Ted Husing and Clem McCarthy were the leading sports announcers. America's top radio entertainment favorites in 1938 were Edgar Bergen and his dummy Charlie McCarthy, Jack Benny, Guy Lombardo and his orchestra, Kate Smith, the Lux Radio Theatre and "One Man's Family" dramatic shows, Burns and Allen, Eddie Cantor, Don Ameche, Nelson Eddy, Bing Crosby, and announcer Don Wilson. But before the end of the year it was Kaltenborn who stole the laurels as the world stopped all else to listen to news of the Munich crisis, which brought Europe to the brink of war.

RADIO NEWS COMES OF AGE

Radio fully met the challenge of diplomatic crisis and worldwide war which began with Adolf Hitler's annexation of Austria and ultimatum to Czechoslovakia in 1938. Beginning with a patched-together but impact-producing coverage of the Munich crisis, the radio networks expanded their news reporting and technical facilities tremendously during World War II. At the station level, newscasts took a place of prime importance.

Network news staffs had continued to develop on a modest scale after the 1933 cut-off of press association news. NBC's Abe Schechter placed staff men in London and Paris, in Geneva for the disarmament conference, and in Shanghai for the Japanese invasion of China. G. W. Johnstone of Mutual was financially handicapped but had reporters in the major news centers. CBS news director Paul White had developed the largest organization for both U.S. and foreign coverage, but its staff was stretched thin.

In 1937 CBS sent a then-unknown Edward R. Murrow to Europe as news chief. For an assistant he hired William L. Shirer, who had been working for the just-closed Universal Service, a Hearst-owned press association. Like the others, they did human interest stories and cultural programs for shortwave broadcasts which were rebroadcast by U.S. stations. Then came Hitler's invasion of Austria and the *Anschluss*. Murrow hustled to Vienna. On March 12, 1938, the first multiple pickup news broadcast in history went on the air. Shirer spoke from London, Murrow from Vienna, and newspapermen CBS had hired gave their impressions from Berlin, Paris, and Rome. The pattern was set for radio's coverage of the fateful 20 days in September beginning with Hitler's demand that the Czechs cede him the Sudetenland and ending with the Munich Pact. Key staffers like Murrow (who went on to become television's best-known commentator and director of the United States Information Agency) and Shirer (author of *Berlin Diary* and *Rise and Fall of the Third Reich*) bore the brunt of the effort, reinforced by the cream of the U.S. newspaper and press association correspondents.

American radio listeners heard news broadcasts from 14 European cities during the 20-day Munich crisis period. Beginning with the plea for support made by President Eduard Benes of Czechoslovakia on September 10 and Adolf Hitler's challenge to the world two days later from Nuremberg, listeners heard the voices of Chamberlain, Goebbels, Mussolini, Litvinoff, and Pope Pius XI. Such broadcasts were not new, but the intensity of coverage was. CBS devoted 471 broadcasts to the crisis, nearly 48 hours of air time; of these, 135 were bulletin interruptions, including 98 from European staffers. NBC's two networks aired 443 programs during 59 hours of air time. On climactic days, these efforts kept the air alive with direct broadcasts, news summaries, and commentaries by the news analysts.

In his "Studio Nine" in New York City Kaltenborn spent the 20 days catnapping on a cot, analyzing the news reports, and backstopping the CBS European correspondents with hours of analysis and commentary. It was Kaltenborn who provided the translations of Hitler's fiery oratory before the Nazi rallies, and who later predicted what diplomatic steps would follow. He was heard 85 times, many of them lengthy commentaries, during the three weeks. A few times he carried on two-way conversations with Murrow, Shirer, and other European correspondents. The CBS "European News Roundup," usually a 30-minute show from three or four points, was matched by NBC after two weeks. Aiding Murrow and Shirer were Maurice Hindus from Prague, Pierre Huss of INS from Berlin, John Whitaker of the Chicago *Daily News* from Paris, and Sir Fredric Whyte from London. Hindus scored a beat on the Czech backdown.

Heading NBC's European effort was Max Jordan, who had a 46-minute beat on the text of the Munich Pact, which he broadcast from Hitler's radio station. He relied especially on M. W. Fodor of the Chicago *Daily News* and Walter Kerr of the New York *Herald Tribune* in Prague, Alistair Cooke in London, and such leading press association men as Karl von Wiegand and William Hillman of INS and Webb Miller, Edward Beattie, and Ralph Heinzen of UP. Mutual had only John Steele in London and Louis Huot in Paris, and used their occasional broadcasts, cabled news, and shortwave pickups to augment the regular press association news flow.

American listeners felt the brutal impact of Hilter's demands when Jordan and Shirer spoke from microphones inside the Berlin Sportpalast against a background of hysterical oratory and frenzied Nazi crowd reaction. They were grave when they heard Murrow describe war preparations in London, relieved when Kaltenborn predicted that Chamberlain, Daladier, Mussolini, and Hitler would find a peaceful solution at Munich. While they devoured columns of type, it was radio that brought them a sense of personal participation in what they realized was the world's crisis, not merely Europe's.

By the summer of 1939 Murrow had a four-man staff: himself, Shirer, Thomas Grandin, and Eric Sevareid, a young newsman who also was to become a leading television commentator for CBS. When German troops marched into Poland, Americans tuned in their radios to hear Prime Minister Chamberlain announce that Great Britain was at war. Bill Henry of CBS and Arthur Mann of Mutual became the first front-line radio reporters. Radio news staffs expanded, and eyewitness broadcasts made history. James Bowen of NBC described the scuttling of the German battleship *Graf Spee* off Buenos Aires. Shirer of CBS and William C. Kerker of NBC reported the surrender of the French to a strutting Hitler in the railroad car at Compiègne. Radio brought news of Dunkirk, of the fall of Paris, Winston Churchill's stirring oratory. And in

August, 1940, Murrow's "This Is London" broadcasts made the Battle of Britain come alive for his American audience. His graphic descriptions of bomb-torn and burning London, in a quiet but compelling manner, did much to awaken a still neutral United States to the nature of the world's danger.

The first news of Pearl Harbor reached Americans by radio bulletins which shattered the Sunday quiet of December 7, 1941. A record audience listened next day to President Roosevelt's war message to Congress. Radio newsmen, using mobile units and tape recordings, joined the coverage of American forces in the Pacific and Europe. There were many memorable broadcasts: Cecil Brown of CBS reporting the fall of Singapore; Murrow riding a plane in the great 1943 Berlin air raid and describing it the next night; George Hicks of ABC recording a D-Day broadcast from a landing barge under German fire. Network reporters made broadcasts and recordings, filed cables, and competed on equal terms with press association and newspaper correspondents.

The demand for news seemed inexhaustible. In 1937, NBC had devoted 2.8 per cent of its total program hours to news; in 1944 the figure was 26.4 per cent. CBS in 1945 spent 26.9 per cent of its network time on news and sports. Variety shows still ranked highest in audience size—Jack Benny, Fibber McGee and Molly, Bob Hope, Edgar Bergen and Charlie McCarthy, and Fred Allen. Dramatic shows and popular music were next. But four of the leading programs in listenership in 1944 and 1945 were news shows: CBS commentator Lowell Thomas, the "March of Time," Mutual's emotional Gabriel Heatter with his human interest commentaries, and the irrepressible Walter Winchell. As the war drew to a close, radio expressed the sorrow of the people by devoting three days of programming to solemn music and tributes to a dead President Roosevelt.

RADIO'S POSTWAR EXPANSION

The war years were exceedingly prosperous ones for radio. Total annual revenue more than doubled between 1937 and 1945, and income on revenues increased from 20 per cent to 33 per cent. When the FCC returned to peacetime licensing procedures in October, 1945, there were 909 licensed commercial standard (AM) radio stations. Sixteen months later there were approximately 600 new stations either on the air or under construction and the FCC had 700 more applications pending.

These mainly were for smaller stations; the number of communities having radio stations nearly doubled in those 16 months. By 1950 there were 2086 AM radio stations on the air and 80,000,000 receiving sets.

Frequency modulation (FM) broadcasting, done experimentally beginning in 1936, was represented by 30 stations on the air in 1942 when wartime necessity brought a freeze in new construction and licensing. In the postwar years many AM stations took out FM licenses and the number of FM stations on the air in 1950 reached 743, a figure which proved to be a high for the ensuing decade. Few of the FM stations were operating independently and giving audiences the selective programming which later was to characterize FM broadcasting.

Radio newsmen, somewhat to their surprise, found listener interest in news sustained during the postwar years. Sponsors, who by 1944 had pushed news and commentaries into third place behind dramatic and variety shows in sponsored evening network time, kept up their interest in news at both network and local levels. The established stations had in many cases developed their own newsrooms during the war, with personnel to prepare both general news summaries and local and regional news shows. The newly licensed stations, often without network affiliation, found news one area in which they could compete. Indicative of the trend was the founding in 1946 of an association of radio news directors, now known as the Radio-Television News Directors Association. Among its early leaders were John Hogan, WCSH, Portland, Maine; John Murphy, WCKY, Cincinnati; Sig Mickelson, WCCO, Minneapolis; Jack Shelley, WHO, Des Moines; and Edward Wallace, WTAM, Cleveland. Part of the stimulus for local station activity was the 1946 FCC "Blue Book," making it clear stations should log public service records, including news and public affairs broadcasts.

Among the network commentators, Edward R. Murrow began his "Hear It Now" program for CBS, where he was joined by his wartime associate Eric Sevareid. H. V. Kaltenborn, who left CBS in 1940, became NBC's leading commentator. Radio listeners who sat glued to their sets all night in 1948, wondering whether President Harry Truman had upset Thomas E. Dewey in the presidential voting, found Kaltenborn one of the first to realize that Truman's popular vote lead would hold up in electoral college totals. ABC had Raymond Gram Swing, one of the finest of the war era commentators. It also obtained Elmer Davis, who had replaced Kaltenborn at CBS before becoming director of the Office of War Information. Davis won high praise for his postwar reporting, his dry humor and telling barbs, and his ability to get at the heart of complex and confusing issues. NBC scored with public affairs programs from the United Nations during 1946 and 1947. The networks and some local stations also offered documentary programs, analyzing important social issues in a semidramatic format.

But television was casting its shadow over radio. Television's "breakthrough" year was 1948, the one in which the value of time sales for the national radio networks reached an all-time high. Competition between the four networks already was intense, and the vogue for program popularity ratings as a means of snaring sponsors led to such devices as the "giveaway" program featured by 1948 radio. The smaller stations found plenty of local advertising revenues in newly exploited markets, fortunately, and after 1947 radio had more revenue from local advertisers than from network advertisers. The networks already in 1948 were shifting their attention to television, and station owners were seeking television licenses until the FCC instituted a four-year "freeze" so that comprehensive plans for television broadcasting could be worked out. In the meantime, CBS forecast the fate of network radio when it made its famed 1948 "talent raid" on NBC to capture such stars as Amos 'n Andy, Jack Benny, Burns and Allen, Edgar Bergen, and Bing Crosby for future television shows.

TELEVISION ARRIVES

Experimental television broadcasting in the United States began in the 1920's. The scientific advances which preceded actual broadcasting stretched back over a century in the fields of electricity, photography, wire transmission, and radio. Early television experimenters used a mechanical scanning disk which failed to scan a picture rapidly enough. The turning point came in 1923 with Dr. Vladimir Zworykin's patenting of the iconoscope, an all-electric television tube. Zworykin, then a Westinghouse scientist, soon joined RCA, where he developed the kinescope, or picture tube. Other leading contributors were Philo Farnsworth, developer of the electronic camera, and Allen B. Dumont, developer of receiving tubes and the first home television receivers.

There were experiments in wire transmission of pictures during the 1920's, which were to lead to the founding of AP Wirephoto in 1935. One of the researchers, H. E. Ives of AT&T, sent a closed-circuit television picture from Washington to New York in 1927. The next year General Electric's WGY began experimental telecasting. In 1930 NBC began operating W2XBS in New York; in 1939 it became the first station to offer regular telecasting schedules. Large numbers of people first saw television that year at the New York World's Fair. Commercial broadcasting was authorized by the FCC in 1941, but the wartime "freeze" left only six pioneer stations on the air. Among them were the first commercially licensed station, NBC's WNBT in New York, and WCBS-TV in the same city. The two big radio networks thus had their entries in television broadcasting.

Because of postwar equipment shortages and industry uncertainties, it was 1948 before television could achieve a significant place among the media. In the meantime RCA's image-orthicon camera tube had appeared to enhance the possibilities of live pick-ups, and AT&T was busily extending the coaxial cables which preceded the microwave relay for transcontinental broadcasting. During 1948 the number of stations on the air increased from 17 to 41, and the number of sets in use neared half a million. Cities with television increased from eight to 23, and the arrival of the coaxial cable and network programming stirred a city's excitement much like the arrival of the telegraph a century before. Cities along the Atlantic coast from Boston to Richmond saw and heard the 1948 political conventions and the Metropolitan Opera. Television's first great star, Milton Berle, stepped before the cameras for NBC in 1948, as did Ed Sullivan at CBS.

Then, in the fall of 1948, came the FCC's "freeze" on additional station authorizations, which lasted until June, 1952. During that time the FCC worked out a comprehensive policy for telecasting designed to give all areas of the country equitable service. In the interval only 108 stations were eligible for broadcasting. A few failed, but many became firmly established. The number of sets in use rose to 15,000,000. The transcontinental microwave relay was completed in 1951, and on September 4 the first coast-to-coast audience saw the Japanese peace treaty conference in San Francisco. NBC also offered the first telecast of a World Series and the first regular coast-to-coast sponsored program, the "NBC Comedy Hour."

The FCC's 1952 plan which ended the "freeze" called for more than 2000 channel assignments to nearly 1300 communities. To do this, the FCC extended telecasting from the established Very High Frequency channels (numbered 2 through 13) to 70 more Ultra High Frequency channels (numbered 14 through 83). There were more than twice as many UHF as VHF assignments, and in addition 242 channels were reserved for educational television stations. But different equipment was needed to tune a set to the UHF and VHF stations, and the established pattern of set making and broadcasting was VHF. The FCC did not require set makers to include both UHF and VHF tuning until 1964; in the meantime UHF languished. In a 1953 decision, the FCC ended a long controversy over color telecasting in favor of the RCA compatible system permitting reception in either black-and-white or color.

Television's great "gold rush" came in 1952–53 with the end of the "freeze." Among the networks, NBC and CBS were well along in their transition from emphasis on radio to emphasis on television. ABC merged with Paramount Theatres in 1953 and took a third-ranking position in television. Mutual did not attempt to enter television; a Dumont network gave up the attempt to compete nationally in 1955. That year there were 439 stations on the air and 33,000,000 receivers. By 1960 there were 533 stations and 55,000,000 receivers. In 1965 there were 588 commercial stations on the air (90 of them UHF), plus 114 educational stations. There were 61,000,000 sets covering 93 per cent of U.S. homes. Television surpassed radio and magazines by 1955 in total advertising revenues and a year later passed newspapers as the number one national advertising medium, although newspapers continued to lead in total advertising thanks to their top-heavy position in the field of local advertising.

TELEVISION AND THE NEWS

Television's first efforts at news shows too often consisted of newsreels supplied by the United Press and Acme Newspictures and still pictures shown while the on-camera announcer read the news script. But television newsmen, equipped with mobile units and magnetic tape, gradually overcame the problems of developing news shows with live film and sound. During the first decade of telecasting, they did far better with on-the-spot broadcasts of major news events, public affairs programming, and documentaries.

In 1951 Edward R. Murrow turned from "Hear It Now" to "See It Now" for CBS. NBC's early morning "Today" show with Dave Garroway, a mixture of news and entertainment, opened in January, 1952.

That year network viewers saw an atomic blast at Yucca Flats, the political conventions, and a heavyweight championship prize fight. An estimated 60,000,000 Americans saw President Eisenhower inaugurated in 1953. Television audiences next followed live broadcasts of the McCarthy-Army hearings, which resulted in the Senate's censure of the Wisconsin senator, and watched a parade of gangsters before Senator Kefauver's crime subcommittee. Crucial United Nations sessions went on camera. At least 85,000,000 Americans saw one of the "Great Debates" between John F. Kennedy and Richard M. Nixon in 1960, with the presidency at stake. President Kennedy opened some of his news conferences to live telecasting in 1961, and used television extensively at the height of the Cuban crisis in October, 1962. An estimated 135,000,000 saw some part of television's coverage of John Glenn's 1962 first manned orbital flight.

If proof were needed of television's ability to report great events, it came on November 22, 1963, when President Kennedy was assassinated in Dallas, Texas. Within minutes the networks began a four-day vigil ending with the burial at Arlington. Many heard the first bulletins on radio, then rushed to watch the unfolding drama and hear news summaries on television. An audience study for New York City homes showed that TV viewing rose from 25 per cent to 70 per cent on Friday after the assassination reports became known. Viewers saw the new President, Mrs. Kennedy, and the casket returning to Washington. They went with the cameras into the White House, saw the Sunday ceremonies at the Capitol. Sunday viewers on NBC (the only network "live" at the precise moment) saw Jack Ruby lunge forward in a Dallas police station to shoot fatally the alleged assassin, Lee Harvey Oswald, and heard reporter Tom Pettit describe the incredible event. Viewership in New York homes jumped to 80 per cent as all the networks ran and re-ran their film. On Monday the funeral of President Kennedy drew a 93 per cent viewership figure, the highest known level in television history. The nation agreed that both television and radio had reported the four days magnificently.

There was far less general approval of television's coverage of the 1964 political conventions, at which the network staffs seemed to dramatize conflicts with picketing groups and relatively minor convention floor disputes at the expense of major convention activity.

By the mid-1960's, CBS and NBC were each budgeting up to

$25,000,000 a year for news and special events (much of it reclaimed from sponsors). ABC was allocating more than $10,000,000. CBS and NBC had some 40 correspondents each and as many staff cameramen in the United States. Fulltime correspondents abroad numbered 21 for NBC, 19 for CBS, and 8 for ABC in a 1963 study. The prestige of each network seemingly depended heavily on its news coverage, and in the 1964 election they spent millions on primary vote-counting before agreeing to a pooled effort with the press associations in November.

After Murrow left the CBS screen in 1958, Walter Cronkite became that network's leading personality. A United Press war correspondent, Cronkite joined CBS in 1950 and became the star of many of its documentaries, including "Eyewitness to History," "The Twentieth Century," and "CBS Reports." He took over the major CBS news program from Douglas Edwards and transformed it into a 30-minute dinnertime show in the fall of 1963. Mike Wallace joined CBS News in 1963 to do its morning show. Other leading CBS newsmen included Eric Sevareid, Charles Collingwood, Harry Reasoner, Bill Henry, Martin Agronsky, Winston Burdett, Robert Trout, Daniel Schorr, and Robert S. Pierpoint. Lowell Thomas held forth on radio. Howard K. Smith and David Schoenbrun, European correspondents for a decade, left CBS in the early 1960's. Fred W. Friendly was producer of "CBS Reports," which had a 30-man staff for its 20 documentaries a season.

NBC's top stars were two seasoned newspapermen, Chet Huntley and David Brinkley, whose mixture of news and comments on the 30-minute evening "Huntley-Brinkley Report" made it the top-rated television news program. They also bested Murrow and Sevareid during the 1960 presidential election and surpassed Cronkite in 1964, on audience ratings. Morgan Beatty and Merrill Mueller had leading newscasts. Other NBC newsmen included Joseph C. Harsch, Irving R. Levine and Elie Abel in Europe, Pauline Frederick at the UN, Ray Scherer, John Chancellor, Frank McGee, Sander Vanocur, Edwin Newman, and commentator Clifton Utley. The "NBC White Paper" was the network's major documentary effort, along with "Project 20." Two 1963 documentary specials winning awards were a three-hour program on civil rights and Piers Anderton's "The Tunnel" from West Berlin, produced by Reuven Frank.

With less resources, ABC has kept pace with such commentators as Quincy Howe and Howard K. Smith, who joined ABC at the close of 1961. James C. Hagerty, former President Eisenhower's press secretary, became news chief after he left the White House and pumped new blood into the operation. Leading correspondents were Edward P. Morgan, William H. Lawrence, John Scali, Robert Clark, Peter Clapper, and Lisa Howard. "ABC Close-Ups" and "ABC News Reports" are major documentary efforts for the network, which has scored with such programs as "The Making of the President" and "The Soviet Woman." John Daly long conducted the network's top television news show.

Westinghouse's Group W (11 television and radio stations headed by KDKA, Pittsburgh, WBZ, Boston, and WJZ, Baltimore) has its own news organization with Jim Snyder as national news director and Sid Davis as White House correspondent. Mutual radio has Stephen J. McCormick as news director and Bill Costello at the White House.

Singling out local station operations for mention is difficult and a list can serve only as an example. Some award winners for news or public service excellence in recent years have been, among television stations: WRCA and WCBS, New York; WBZ and WGBH, Boston; WTVJ and WCKT, Miami; WHAS, Louisville; WGN and WBBM, Chicago; WCCO and KSTP, Minneapolis-St. Paul; WMT, Cedar Rapids; KLZ, Denver; KSL, Salt Lake; KHOU, Houston; WBAP, Fort Worth; KNXT, Los Angeles; KPIX, San Francisco; KING, Seattle. Among radio stations: WNEW, New York; WAVZ, New Haven; WCAU, Philadelphia; WBZ, Boston; WMAQ, Chicago; WCCO, Minneapolis; WOOD, Grand Rapids; WBT, Charlotte; KPHO, Phoenix; KIRO, Seattle; and KNX and KPFK-FM, Los Angeles.

News by satellites became television's most sensational achievement of the 1960's. The successful launching of AT&T's Telstar on July 10, 1962, permitted the first live transmissions between the United States and Europe. These were "staged" shows of a few minutes' duration while the signals could be bounced off the satellite, but they thrilled TV audiences. RCA's Relay carried pictures of the Kennedy assassination to 23 nations. Howard Hughes' efforts to launch a satellite that would achieve a fully synchronous orbit (an orbit and speed that keep the craft directly over one point on earth) met near-success with Syncom II in 1963 and full success with Syncom III in 1964. Three such satellites, equally spaced around the world, could provide television coverage to all inhabited portions of the planet. The Communications Satellite Corporation, formed by Congress in 1962 to unify the U.S. effort, expected to launch a successor to Syncom, called Early Bird, in 1965, which would double the number of phone circuits across the Atlantic and permit the first regularly scheduled telecasts between America and Europe. Television news was at last catching up with radio's "instantaneous coverage," even from abroad.

TELEVISION AND ENTERTAINMENT

The period from the end of World War II to the present has been one of turmoil and indeed revolution in the world of visual entertainment. Television's sudden emergence as a major home entertainment medium affected all other media, but particularly radio and the motion picture. In the years after 1948 the aerial became a fixture atop almost every roof; inside the living room the TV screen grew from 7 inches in width to 12, to 17, to 21, and in some cases to 24 inches. During the first years of television's popularity, at least, the presence of such free entertainment had a profound effect upon American social habits. Some families planned their day's activities so that they could be at home for favorite programs; that gastronomical phenomenon, the TV dinner, was marketed to be eaten by families sitting in partially darkened rooms with eyes focused on the screen. Gradually audiences became more selective but the average set still remained on in the mid-1960's for some six hours each day.

Having captured a very large portion of the entertainment-seeking audience, television too found many serious problems. Program directors discovered that operating as they did many hours a day, the television stations devoured good program material faster than it could be created. The writing and producing talent drawn into the television industry simply could not conceive enough fresh material of broad general appeal to fill the stations' program time.

As a result the mass of television programming offered to the public was uneven in quality. Much of it was trite, inane, and repetitious. The critics denounced it vehemently, with good cause. Yet every week, at least during the winter months, a selective viewer could find many hours of literate, provocative, informative, and frequently very entertaining programs. Some of the best were the "spectaculars" or "specials" originated by Sylvester (Pat) Weaver for NBC to break the monotony of regularly scheduled series. The cost of these lengthy and star-studded productions also could be spread to several sponsors.

Television programming suffered from two major difficulties: (1) the tendency of many program directors and sponsors to underestimate the intelligence of the audience and (2) a severe case of overexposure— too many hours of program time in relation to the amount of good-quality program material, even when old Hollywood movies were added to the fare.

New program ideas quickly attracted imitators. The public was subjected to cycles of entertainment, a number of programs similar in nature. For two or three seasons in the late 1950's quiz programs were extremely popular; these gave away fantastic amounts of money to contestants who made the correct replies to many kinds of questions. But the public began to grow weary of these giveaways, and when revelations of unethical assistance to some contestants were made, most of the quiz programs disappeared from the air. Western programs, a modification of the Western movie or "horse opera" that long was a standard item in the motion picture industry, came into vogue. Soon the obvious tales of the Old West were exhausted, and producers took to exploring many ramifications of life, translated into a Western setting. In some cases they took classic fiction plots and reworked them as Westerns. At the peak of the Western craze, so many of these "oaters" (as the industry called such horse pictures) were being shot around the overcrowded Hollywood outdoor locations that the casts of competing shows had to wait in line for turns to perform their heroics before the camera.

Milton Berle was television's first great star, going on the air for NBC in 1948. During the medium's first decade the top audience ratings went to variety shows and comedies. Holding steady places for several years each were Berle, Groucho Marx, Ed Sullivan, and Arthur Godfrey. "I Love Lucy," starring Lucille Ball, held first-place rating for five years. Then, in 1958, came the Westerns, led by "Gunsmoke," and in 1959 half the "top ten" were action-filled, bullet-punctuated tales. "Wagon Train" took top honors for four years, then gave way to "Bonanza." The "private eye" dramas headed by the "Perry Mason" and "77 Sunset Strip" shows were popular in the 1960's. Hospital-based dramas—"Dr. Kildare," "Ben Casey," and "The Nurses"—were next on the popularity cycle. Situation comedies meanwhile continued to hold their own.

But not all of television entertainment was keyed to the audience ratings. The educational program "Omnibus" was a rewarding contribution of the 1950's; so was "Playhouse 90." There were such artistic productions as "Peter Pan" and "Victoria Regina." Leonard Bernstein and the New York Philharmonic orchestra played for appreciative television audiences. Walt Disney's "Wonderful World of Color" even made the "top ten" lists of the 1960's. Such shows, combined with the news and documentary programs, gave television some claim to a role more socially useful than the casual entertainment role identified by critics as a "vast wasteland."

RADIO'S NEW PATTERN

Within the few years between 1948 and 1955, virtually all radio network drama, comedy, musical, and suspense shows were dropped, as the sponsors switched to similar programs on television for larger audiences at much higher cost and with a presumption of stronger impact on the viewer. The radio networks declined sharply in importance and many local stations adopted the "music, news, and sports" format which kept costs in line with decreased revenues. But far from fading away in the face of television's popularity, radio expanded. The number of AM stations increased from 2086 in 1950 to 4046 in 1965. FM broadcasting found sharply increased audience favor in the 1960's and by 1965 there were 1280 FM stations on the air. Radio sets were everywhere—an estimated 228,000,000 of them in homes, cars, and coat pockets.

Radio found it could best sell brief time slots and spot announcements to sponsors. The result was the rise of the disc jockey, a glib fellow who could project a vocal personality on the air and through his chatter give a semblance of unity to a melange of popular recordings, commercials, and news summaries. Many stations became more profitable for their owners with this new style of programming.

Network radio news programs conformed to the new pattern. NBC in 1957 began offering news on the hour for 18 hours of the day, in five-minute segments. Stations added local news, weather, and sports coverage. Bigger stations maintained more comprehensive news shows for morning, noon, and evening audiences but many smaller stations failed to get beyond the headlines. In the mid-1950's CBS offered a news analysis in depth, "The World Tonight," and NBC introduced its weekend "Monitor" show with a substantial news-and-comment base. Each of the networks developed a four-minute information program fitting the new sponsors' time desires—"Dimension" on CBS, "Emphasis" on NBC, and "Flair" on ABC.

With mobile units, beeper phones, and tape recorders, radio can go where the news is with little difficulty. Radio has continued to offer coverage of major news events as they happen. Enterprising stations cover home town meetings, air interviews, and conduct "open mike" opinion shows. With its widespread listening availability, radio continues to be an important news medium.

CHANGES IN THE MOTION PICTURE

The changes wrought by television in the Hollywood motion picture studios have been equally profound. During the first part of the postwar decade, the major Hollywood studios avoided television like a poisonous thing. They forbade their stars to appear on TV shows and refused to release their old films for rerunning on television. This resistance broke down under economic necessity. Having failed to defeat television by these tactics, the motion picture industry decided to join it. One by one the major studios sold their backlogs of old films to television for huge sums, and immediately millions of American families saw on their home screens the same motion pictures they had paid admission fees to watch in theaters two decades earlier. Entertainers, especially comedians, who had long been forgotten by the public suddenly regained prominence through revival of their old pictures, and in some cases they began their careers afresh as a result.

The huge motion picture lots in and around Hollywood became devoted more and more to the production of filmed television programs and TV commercials. One of the largest and most spectacular, the back lot at Twentieth Century-Fox where frontier towns, streets in old New York, small midwestern villages, and southern plantation homes stood side by side in an anachronistic jumble of stage settings, gave way to a vast apartment and residential development.

The changes in Hollywood's film output were equally drastic. The theme for the major producers became "fewer and bigger pictures," many of them filmed in Europe because of tax considerations and a favorable labor market. The producers found their market for the routine Class B drawing room drama and adventure tale taken over by the televised half-hour show, which the home audience could watch free. So the major studios turned to producing pictures of epic proportions in color, shown on gigantic screens. Here was sweep and grandeur the TV screen could not match, qualities sufficiently alluring to draw the viewer away from his easy chair and the admission fees out of his pocket.

A segment of the film industry went off in another, less desirable direction in pursuit of ways to draw the viewer from television. These film makers tried to achieve shock value with material that was too grotesque, socially daring, or close to obscenity for the home TV screen.

One result of the film industry's struggle for survival was a breakdown in the self-imposed censorship code by which the producers policed themselves. This had been adopted in reply to outcries by organized religious and social groups against a too-liberal treatment of sex in some films. For years some producers grumbled that the code was unrealistic in many respects, but generally it was respected and obeyed. Then, in the late 1950's, certain producers intentionally violated its strictures. Sensing a more liberal attitude among the citizenry, and arguing that they were dealing with socially significant subjects which had been forbidden unwisely, these film makers plunged ahead. One of these "breakthrough" efforts was Otto Preminger's picture on the previously banned topic of narcotics, *The Man with the Golden Arm*.

In the 1960's, numerous films were being released by European and Hollywood producers and accepted by the public which would have been taboo a decade earlier. Some of these rightfully could be credited to a more adult and open attitude toward social problems and were sponsored by men willing to fight against censorship barriers they believed to be outdated and unreasonable. Certain legal decisions hitting at film censorship practices in some states, such as that permitting the showing of the controversial British film, *Lady Chatterley's Lover,* broke down the barriers even further. These developments created a more friendly atmosphere for such films as the British *A Taste of Honey,* the American *Lolita,* and Ingmar Bergman's Swedish-produced psychological studies like *Through a Glass Darkly* and *Wild Strawberries.* Unfortunately they also opened the way for pictures which had no social purpose but which blatantly exploited the market for lustful crime and sex films.

SUMMARY

Both film and radio were used to transmit news almost as soon as they were developed as means of communication. The first news broadcast in the United States, in 1916, is generally credited to Dr. Lee De Forest, the inventor of the vacuum tube, which made voice broadcasting possible. Regular news broadcasting by licensed stations began in 1920.

In the 1920's, radio concentrated on dramatic news events and on-the-spot sports coverage rather than news summaries. Growth of radio networks, and standardization of broadcast practices under the authority of what became the Federal Communications Commission, were important elements in the growth of radio news.

A bitter war between newspapers and radio over broadcasting of news led to creation of a Press-Radio Bureau to provide the networks only a limited amount of news summaries. The move failed, and after 1935 stations could buy the news reports of the press associations. Columbia Broadcasting System led in developing its own news-gathering organization after 1933. With H. V. Kaltenborn and Edward R. Murrow as leading figures, radio news achieved maturity during the Munich crisis and war years. Radio enjoyed a boom during the war and postwar years; public attention to broadcast news continued at a high level and local stations built up their news bureaus and coverage.

Experimental telecasting began in the 1920's, but it was 1939 before NBC offered New York City the first regular telecasting schedules. A wartime "freeze" prevented expansion until 1948, the year the coaxial cable linked east coast cities. A second "freeze" to give the FCC time to plan nationwide television lasted until 1952; during that period the transcontinental microwave relay was completed in 1951. Television's great expansion was under way in 1953 and emphasis on broadcast news by the networks shifted to the new medium. Such leading personalities as Murrow, Kaltenborn, Walter Cronkite, Chet Huntley and David Brinkley, and Howard K. Smith became familiar visitors to American homes on news and documentary shows. Europe was linked to America for "live" television viewing through the successful launching of communications satellites, beginning with Telstar in 1962. While television developed considerable programming of high quality, it also featured Westerns and old movies.

Despite a sharp decline in the importance of their networks, radio stations survived the spread of television by adopting a "music, news, and sports" format which kept costs in line with decreased revenue. The number of radio stations on the air nearly doubled between 1950 and 1965, and FM radio enjoyed an upturn in popularity. Motion pictures suffered from decreased theater attendance, but found new formulas by producing wide-screen spectaculars and films of a more provocative nature.

STUDY QUESTION

How well, in your opinion, do the television and radio stations you listen to or watch keep you informed about news and public affairs? Do you turn to newspapers or magazines for some particular kinds of information?

PROJECTS

1. Listen to a substantial evening newscast, either on radio or television, and keep a record of the stories covered and the approximate amount of time given to each. Compare these results with the next morning's newspaper. How many of the same stories appear and what prominence do they have? What prominent stories in the newspaper were not on the broadcast?

2. Watch a television program or listen to a radio program and write a brief analysis of the educational level of the viewers or listeners at whom the program seemingly is aimed. Name a program that appeals to persons of another educational level.

PART III

CURRENT PROBLEMS
AND CRITICISMS

CHAPTER 7

THE MASS MEDIA: CURRENT PROFILES

WHO READS, LISTENS, LOOKS?

Newspapers, radio, and television come close to being universal media in the United States. Nine out of 10 American adults see a daily newspaper regularly; of those who do not, a majority read a weekly paper. Radios are found in 98 per cent of homes; television sets, in 93 per cent. Again, the adult audiences come close to the total potential.

Magazines rank next in appeal; the best available survey figures show that from 60 to 70 per cent of adults read at least one magazine regularly. Approximately 50 per cent of American adults, when asked, say they have attended a movie during the previous month; a fourth have seen one or more each week. Only 25 per cent report they have read a book during the past month, and book readership is estimated at about 30 per cent of the American adult population.

These figures constitute both a tribute and a challenge to the mass media. Certainly they point to widespread public support of the communications industries. But they immediately pose problems for those who must produce publications, programs, or films for mass audiences with diversified interests and varying expectations of what they want to read, see, or hear: the single newspaper, radio station, or television station serving an entire community; the network television or radio program seeking acceptance in tens of millions of homes; the nationally read magazine reaching out for several millions in circulation; the "smash hit" motion picture and the "best seller" book which are the hopes of those industries. Some mass media products—particularly in the magazine, film, and book fields—are designed for small and essentially homogeneous audiences, but the characteristic tendency is toward "bigness" of audience and the finding of a common denominator of appeal.

The 1750 daily newspapers print approximately 59,000,000 copies each week day and the 550 Sunday papers print 47,000,000 copies— enough to make the average per family 1⅓ daily copies and slightly more than one Sunday issue. Another 18,000,000 circulation weekly is added by the 8500 weekly newspapers. Readership surveys for metropolitan dailies show the average reader (excluding nonreaders of the issue being surveyed) spends from 25 to 35 minutes with his newspaper —perhaps a minute a page. He is a single individual in a heterogeneous audience; he selects the articles which interest him, the advertisements which catch his eye, the pictures which tell their stories quickly. The editor can appeal to him with the one-fourth of the items in a typical daily which gain no more than 4 per cent readership and with the one-fourth which are read, at least in part, by 30 per cent or more of the potential audience. The Continuing Study of Newspaper Reading, conducted for 11 years by the Advertising Research Foundation, found that men read an average of 14 per cent of all the items in a daily paper, and women read 11 per cent. No story gained more than 90 per cent readership.

The large newspaper, like the leading department store, must be "all things to all people" if it is to win the maximum attention in terms of reading time from its diverse audience. Some of its readers wish mainly to be entertained when they sit down with the paper; at the other end of the scale is a group which reads magazines, books, and other newspapers and follows television and radio public affairs programs. Its expectations in the news and opinion areas are far more demanding than the average. Striking a balance is not an easy task for an editor. Weekly newspapers, concentrating on telling local news to smaller and more intimate audiences, are more thoroughly read than are dailies; small-town dailies, in turn, draw a higher readership per item than the metropolitans of bigger bulk and more diversity of offerings and audiences. With less space, however, these smaller papers are less likely to satisfy the special interests of differing groups of readers.

In the vast majority of towns and cities where weekly and daily newspapers are published, everyone reads the same paper. But when radio and television sets are turned on, there is more choice; relatively few listeners or viewers are restricted to a single choice among the 4000 AM radio stations, 1280 FM stations, and 700 television stations. Some 228,000,000 AM radio sets, 25,000,000 FM sets, and 61,000,000 television receivers snap on and off—the average family listens to the radio for approximately one and a half hours a day and watches television for almost seven hours each day. Programs of limited appeal cannot be aired except at the peril of boring and losing a good deal of the audience. When broadcasting news, radio and television must concentrate on the type of story which gains 30 per cent or more of the newspaper readers' attention.

There are some 8000 periodicals published in the United States that have a total circulation of upward of 400,000,000 copies per issue. Of these, approximately 600 are classified as general interest magazines; the remainder appeal to specialized audiences. About 50 have a circulation of 1,000,000 or more, the largest running to 15,000,000 copies. The 1500 book publishing firms produce more than 1,200,000,000 copies yearly, with some paperbacks and occasional "best sellers" selling a million or more copies. The general interest magazines and mass-sale books encounter the same problems faced by newspapers, radio, television, and motion pictures in satisfying large-scale audiences which are made up of many individuals with varying interest levels and desires.

An opinion attitude survey made on a national basis by the Survey Research Center of the University of Michigan for the National Association of Science Writers in 1957, as part of a study of science news by Professor Hillier Krieghbaum of New York University, provides a reliable check on how the public rates four of the mass media. Asked which was their favorite for obtaining general news, those queried answered in these percentages: newspapers, 57 per cent; television, 22 per cent; radio, 16 per cent; magazines, 4 per cent. For those who had a favorite source for obtaining science news, the percentages ran: newspapers, 34 per cent; television, 22 per cent; magazines, 21 per cent; radio, 3 per cent. In this specialized area, magazines had an advantage in giving perspective to the news. But the tables turned when each respondent was asked to name his favorite source for entertainment. The percentages were: television, 74 per cent; radio, 14 per cent; magazines, 6 per cent; newspapers, 5 per cent. This survey confirmed what the mass communications industries already knew: television had won supremacy as the primary media source of entertainment, and other media were wise not to attempt to compete with it for audience attention on that basis alone.

WHO OWNS THE MEDIA?

One of the major challenges to the mass media in recent years has been sharp criticism of the trend toward their control by relatively small groups of individuals. Newspapers have drawn the heaviest fire on the issue of ownership concentration. But similar trends have occurred in all the mass communications industries, as they developed in a society whose economic atmosphere encouraged mass production and bigness of business enterprises.

More detailed examinations of the present-day positions of each of the mass media will be presented in later chapters dealing with each medium individually. But historical trends, particularly in newspaper ownership, and a comparative summary can be noted now so that the criticisms may be evaluated.

In 1880, when the New Journalism era was developing, there were 850 general circulation English-language dailies in the United States. The number jumped to 1967 by the year 1900, and reached a peak of 2200 in 1910. By 1930 there were 1942 dailies; a low of 1744 was reached in 1945 before a stabilizing process leveled off the number at 1750 (a few more in some years).

The number of one-daily cities stayed fairly constant until 1920 at about 40 per cent of the total. It jumped to 71 per cent by 1930 and to 84 per cent by 1965. The number of cities with more than one daily, but with a single owner, was negligible until the 1920's, but reached 12 per cent of the total by 1965. This left only 50 cities, or fewer than 4 per cent, with competing daily newspapers under separate ownerships, as compared to 20 per cent in 1930 and some 60 per cent at the turn of the century. Community weeklies reached a peak of 11,800 in 1910 and leveled off at 8500 by 1960, with only 4 per cent of weekly newspaper towns supporting competing papers.

More cities had daily newspapers in 1960 than in 1910—1470 as compared to 1207. Circulation of dailies had jumped from 24,000,000 to 59,000,000 copies, a sharper increase than was recorded in population growth. But there were 450 fewer dailies, and there was considerably less choice in the big cities which had supported a variety of newspapers a half-century before. In four out of five towns and cities, there was no choice at all of local newspapers; in 19 out of 20 there was no choice between competing publishers. Diversity of viewpoint had to come from out-of-town newspapers, magazines, books, radio, television, film, and other cultural contacts.

Group ownership of newspapers has been a much-debated subject. A group, or chain, is defined as two or more newspapers published in different cities by the same owner. In 1900, when Scripps and Hearst were organizing their groups, there were just eight in the country, controlling 10 per cent of the total daily circulation. By 1935 there were 63 groups, controlling 41 per cent of daily circulation and 52 per cent of Sunday circulation. This was the peak year for the national chains, led by Hearst and Scripps-Howard. Hearst's 26 dailies had 13.6 per cent of the country's circulation and his 17 Sunday editions had 24.2 per cent. The smaller Scripps-Howard papers had 5.1 per cent of total daily circulation with 25 dailies.

By 1965 there were more groups listed, in part because better records of newspaper ownership had been kept. The 135 groups (one-third consisting of just two papers) controlled some 660 dailies, with 45 per cent of total daily circulation and 50 per cent of Sunday circulation. The Hearst dominance had been sharply curtailed, however; that group's 10 remaining dailies had 4.7 per cent of daily circulation, and its 8 Sunday papers had 6.5 per cent of the Sunday total. The Patterson-McCormick group (with the *Daily News* in New York and the *Tribune* and *American* in Chicago) was largest, with 5.4 per cent of the country's daily circulation and 9.9 per cent on Sunday. Scripps-Howard had the largest number of dailies, 18, with 5 per cent of daily circulation and 7 Sunday papers with 4 per cent of the total.

Rising among the group owners was Samuel Newhouse, who added the dailies in Portland and New Orleans, the St. Louis *Globe-Democrat,* and the Birmingham *News* to his earlier holdings in New Jersey, on Long Island, and in Syracuse. His 16 dailies had 4 per cent of total daily circulation and 5.3 per cent of the Sunday total. In round numbers, the leading group owners had total circulation as follows: Patterson-McCormick, 3,200,000 daily, 4,600,000 Sunday; Scripps-Howard, 3,000,000 daily, 1,860,000 Sunday; Hearst, 2,800,000 daily, 3,000,000 Sunday; Newhouse, 2,350,000 daily, 2,500,000 Sunday.

In the vicinity of the 1,000,000 mark for both daily and Sunday circulation were three other prominent group owners. John S. Knight had four large papers in Detroit, Miami, Charlotte, and Akron. John and Gardner Cowles had four in Minneapolis and Des Moines. The Ridder family had

14, centered in Minnesota and California. Next in order of circulation importance were the holdings of the Cox, Gannett, and Block groups, all above a half-million.

Some owners in single cities had circulations bulking as large, however; Marshall Field's *Sun-Times* and *Daily News* in Chicago ran above 1,000,000 combined daily circulation to lead this list. The Chandler family's Los Angeles *Times,* the McLean family's *Bulletin* and the Annenberg family's *Inquirer* in Philadelphia, and the Ochs-Sulzberger family's New York *Times* all topped the half-million mark daily.

If large units of ownership and lack of local competition seemed to be growing characteristics of the newspaper industry (although the average daily paper had only 10,000 circulation), the same was equally true of the other mass media. In magazine publishing, 10 large firms dominated the field, with two of them—Time Inc. and the Curtis Publishing Company—taking in more than 40 per cent of the money spent on national advertising in general interest magazines. Ranking behind them were the Hearst magazine group, largest in point of numbers of magazines, and the *Reader's Digest,* largest in circulation with 15,000,000 circulation in the United States and 11,000,000 overseas. Among the country's other most influential magazines, Time Inc. controlled *Life* and *Time;* Curtis, the *Saturday Evening Post* and *Ladies' Home Journal;* Cowles magazines, *Look;* McCall Corporation, *McCall's;* and Hearst magazines, *Good Housekeeping. Newsweek, U.S. News & World Report,* and the *New Yorker* were independents. The number of major competitors in various magazine fields tended to decline; readers had from two to four choices in each of the general interest, news, women's, and quality magazine areas.

Radio and television, as we have seen, quickly established patterns of network broadcasting. Under Federal Communications Commission policy, one ownership is limited to no more than seven AM, seven FM, and seven TV stations (five VHF, two UHF). Thus the four major networks themselves owned only 19 radio stations and 15 television stations. But stations affiliated with them under contracts totaled, in the radio field, 228 in 1934, 702 in 1944, and 1334 in 1953. Virtually all of the powerful clear-channel radio stations were network-owned or affiliated. Television's ascendancy in the 1950's brought a decline in radio network programming and a consequent lessening of network influence, but there were still 1351 radio stations affiliated with the national networks in

1965. The three television networks had a total of 645 outlets. There were, in addition, 58 regional radio networks and 10 regional television networks. The rapid increase in the number of radio stations (up from 2375 to 4000 between 1953 and 1965) gave listeners a widening choice, however. Television is a one-station "monopoly" outside the major cities, except in towns served by community antenna television systems (CATV).

In book publishing, no more than two dozen firms account for two-thirds of the grand total each year. Eight large studios have dominated the motion picture industry historically, producing 80 per cent of feature films and distributing 95 per cent of films reaching the public, although independent production by stars and the inroads of television have tended to break down the major-company system in recent years. The mass media which receive news reports from the press associations have just two to choose between—Associated Press and United Press International. The feature syndicates, although numerous, have developed a few major suppliers of columns, comics, and other entertainment materials. In the world of advertising, a small number of the hundreds of advertising agencies dominate the placing of the large national advertising appropriations in the mass media.

Cross-channel ownership is another characteristic of the mass media. Newspapers and magazines are associated in common ownership with 9.8 per cent of the AM radio stations, 13 per cent of FM stations, and 31 per cent of television stations. The Hearst group owns both major newspaper and magazine properties, radio and television stations, a news service, a photo service, a feature syndicate, a paperback book publishing firm, and a newsreel. Scripps-Howard is in the newspaper, radio, television, press association, photo, and feature syndicate fields. The Cowles brothers own newspapers, magazines, and radio and television stations; Samuel Newhouse also is in all these fields. Time Inc. and Meredith Publishing Company are in radio, television, and book publishing, as well as being leaders in magazine production.

SOCIAL AND ECONOMIC PRESSURES ON THE MEDIA

Obviously the mass media are not free agents, able to produce their publications, programs, and films exactly as their owners would like to do, or in the manner they might seek to reach in keeping with their social role as described by the philosophers. They are part and parcel of a society which exerts strong social and economic pressures upon them while it commands them to be free from pressures which would inhibit full exercise of their responsibilities.

The public interest and the public's interests are often two very different things. The editor is expected to present a full, comprehensive, and intelligent account of all the day's events—to do so is in the real public interest. Yet various groups with personal interests in a thousand and one different activities seek to gain space within the newspaper's columns for their projects. Much of this activity is well intentioned, but the pressures brought upon the news media inevitably affect total performance. If a newspaper gives several columns of space to a pleasurable but relatively unimportant civic function, some other kind of news will not appear. Social workers, educators, foreign affairs specialists, scientists, businessmen, political partisans, and many other citizens are convinced that the kind of news and opinion they are most interested in deserves more space than it is getting. The editor, be he at the newspaper or the radio or television station, can only seek to balance these pressures against his obligation to handle the main flow of the news.

News people must also contend with organized pressures. So must the people who produce magazines, books, films, and radio and television programs. Discussions of controversial issues are often impeded by groups or individuals who bring powerful pressure to bear upon the mass media. Editors who seek to do a conscientious job of analyzing touchy political issues run afoul of groups of citizens who seek to punish them for speaking out in behalf of the public welfare. Radio and television have been subject to organized pressures which sometimes have led the media to avoid controversial programming. Motion picture operators know full well the power of religious groups and other organizations which effectively dictate in matters of taste; this censorship extends at times into matters of subject material. Magazine and book publishers likewise must contend with informal censorship through social pressure. The entire field of public relations and publicity writing is a form of organized pressure upon the mass media which institutions and companies seek to use to carry their messages. Organized groups, like individuals, can be useful at times in supplying information to the media and in convincing media people that they should or should not carry out specific undertakings, but they can also prevent the media from doing the most effective jobs they are capable of doing in serving the over-all public interest.

Economic pressures are inevitable for all of the mass media. They must make a profit; they must have adequate capital if they are to improve their products. The competition for sales and advertising revenues is intense between media and among units in the same medium. In each of the media there must be a balance struck between what should be done and what can be done if the product or service is still going to have sales value and adequate public support. Without a reasonable number of readers or viewers, a newspaper or television station cannot have advertisers, for example. Neither can a magazine or a radio station. Films or books, no matter how socially desirable they might be, must have viewers or readers who will pay cash for the privilege. Many of the media units exist on small margins of profit; even as great a newspaper as the New York *Times* returns as little as $1,500,000 profit on a $120,000,000 annual gross. Each book published represents a gamble for a narrow profit return—unless a "best seller" comes along—and too many bad gambles can lead a publishing house into bankruptcy. Quality magazines likewise run close races with the red ink in many cases.

Changes in the pattern of media use by advertisers bring strong economic pressures on the media, which are competing for the revenues involved. Some figures will illustrate the point. The first set of figures covers the total of expenditures for all forms of advertising by both national and local advertisers. The compilations, made for *Printers' Ink* by the research department of McCann-Erickson Inc., are informed estimates based upon the best available statistics. They show that newspapers, in the three decades since 1935, began with 45 per cent of all advertising expenditures in the country, dropped to 36.5 per cent by 1953, and to 29 per cent by 1963. Magazines started at 8.3 per cent of the total, rose to 13.8 per cent by 1946, and dropped back to 8 per cent by 1963. Radio began at 6.5 per cent, increased to 15.7 per cent by 1946, and fell to 5.9 per cent by 1963. Television, starting with 3 per cent in 1950, had by 1963 taken over 15.8 per cent of all advertising expenditures. The "all others" category of some 40 per cent includes direct mail (15.5 per cent), business papers (4.7 per cent), outdoor advertising (1.3 per cent), and other miscellaneous forms of advertising. In dollars, the four major media were estimated to have received these sums in advertising expenditures in 1963: newspapers, $3,800,000,000; television, $2,000,000,000; magazines, $1,000,000,000; radio, $780,000,000. The total for the four was more than double that for 1950.

But another set of figures shows a much different relationship among the four major media. These deal with just national advertising expenditures in newspapers, magazines, radio, and television. Out of the total amount spent by national advertisers each year in just these four media, how much did each of the media receive? National advertising forms a crucial part of their total revenue pictures and there is intense competition for the pieces of the "pie" assigned to the major mass media by the advertisers. The figures show that in 1929, newspapers received 54 per cent of national advertising revenues going to these mass media; magazines, 42 per cent; radio, 4 per cent. Ten years later, in 1939, the figures were: newspapers, 38 per cent; magazines, 35 per cent; radio, 27 per cent. Radio had become a powerful new advertising medium. This relationship continued with only small percentage changes until television arrived on the scene. By 1953 the line-up was: magazines, 30 per cent; newspapers, 29 per cent; television, 24 per cent; radio, 17 per cent. By 1963 the relationship seemingly had leveled out at these figures: television, 45 per cent; magazines, 27 per cent; newspapers, 20 per cent; radio, 8 per cent. Television had replaced radio as a major national advertising medium, and had eclipsed newspapers in that field. Over three decades newspapers had seen their share of this particular advertising "pie" cut to less than half; even though their dollar take had tremendously increased, their potential in national advertising revenues had greatly declined. The same was true to a lesser extent of magazines. Newspapers received 80 per cent of their total advertising revenues from local advertising; radio, 63 per cent; television, 16 per cent. In the local field, television was no particular menace. Magazines developed regional editions to cater to regional advertisers, and split-runs for localized advertising, in an effort to add to their revenues.

Advertisers are hard-boiled about where they spend their money. They study the various media and make decisions, such as to switch their magazine appropriations into television, or to increase their newspaper expenditures at the expense of television and radio. They can choose between putting ads into the big Sunday magazine supplements or into a long list of smaller newspapers. Such decisions depend upon the type of advertising and the type of audience appeal the product might require. Eventually the agencies must select individual units within each medium —will it be *Life* or *Look,* or both, or the *Reader's Digest* instead? How about the weekly newspapers—how many and how much for each? The media do intensive promotional work, as industry groups, and as in-

dividual publications and stations. All of this contest must be carried on
—and successfully—before the editors can do their jobs of supplying
news, opinion, and entertainment.

The mass media are also subject to certain economic pressures imposed by government. It is clear that the Supreme Court will permit
government regulation of the press for ends which it regards as desirable;
it is equally clear that the media are not exempt from regulations which
affect their businesses (taxes, wage and hour laws, collective bargaining
laws, etc.) any more than any other industries. Ownership of newspapers,
magazines, and radio and television stations must be made public—a desirable form of pressure from government. The provisions of the antitrust
laws were applied to open the Associated Press membership more widely.
They were also used in the case of the Lorain, Ohio, *Journal* to prevent
the paper from coercing advertisers who were also patronizing a local
radio station. They were used again in the Kansas City *Star* case to bring
an end to what the court held was a local advertising monopoly, reacting
adversely against possible competitors, through forced tie-in of advertising in morning and evening papers and radio and television stations
owned by the publishing company. In cases of consolidations of both
newspaper and magazine properties, the government has attempted to
intervene in the interests of preserving competition; so far, it has been
unsuccessful. The Federal Communications Commission forbids one licensee from holding more than one radio and one television license in
each community and limits the total number of licenses one person or
firm can hold. The FCC has also scrutinized carefully the applications of
newspapers to hold radio or television licenses, but generally it has not
discriminated against valid applications which have more merit than
those of other applicants for the same wave lengths or channels.

One final charge concerning economic pressure should be noted. This
involves pressures brought by advertisers upon the mass media. Much
more emphasis has been placed upon this subject than it deserves. A
generation ago many more instances of "censorship" by advertisers who
wanted something kept out of the news columns could be cited than
today. Neither large nor small newspapers need submit to outright threats
by a single advertiser—even their largest—for the advertiser needs the
paper as much as the paper needs the advertising. An ordinary advertiser
has no power to make threats at all, if they involve the paper's integrity.
Requests from advertisers are another matter. Some want publicity as

well as paid space, and sometimes newspapers and other media oblige. Requests and publicity releases from advertisers can be as legitimate as those from other members of the community. This is a matter of news judgment, tempered in some instances by business office efforts to please a customer. The supposition that advertisers exercise "thought control" over newspaper publishers and editors is greatly exaggerated; after all, the publisher is a member of the same business and social community as the advertiser and he is likely to hold the same basic viewpoints in economic and political matters. Assuming that the paper has conscientious editors, it is unlikely that pressures brought by advertisers will be any more effective than those brought by other groups in the community.

In television and radio, the advertiser controls the content of the program put on during the time span he has purchased (this control of the time surrounding his advertising messages is in sharp contrast to the practice in the print media, where the advertiser has no control over the space surrounding his ad). His advertising agency advises him on the type of program most likely to do the job of attracting listeners or viewers. This development has such deep historical roots in the two industries that it is unlikely that the practice can be changed, although such groups as the Commission on Freedom of the Press have called for the networks and the stations to take control of their time and limit the advertisers to control of brief advertising message periods. Those who dislike the quality of television and radio programs can blame the advertisers and bring pressure upon them, as well as upon the industry, to improve their offerings. Disclosures of unethical practices on television quiz and give-away shows during the late 1950's brought an awakening of public interest in the subject of program control and threats of governmental intervention if the networks, advertising agencies, and advertisers did not find a way to assure the integrity of their programs. Continuing controversy over the amount of violence and other antisocial actions presented in television shows kept the issue alive, a criticism which will be discussed in the next chapter.

SUMMARY

The mass media are well accepted by their readers, listeners, and viewers in the United States. Newspapers, radio, and television come close to being universal media, with 90 per cent or more of homes exposed to each. Magazines reach 60 to 70 per cent of adults; motion pictures, 50 per cent; and books, 30 per cent. These figures are both a tribute and a challenge to the communicators, who know full well that there are difficulties to overcome and criticisms to meet in the serving of such diversified audiences.

One of the major challenges to the mass media in recent years has revolved around the problems of declining competition and control by relatively small groups of individuals. Our 1750 dailies appear in 1470 cities and towns, but only 4 per cent of those cities have competing, separately owned papers. Similarly, only 4 per cent of towns with weeklies still have competing papers. Group ownership of newspapers is substantial but the largest group of dailies, owned by Scripps-Howard, numbered 18 in 1965 and no group owner controlled more than 5 per cent of the total circulation.

Similar characteristics can be observed in the other media. Ten large firms dominate magazine publishing, led by Time Inc., Curtis, Hearst, McCall, and Cowles. Television and radio stations, particularly the larger ones, are affiliated with three big networks. Two dozen book publishing houses account for two-thirds of the books produced each year. Eight large studios have dominated the motion picture industry historically. Cross-channel ownership further concentrates media ownership.

There are many pressures exerted on the media by society, including pressures by individuals, organized groups, and government. Economic pressures must be taken into account in evaluating the performance of the media. Newspapers obtained 45 per cent of all advertising expenditures in the country in 1935, but only 29 per cent in 1963 as television emerged to take 15.8 per cent. Television is now the dominant national advertising medium; newspapers are the overwhelming choice for local advertisers. Radio has become primarily a local advertising medium.

STUDY QUESTION

To what extent are large units of media ownership a natural development of modern American life?

PROJECTS

1. Consult the newspaper and broadcasting directories listed in the bibliography and determine the ownership of the newspapers and broad-

casting stations in your community. Are any of the papers group-owned? What network affiliations do the stations have?

2. Examine three issues of a newspaper and list items which you think were published for very small groups of readers either at their request or in an effort to provide diversity of content. Examples might be an article about art, a column about stamp collecting, or a story about the activities of a minority political party.

CHAPTER 8

CRITICISMS
AND CHALLENGES

CRITICISMS CONCERNING DIVERSITY

With all of the evidence about ownership and control of the mass media before them, critics of the print and electronic media cannot be blamed for raising their voices in protest. The complaints have centered about the charge that newspapers have become a "one-party press" in expressing their opinions about political candidates, about the lack of outlets in the mass media for expression of minority viewpoints, and about the lack of diversity of offerings for readers, viewers, and listeners of different cultural levels. The complaints all add up to a common one: the mass media have become standardized in content and outlook because control has been concentrated in relatively few ownership groups, all seeking to reach large common-denominator audiences.

Certainly there is merit in general discussion of these and other problems facing the mass media. Those owning and working in the various media recognize the existence of the problems, and some, at least, have attempted to meet the challenges insofar as they can be acted upon. They resent the excesses of criticism from some quarters, particularly when there is no reasonable solution to a problem, or when the critics fail to recognize that changing social and economic conditions have forced acceptance of changes in the mass media not to anybody's liking. An arbitrary assumption that a "monopoly" newspaper situation is automatically bad for a community is an unfair generalization; so is the assumption that "bigness" is correlated with antisocial conduct. The best of the mass media's offerings are both competitive and noncompetitive, both large and small. So are the worst. What is important is the amount of responsibility accepted by the owners and workers in the mass media for carrying out their obligations to the society which they serve.

Criticisms of newspapers since the 1930's have been focused most often on their editorial positions in political campaigns. Figures compiled by *Editor & Publisher* magazine each presidential election year explain why. Historically the majority of daily newspapers giving editorial page support to a presidential candidate has been on the side of the Republican party. In 1932 the Democratic candidate, Franklin D. Roosevelt, had the active support of 38 per cent of the daily circulation represented in the *Editor & Publisher* poll; his Republican opponent, President Herbert Hoover, had 55 per cent (the remainder represented newspapers making no endorsement editorially). This seemed to be a fairly reasonable division of newspaper editorial opinion, although some critics contended the newspapers should reflect the outlook of the majority of the electorate, despite the fact that publishers and editors might personally have arrived at an opposite conclusion regarding what was best for the country.

As Roosevelt ran in his second, third, and fourth campaigns, his editorial page support dwindled, dropping to 25.2 per cent in 1940 and 17.7 per cent in 1944. When President Harry Truman upset Republican Thomas E. Dewey in 1948, he had the backing of only 10 per cent of daily newspaper circulation, whereas Dewey was actively endorsed by papers with 78.5 per cent of the polled circulation. In 1952, Dwight D. Eisenhower won with the backing of 80.2 per cent of daily newspaper circulation, while Democrat Adlai E. Stevenson could muster only 10.8 per cent. It was then that Stevenson made his charge about a "one-party press in a two-party country." In 1956 President Eisenhower's total dropped to 72 per cent of the polled circulation; Stevenson had 13 per cent, and 15 per cent represented papers not actively endorsing either candidate (the largest such total to that time).

In 1960 Vice President Richard M. Nixon had the support of papers with 70.9 per cent of the polled circulation in his unsuccessful race against Democrat John F. Kennedy, who had 15.8 per cent. Kennedy was endorsed by 22 of 125 dailies above 100,000 in circulation, Nixon by 87. No stand was taken by 12 and 4 went unreported. This represented more large pro-Democratic papers, with a better geographic spread, than at any time since 1944. But Democrats still grumbled.

Then came the dramatic reversal of 1964. President Lyndon B. Johnson and Senator Hubert Humphrey were the Democratic nominees in the wake of Kennedy's assassination. The Republicans turned to candidates from their conservative right wing, Senator Barry Goldwater and William Miller. *Editor & Publisher's* poll was as clear-cut as the election results. Johnson had the support of dailies representing 61.5 per cent of the polled circulation, Goldwater 21.5 per cent. Among the 125 dailies above 100,000 in circulation, 82 endorsed Johnson, 12 endorsed Goldwater, 8 said they were uncommitted, and 23 remained undecided or unreported. Because papers representing only 76 per cent of the total daily circulation answered the 164 poll (compared to 92 per cent in 1960), it is also useful to compare each candidate's committed circulation to the total circulation of all 1750 dailies. In 1960 these figures were: Nixon, 65.2 per cent; Kennedy, 14.5 per cent; independent and unreported, 20.3 per cent. In 1964 the figures were: Johnson, 46.8 per cent; Goldwater, 16.4 per cent; independent and unreported, 36.8 per cent. In numbers of papers endorsing candidates, the figures for 1960 were 731 for Nixon and 208 for Kennedy, and the figures for 1964 were 445 for Johnson and 368 for Goldwater. For at least that one election, the shoe was on the other foot and it was Goldwater who cried out against a "partisan press."

What could be done? If publishers and editors conscientiously believed Candidate A should be elected over Candidate B, they scarcely could be asked to endorse Candidate B just to give him a better split of the editorial page support across the country. They could take steps to see that their editorial pages, outside the column of editorials themselves, gave due expression to viewpoints of all political factions. They could make every effort to back up their own editorial opinions with full discussions of the issues, honestly and fairly weighed. Most importantly, they could take every precaution not to let the newspaper's editorial preferences affect in any way the selection and presentation of news stories.

However one-sided the newspapers lined up editorially, they did not do so in their news columns. The weight of the evidence in various studies made of press performance in covering recent campaigns shows a reasonably creditable job on the news pages. Only a very small minority of newspapers could be accused of deliberate bias. Most presented the news as it happened, without regard to the candidate the paper might be supporting. Unhappily, the nation's publishers turned down an opportunity for a large-scale study of their performance in a political campaign, proposed by the professional journalistic society, Sigma Delta Chi, and blueprinted by a group of leading social scientists and journalism educators. This reluctance to accumulate factual evidence cost the newspapers a chance to be cleared of some of the more extreme charges leveled against them and cost all students of the press, in and out of the media ranks, an opportunity to learn more about the problem of improving political reporting and press performance during election campaigns.

It should be noted in passing that American readers do not support newspapers purely on political grounds. In many cities, the last pro-Democratic paper disappeared a half-century ago. New York City's many Democratic voters permit the *Post*, most consistently liberal of the city's six dailies and the only one to support Stevenson in 1952 and 1956, to run a weak fifth in circulation. In Los Angeles, the pro-Democratic *Daily News* went bankrupt in 1954 even though it stood alone among five papers in a metropolis with a good split of political partisans. Really radical newspapers have had even less success in attracting reader support. The proposal by some press critics that "new newspapers" be established to redress the political balance on editorial pages is as unrealistic in terms of gaining paid-in-advance subscriptions as it is in terms of finding ways of reversing the trend toward reduction of competing units.

Finally, it should be noted that editorial pages have been given credit for more influence than they have. Research studies show that many other factors besides newspaper reading enter into the formation of voter decisions in a national political campaign. Voting behavior is most strongly affected by social pressures and group associations and by opinion leadership. Radio and television, with their direct broadcasts of candidates' speeches, are another important factor. Magazines are an important source of information for the opinion leaders. The impact of events, as reported by the news media, can produce a tide of public opinion which editorial pages could scarcely be expected to reverse. Certainly the voter has a variety of exposures to information and opinion outside the columns of his newspaper.

The complaint that the mass media, in general, do not provide sufficient outlets for the expression of minority viewpoints is a valid one. Splinter groups in politics find themselves virtually ignored both in the news columns and in gaining any sort of editorial page support. Those to the far right or left in economic matters, or in suggesting solutions to social problems, meet the same fate. This is not to say that the mass media shun minority viewpoints and radical proposals, for they do not.

But by the very nature of their relationship to their mass audiences they scarcely can give the amount of space zealous advocates of such viewpoints would like to see devoted to their causes and opinions.

Perhaps most serious is the complaint that the mass media lack a diversity of offerings for readers, viewers, and listeners of differing cultural levels. The high-level reader who finds the *Times* or *Herald Tribune* in New York City to his taste is shocked to discover that in many other American cities no newspaper appears which he finds worth-while to read. Even in cities with three or four newspapers, all will be aimed at a too-low level of appeal, both in the exercise of the news function and the editorial function. This same charge is the most prevalent one made against television and radio—programming is aimed at the intellectually immature and entertainment-seeking people and cannot satisfy those who wish higher levels of cultural performance and information-giving. Magazines, books, and films can be produced more easily for different cultural groups but excessive popularization has also been charged against those media.

One bright spot in television and radio diversity has been the noncommercial educational station. But only 114 of the 242 television channels reserved for this type of station had been claimed by 1965, a disappointing result for those who wished a more intellectual television fare.

It is hard to estimate how much "bigness" and concentration of ownership of the mass media have been responsible for lack of diversity. Certainly in television and radio, some of the most effective programming has been supported by the networks. Presumably big book publishing firms, major motion picture producers, and the leading magazine publishers would not shun an opportunity to make a profit by catering to the desires of those who wish products deviating from the mass-desired norm. And certainly conscientious newspaper publishers do not want to stand accused by the most intelligent persons in the community of producing their newspapers at the dull level of mediocrity.

Too much concern probably has been shown over the decline in newspaper competition. It is true that in New York City, for example, the number of newspapers has been reduced. The death of any newspaper is a sad event; the passing of Joseph Pulitzer's New York *World* in 1931 was particularly grievous. But the merging of Bennett's *Herald* and Greeley's *Tribune* to form the *Herald Tribune* gave New York an outstanding newspaper to replace its losses. The merging of Pulitzer's *World*, Bennett's *Telegram,* and Dana's *Sun* to form a single paper did not result in such a gain, but it reduced the stress of economic competition for such papers as the *Times,* the *Herald Tribune,* and the *Post,* in their jousting with the popular tabloids. The best available studies indicate that the emergence of the "natural monopolies" in the newspaper publishing industry has brought it to the highest point of economic stability in its history, and such stability is necessary for the improvement of press performance.

Opinion surveys of readers of noncompetitive papers in Minneapolis, Louisville, Des Moines, and Atlanta show they have highly favorable attitudes toward their newspapers. It is a matter of demonstrated record that many of the highly regarded newspapers are noncompetitive (the *Christian Science Monitor, Wall Street Journal,* Milwaukee *Journal,* Louisville *Courier-Journal* and *Times,* Minneapolis *Star* and *Tribune,* Kansas City *Star,* Toledo *Blade,* Des Moines *Register* and *Tribune,* Providence *Journal,* Atlanta *Constitution*). Others of the leaders have no direct competition in their own publishing time cycles (the Washington *Post and Times Herald,* St. Louis *Post-Dispatch,* Baltimore *Sun,* Los Angeles *Times,* Denver *Post,* Miami *Herald*). Some maintain top levels of performance in directly competitive situations (the New York *Times,* New York *Herald Tribune,* Chicago *Daily News*), but in most of the highly competitive cities, the quality of newspapers suffers. Studies comparing the amount of space allotted to different kinds of content in noncompetitive and competitive papers show, however, that for dailies as a whole there is little difference in either news or editorial content; in many cases publishers relieved of the problems of direct competition have not taken the opportunity to improve their products as they argue they can do in "natural monopoly" situations, and as papers like those cited have done.

GENERAL CRITICISMS OF CONTENT QUALITY

Any summary of challenges to the mass media must focus on the criticisms leveled against the quality of their content. These criticisms fall into the following general areas: (1) over-emphasis on entertaining rather than informing, (2) sensationalism rather than effective popularization, (3) insufficient interpretation and reluctance to exercise the opinion function, and (4) lack of both quantity and quality of media content in smaller communities.

The Commission on Freedom of the Press, financed by Henry R. Luce of Time Inc. and chaired by Chancellor Robert M. Hutchins of the University of Chicago, considered these questions in its 1947 summary report, *A Free and Responsible Press,* a general statement of principles for consideration of mass media problems. This important private study was directed by 13 men, principally social scientists from outside the field of journalism, lawyers, and philosophers. They subscribed to the Jeffersonian concept of a free press that is responsible for providing the current intelligence needed by a free society and listed society's five requirements of the mass media: (1) a truthful, comprehensive, and intelligent account of the day's events in a context which gives them meaning; (2) a forum for the exchange of comment and criticism; (3) the projection of a representative picture of the constituent groups in the society; (4) the presentation and clarification of the goals and values of the society; and (5) full access to the day's intelligence.

This philosophical statement viewed the agencies of mass communication as "an educational instrument, perhaps the most powerful there is." The images created by the mass media can be helpful or detrimental in the making of public decisions and in the maintenance of social goals and values. The obligation to inform, the commission emphasized, extends beyond mere relating of current news, or mere entertainment in the cases of magazines, books, film, radio, and television. Entertainment can also be informative in nature, but that type of approach does not meet the full obligation of the mass media to reflect educational leadership.

In a statement about sensationalism, the commission commented:

To attract the maximum audience, the press emphasizes the exceptional rather than the representative, the sensational rather than the significant. Many activities of the utmost social consequence lie below the surface of what are conventionally regarded as reportable incidents: more power machinery; fewer men tending machines; more hours of leisure; more schooling per child; decrease of intolerance; successful negotiation of labor contracts; increase of participation in music through the schools; increase in the sale of books of biography and history.

In most news media such matters are crowded out by stories of night-club murders, race riots, strike violence, and quarrels among public officials. The Commission does not object to the reporting of these incidents but to the preoccupation of the press with them. The press is preoccupied with them to such an extent that the citizen is not supplied with the information and discussion he needs to discharge his responsibilities to the community.

Effective popularization would be the reporting of such activities of "utmost social consequence" as the commission lists in a manner which would make the stories interesting and readable. Certainly the news media do report in these and other significant areas of human activity, but it is also true that in many newspapers, and television or radio newscasts, there is preoccupation with the interesting but more transitory events to such an extent that too little attention is paid to the more significant news. Crime news occupies only a small percentage of space in newspapers but the prominence given it often makes it appear to "crowd out" more basic news; the same is true of news of controversy as opposed to the news stories that record progress.

The duty to present "a truthful, comprehensive, and intelligent account of the day's events in a context which gives them meaning" involves both the use of interpretative news accounts and the exercise of the opinion function. The trend toward interpretative reporting has been a substantial one; but any thoughtful newsman would agree that much remains to be accomplished. If space limitations prevent the use of interpretative material, then the news medium fails in part of its duty. Radio, by reverting to five-minute newscasts on the hour—even at the network level —took a step backward in its social performance. Even though radio claims it has increased the volume of its news operations, any five-minute broadcast must necessarily be more shallow than a 15-minute news program or news analysis broadcast. Newspapers which permitted the ratio of advertising to news to reach two-to-one levels thereby curtailed available space for significant news and interpretation to such an extent that only the most careful regulation of entertainment and feature material and human interest news could salvage the situation.

The smaller community has problems of obtaining both quantity and quality of media content which are not so pressing in big cities. Dailies of limited size must curtail the length of some of their news articles, and their editors must pick and choose a few stories from among a large number of worthy ones because of space limitations. Motion picture operators in smaller communities — and even in some larger ones — cannot profitably show foreign or out-of-the-ordinary films which are of higher quality than the usual Hollywood fare. But this is a problem which extends to other cultural and educational areas for the non-metropolitan population. Those who wish may subscribe to larger nearby newspapers or to journals like the New York *Times* or *Christian Science Monitor*. They may read magazines, books, and news magazines. They have access to television and radio. They may go to the city for films, art, plays, and musical events. A study of Paducah, Kentucky, a city of

33,000 people, showed it received 1800 copies of daily newspapers and more than 5000 Sunday papers from outside the community (the Paducah paper itself sold 12,000 copies within the city), 430 news magazines, almost 2000 picture weeklies, some 1750 other general weeklies, and 13,000 monthly magazines. Its public library had 110 magazines on file and circulated about 10,000 books a month. These facts do not absolve the local mass media from attempting to do the best possible job in presenting information, but they point up the reality that the smaller newspaper must be supplemented with other kinds of mass media, no matter how conscientiously it is edited.

WHAT IS THE ENTERTAINMENT FUNCTION?

Much of the criticism of the mass media revolves around their entertainment content: overemphasis on entertaining rather than informing; lack of diversity of offerings for readers, viewers, and listeners of different cultural levels; lack of meaningful social purpose in much of what is offered; outright poor taste and antisocial conduct in making appeals to audiences on sensational or emotion-arousing bases. It is necessary, while examining these criticisms, to recognize the nature of the entertainment function.

Historically the mass media through which news and opinion are circulated also have entertained their readers, viewers, and listeners. Some media, in fact, devote the bulk of their time and space to entertainment, assigning only a relatively small portion to the dissemination of news and opinion. In other media, notably newspapers, the news and opinion functions dominate. The degree and quality of what we call entertainment vary widely, even within a single medium, according to the character of the offering and the intent of the media producers.

In some cases the goal is primarily a fulfillment of aesthetic pleasure— the audience receives a sense of enjoyment as a dominant reaction. Examples would be reading good fiction or poetry in books and magazines, viewing some motion pictures, hearing radio music or viewing television drama of quality, seeing some types of photographs. In other cases a simpler definition of entertainment prevails: "to amuse, interest, divert." This is true of much of the offerings of the print media, films, radio, and television, including those in which an entertainment quotient is sought to accompany news and opinion.

Indeed, the more deeply we probe the relationship between entertainment and news-opinion, the thinner the line of separation appears. Printed and broadcast material which the recipient believes to be solely for his entertainment may in fact carry a social or political message and be closely linked to the news of the day. In reverse, the purveyors of news often use the techniques of the entertainers—such as suspense, change of pace in delivery, conflict, and incongruity—to dramatize their information. Thus they strengthen its impact on many of their readers and listeners.

A study of the daily newspaper shows that the definition, "to amuse, interest, divert," can be applied to many of the news stories published, especially those human interest items which most editors print as spice for the heavy menu of serious political and economic news. The words apply directly to the layouts of comic strips, cartoon panels, whimsical columns, and crossword puzzles that appear in most daily newspapers. This same definition also applies to magazines in which comic drawings, light verse, and fluffy satirical essays are published in the same issue as serious articles on politics; in fact, these bits of sheer entertainment are often inserted in "back of the book" pages to lighten the appearance of the long articles and to help carry the reader through the advertisements. Similar overlapping of the entertainment and news-opinion functions, both intentional and incidental, can be found in the other media—motion pictures, television, radio, and books.

To understand fully the dual role of the mass media, it is necessary to remember that a human is learning something most waking moments of his life, whether he realizes it or not. This is especially true when he is exposed to the offerings of the mass media. Even while watching a horror movie in a drive-in theater, he is acquiring some new bit of knowledge or insight into human behavior, if nothing more than a fresh realization that many of his fellow men are so anxious to escape the dull realities of everyday life that they will pay to sit in the dark and have a monster of cardboard on a canvas screen frighten them. The newspaper reader who turns to the crossword puzzle for a few minutes of relaxation finds himself learning such words as emu, ibis, and gnu because the puzzle designer had trouble making his pattern come out even. The television viewer sees and hears a newscaster quote an American official to the effect that the Soviet Union is 20 years behind us in the material aspects of life. Later in the evening a rerun of an old motion picture brings home to him graphically how much the designs of our automobiles and household appliances have progressed in two decades. This bit of insight, gained while he is pursuing his main purpose of being entertained, helps him to comprehend better the flow of twentieth-century history: the old TV film gives the viewer a visual frame of reference for the news report.

ENTERTAINMENT IN THE PRINT MEDIA

Earlier chapters have already suggested the uses made of the printing press in supplying entertainment to readers. Many of the incunabula, the books published before 1500, were cheap, popular editions. Although books historically have represented a treasure house of our civilization, they have also provided entertainment, ranging from the level of highest aesthetic enjoyment to that of momentary diversion. Many novels appear every year with the sole purpose of providing escape and entertainment for the reader. Development of the low-priced, paper-bound book in the nineteenth century and its current strong revival have helped the authors in the "escape" field, some of whom are as adroit in their craftsmanship as are the writers of fiction and nonfiction which has a serious social purpose. There are few creative outlets equal to the well-written novel as a purveyor of opinion, information, and social purpose, partially concealed by the cloak of entertaining action. Many motion picture producers have turned to novels for source material. The same range of quality and emphasis upon the entertainment function has also been exhibited by the thousands of magazines which have been founded as publishing ventures since the 1700's, ranging from the literary journals to the cheap pulps playing on interest in sex and crime.

In the newspaper area, what we call "human interest" news has always been in reader demand. Before newspapers were established, the casual news sheets and flyers which printers produced often dealt with sensational events: violent crime, "miracles" and rumors based on lack of scientific knowledge of physical phenomena, wars and battles, doings of the famous. Crude woodcuts were used early to attract and entertain audiences through illustration. Throughout newspaper history, as the chapter on development of the news function has already indicated, editors and reporters have used the news columns themselves for their entertainment value, either through selection of story material or through use of writing skills.

The newspaper today, as yesterday, also has a budget of non-news entertainment material: comic strips, puzzles, humorous columns, cartoon panels, short stories, advice to the lovelorn, "how-to-do-it" articles in the family and women's sections, travel articles, fashion and cooking hints, and other offerings which fall outside the definition of news. One of the problems of the modern editor is to keep this sort of material in proper balance. Studies of representative samples of daily newspapers show that only 55 to 64 per cent of nonadvertising space is devoted to "spot news," meaning local and nonlocal stories and pictures with definite timely elements. The remainder goes to the editorial page and opinion features, informative material, and entertainment items. Undeniably, readers expect their newspapers to entertain them to a degree. But they also can turn to other media for entertainment, notably to television in recent years. Studies of circulation trends in the 1950's show clearly that those newspapers published in big cities which had sacrificed their news-opinion role in order to entertain their readers, or had over-emphasized entertainment, were the heaviest losers of circulation. Copy sales of the New York *Daily News* and of a group of Hearst-owned newspapers declined in numbers ranging into the hundreds of thousands over a single decade.

Throughout much of its history, the newspaper has supplied literary material to a hungry reading public. The *Tatler* and the *Spectator,* produced by Joseph Addison and Richard Steele for early eighteenth-century readers, depended upon "essays" for their enormous popularity in London. James Franklin in Boston and Benjamin Franklin in Philadelphia reprinted English authors and modeled their own writing on the same literary style. Daniel Defoe's *Robinson Crusoe* was printed serially in many colonial weeklies. Magazines and books were still hard to come by in nineteenth-century America, particularly on the frontier, and as much as a third of newspaper content might be literary in character: short stories by James Fenimore Cooper, Rudyard Kipling, Robert Louis Stevenson, Bret Harte, Mark Twain; essays and poems by Emerson, Hawthorne, Whittier, and Whitman; and a mass of far less famous material.

The syndicates which supply non-news material to newspapers got their start with literary offerings. S. S. McClure and Edward W. Bok of magazine fame began two of the syndicates of the 1880's. Readers throughout the country came to know the work of newsmen turned columnists and humorists: Opie Read, Joel Chandler Harris, Finley Peter Dunne ("Mr.

Dooley"), George Ade, Eugene Field, Edgar A. Guest. Gradually the magazine replaced the newspaper as the medium offering literary fare, but vestiges of this traditional role still exist in the daily and weekly press. The syndicates shifted their attention, in turn, to humorous columns, cartoons and comic strips, gossip columns from Broadway and Hollywood, and political columns, in addition to the welter of special-interest material ranging from crossword puzzles to cooking hints. Among the leading syndicates over the years have been Western Newspaper Union (primarily for weeklies), Hearst's King Features, Scripps-Howard's United Features, Bell, McNaught, and the Chicago *Tribune*-New York *Daily News* Syndicate.

The "funny papers" first appeared as a part of the Sunday newspaper package of the 1890's—the same package which contained magazine supplements like Hearst's *American Weekly* and other entertainment sections. Joseph Pulitzer and William Randolph Hearst built the Sunday edition to its omnibus status during their circulation war in New York City which was highlighted by their struggle over possession of Richard F. Outcault's "Yellow Kid" cartoon. The "Katzenjammer Kids," "Happy Hooligan," "Bringing Up Father," and "Barney Google" were all early Hearst successes; "Mutt and Jeff," the first daily strip, and "Toonerville Folks" were given national distribution by Bell Syndicate. Immediately after World War I, Robert R. McCormick of the Chicago *Tribune* and Joseph Medill Patterson of the New York *Daily News* gave the reading public "Andy Gump," "Gasoline Alley," "Harold Teen," "Winnie Winkle," "Moon Mullins," and "Little Orphan Annie." Hearst retaliated with "Toots and Casper," "Thimble Theatre" featuring Olive Oyl and Popeye, "Tillie the Toiler," "Boob McNutt," and the most successful of all American comic strips, "Blondie."

The "funny papers" changed character in the 1930's with the entry of countless strips involving detectives, gangsters, cowboys, adventurers, and supermen. McCormick-Patterson's "Dick Tracy" started one trend and the same syndicate's "Terry and the Pirates" another. But such familiar characters as "Henry," "Skippy," "Little Iodine," and H. T. Webster's "Casper Milquetoast" continued to appear, followed by "Dennis the Menace" and the little folks of "Peanuts," reversions to the 1890's pattern. United Features' "Li'l Abner" and Post-Hall's "Pogo" offered social messages in addition to humor. With circulations ranging to 40,000,000 and 50,000,000 readers, the comic strip characters have become a part of American life (and in some instances, life in many countries overseas). In all except a few daily newspapers (notably, the New York *Times*), they remain an important circulation-drawing feature. When Li'l Abner married Daisy Mae in 1952 the event was featured as a news item in many papers.

Syndicates have also made famous such editorial page cartoonists as Rollin Kirby, Edmund Duffy, Nelson Harding, Daniel R. Fitzpatrick, Herbert L. Block, and Bill Mauldin, whose influence extends far beyond their home newspapers. The political columnists—Walter Lippmann, Drew Pearson, Joseph Alsop, Doris Fleeson, Marquis Childs, and the rest—likewise owe their fame to syndicates. So do the columnists of the entertainment area: Walter Winchell, Dorothy Kilgallen, Louella Parsons, Hedda Hopper, and the advisers of the lovelorn and "I have a problem" readers, Dorothy Dix, Ann Landers, and Abigail Van Buren. It is a hard fact that offerings like "Blondie" and "Dear Abby" draw some of the highest ratings in readership surveys, and the modern newspaper executive must study the syndicate offerings as carefully as he watches the main flow of the news.

Granted the necessity of providing entertainment, the newspaper editor merits criticism when he runs too many comic strips, gossip columns, and non-news features at the expense of adequate coverage of the news; when he selects too much of the flow of human interest news and cuts short news of social and political importance; when he resorts to headlining of murders, sexual misconduct, and other sensational events for purposes of arousing emotions and selling papers rather than illuminating antisocial problems. Those concerned with the adverse effects of overemphasis on the themes of sex and violence also point to magazines and paperback books as conspicuous culprits.

A recent study of "Sex and Violence on the American Newsstand" by a sociologist, Herbert A. Otto (summarized in *Journalism Quarterly,* Winter 1963), provides a comparison among different segments of the print media. The researchers analyzed issues of 55 representative magazines and found a total of 2524 incidents of violence and 1261 incidents dealing with sexual themes. Police and detective magazines contained an average of 77 incidents of violence per issue and 15 involving sex; men's magazines, 63 involving violence and 19 involving sex; romance magazines, 33 involving violence and 50 concerned with sex. The highest quality magazines—*Atlantic, Harper's,* and *New Yorker*—averaged 15 incidents of violence and 5 involving sex. Family magazines scored 12 and 4, respectively. Of a sample of 300 paperback books found on a representative newsstand, 44 per cent had covers or illustrations with a seductive, sadistic, or violent theme.

Turning to issues of 10 representative metropolitan newspapers, the researchers found that on the average they devoted 5 per cent of their news space to stories dealing with incidents of violence, including accidents and war as well as crime. One, the New York *Daily News,* used a third of its news space for such stories; the other nine used from 2 to 8 per cent. The *Daily News* devoted 3.3 per cent of its space to subjects dealing with sex, the other nine less than 1 per cent. These figures should surprise many critics of the newspaper press.

CRITICISMS OF FILM AND TELEVISION

Of all the mass media, the motion picture and its first cousin, television, are the most extensively devoted to the entertainment function. In the large majority of motion pictures the primary purpose is to give aesthetic pleasure or simply "to amuse, interest, divert." Even when the producer of a motion picture intends to deliver a social message, he does so with a strong narrative line, so that viewers who fail to absorb or appreciate his editorial message will nevertheless leave the theater with the feeling that they have had their money's worth in entertainment.

Many motion pictures and television programs have a goal no more ambitious than to give the viewers a period of relaxation, through comedy, romantic drama, or suspense shows. This purpose is laudable and requires a large amount of technical and story-telling skill to be accomplished successfully. Those who condemn the motion picture and television fare being offered to the American audience today do not quarrel with the fact that such light diversions are presented but with the fact that in their view far too much of the available time is devoted to this frothy, almost meaningless entertainment. They contend that the expensive, proficient technical facilities of motion picture and television studios should be put to a meaningful social purpose more frequently than they are.

But does the mass of the public really want more adult and provocative film fare? Many of the men who direct the motion picture and television industries contend that their primary role is to sell entertainment, not to conduct an educational institution. They cite viewer polls which show large followings for films and TV shows the critics condemn as inane. With the extremely heavy investment involved in producing films, these purveyors of entertainment say they cannot afford to give the public pictures which win critical acclaim but fail financially because too few people view them. Unfortunately that has been the fate of some of Hollywood's most literate film offerings. A man who invests $6,000,000 in producing a motion picture usually protects his investment by aiming his product at an educational level sufficiently broad to attract huge audiences.

No matter what position a debater takes in this perennial argument about the "age level" of film fare, notable examples are available in history to contradict his argument. Every year a few motion pictures are made whose success shows that a film can be literate, witty, and even socially significant and still earn large profits. Historically, however, Hollywood has produced few films which match the artistic qualities and aesthetic level of even its pioneer film, D. W. Griffith's *Birth of a Nation,* or Charlie Chaplin's later successes in *The Gold Rush* and *Modern Times.* Those interested in this level of experimental quality and aesthetic achievement must turn to the European film producers, who have given us such widely acclaimed pictures as *Open City* and *The Bicycle Thief.* Such directors as Sweden's Ingmar Bergman, Italy's Roberto Rossellini and Federico Fellini, France's Jean Renoir, Britain's Tony Richardson, and Spain's Luis Buñuel have had great cultural impact and influence on film-making, as have film producers in Japan, India, Mexico, and Poland. Fellini's *La Dolce Vita* and Richardson's *Tom Jones* were major U.S. box office attractions; usually, however, foreign films appear only in larger cities despite growing U.S. interest in them.

In recent years, to offset the inroads of television on theater attendance, U.S. motion picture producers have been making spectaculars—long films in color, employing wide-screen processes and stereophonic sound, in which the viewers find themselves almost engulfed by sight and sound. Many of these have been loud, dull, and almost pointless; an example is *Cleopatra,* which nevertheless is paying back its $50,000,000 investment. Some, like *The Diary of Anne Frank,* have been artistic successes and box office disappointments. Others—including the early Cinerama travelogues, *Around the World in 80 Days, Ben Hur,* and *West Side Story*— have been successful from both critical and financial aspects. *Ben Hur* reclaimed its investment from road showings at advanced prices and sub-sequently passed *Gone With the Wind* as the top income-producing film in motion picture history, a record which has kept Hollywood's focus on spectaculars. Hollywood has produced such fine less costly films as *Lilies of the Field* in recent years, yet it knows that such an urbane and witty film as *Gigi* played on double features with a cowboy picture in some rural areas in order to draw a crowd.

More disturbing to discerning critics of Hollywood than the relatively low intellectual level and the emphasis upon broad mass appeal by pic-tures as a whole is the readiness of some producers to exploit the baser human emotions. The films these men put into the theaters are contrived mixtures of brutality, sex, and depraved horror. These films no more qualify as escapist relaxation for most viewers than they do as social documents. They appeal only to the desire among some portions of the population for vicarious adventures in lust and corruption. It is such films which have done the most to discredit the reputation of American mo-tion picture producers.

Television has faced criticism of its entertainment fare since its incep-tion, but not until 1959 did the new medium become involved in wide-spread controversy. That year public attention was focused on scandals involving "fixing" of contestants on the popular quiz shows. At the same moment those who were already critical of the frothy nature of the top-rated variety and comedy shows were horrified to find them succeeded in network prime time preference by the Westerns. An increase in detec-tive and murder mystery dramas added fuel to the controversy. Investiga-tions of the quiz shows, of the role of advertisers in dictating content of television's offerings, and of the amount of crime and violence shown on the nation's screens followed each other in rapid order.

In May, 1961, the then chairman of the Federal Communications Com-mission, Newton N. Minow, stunned a National Association of Broadcas-ters audience with this indictment:

When television is good, nothing—not the theater, not the magazines or newspapers—nothing is better. But when television is bad, nothing is worse. I invite you to sit down in front of your television set when your station goes on the air and stay there . . . until the station signs off. I can assure you that you will observe a vast wasteland.

You will see a procession of game shows, violence, audience-participation shows, formula comedies about totally unbelievable families, blood and thunder, mayhem, sadism, murder, Western badmen, Western goodmen, private eyes, gangsters, more violence, and cartoons. And, endlessly, commercials—many screaming, cajoling and offending. And most of all, boredom. True, you will see a few things you will enjoy. But they will be very, very few.

The "vast wasteland" speech, carrying with it an implied warning from the chairman of the regulatory commission for television to police itself or be policed, brought a spurt of reform. It also brought out some counter statements, such as this one by Robert W. Sarnoff, NBC board chairman:

Television is a huge communications system that serves the public interest and must reflect to a fair degree the mass audience's preferences. . . . The best a network can do is to produce a balanced blend of light and high-brow entertainment, public affairs and news that gives reasonable satisfaction to all elements of the audience. . . . The schedule offers something for everyone. . . . What do you want from TV? No matter how elevated your tastes are, I guarantee that it offers more than you have time to watch. . . . It merely involves consulting the schedule in a newspaper.

The Television Information Office, spokesman for the industry, asked public opinion pollster Elmo Roper to put these two statements to a test. Respondents in a national sample were asked to read them and to indicate with which they were inclined to agree. In November, 1961, 55 per cent agreed with Sarnoff's defense; two years later the figure was 65 per cent. Minow's "vast wasteland" indictment won agreement from 23 per cent in 1961, from 18 per cent two years later. Other respondents agreed with both, neither, or did not reply.

A fresh attack on the amount of crime and violence portrayed on television screens came in October, 1964, from a Senate subcommittee investigating juvenile delinquency. The report was based on monitoring of programs shown in four major cities from 7 to 10 p.m. over a seven-day span. Programs featuring violence accounted for 46.8 per cent of those shown in this 1964 test period, the committee said, compared to 48.6 per cent reported in a similar 1961 monitoring. Both ABC and NBC devoted 55 per cent of prime time programming to programs emphasizing violence and related antisocial behavior; CBS, in sharp contrast, 26.5 per cent. The committee pointed out that these shows were televised, to an overwhelming degree, during time periods in which the children's audience was a large one. Television, the senators said, should improve its content before the patience of the Congress wore too thin.

CRITICISMS OF ADVERTISING

Criticisms of advertising have been widespread. Let us consider some of the more common complaints and the replies that have been made to each in the literature of the field: (1) *Advertising persuades us to buy goods and services we cannot afford.* Persuasion is present, but never coercion; it is up to each of us to exercise self-control and sound judgment in our purchases. (2) *Advertising appeals primarily to our emotions rather than to our intellect.* Since all of us are motivated largely by emotional drives, it is only natural that advertisers should make such appeals. Again, a cautious buyer will avoid obvious "plays" to his emotions. (3) *Advertising is biased.* This, too, is natural; everyone puts his best foot forward in whatever he says or does. Being aware of this bias, we can discount some of the superlatives in advertising. (4) *Advertising involves conflicting competitive claims.* But advertising is "out in the open," never hidden as are some forms of propaganda, and we can decide for ourselves. (5) *Advertising is unduly repetitious.* That is because the public is essentially a passing parade, not a mass gathering; there are always new users whom the appeal has never reached. And slogans like "It Floats" have sold goods successfully for generations. (6) *Much advertising is vulgar, obtrusive, irritating.* Actually, only a handful of advertisers employ poor taste in their appeals; their excesses damage the higher standards of the many. And the very nature of radio and television, whose commercials cannot easily be turned off, accounts for much irritation; this complaint is seldom voiced in relation to printed advertising, which can be ignored.

There are other criticisms, relating primarily to the role of advertising itself rather than to its content. Certain economists, especially those who nourished the vision of a planned, controlled society, have charged that advertising is wasteful and unnecessary, adding to the cost of goods and services. This is true in some instances, when business uses the advertising tool foolishly or for the purpose of maintaining an inflexible high price on a product. But as a general criticism, it is answered with the statement that advertising serves a socially desirable purpose: Our entire economy is geared to a fast turnover of merchandise; advertising provides selective buying information, assures us of uniform quality, saves us time in shopping, helps to lower prices through mass production and mass selling techniques, improves our standard of living by educating us concerning new products, serves cultural and intellectual ends as well as those of a purely material nature, and enables us to enjoy the mass media at small expense.

Other criticisms are directed at advertising by those who fear that their very lives are being manipulated by clever and unscrupulous Madison Avenue word-wizards whose only objective is to sell goods and ideas regardless of the social consequences. These critics are generally intellectual men and women who resist classification among the masses at whom the communications media are directed. Their intense desire to think and act of their own volition in an increasingly monolithic world leads them to attack advertising—"mass" by its very nature—at every turn, with little thought of the inevitable consequences of a society in which advertising became unduly shackled.

Many opinion leaders consider that advertising is almost wholly devoid of ethics. Who has not read Frederic Wakeman's 1946 best seller, *The Hucksters,* or one of the series of anti-advertising novels which it spawned? Who does not recall the rigged quiz shows and the disk jockey payola scandals of the late 1950's, for which advertisers and the communications industry were blamed? The image of the earnest young man-about-Madison Avenue complete with gray-flannel suit, attache case, sincere smile, and lavish expense account is not one to inspire confidence. Set against the background of yesterday's patent medicine quackery, extravagant advertising, and the *laissez faire* doctrine of *caveat emptor,* and today's allegations of misleading drug and no-warning cigarette advertising, the bill of indictments is devastating.

Add to that the questions of good taste in broadcasting—the jarring loudness of some commercials, the so-called insulting and obnoxious advertisements, the cramming of too many commercials into segments of broadcast time, and the clutter and length of some TV program credit crawls—and many persons have declared an anti-advertising Roman holiday. "TV is a series of tasteless and endless interruptions," cried one critic. "The people are tired of being screamed at, assaulted, and insulted by commercials," exclaimed another.

The Federal Trade Commission has become the principal Washington guardian over advertising, instituting "corrective" suits on numerous occasions. Senate groups have conducted hearings about drug advertising. The Federal Communications Commission has threatened to curb broadcast "overcommercialization," but mainly has looked to the FTC for action against advertising content. In all, more than 20 federal agencies, including the Internal Revenue Service and the Securities & Exchange Commission, have taken some steps to regulate advertising.

In reply, the advertising industry has pointed to its long tradition of cooperation and self-policing and raised two defenses: that all advertising should not be smeared due to the derelictions of a few, and that government "does not understand advertising." Industry leaders point out that, just as we have some quack doctors, shyster lawyers, and unethical business men, so there are advertising men without a sense of social responsibility. This minority tends to give a "black eye" to the entire industry, which in its associations and individually has been raising standards for several generations.

Morton J. Simon, Philadelphia lawyer and author, has cited, in a *Printers' Ink* article, six principal reasons for the current unfavorable governmental climate toward advertising: (1) *Advertising is a horizontal industry.* It cuts across almost every business and service, so an attack on any industry almost always includes advertising. (2) *Advertising represents a lot of money.* It spends billions of dollars annually and some persons view these funds as apparently untaxed and above the grip of the government. (3) *Advertising lives in a glass house.* By its nature it cannot hide its sins. (4) *The gray-flannel-suit image is pervasive.* Many consider that advertising men live lavishly and improperly on tax-deductible expense accounts. (5) *Advertising is not constitutionally protected.* Some in government believe that advertising is somehow tainted by its commercial purpose and therefore is not protected by the First Amendment; its legal status in this regard has not been made clear. (6) *Advertising has rarely lobbied.* Unlike most other major segments of the economy, advertising has never maintained a Washington lobby.

The industry is acutely aware of the many criticisms directed against advertising, but insists that censorship and other governmental restrictions are not the answer. Only through continued voluntary pressures exerted by advertising groups and through the steady growth of a sense of social responsibility, it is maintained, will the abuses eventually be reduced to a minimum.

EFFORTS TO IMPROVE

It is generally agreed that government can play only a minor role in efforts to improve the mass media, if they are to remain free. This means that efforts at improvement must come from within the media themselves or must be generated by groups outside the media that represent the general public. In each of the media there are groups and individuals who are contributing to the efforts to meet the challenges raised by society.

One group is composed of the various trade associations. For newspapers there are the American Newspaper Publishers Association, representing the dailies; the National Editorial Association, for weeklies and small dailies; and two subsidiary national daily groups, the International Circulation Managers' Association and the Newspaper Advertising Executives Association. There are also strong regional associations—Inland Daily Press Association, Southern Newspaper Publishers Association, New England Daily Newspaper Association, Northwest Daily Press Association—and state associations (usually emphasizing problems of weeklies).

The trade associations for other media include the National Association of Broadcasters, the Magazine Publishers Association, the American Book Publishers Council, the American Textbook Publishers Institute, the Motion Picture Association of America, the American Business Press, Inc., the American Association of Advertising Agencies, and the Advertising Federation of America.

Each trade association speaks for its industry in affairs of general interest to the members. The staffs represent the industries when necessary at congressional hearings and before other government bodies. The associations develop promotional materials for their media and operate central offices which act as clearing-houses for information about the industries. The daily newspapers organized a Bureau of Advertising which promotes their media; the Magazine Advertising Bureau, the Radio Advertising Bureau, and the Television Information Bureau do the same in their fields. The National Association of Broadcasters, the Motion Picture Association of America, and the American Association of Advertising Agencies have developed codes of conduct; in the case of the motion picture group, the strict code regulating production of films is the primary reason for its existence. While they are primarily concerned with business matters, many of the associations sponsor discussions aimed at improvements of their media and encourage individual activities aimed at raising the standards of members.

There are also groups of editors and newsmen. Most prominent is the American Society of Newspaper Editors, limited primarily to editors, editorial page editors, and managing editors of dailies of 50,000 or more circulation. The ASNE formulated the "Canons of Journalism" in 1923 and attempted to regulate the professional conduct of its members but found it could not expel an accused editor. Its thoughtful discussions in annual meetings of news and editorial problems are reproduced in book form in the *Problems of Journalism* series.

Editorial page editors and writers also formed the National Conference of Editorial Writers, which meets annually in sessions featuring small-group critiques of the editorial pages of the members. It publishes a quarterly, the *Masthead,* and has a code of principles "to stimulate the conscience and the quality of the American editorial page." Managing editors of newspapers belonging to the Associated Press have organized the Associated Press Managing Editors Association, which has made a continuing study of the AP news report and has published the *APME Red Book* reporting on committee findings and convention sessions.

The Radio-Television News Directors Association is the equivalent organization for the electronic media. It has sought to elevate standards through adoption of a code of principles and has been instrumental in forwarding the position of news and public affairs broadcasting in the industry. Among magazine people, the International Council of Industrial Editors has set standards of performance and has held annual sessions for men and women who edit company publications. Both groups issue magazines for their members.

The American Newspaper Guild has done much to improve the standards of the newspaper business through the raising of salaries and has attempted to carry out programs of self-improvement. Its publication is the *Guild Reporter*. Membership is limited primarily to workers in larger daily newspapers and the press associations. Its role as a trade union will be discussed in greater detail in Chapter 9, which is devoted to the newspaper industry.

There are other groups: the professional journalistic societies, Sigma Delta Chi for men and Theta Sigma Phi for women, both a half-century old and both operating chapters for working journalists as well as on campuses; Pi Delta Epsilon, honorary collegiate journalism fraternity; Kappa Tau Alpha, journalism scholastic society; Alpha Delta Sigma, professional advertising fraternity; Gamma Alpha Chi, professional advertising sorority; Pi Alpha Mu, professional fraternity for men and women in the publishing, advertising, and journalistic management fields; and Kappa Alpha Mu, professional photographic fraternity for men and women. All issue publications, the *Quill* of Sigma Delta Chi being the best known. The Nieman Fellows, alumni of the Nieman Foundation program for giving newsmen a year of study at Harvard University, issue an important quarterly, the *Nieman Reports.* The Commission on Freedom of the Press, cited earlier in this chapter, made the most notable effort by a group outside the media to influence their conduct. The role of journalism educators in universities and colleges and the cooperation extended to them by the mass communications industries is detailed in Part V of this book.

Any attempt to name individuals within the media who have demonstrated leadership in responding to the challenges raised by society and in urging programs of self-criticism and improvement is difficult. But some can be singled out as examples. Among owners and publishers, there have been Barry Bingham of the Louisville *Courier-Journal,* Arthur Hays Sulzberger of the New York *Times,* and John Cowles of the Minneapolis *Star* and *Tribune.* Among editors, Erwin D. Canham of the *Christian Science Monitor,* Herbert Brucker of the Hartford *Courant,* J. Russell Wiggins of the Washington *Post and Times Herald,* and Norman Isaacs of the Louisville *Courier-Journal* and *Times.* Among other newsmen, James B. Reston, associate editor of the New York *Times,* editorial writer Alan Barth and cartoonist Herbert L. Block of the Washington *Post and Times Herald,* Washington correspondent Clark Mollenhoff of the Des Moines *Register* and *Tribune,* and columnist Marquis Childs of the St. Louis *Post-Dispatch.* In the magazine world, the voice of Ben Hibbs, former editor of the *Saturday Evening Post,* has been heard. Chief spokesmen in the field of radio and television have been Dr. Frank Stanton, Edward R. Murrow, and Eric Sevareid of CBS; Chet Huntley of NBC, and Howard K. Smith of ABC.

Many more individuals could be named, for in all the mass media there are conscientious and talented men and women who are as anxious as any of the philosophical critics of the press that a better job be done of informing the public and of giving it the basis for making proper decisions. They need the help of all readers, listeners, and viewers who make up the general public which the mass media serve.

SUMMARY

Criticisms concerning diversity of media content have arisen, particularly focusing on the newspaper editorial page. A tendency toward a "one-party press" during national political campaigns compounded the difficulties of newspaper editors, who obviously could not cater to all points of view in mass circulation "monopoly" journals. Some of the critics, it should be noted, placed undue emphasis upon the "power of the press" to control voting.

Quality of media content has been criticized on the following points: overemphasis on entertaining rather than informing, sensationalism rather than effective popularization, insufficient interpretation and reluctance to exercise the opinion function, lack of both quantity and quality of media content in smaller communities, and bad taste and lack of social purpose in advertising. The Commission on Freedom of the Press made a thoughtful philosophic report on these problems in 1947.

No matter what physical and commercial changes occur in the mass media, it can be assumed that the entertainment function will continue to be a significant factor, both in its own right and as a means by which writers and performers can deliver facts and viewpoints in a manner palatable to mass audiences.

In some media, particularly television and the motion picture, the entertainment function predominates. In others, notably the newspaper, it plays only a related role to the news and opinion functions. The degree and quality of what we call entertainment vary widely; in some cases the goal of fulfillment of aesthetic pleasure is accomplished; in others the object is simply to amuse and divert.

Relatively few motion pictures achieve a high artistic and aesthetic level, and the same criticism is true of television offerings. Those who work in these media point out that too often pictures and programs which win critical acclaim fail at the "box office."

Throughout newspaper history, the news columns have been exploited for their entertainment value, either through choice of stories to be published or through the way the stories are written. Newspapers have always had, in addition, a budget of non-news entertainment material. The older literary offerings have given way to columns, comic strips and cartoon panels, advice to the lovelorn, "how-to-do-it" articles, and the countless other offerings of the modern syndicate. Readers expect their newspapers to entertain them, but those editors who go too far in emphasizing this function find they are losing ground in the competition for audience attention. The reader turns to the newspaper for news and opinions and a degree of entertainment; if it is entertainment alone that he wants, other media claim his eye and ear.

It is generally agreed that efforts at improvement of the mass media must come from within the media themselves or be generated by groups representing the general public. Government can only play a minor role in efforts to improve the media, if they are to remain free. In each of the media there are organized groups and individuals working for better performance: trade associations, organizations of editors and newsmen, professional societies, and outstanding individuals who have demonstrated leadership in responding to the challenges raised by society.

STUDY QUESTION

How valid, in your opinion, is the argument that the mass media, by their nature, must reflect the average level of tastes in their presentation of entertainment?

PROJECTS

1. Write a 300-word essay describing the types of comic strips published in the newspaper you read. How many depend on humor, for example?

2. Clip an advertisement from a newspaper or magazine and write a brief commentary about its value to society.

PART IV

THE MASS COMMUNICATIONS INDUSTRIES AND PROFESSIONS

CHAPTER 9

NEWSPAPERS

THE NEWSPAPER'S ROLE

The term "newspaper" covers a surprisingly broad range of publications. It includes the small weekly in which every task from gathering news to running the press is done by two or three people and the huge metropolitan daily with a staff of more than a thousand and a daily circulation of a million copies. Between these extremes are hundreds of daily and weekly newspapers of many sizes and degrees of prosperity.

No matter what their circumstances, all of them are akin: they are made of type, ink, and newsprint. They exist to inform and influence the communities in which they are published, and the men who produce them share a common urge to get the news into print. Into the pages of every newspaper goes an essential but intangible extra ingredient, the minds and spirits of the men who make it.

Newspaper work is an adventure, so full of fresh experiences that men and women who have been in it for years still come to work with a subconscious wonder about what unexpected developments the day will bring. It is based upon a firmly disciplined routine, because "getting the paper out" on time is paramount, and this can be done only if a definite work pattern exists in all departments.

The exciting things that can happen within that framework are innumerable. For the newsman there is the stimulation of being on the inside of big developments, of watching history being made, and of meeting intriguing people. For those who work in advertising and circulation, there is satisfaction in conceiving and executing ideas that bring in money and influencing people through skill with words. Working on a newspaper is an open invitation to create ideas and put them to work.

The newspaper people who succeed best are those who handle the necessary routine meticulously and bring to their jobs an extra spark of creative thinking. Those for whom the atmosphere and work lose their excitement frequently move on to other media or occupations.

As one of the mass communications media, the contemporary newspaper has three fundamental functions and some secondary ones. The basic ones are: (1) to inform its readers objectively about what is happening in their community, country, and world; (2) to comment editorially on the news in order to bring these developments into focus; (3) to provide the means whereby persons with goods and services to sell can advertise their wares. The newspaper's less vital roles are: (1) to campaign for desirable civic projects and to help eliminate undesirable conditions; (2) to give the readers a portion of entertainment through such devices as comic strips, columnists, and special features; (3) to serve the reader as a friendly counselor, information bureau, and champion of his rights.

When a newspaper performs all or most of these tasks well, it becomes an integral part of community life. For most people the newspaper has a more vivid "personality" than any of the other media. The temporary disappearance of newspapers from a city, because of labor trouble or a mechanical breakdown, creates confusion in business life and in the ordinary flow of social and civic affairs. The subscriber without his newspaper feels as lonesome as a person whose best friend has left town.

The printed word has a lasting power far beyond that of the spoken word or the visual image. Readers can refer to it again and again. Thus one of the satisfactions of newspaper work is that the stories printed in today's columns may be clipped and saved by readers for many years and may be readily examined in the newspaper's files decades later. This fact increases the reporter's feeling that he is writing history and contributes to the newspaper's position as a stabilizing, continuing institution in the community.

GENERAL ORGANIZATION OF NEWSPAPERS

The newspapers in the United States can be divided roughly into four categories: weeklies and semiweeklies, small dailies, larger dailies (mostly in the submetropolitan areas), and the gigantic metropolitan dailies. Each of these newspapers has a definite purpose and is tailored to the needs of the community it serves. The size and frequency of a newspaper's editions depend upon the amount of advertising and circulation revenue it commands; trying to publish a newspaper on a grander scale than its community can support is a sure and swift way to bankruptcy.

Most American newspapers have a page that is eight columns wide and 20 to 21 inches deep; the normal column width is slightly less than 2 inches. This is called a standard size page. A rather small minority of newspapers are tabloid in format, usually five columns wide and 15 inches deep, or approximately half the size of a standard page. Although it is widely agreed that the tabloid size newspaper is very easy for the reader to handle, the problems of printing it and the limitations on its advertising potential have kept many publishers from adopting this format. In spite of these limitations the newspaper with by far the largest circulation in the United States, the New York *Daily News*, uses the tabloid format.

Unfortunately because of the editorial approach used by some tabloid metropolitan newspapers, the word "tabloid" has taken on a connotation of sensationalism. This is unfair to many tabloids whose content is no more sensational than that of standard size dailies, even less in some cases. Equating physical size and content is a false approach, too often practiced.

No matter what their size, all newspapers have a fundamental organization in common. Each has five major departments: *editorial,* which gathers and prepares the news, entertainment, and opinion materials, both written and illustrated; *advertising,* which solicits and prepares the commercial messages addressed to readers; *circulation,* which has the task of selling and delivering the newspaper to the readers of a community; *production,* which turns the editorial materials and advertisements into type and prints the newspapers; and *business,* which oversees the newspaper's entire operation.

Newspaper stories are written to include the "5 W's and H"—who, what, when, where, why, and how. Their purpose is to present a report of an action or a situation in simple, easily understood language that can be comprehended by a mass audience of different educational levels. Increased emphasis has been placed upon simplicity of writing in recent years and upon explaining the "why" of news situations. Stories should be written objectively without showing the personal beliefs of the writer or his publisher; the paper's opinions concerning the news it is reporting should be reserved for its editorial page and signed opinion columns. These principles should apply on newspapers of all sizes. As a whole, contemporary American journalism adheres to them quite well, although there are some glaring exceptions.

Newspaper advertising is divided into two types, display and classified. The former ranges from inconspicuous one-inch notices to multiple-page advertisements in which merchants and manufacturers proclaim their goods and services. Classified advertisements are the small-print, generally brief announcements packed closely together near the back of the paper; they deal with such diverse topics as help wanted, apartments for rent, used furniture and automobiles for sale, and personal notices. On almost all newspapers except the very smallest, display and classified advertising are handled by different staffs. Most newspapers receive about three-fourths of their income from advertising and one-fourth from circulation.

Display advertising in turn is broken into two categories, retail and national, sometimes called general. Retail advertising, often called local, comes from the sources its name implies, local merchants and service companies. National advertising comes primarily from manufacturers and other commercial organizations selling brand-name merchandise and services over wide regions or the entire country. Much of this advertising is placed through advertising agencies. Local advertising is usually discussed in terms of column inches whereas national advertising is measured by agate lines, 14 to the inch. A column inch is a space one column wide and one inch deep.

The organizational setup of all newspapers is basically the same, although naturally the larger the newspaper, the more complex its staff alignments. The top man is the publisher, and, in many cases, he is also the principal owner of the newspaper. On some papers the publisher's decisions on all matters are absolute, whereas in other instances he must answer to a board of directors. The publisher's task is to set the newspaper's basic editorial and commercial policies and to see that they are carried out efficiently by the various department heads. On quite a few newspapers, especially smaller ones, the publisher is also the editor; he is then usually referred to as "editor and publisher," a nice tribute to the importance of editorial content in the newspaper.

Frequently there is a business manager or general manager under the publisher to administer the company's business operations, which range all the way from obtaining newsprint to the purchasing of tickets as the newspaper's contribution to a community concert series. The heads of the advertising, circulation, and production departments answer to the publisher through the business manager, if there is one. But the editorial department, jealous of its independence to print the news without being subject to commercial pressures (theoretically), demands and generally gets a line of command directly to the publisher. When editorial and business departments clash, as they sometimes do over ways to handle news situations and expenses, the ultimate decision is made by the publisher. The titles of executive editor and managing editor are most commonly used to designate heads of the news operation.

THE CHANGING NEWSPAPER PATTERN

The year 1910 was the peak year, as we have seen, in numbers of newspapers published in the United States: 2200 general circulation English-language dailies and 11,800 weeklies. By 1965 the figures were approximately 1750 dailies and 8500 weeklies. Since during those 55 years the population of the country doubled, one might assume that newspapers were losing their place in American life. But this is not so; the daily papers of 1965 had 150 per cent more readership than those of 1910, and both daily and weekly newspapers are established as firmly today as the basic means of news and advertising communication as they were a half or a quarter of a century ago.

The 1750 dailies appear in 1470 cities and towns. Most of these fall into the category of "small city dailies." Nearly a thousand are published in towns of less than 25,000 population. Only 280 appear in cities of 100,000 or more; the bulk of these make up the submetropolitan and metropolitan classes of dailies. Half of the American dailies have circulations of 10,000 copies or less; another quarter range in circulation from 10,000 to 25,000. Only 125, or 7 per cent, rank above 100,000 in circulation; only 30 have a circulation above 300,000.

If there is an average American daily (and the individualistic patterns of journalism make the description of an average or typical newspaper virtually impossible), it has a circulation of not more than 10,000 copies and serves a town of about 20,000 population and its surrounding trade area. A typical weekly has a circulation of some 1500 copies in a small town and an agricultural countryside dotted with smaller villages. Neither has direct competition in its own community; only approximately 4 per cent of both daily newspaper cities and country weekly towns have competing newspaper ownerships.

There are approximately 300 morning dailies in the United States, but they have 40 per cent of the circulation of all dailies—a circulation of about 23,500,000 copies in 1964. The 1450 evening dailies had 35,500,000 of the total 59,000,000 circulation. The 550 Sunday editions had a circulation of approximately 47,000,000.

There were in 1965 still 50 cities with separately owned and competing general circulation daily newspapers. But competition was still the rule only in cities of more than 500,000 population, and even there it was restricted. New York City had six dailies with six separate owners, Boston five dailies with three owners, and Washington three dailies with three owners. No other city had more than two ownerships and seven of the largest 25 cities had a single ownership. In 1235 of the 1470 cities with dailies there was just one paper, and 185 had morning and evening dailies published by the same owner or in joint printing arrangements.

As Professor Raymond B. Nixon of the University of Minnesota has pointed out in the *Journalism Quarterly* (Winter 1961), the trend toward consolidation of ownerships is virtually completed. He predicts that the number of daily newspapers will remain stabilized at 1750, with births of new dailies offsetting the deaths of others. Rapidly rising population figures mean more reader support for smaller dailies, the fastest growing group; and newly created population centers will contribute new dailies to balance the remaining few losses in older established cities. Similarly, the number of weeklies has remained steady during the past decade. Each newspaper can look forward to some additional circulation. Serving both a growing population and a steadily expanding national economy, the newspaper can expect to remain a powerful and profit-making institution if the proprietors can keep improving the production techniques to offset higher costs of operation.

The chief immediate reason for the disappearance of many newspapers is the constantly rising cost of production. The wages of the men who write and print them, the cost of newsprint, the metal for the typesetting machines, gasoline for the delivery trucks, taxes, the news and picture services—these and a hundred other expenses of a newspaper have become higher and higher. The price of newsprint has tripled in the past

25 years, for example, but the price at which most newspapers are sold to the public has not risen at the same pace. Nor has the cost of an inch of advertising. Thus to maintain the same profit margin as he had 25 years ago, the publisher must sell more newspapers and more advertising or find ways to cut his production costs. Competition by television and radio for the advertiser's dollar has given the publisher another thorny problem.

Many newspaper proprietors have found ways to overcome these difficulties, and their newspapers continue to be profitable business ventures. Others have been less fortunate, either through lack of skill and vision as publishers or because the markets in which they operate simply do not have enough potential advertising and circulation revenue to offset the rising costs. They have been forced to close their newspapers or to combine them with others in the same community.

In many cities where two newspapers were competing for advertising and circulation, and both were struggling to stay solvent, the two owners have seen the financial advantage of combining forces into one publication. One sells out to the other, or they make a partnership arrangement of some sort. The city is left with only one newspaper. Critics of the American press look upon the rise in the number of one-newspaper cities as an unwholesome trend because it subjects the readers to the whims of a monopoly publisher if he chooses to twist or conceal news. There is reason for worry in this trend. Competition between two or more newspapers to cover the news usually gives the readers better assurance of being kept fully informed about what is happening in their community.

There is a substantial argument on the other side, however. One strong newspaper in a city, if the publisher and editor are conscientious men sensible of their responsibilities, can often provide better news coverage and community service than two weak ones. Also, a financially strong paper is sometimes more willing to attack entrenched and harmful interests in a city, because it is able to absorb the financial retaliation its foes aim at it by trying to undercut its advertising and circulation income. A paper that is weak financially is usually a timid paper editorially.

Concurrent with the reduction to one newspaper in many cities is the rise of local news coverage by television and radio stations. Thus in many cases the citizens do have an alternate source for local news. In the event that a newspaper attempts to ignore or twist a local news situation for a policy reason, an attitude much less frequent than the more vehement critics of the press claim, the news coverage by television and radio stations can expose this irresponsible action.

There are deeper factors, too, which help explain the diminishing number of American newspapers. A half-century ago before the development of fast automobile and truck communication, every city was a self-contained unit, of which the local newspaper was a basic part. Today, however, in many states the metropolitan newspapers can circulate swiftly over such large regions that they provide readers in the smaller nearby cities with bigger, more comprehensive, and better edited editions than the home-town papers can offer. The local paper's greatest advantage is its more detailed presentation of home-town news, which many readers consider the most important ingredient. If the home-town paper is forced to quit business, the readers still have access to a metropolitan paper that satisfies part of their needs, although home-town news suffers. From a cold-blooded, dollars-and-cents standpoint, this sometimes means the elimination of marginal newspaper operations, just as marginal grocery stores are driven out of business by the supermarkets.

In the sprawling urban complexes that have grown up around some of the country's great cities, this process is working in reverse. Suburban towns spring into being almost overnight with their shopping centers and branches of major chain stores. They are close geographically to the core city, such as Los Angeles or Detroit, but they develop a substantial business district and community interest of their own. A weekly newspaper is started, and after three or four years it may be converted into a daily, serving an area which previously was dependent entirely upon a metropolitan paper. In the listings the new city appears as a one-newspaper town, even though the new daily is in heavy competition with the nearby metropolitan press for news and advertising.

Growth of these fringe dailies cuts into circulation and advertising revenues of the older metropolitan papers and is sometimes the factor which pushes them into consolidation. Thus it can be seen that the newspaper population of the United States is constantly in flux, changing to meet the evolving patterns of our population shifts and contemporary living conditions.

In examining the structure of the newspaper industry in the United States, two things should be remembered: (1) Newspapers do not necessarily increase in excellence as they grow larger. Some of the finest, best edited, and most influential papers in the country have relatively small circulations. (2) As a commercial venture a large newspaper is not necessarily more profitable than a small one. Many small city dailies return a greater annual profit to their proprietors than certain metropolitan dailies with famous names, although the latter have vastly heavier investments in equipment and manpower. In relation to their investment, some weekly newspapers are among the most profitable of all publishing operations. They are less glamorous places to work than the metropolitan papers, and usually their technical standards are lower, but as business ventures they may be superior. Also, they are often closer to the real needs and feelings of their communities than the huge dailies.

The majority of American newspapers are owned by people whose principal business is putting out the newspaper. Control is usually held tightly by an individual, a family, or a small group of investors whom the publisher has invited to share in the ownership. Only infrequently is the stock of an individual newspaper offered on public sale. The nature of newspaper publishing makes widespread public participation in the ownership, such as that found in railroads or manufacturing companies, impractical and undesirable. An effective newspaper's editorial policy cannot be subject to the whims of stockholder battles. Newspapers are more the reflection of personal ownership than almost any other major segment of American business life, and owners as a group are not anxious to share ownership unless financial necessity requires this.

Some successful publishing families branch out into other business fields, using the newspaper as the foundation for their financial and political operations. If they allow these outside interests to influence the editorial policy of their newspapers, this can be a disservice to the public. This sometimes happens. As a whole, however, American publishers put the task of bringing out the newspaper ahead of their other interests.

The market prices of successful newspapers have risen so sharply that it is difficult for an individual to purchase an important daily newspaper property today unless he is very wealthy or has substantial financial backing. A small daily with a circulation of 5000 will cost at least $100,000 if it is in a "live" business community. The total cost of stock in the recent sale of the Chicago *Daily News* to Field Enterprises was $24,000,000. Weekly prices are lower because the papers usually have less mechanical equipment and are situated in towns where the advertising potential is limited. The selling price of an average moderately successful weekly is about $25,000 to $50,000; prices go to $100,000 or more in some cases.

Although there still are occasional stories of men who start a small local newspaper on a shoestring and build it into a notable financial success, these have become rarities.

Starting a daily newspaper from scratch today with a capital outlay of less than $150,000 is virtually impossible because of the high cost of mechanical equipment; most likely the figure would be higher. The publisher must also be prepared for operating losses until his advertising income is developed. Establishment of a completely new metropolitan newspaper would require an outlay of $10,000,000 or more before the publication could stand on its financial feet, which explains why no new papers are being born in our large cities.

Despite all the difficulties, newspaper publishing remains an attractive business. Few great fortunes are made in the field today, but well-managed publications in active communities yield their owners a substantial living with a strong measure of prestige attached. There are instances where a hard-working weekly publisher has improved his capital position by as much as $75,000 over a 15-year period of economic growth in his community.

OPPORTUNITIES IN NEWSPAPER WORK

One of the baffling misconceptions which has been held by many young people in recent years is that "you can't get into newspaper work." This despite the fact that newspaper publishers literally have been begging journalism schools to supply them with new talent for the past decade. The misconception probably took root during the years of the great depression of the 1930's, when jobs everywhere were scarce. Coupled with reports of relatively low starting pay in newspapers—a handicap now being overcome as more publishers realize college-trained beginners are worth more pay—and a feeling that progress is slow and opportunities to accomplish socially desirable results are few, the basic misconception of "I can't even get started" has kept many a promising prospect from the newspaper field.

Certainly there is no dearth of starting positions on the 1750 dailies and 8500 weeklies in this country. Normal turnover creates hundreds of openings each year, as "help wanted" ads in the industry's trade journals testify. Weeklies and small dailies are the most frequent users of journalism school placement services, both for news and business department personnel. In addition, the prosperous era through which newspapers have been passing has brought sizable staff additions for both smaller and larger papers. When you stop to think that the 8500 weeklies average several employees each, that the smaller dailies often have from 10 to 25 news department workers and an equal number in their business departments, and that metropolitan daily staffs run into the hundreds, you should realize that an ambitious, college-trained man or woman can find a suitable starting place in the newspaper world. Those with persistence and talent can rise to satisfying levels both in pay and in opportunity to perform work of a rewarding nature both to themselves and society.

Daily newspapers in the United States employ more than 230,000 persons, according to a survey by *Editor & Publisher*. Of these, at least 36,000 were tabulated as being in news departments, 26,000 in advertising, 19,000 in other business departments, 31,000 in circulation, and 93,000 in mechanical departments. Women number 22 per cent of news department employees and 38 per cent of advertising workers. Census figures indicate that another 50,000 persons are employed by weeklies and their printing establishments. The 1960 census counted 49,000 reporters and editors working for all types of newspapers (17,000 of them women) and 3700 newspaper photographers.

The men and women who work on newspapers are drawn from many backgrounds and are of many temperaments. Those in the editorial department need a strong sense of curiosity about their fellow beings and a sympathy for them; other qualifications include a good command of English, an interest in government, a desire to know why things happen, a high respect for accuracy, and an aptitude for personal communication with other people in order to obtain news from them. A reporter must be both a willing listener and an alert poser of questions.

Many of these same abilities are helpful in the commercial side of newspaper work. Those who sell advertising space and engage in circulation operations need an aptitude for salesmanship, a knowledge of economics and commerce, and the ability to handle detail swiftly and accurately.

Increasingly newspapers seek employees for all editorial and "front office" departments who have had at least some college education. Many editors make college training a requirement for all reporters they hire. This does not necessarily mean journalism school experience, however;

an applicant who is well trained in liberal arts, with emphasis on English and political science, is welcomed in most newsrooms. The percentage of college-trained men and women in the commercial departments is lower, but it is rising steadily.

News and editorial. There are two main divisions of newsroom work— *reporting,* which includes gathering and writing news and feature stories and the taking of news and feature photographs; and *desk work,* which is the selection and preparation for printing of the written material and photographs submitted by the reporters, photographers, and the wire and syndicate services. The men who do the desk work are called editors.

This distinction between the newsgatherers and the news processors is quite sharp on large daily newspaper staffs. Some editors will go a year or more without writing a single news story, and metropolitan reporters have nothing to do with the selection of a headline or page placement of the stories they write. On smaller papers the distinction is less pro- nounced, and in many cases an editorial man spends part of his day as a reporter, photographer, and writer and the other part in selecting and processing the news for publication. The smaller the paper, the greater the need to be the proverbial "jack of all trades."

Some men and women find their greatest satisfaction in being reporters all their lives—probing for information, being close to events as they happen, and mingling with the people who make news. Theirs is the most exciting part of newspaper work, when big stories are breaking, and they are the ones the public knows as newspapermen. Few laymen have any concept of the inside office workers who really put the paper together. Many of the finest reporters in the country abhor the idea of being bound to a desk all day, shuffling paper and fighting the mechanical demands of type and newsprint. In fact, some cynical metropolitan reporting veterans have a tendency to look upon desk men as slightly deficient in intelligence and very deficient in a zest for life.

The fact remains, however, that a reporter rarely is promoted directly to a high editorial place on a large or medium-sized daily. The top jobs go to the men who have had desk experience. They are the organizers, the planners, the men and women who think automatically of whether a headline will "count" and whether all the essential stories for an edition are moved out to the composing room before deadline so the papers will come off the press on time. By the same token, few desk men are truly successful unless they have had a thorough grounding in reporting, so they can know the problems a reporter faces on a story and can feed him useful suggestions.

A beginner can start as a city hall beat reporter for a small daily; he can also start as the telegraph editor, handling the news wire and writing headlines. If he chooses and sticks to reporting, he may graduate eventually to a metropolitan reporting staff; if he selects the editing path, he may advance to a large paper's copy desk. Or, in either capacity, he may remain with the small daily and soon rise to editorial management status.

On most daily newspapers there are specialized editing-reporting jobs, where the editorial worker gathers his own news and also helps in preparing it for print. The woman's page, the sports page, the business page, and the entertainment page fall into this category. Some men and women prefer to become specialists and do their reporting in one area. The woman's pages of a modern daily offer many opportunities for stimulating writing; sports always has been a magnet for prospective young men reporters. Business news has become a specialty on many papers, with staffs of as many as six or eight assigned to the area. Some metropolitan papers offer opportunities for critical reviewers of films, television, the drama, and books. There are also varied opportunities to specialize in one of the broader general news areas: politics, science, labor, religion, space and aviation, social work, and public health. Many a general assignment reporter has become a recognized expert in one of these fields and thereby has found a satisfying career.

A very important area of work is that on the editorial page. Editorial page staffs run to eight or ten men (and occasionally a woman) on metropolitan papers which pride themselves on the quality of their opinion offerings. Some specialize as writers of editorials on international affairs; others specialize in economics and business, or perhaps local subjects. The editorial page director coordinates their work and consults with the publisher on major policy decisions. Editorial page staffs of this size usually have a make-up editor who selects the column materials and "letters-to-the-editor" and produces the page. They also may have a staff cartoonist. Papers which place less emphasis upon the editorial page will have fewer editorial writers. And at the smaller daily level, there may be only one editorial writer, plus a managing editor who also attempts to comment on the day's news. Weekly newspaper editors sometimes write and publish regular editorial columns; others prefer to write what they call "personal columns" in a more informal style.

The opportunities to advance on an editorial staff come in many forms. A reporter may eventually earn a staff assignment in Washington, at the United Nations, or abroad; an increasing number of these jobs is becoming available. He may work his way up through the desk jobs to become city editor or even managing editor; he may become a top-flight political or science writer; or he may move into the editorial page staff or one of the specialized departments for a stay of many years. Much depends upon his temperament, and a bit of luck. As a rule the editorial management chooses for promotion, when an important vacancy occurs, a man or woman with all-around experience and a record of dependability and creative thinking.

Photography. The newspaper photographer fills a large and growing role on the staff of every daily newspaper, large or small, as the field of photojournalism expands. On a newspaper, the photographer's primary task is to record in a single picture or a sequence, rapidly and factually, the news and feature developments of the day that lend themselves to pictorial treatment. He may take pictures for the news, sports, woman's page, and entertainment editors, as well as for the promotion and advertising departments. On large staffs, employing 20 or more photographers and technicians, individuals may develop specialties and be assigned primarily in these fields. One man demonstrates a knack for catching vivid sports action from unusual angles; another may be especially skillful at taking fashion and social pictures to avoid the "waxworks pose" that is so deadly in many prearranged feature photographs.

Planning of photographic coverage on good newspaper staffs is as meticulous as the arrangement of coverage by reporters. Memorable news photos usually are the result of having a photographer assigned to the right place at the proper time, plus the photographer's instinct for the climactic moment in the news situation and his technical ability to take an effective picture when that moment comes.

Newspaper photography has advanced far from the days when an aggressive copyboy of limited education could be taught the rudiments of a camera and turned loose as an ambulance-chasing photographer. Today many news photographers have college educations or have attended professional photography schools. They look upon photojournalism as a satisfying career and know that their income will increase with their skill. News photography is not a field for a shy person. The photographer must be ready to fight for his picture at times. However, the widely held concept of the photographer as a rough, brash fellow shoving heedlessly into the middle of things is inaccurate and misleading.

On the larger papers, the photographer's equipment ranges from the 5 × 7 Big Bertha camera with a 28-inch lens to the 35 millimeter or 2¼ × 2¼ camera. The trend is toward the use of small, inconspicuous equipment. His assignments range from aerial photos to close-ups of tiny objects such as rings. Two-way radio may keep him in constant touch with his office. Smaller dailies may have only one or two photographers, and on many weeklies the editor takes his own pictures. The reporter who can take photographs, and the photographer who can report, are in especial demand on small papers and are often paid more than those with a single ability.

Newspaper photographers receive the same salaries as reporters under Guild scales. They frequently supplement their salary checks with overtime assignments and with after-hours jobs such as photographing weddings. Free-lance photographers, not on the newspaper payroll, are paid for newsworthy pictures that they submit for publication. Large papers also employ picture editors, who give and coordinate assignments and supervise the publishing of all pictures, including photo pages.

The movement of experienced photographers between media compares to that of writers and editors. A photojournalist may remain on newspapers for his entire career. He may move to the photographic staff of a television station or a magazine. Perhaps he may choose to enter the commercial or industrial photographic field. Wherever he goes with his camera, his newspaper experience in judging situations and people quickly is invaluable.

Advertising, circulation, management. Although news reporting is the most glamorous and best publicized part of newspaper work, there are many other opportunities for young men and women in advertising sales and copywriting, circulation, promotion and public relations, personnel, research, production, and general business management.

The advertising department is one of the most attractive for sales-minded persons. A good newspaper space salesman must be much more than a glib talker. He must know as much as possible about the paper's policies and features. He must be able to supply the potential advertiser with abundant and accurate figures about the paper's circulation pattern and totals, the advertising rates, and the kind of merchandising support the advertiser will receive. He must know at least the rudiments of layout and art work. In addition, he should be an idea man, enthusiastic and able to give the merchant ideas about how best to use his advertising budget. Selling newspaper advertising requires the art of persuasion, a briefcase well loaded with facts and ideas, and a strong personal belief that the newspaper space he is selling will move goods off the merchant's shelves. The more he knows about his client merchant's business and problems, the more effectively he can serve him. In fact, it is not unusual for an advertising man to join one of the firms to which he has been selling advertising.

Advertising work for weeklies and small dailies is an excellent training ground for any kind of advertising man. Some young college graduates become advertising managers of weeklies, handling all types of business for their papers, from classified ads to the major local accounts. The same sort of opportunities for diversified experience come on small dailies, although as they increase in circulation the dailies tend to specialize in their advertising staff functions. On smaller papers, the advertising salesman is likely to be his own copywriter; on larger dailies there are positions for copywriters, both men and women, and artists.

Many advertising men get their start in the classified department of larger newspapers, where they deal with many small accounts in a wide variety of fields. A certain amount of classified advertising comes in voluntarily but most of it must be solicited. Classified is sold on a day-to-day basis with deadlines only a few hours before publication. Salesmen have territories and detailed lists of accounts to cover, much like a reporter's beat.

The young salesman is often promoted from classified into the local display department, and later perhaps into the smaller and more select national (or general) department. While in the classified ad department he scrambled to meet his daily quota of lines for the next day's paper; in the national advertising department he works with manufacturers and distributors of brand-name products, often weeks in advance of publication. He is selling schedules of multiple insertions, sometimes in color. A newspaper's national sales staff works in conjunction with its national newspaper representatives, who solicit advertising for it in other major cities.

Promotions to the top ranks in the business department of a newspaper come for those who have demonstrated their ability in classified, local display, and national advertising. Heads of those departments report to the business manager, one of the key men in the organization.

The circulation department offers some opportunities for college-trained men with organizing ability, promotional ideas, and a liking for detail. Men who have a knack for working with carrier boys on a friendly basis, much like a coach with a high school football team, are in demand. While the top circulation jobs on large newspapers carry high salaries, the number of jobs available in this department for the college-trained man is somewhat less than in editorial and advertising. Few women work in circulation except in clerical capacities.

On larger dailies there are well-paying and interesting jobs in such supplementary departments as promotion and public relations, personnel, research, and administration. Some newspapers put out their own institutional publications for employees.

Roughly half the jobs on a metropolitan newspaper are in the production department, yet few men with college training in journalism find a place in this half of newspaper operation. The men who work in the composing room, the stereotype department, the engraving section, and the pressroom are drawn largely from the trade schools. The work is mechanical in nature, demanding a high degree of technical skill. The men who hold top positions in the production departments usually come up through the ranks, although graduate engineers sometimes find their way into newspaper production offices.

Cost control is extremely important in newspaper production, just as in any manufacturing operation. Elaborate accounting sheets are kept, showing the costs of setting a column of type, making up a page, printing a thousand papers, increasing the size of an edition by two pages, working a press crew overtime because of a missed deadline, and a hundred other expense factors. All these costs are weighed carefully in setting the newspaper's advertising rates. If the publisher pegs his space rates very low he will attract extra advertising, but he may find that he is spending more to print each advertisement than he is being paid for it. If a loosely run production department has such large costs that the publisher must charge unusually high advertising rates to cover them, he forces the advertisers to use other media.

Most editorial people on large newspaper staffs, it might be added, know little and care less about such production and cost problems. They regard the business aspects of publishing as something remote and of scant concern to them. This is unfortunate, especially if they have thoughts of striking off on their own some day on that small country weekly of their dreams.

Salaries. Newspaper salaries, while not at the top of the list, compare favorably as a whole with those in other businesses and professions that require a good education and creative thinking. They have improved steadily and at times quite sharply during the past 25 years.

The activities of the American Newspaper Guild have been an important factor in this improvement. Organized in 1933, during the depression when editorial salaries in particular were low, the Guild has campaigned as an organized labor union for higher wages and more favorable working conditions. It has called strikes against newspapers to enforce its demands. A rise in newspaper salaries was inevitable, even without the existence of the Guild, or the industry could not have held its workers as economic conditions improved. But the activities of the Guild speeded the process.

Today the Guild has 30,000 members, mainly on larger papers. Its contracts with management cover salaries, vacations, severance pay, and working conditions. The salary levels are minimums, covering all men and women in the categories specified. Some Guild contracts cover just editorial departments; others, all nonprinting employees. The basic contract provides a graduated pay scale, with automatic annual steps from the starting minimum through five or seven years to a top minimum. Salary advancement faster than, and beyond the top of, Guild scales is by individual negotiation with management.

Top minimum salaries on the 180 dailies with Guild contracts (1964 pay scales) run from $120 to $185 a week. The median is $140 a week (for the smallest dailies under 25,000 circulation the median is $125 a week, for metropolitans over 250,000 circulation it is $165 a week). These are for reporters and photographers; desk men run a little higher. Converted into an annual basis, $140 a week is $7280 a year, and $185 amounts to $9620 a year. The Guild's stated goal for new contracts is $200 a week top minimums, or $10,400 annually.

The starting minimums under the Guild contracts vary widely, from a ridiculously low $46 a week on a New England daily to $115 a week on the New York *Times*. The median is $80 a week (for the dailies under 25,000 circulation $70 a week, for the metropolitans $100 a week). Many of the papers with low starting minimums make higher offers to journalism school graduates and in some areas of the country weeklies and small dailies are willing to pay $100 a week or $5200 a year to attract promising young people. The $80 a week, or $4160 a year, median is a lower starting level than in other professional areas, but Guild contracts call for annual increases of $10 to $15 a week to reach the top minimums in five to seven years—a more rapid advance than in most areas of work. The Guild's objective in new contracts is $100 a week starting minimum. On the advertising side, newspapers start competent college graduates at from $4500 to $5500 a year in many cases.

The Guild salaries quoted are for 40-hour weeks, for average people. Superior people get above-minimum salaries and can rise to five-figure pay. But as in all professions they must expect to work more than a mere 40-hour week to get five-figure pay. Any newspaperman can add to his income by becoming a specialist, doing outside writing and speaking. He thus enhances his value to the newspaper and likely becomes one of the above-minimum newsmen, who constitute a third to a half of many metropolitan staffs. Another route to the top pay levels is through skilled desk work.

A recent survey showed that on small newspapers doing less than $250,000 annual gross business the pay for the publisher ranged from $7500 to $12,000; for the managing editor, from $5200 to $7200; for the city or news editor, from $4200 to $5000; for the business manager, $5200 to $7900. At the other end of the line, on the largest metropolitan papers, the range for the publisher was $30,000 to $52,000; editor, $15,000 to $25,000; managing editor, $11,000 to $18,000; city editor, $9000 to $13,000; business manager, $20,000 to $30,000.

A committee on recruitment for journalism reported to the Association for Education in Journalism the results of a survey showing that 11.2 per cent of newsroom employees are paid $10,000 a year or more.

Opportunities for women in newspapers have expanded in recent years; weeklies and small dailies in particular have accepted women as general editorial workers, both as reporters and on desk jobs, frequently taking them right out of college. Many weeklies are run by husband-and-wife teams. There are relatively fewer places on metropolitan staffs for women, but there are some on almost every paper; many do specialized work but some hold down regular news beats and desk assignments. Quite a few have become telegraph editors on small dailies.

Although many men and women spend their entire careers in the newspaper business, others move on from it into related fields. Newspapers are one training ground for workers in all mass communications media. In the newsroom they learn the art of reporting, the basic skill for all communication, and in the advertising department they develop their techniques of selling and presentation.

Why do men and women move from newspapers into related fields? Generally they are drawn by higher pay, the possibility of increased freedom as writers, or the opportunity to go into business for themselves. Public relations offices, magazine staffs, and radio and television news staffs are heavily loaded with former newspapermen and newspaper-women. The press associations reach into the newspapers for their staffs; in turn, there is a steady movement of experienced press association men to the newspapers in the higher bracket editorial posts. Some faculty members in journalism schools are recruited from newspapermen who return to college for graduate work, then stay on to teach. Advertising agencies draw much of their manpower from the staffs of daily news-papers. Some newsmen enter politics, obtaining appointive jobs through friendships made as reporters and editors, and possibly later running for elective office. The newspaper has always been a fountainhead from which manpower flows into all areas of mass communications.

THE WEEKLY NEWSPAPER

In thousands of American towns the weekly newspaper is at the core of community life. It is the chief source of information about the activities of individuals and organizations, and the merchants look to its advertising columns as a major tool for selling goods. In the files of a small-town weekly are recorded the vital statistics of the town's life—the births and deaths, marriages, social events, tragedies, and the ludicrous moments that give life zest. The editor knows almost everyone and they all know him; the relationship between the small weekly newspaper and its audi-ence is closer than in any other type of publishing. Even when it is overshadowed by a big city daily a few miles away, the weekly news-paper often has a secure place in the heart of its community and can continue to thrive. The chief stock in trade it has to offer is names: sub-scribers reading about their neighbors and about themselves. The larger the newspaper, the less impact the names in news stories have on the readers, because they do not know all the people mentioned. This per-sonal link is an advantage the community weekly paper has over its larger, more sophisticated big city cousin.

The weekly newspaper is editing and publishing in its simplest form, although anyone who believes that putting out a weekly is easy has been badly misled. All the jobs involved in any newspaper must be done: getting news and editing it, selling advertising, handling circulation, and seeing to it that the paper is printed on time. On the large daily there are many people to handle each of these operations, but on the weekly everything is done by a handful of workers. The editor may also sell advertising, read proof, take pictures, haul the papers to the post office for mailing, and pitch in to help the printers put type into the forms on publication day. In some cases he also runs the press. The 40-hour week is only a dream to the men who edit and publish weekly newspapers. After the day's work at the office is finished, the weekly editor covers civic meetings, attends social functions in the hope of getting news, and listens to the complaints of fellow townsmen who consider him a referee of local disputes. The very fact that he is a newspaperman adds a certain aura to his name.

Many weekly newspapers are published by husband-and-wife teams. In some cases they share billing in the paper's masthead as joint editor and publisher; often the wife's aid is more informal, such as helping in the office with the advertising and circulation billing or gathering local news items by telephone. The work hours she contributes reduce the cost of hired help that much, and in an operation where the margin of profit is small that saving may have a significant influence on the year's earnings.

Another common arrangement is a partnership between a printer and a front-office man. One handles the mechanical operations while the other does the editorial and advertising work. In the past many weeklies were started by printers who set most of the type themselves and hired some relatively inexperienced person at a low salary to handle the front-office duties. A more common procedure now is for the publisher to be an advertising man who has decided to strike out on his own and who either handles the editorial work himself or hires someone to do it.

Most weekly publishers are also in the job printing business, and indeed they make a large percentage of their annual profit from this side of the operation. The same printing plant which publishes the paper once a week also prints programs and yearbooks for local clubs, wedding announcements, business cards, and other types of printing needed in every community. By doing job work the publisher keeps his machinery busy and has enough work to give his printers full-time jobs. The shop foreman, or the publisher himself if the paper is small enough, organizes the flow of printing work so the commercial jobs mesh with the weekly production of the paper. Relatively few daily newspapers do extensive job printing work unless they have a separate division especially set up for it with equipment of its own, because the task of producing a daily paper is too great a burden on the equipment.

Weekly newspaper publishing is a risky enterprise for a man who thinks only in editorial terms; he must learn the business tricks of obtaining revenue from advertising and circulation or his paper won't stay alive very long.

One of the clichés of newspaper work is the big city newsman who dreams of getting away from the hustle and bustle and settling down to an easy life in a small town with a weekly newspaper of his own. He envisions himself as a man of power in the community, leisurely writing editorials and going fishing for the week-end as soon as the week's edition is printed. Nothing could be further from the truth. The minute one week's edition is out he begins churning out copy for next week's paper so the Linotype operator can set it into type without drawing overtime pay on press day; talking to county political leaders about printing the delinquent tax list, a lucrative annual plum for newspapers in many communities; or soothing an angry mother whose daughter's name was misspelled in a wedding story. Instead of fishing he may spend his Saturday trying to collect a bill from a delinquent classified advertiser, repainting the office furniture, or attending a church picnic to prevent gossip that he was ignoring that particular denomination.

Good clues to the type of opportunities for ownership available in the weekly field are to be found in the columns of the *Publishers' Auxiliary,* a trade publication in the small newspaper field. The advertisements of newspapers for sale contain such phases as these: "profitable if publisher can help some in back shop" . . . "golden opportunity for good man-and-wife team" . . . "present owner here 50 years will sell one-fourth interest with option on balance to qualified printer-manager who can eventually take complete control. Will sell paper separate without plant to good newsman" . . . "lots of legal advertising, lots of printing, machinery in good condition. Present owner must slow down."

As an indication of the jack-of-all-trades ability required on small weeklies, here is an actual example of the setup of a weekly paper in a small southern town. The staff consisted of five persons: three were apprentice printers who did job printing as well as making up the newspaper; the fourth was a part-time woman who wrote society news, which she brought to the office once a week. The remaining staff member was editor, columnist, advertising solicitor, proofreader, reporter, photographer, typesetter, pressman, and bill collector. This wasn't much of a newspaper by usual journalistic standards, but it did manage to come out every week and provide the community with information it could receive in no other way.

The weekly editor and publisher cannot easily escape his audience, as can the metropolitan newspaperman. His contacts with the community are too many and too deep. Even though these sometimes are a nuisance so far as demands upon his time are concerned, they are the very essence of his success.

Most weekly newspapers are published on Thursday, not merely from tradition but for a sound commercial reason. It is the day on which the local merchants want to reach readers with news of their week-end sales. The grocery stores in particular key their marketing pattern to their Thursday newspaper advertisements, offering special items on sale Thursday through Saturday. This pattern runs through newspapers of all sizes, in fact; Thursday is usually the biggest advertising day of the week, and as a result the papers issued on that day have more pages. Recently, however, food stores in some parts of the country have switched their advertising to Wednesday afternoons, some even to Tuesdays, in the struggle for competitive advantage.

Basic printing methods. The operating schedule of a weekly newspaper is determined largely by the capacity of its mechanical department. Many weeklies are published with an absolute minimum of equipment, a single Linotype machine to set both news and advertising matter and a limited supply of handset type. Since printing equipment is so expensive that a struggling newspaper cannot afford the luxury of all it needs, the men who put it out must adjust their work schedules to fit the amount of type the machinery can produce.

Two traditional kinds of newspaper presses are currently in use in this country. One is the flatbed type. On this the pages of type are laid flat on a tray, side by side, and the web of newsprint from a large roll is pressed down on them by a roller moving back and forth. A simpler flatbed press, widely used by small weekly newspapers, prints on single sheets of newsprint rather than on a roll. This is direct printing; the paper is in contact with the original type. The other, faster method is the rotary press. This type of press is rarely used by weekly newspapers. Here a mat is rolled from the original page of type, and from that mat in turn a semicircular stereotype cast of lead is made. The full-page cast is locked onto a rotating cylinder on the press and prints onto the moving web of newsprint. All large dailies and most smaller ones use rotary presses, which operate at much higher speed than the flatbed type, can handle more pages at one time, and generally provide a better job of reproduction. Another advantage of the rotary press is that several casts can be made from the same page of type, so that different press units can print the identical page simultaneously.

Flatbed presses are used on most weekly newspapers because they cost less, and most papers have a press run too small to obtain the full advantages of rotary press operation. Whereas some rotary presses can turn out 35,000 papers an hour or more when running at full speed, the normal flatbed web press produces about 3000 an hour. The single-sheet flatbed is even slower. But even at this slow rate an hour's press run will handle full circulation of many weeklies.

A significant trend in the printing of weeklies and small daily newspapers by the offset process developed during the first half of the 1960's. A steadily growing list of newspapers were being printed by this "cold type" process, after the appearance of several web-offset presses on the market. In the traditional or "hot type" method, type is set on a line-casting machine and locked into forms for the press. In the offset process news copy is typed onto paper by a typewriter-like machine that "justifies" the lines so that the right-hand margin is even. Pasteups of this typed material are made and photographed; offset plates are made from the negative and placed on the web-offset press.

Once the original investment in offset equipment is made, small papers can be produced at lower cost than with hot type because fewer skilled printers are needed. A common practice is for several weeklies to be printed in a centrally located offset plant. The editors send their "camera-ready" pages to the plant and a few hours later the circulation department carries away a printed edition ready for distribution.

As the offset process improved during the 1960's, more and more small dailies turned to it. Although offset was not yet considered sufficiently well-developed for large daily newspaper use, many large dailies were employing the cold type process for preparation of some advertising and editorial material.

The weekly's editorial problems. When we add up all the difficulties the weekly newspaper publisher has in keeping his small enterprise operating at a profit, it is not surprising that the editorial aspects of his newspaper sometimes suffer. The editorial department costs money but takes in nothing—nothing directly, that is, except for the fundamental fact that without it there would be no newspaper. The tendency of many weekly publishers, especially those whose experience runs largely to printing or advertising work, is to "get by" with the lowest editorial cost possible. They employ inexperienced help to write a few columns of front page news a week and fill the inside pages with "canned" material from commercial sources and articles contributed by local residents. The latter material is put into the paper with a minimum of editing.

Weekly newspapers do not have the news reports of the press associations to help fill their pages. Everything they print must be written locally or obtained from such sources as the editor can develop. Some small printing plants, operating with only a single typesetting machine, cannot produce enough type for the paper unless the printers work overtime at bonus wages, and so the editor must depend upon matted feature "boiler plate" material to fill the gap.

Because a portion of our weekly newspapers is forced to operate on such an extremely skimpy basis, it should not be assumed that all do so. The range in editorial excellence among weeklies is very wide. Notable examples of splendidly edited weeklies are to be found throughout the United States, as can be seen by an examination of the entries submitted in the annual contests conducted by the state press associations. The writing, editing, and make-up in these weeklies is the equal of that found in many large dailies.

Rarely are weekly newspapers of the crusading type. Most editors see their role as that of printing the constructive, orthodox news of the community without dealing in what often is called sensationalism. Their circulation is almost exclusively among families, and their personal contacts among the townspeople are so intimate that they sometimes omit stories which might be embarrassing. Also, in a tightly knit small community the commercial and social pressures on an editor to "stay in line" are exceptionally heavy. In some cases the newspaper's profit margin is so thin that the publisher cannot risk irritating an important advertiser by printing something he dislikes.

Often the editor-publisher is so busy with his business responsibilities that he neglects the editorial vigor his newspaper should have. This is understandable but nevertheless it is a decided weakness in the functioning of our weekly press. Without resorting to big city street sensationalism, many weekly editors could serve their communities better if they dealt in print more bluntly with local problems and tackled controversial issues head-on. The American weekly press as a whole is conformist and conservative.

Circulation for weeklies. The advertising rates a newspaper can charge depend upon the number of copies it sells, so it follows that the task of building the largest circulation possible is fundamental. This is a serious problem for most weeklies, because the sales potential in a small community is limited, and because circulation building is a specialized skill in which many weekly publishers are not well versed. For many years most weeklies followed the traditional policy of selling subscriptions to local residents and delivering the paper each Thursday in the regular mail. All too often the publisher let his circulation lists get out of date and failed to push his annual collections. Some progressive weeklies switched to delivery by carrier boy, a practice which has worked more successfully in some communities than in others.

More recently, especially in the suburban areas, some weeklies have changed to a free distribution basis, having a carrier boy deliver a newspaper automatically to every home in the community. Those who have adopted this practice prefer to call it "controlled circulation" while their opponents use the derogatory term "throwaway."

The publisher who distributes his newspaper free accepts three financial disadvantages to gain one important advantage. His newsprint bill rises and his income from circulation virtually disappears, and if he distributes copies by mail his postal costs rise, too. But by convincing advertisers that he has blanketed the town with copies of his newspaper he can obtain a higher advertising rate and more linage. If he can raise his advertising income sufficiently, his net profit rises.

A common practice of such free delivery weeklies is to have carrier boys call at each home every month to collect a small sum, frequently 25 cents, from those householders who volunteer to pay. Technically the money is for the delivery service, not for the newspaper itself. Those who do not pay continue to receive the paper anyway unless they specifically order it stopped. Usually the boy is paid a guaranteed sum for his work and anything he collects above that amount is turned in to the paper. Such free distribution methods are impractical for daily newspapers because of the high newsprint costs and the lack of circulation revenue. They work well on weeklies only in those areas where there is a large concentration of homes.

Many of the most profitable weekly newspaper enterprises are combination operations in which one company prints weekly papers for several communities in a single plant. Each newspaper has a separate identity and is filled with news of its own community, gathered by an editorial staff on the spot. The typesetting and printing are done in a centralized plant, sometimes quite a few miles distant from the town of publication. Advertising in one paper of the group can be published in one or more of the others for a small additional fee or "pickup rate."

The advantages of such an operation are many. Because each piece of his equipment is used with greater frequency during the week, the publisher can afford better printing tools and so can put out a more attractive newspaper. By coordinating the editorial and advertising efforts of the various papers, and picking up some news from one edition to another, he can employ better qualified staff members. Some weekly group plants operate almost on a daily newspaper schedule with rotary presses and tightly planned deadlines. Suburban areas lend themselves especially well to group operation.

The next step above the weekly newspaper is the semiweekly, published twice a week rather than once, frequently on Monday and Thursday, or sometimes with a Sunday edition. There are relatively few semiweekly and triweekly publications in this country, because usually a weekly which seeks to expand into broader fields makes the jump directly to daily operation. Many semiweekly papers are the result of the combination of two competing weeklies in a town. Some come into being when a publisher learns to his sorrow that his city cannot sustain a daily and so cuts back to twice-a-week publication.

The semiweekly is related to the weekly in content, rather than to the daily. Usually it receives no wire service reports and is dependent upon local news to fill its columns, like the ordinary weekly. Because it has many of the advantages of group weekly publication, the semiweekly's standards of content and appearance are relatively high.

THE SMALL DAILY NEWSPAPER

The differences in operation of the weekly newspaper and the small daily newspaper are great, because the fundamental element of timeliness has been added. The principle of "today's news today" dominates the minds of daily newspapermen, no matter how small their paper may be.

Because the process of assembling and printing the newspaper is done six or seven times a week, instead of once, the thinking of the men who do the job is accelerated. Working on a daily does not necessarily make a reporter or an advertising solicitor a better newspaperman than his colleagues on the weeklies, but it does tend to make him a faster one. Deadlines take on a fresh, compelling meaning. A weekly may define its news deadline as "Tuesday afternoon," and still be able to slip through a couple of late columns Wednesday morning without seriously disturbing the rather flexible press time. Not so on the daily; if the copy deadline is 12:40 p.m., any stories sent out to the composing room after that minute may make the press start late. That in turn can mean missed bus connections and lost street sales for the circulation department. However, in the 24 hours before publication a weekly newspaperman turns out a large amount of copy, probably more than he would on a daily.

A substantial overlapping exists between the weekly and small daily fields, in the sense that weekly cities sometimes are larger than small daily cities, and some weeklies have more circulation and advertising linage than small dailies. Yet, given a choice of jobs at identical pay, the majority of newspapermen would probably choose the daily. They find more stimulation in the faster pace, in seeing their stories in print shortly after they have written them, and in having a greater kinship with world affairs through the presence of wire service news teletypes in the office.

What, then, causes some towns to have daily papers and other larger towns to have only a weekly? Essentially it is a matter of geography, supplemented at times by the commercial audacity of the publisher. When a good-sized town is close to a large city, competition from the big neighboring paper may make successful operation of a small city daily financially impossible. Yet there is room for a weekly newspaper to present community news and the advertising of local merchants. A small daily in a relatively isolated region may operate at a profit, whereas the same paper would fail if it were published in the shadow of a large city daily.

Perhaps there would be more daily newspapers in operation if more weekly publishers were willing to gamble by "going daily." But they look at their present comfortable incomes, calculate the sharply increased costs of daily operation, and worry about whether they can obtain enough additional advertising and circulation revenue to cover this expense increase. Many of them decide to play it safe and remain weeklies, even when a daily operation might succeed. The economics of newspaper publishing is such, however, that elemental research shows that many towns which support a profitable weekly simply could not support a daily. Nevertheless, across the United States there are quite a few cities which have both a daily newspaper and a weekly. The latter is usually financially weak and manages to stay in business by picking up the "leavings" in advertising by local merchants and public utilities.

The primary problem a daily newspaper publisher faces is that the cost of producing his paper goes on every day, regardless of how much or how little advertising each issue carries. A "fat" paper one or two days a week cannot carry all his burden if the other issues have only a skimpy advertising content. Most newspapers try to average at least a 50-50 ratio between the amount of editorial and advertising content. This may rise as high as 65 per cent advertising or a trifle more on some days.

A small daily newspaper in the proper geographical setting can be financially successful in a modest way with 5000 circulation if it is efficiently operated. Of course, it cannot give its readers as much news, background material, and advertising as they would receive from a metropolitan paper. It can give them the highlights of world and national news from a press association wire without the detailed background they find in a large city daily, plus thorough coverage of local news and the advertisements of local merchants. For most residents in the community that is sufficient. If they had to depend upon a large city newspaper hauled in from 50 or 100 miles away, they would get more news about the rest of the world but would be deprived of news about their neighbors and local school, church, and civic affairs.

To illustrate how a very small daily works, here is the actual staff line-up and working procedure of a successful newspaper with a daily circulation of less than 5000. Notice that the staff members, although relatively few in number, work in their own specialized fields without the "doubling in brass" so necessary and so commonplace on weekly newspapers; an editorial man rarely handles any advertising work, and an advertising salesman rarely concerns himself with circulation problems.

This paper has four editorial staff members: the managing editor, a general reporter who helps with the task of editing certain pages, a woman's section editor who also handles some spot assignments, and a beginning reporter who handles local sports and the police and fire beats as well. All three men take pictures; the Number Two man on the staff does most of the darkroom work.

The key man on the editorial staff is the managing editor. His tasks are varied and complex. On a large daily they would be handled by several different men, perhaps including the janitor, but he manages to get them all done and still get the paper to press on time. He makes assignments for the reporters, selects and edits stories from the press association wire, lays out the news pages, writes headlines on news stories, handles telephone calls, writes an occasional story, confers with the business staff on future projects, writes editorials, checks with the composing room foreman frequently during the day, and, at deadline time, supervises the make-up of the front page. Several nights a month he covers civic meetings.

Usually the managing editor of even such a small daily has at least some college education and five years or more of newspaper experience. He is managing editor, city editor, and copy desk all rolled into one, a combination of tasks impossible to maintain on papers much larger than this. The newspaper has at least six pages daily and on heavy Thursdays runs 14 to 16 pages; on a few special days each year it may publish as many as 20 pages.

The advertising staff of this very small daily consists of a business-advertising manager who handles most of the large accounts, another display advertising salesman, a clerk-secretary, and a classified advertising manager. Also in the front office there are a circulation manager, two women clerk-bookkeepers, and a proofreader. In the mechanical department there are four printers and one press operator. This force of 17 men and women brings out a daily newspaper six afternoons a week which, although modest in scope, is an essential part of the city's life.

Nowhere can a young man or woman interested in editorial or advertising work get finer, more rounded experience than on such a small daily. Since mechanical facilities are limited, the flow of copy must be closely scheduled and controlled, giving the beginner valuable experience in the extremely important matter of meeting deadlines. He learns to "make do" with the time and equipment at his disposal. In the editorial department he has an opportunity to cover local stories, observe the workings of a press association wire, and write headlines. His mistakes in news stories are brought to his attention very quickly, since in the small city he is in frequent business and social contact with the people about whom he writes. Also he has an excellent opportunity to practice photography. His ability to take pictures will help him throughout his career; the field of photojournalism, in which a man uses both reporting and camera skills, is growing more important. If a beginner has that extra spark of creative imagination so sought after by newspapers of all sizes, it will shine forth more quickly on a small daily than almost anywhere else in journalism that the young man or woman might work.

Small daily editorial problems. Perhaps you wonder how a four-man editorial staff can produce enough copy day after day to fill the newspaper. A six-page paper with 50 per cent advertising content requires 24 columns of editorial matter. Where does this small staff in a little city finds that much news or more day after day, and get it all written fast enough to make the daily deadline? The answer is that it doesn't need to do so. Part of this editorial hole is filled with feature material purchased from the newspaper syndicates and part is filled by wire service stories selected from the global news reports on the AP or UPI teleprinter which chatters away hour after hour in the newsroom.

Comic strips and syndicated feature columns, such as political commentary and personal advice, may take five to eight columns of that space. Pictures require the equivalent of three or four columns. Some are local photographs taken by staff members or are supplied to the newspaper by commercial photographers; others are feature mats or glossy prints purchased from the news picture services. A three-column picture 6 inches deep occupies 18 column inches, or almost the equivalent of a full column of type. (A column inch is the width of a single newspaper column, one inch deep.) Whereas the weekly editor must fill his entire paper with stories written or assembled by his staff, the daily editor has the resources of the press association teleprinter. It is quicker and easier to tear a 500-word story off the teleprinter and send it out to the composing room than to report and write a local story of the same length. A daily newspaper undertakes to give its readers a picture of the entire world, and to do so it must use much of the material supplied by the wire service, which has correspondents throughout the United States and around the world. But because wire service copy is easy to use, some small daily editors tend to fill their pages with second-rate telegraph stories when their readers would rather have well-developed local "enterprise" stories and interviews.

The staff which has been described is about the smallest possible one with which to publish a daily newspaper. As the circulation of a paper rises, so does the size of the staff. Any newspaper with less than 25,000 circulation falls within the general category of the small daily; a very large percentage of them are in the range from 7500 to 15,000. A recent survey of newspapers in this latter classification shows that about a third of them have either six or seven men in the newsroom and most of the others report that they have eight to twelve men.

In these somewhat larger staffs, the tasks performed by the managing editor of the very small daily are divided among several men, and the functional organization which reaches its peak in the staff of a huge metropolitan newspaper begins to emerge.

The managing editor's primary purpose is to oversee all the operations. Under him he has a city editor to direct the work of the local reporters and photographers and a telegraph editor who does the detailed job of selecting and editing stories from the press association wire. As the staff grows, a copy desk is set up to handle the task of editing copy and writing headlines, thus relieving the editors of this onerous but extremely important work. With specialists at work, the result is a better edited newspaper. But our six-page, 5000-circulation daily simply couldn't afford to operate with such a large news staff, and anyway there wouldn't be enough work to keep all these specialists busy. So the jack-of-all-trades managing editor does a little bit of everything.

Advertising staff. Advertising staffs grow, too, as a newspaper's circulation rises. The survey of dailies with circulations of 7500 to 15,000 showed an average of four retail display salesmen on each staff. The number of salesmen in the classified departments varied from two to five. Although most of the sales personnel in display advertising are men, women play a large role in classified work. Much classified selling is done by telephone. A pleasant feminine voice, projected over the telephone by a woman trained in the techniques of selling, can bring much additional linage into the paper. In many cases the manager of the classified department is a woman, almost the only department of an American newspaper in which women are likely to reach the top position.

On small dailies, the sale of local and national display advertising is handled by the same men, working in the latter case with the paper's national sales representatives. Because of the volume of the work involved, larger newspapers divide their display sales staffs into local and national sections.

Mechanical production aids. In recent years an important development has come into the offices of many daily newspapers, the teletypesetter. On the smallest dailies its role in bringing out the newspaper is very important, and a substantial number of the country's larger publications also use it in some form. This machine is known around newspaper shops as the TTS.

Traditionally, since the development of the Linotype and the Intertype, the process has been for stories prepared in the newsroom to be sent to the composing room and there they are put into solid lines of type by an operator tapping them out on the keyboard of a typesetting machine. Under TTS operation, a special appliance known to printers as a "bug" is attached to the typesetting machine, and through it is run a perforated tape which activates the keys. The machine casts lines of type automatically at a steady pace without a man touching the keyboard, and it works at a slightly faster pace than many operators can. In composing rooms where multiple TTS machines are operating, one printer can monitor several machines, instead of having a man at the keyboard of each. This speeds up the operation of setting type for the newspaper and makes it more economical.

The tape fed into these TTS-equipped typesetting machines comes from two sources. Local stories are punched into tape form by a man or woman operating a TTS keyboard, and rolls of the tape are then put on the typesetting machine. Both the AP and UPI run special newswires in some areas designed for TTS use. A newspaper subscribing to this news report receives dispatches teletyped on a roll of paper, just like the ordinary news report except that the lines are shorter and in upper and lower case, rather than the traditional all-capitals style of press association copy. Simultaneously, a perforating machine nearby, operated by telegraphed electrical impulses, is turning out a TTS tape of each story on the wire. The editor sends this tape to the composing room along with the printed copy of the story, and the tape is put onto the typesetting machine. Although the use of such tape on press association stories speeds the production of the newspaper, it reduces the amount of editing flexibility each newspaper has because trimming phrases, sentences, and paragraphs from the tape is time-consuming and expensive. Use of computers to speed up typesetting by tape has begun in metropolitan newspapers, whose typesetting load justifies the heavy investment.

Another development in small daily newspapers is use of the Fairchild engraving machine, which enables these publications to publish pictures taken by their own photographers at a relatively small cost. In the past, many newspapers found the cost of operating a photoengraving plant to produce zinc halftone cuts for picture reproduction prohibitive. They had to send their staff pictures out to a commercial engraver, which frequently resulted in delays and often involved a high cost. As a result, they published fewer pictures than their readers and editors desired.

The Fairchild machine reproduces a photograph on plastic rather than on zinc; these plastics can be placed directly into the newspaper form and on the press. The process is an electronic one in which a light beam scans a photograph fastened to a revolving cylinder. A cutting needle makes an exact reproduction of the photograph on a sheet of plastic wrapped around the other end of the cylinder. Although there are limitations on the jobs it can accomplish, and some printers contend that the quality of the plastic mats is not quite the equal of metal halftone cuts, the Fairchild machine enables many small dailies to give their readers much better picture coverage than ever before. The machines can be leased from the company which manufactures them, at a fairly high monthly fee, or can be purchased. Any staff member can operate a Fairchild machine after one instruction session, so no special labor cost is involved.

A European engraving machine rather similar to the Fairchild process has been placed on the American market, but by the mid-1960's it had made only relatively small inroads into the Fairchild market.

Selling the papers. Circulation procedures on daily newspapers are much better organized than on most weeklies, because the task of distributing and selling the paper must be done every day. There are several commonly used methods of selling a daily paper. Most of these are based upon the principle of having the publishing company sell copies of the paper to a distributor or delivery agent at a wholesale price several cents below the announced price per copy. The selling agent—home delivery carrier boy, street corner vendor, or store—sells papers to the public at the published price; the difference between wholesale and retail prices provides his profit. About one-third of the American daily papers sell for more than 5 cents a copy, and most of the rest at that price; many offer reduced prices for home delivery.

The backbone of a successful circulation system in most cities is the home delivery subscription list. Single-copy street sales are affected from day to day by the weather, traffic and shopping conditions, holidays, and the nature of the banner headline. Home delivery papers are sold to subscribers on a weekly, monthly, or even an annual basis; they give the newspaper an assured income and a firm circulation figure to quote to its advertisers, who want to know exactly how many newspaper purchasers will receive copies of their messages.

A few decades ago in the fight to win circulation and outdo their rivals, some newspapers resorted to making exaggerated claims about their sales. Since advertising rates are based upon circulation figures and upon the cost of reaching each thousand readers, this led to many discrepancies and a chaotic situation in which honest publishers were placed at an unfair disadvantage by the unscrupulous operators. To correct this problem the Audit Bureau of Circulations was formed in 1914.

Newspapers which belong to the ABC, as all larger dailies do, submit detailed reports of their circulation every six months and open their books to a detailed examination by ABC auditors every year. Rigid rules are enforced. The organization puts limits on methods of solicitation, the number of low-cost subscriptions, bulk sales, and other devices used by some publishers to inflate their circulation figures. Types of circulation which fail to meet these standards are disallowed, and others of a somewhat transitory nature are appropriately indicated on the statements published by the ABC about each paper.

In their constant battle to build circulation, some daily newspapers use many kinds of prize contests; others never use this kind of sales stimulant. A favorite device is the picture puzzle series or rebus type of puzzle; this starts simply to attract contestants and grows more difficult as later puzzles are published. Readers who participate must buy the newspaper daily during the contest or subscribe for a stated interval. The prizes are high, totaling more than $25,000 in some metropolitan promotions, but are paid out only after an elaborate series of "tie-breaker" supplementary puzzles.

The experience of many newspapers is that such contest-created circulation does not turn into permanent readers. Yet in the fight to keep their sales figures high, some big city publishers keep throwing in one contest after another at great expense. Others use trick weekly crossword puzzles, called by such names as Cashword or Baffler, or give cash to readers who find their Social Security numbers or automobile licenses in the daily printed lists.

Although some publishers and circulators consider such promotions an essential part of their newspaper-selling methods, others prefer to build readership more slowly but solidly through their carrier boy and street-outlet organizations. The decision is usually made on the basis of the local competitive situation and the state of the paper's circulation health. No newspaper can afford to have its advertisers see that its daily sales are slipping. If that happens, the advertiser demands lower rates and the financial woes multiply. In the recent history of American newspapers there are many proofs of the fact that once a newspaper goes into a prolonged circulation decline, its prospects for survival are slim.

One widely used method of handling home delivery is known as the little merchant system. A carrier boy has a route covering several city blocks and is responsible for delivery of the newspapers over that route, as well as making weekly or monthly collections of subscription fees from his customers. The publishing firm bills him at the wholesale rate each month for the number of copies he draws from it, and he collects the full subscription price from the readers. The difference is his monthly profit. The more new subscribers or "starts" he obtains, the more his monthly income will be. In effect he is an independent businessman in a small way. The newspaper circulation departments conduct prize contests to stimulate production of new orders, giving rewards such as sporting equipment, bicycles, and special trips to ball games or popular recreation areas to boys who reach specified quotas. Some papers give special awards to carriers who succeed in obtaining a subscription from every house along their routes.

The underlying premise in this circulation system is incentive: the paper tries to provide an incentive to make it worth the boy's while to give up part of his free hours, or to rise very early every morning, in order to deliver papers. Many boys have paid part of their way through college with earnings from their paper routes. Not only must they build their routes by obtaining additional starts, but they must keep their subscribers satisfied by giving them prompt and dependable delivery service.

In this respect newspaper publishing is unique; it hires expensive, highly experienced men to create its product and then depends upon young boys, many of them not yet in their teens, to sell it to the public. In other types of business such a practice would result in commercial failure. Given proper adult supervision, however, it works successfully for newspapers because the product is partially presold. There is an appetite for news, and in most communities the newspaper is a household word; the carrier boy's task is to turn this latent interest among potential readers into actual subscriptions. His own boyish appeal is often the decisive sales factor. Some observers, however, contend that overheavy reliance upon juvenile salesmen has held back newspapers from reaching their full sales potential.

The circulation department of a daily newspaper provides good opportunity for young men with sales and promotional instincts. A successful circulator must also have ability to handle detail, since much of the department's work involves accurate record keeping. Men who rise to the position of general manager in newspaper organizations frequently start in circulation or advertising work. Within the circulation departments of larger papers there are positions as district supervisors who oversee groups of carrier boys, and street sales supervisors whose responsibility it is to see that the paper is properly distributed on news racks and sold by vendors at places where foot and automobile traffic is heavy.

Few people will come to a newspaper office to buy a paper; the paper must be taken to them, and it must be put before them while it is fresh off the presses. To most circulation men the most sacred minute in the day is the moment the press is scheduled to start. Their entire distribution system is keyed to a prompt press start; if the papers begin rolling off a few minutes late, they may miss train or bus connections for out-of-town delivery, or fail to reach a busy sales spot in time to meet the outpouring of potential buyers from a factory or office building. That is why editorial deadlines must be met so diligently. Publication of a daily newspaper is a tightly scheduled operation in which every step is calculated and timed as closely as in an automobile factory assembly line. Failure or delay in any step of this flow disrupts the entire operation, sometimes with a direct loss of sales.

THE SUBURBAN DAILY

One of the bulwarks of American journalism is the group of middle-sized daily newspapers, ranging in circulation from 25,000 to 100,000. These are published largely in state capitals, or in the second- or third-ranking cities in some large states, and more recently in the suburban fringes of our metropolitan areas. In many instances their influence reaches far beyond the city limits because they are distributed by mail, bus, truck, and even airplane to large surrounding rural areas. A motorist driving along a country road can often judge the impact of the newspaper published in the nearby city by the number of bright yellow tubes nailed on posts outside the farmhouses to receive delivery of the daily editions.

Papers of this size are financially strong enough to have editorial staffs of considerable scope, usually with several men of outstanding ability. Some of these may eventually move on to metropolitan papers. Others are content to spend the rest of their working lives in the congenial atmosphere of the middle-sized paper in a community sufficiently large to have some urban flavor, yet small enough for comfortable living.

The rise in operating expenses which has plagued newspaper publishers and narrowed their profit margins is especially well demonstrated on small and middle-sized papers. A study of nonmetropolitan newspapers for 1963, compiled by a Chicago accounting firm, showed that the profit margin of many newspapers is relatively small, especially in relation to the heavy investment in plant and equipment. This study divided the newspapers into 11 groups by circulation, from the very small daily of 3500–5000 circulation up to the 75,000–130,000 group. Average profits for these groups *before taxes* ranged from 6.41 per cent up to 13.15 per cent, with the profit figure rising as circulation increases.

The changing pattern of American urban population has created a new and highly successful category of daily newspapers, those published in the fringes of our sprawling city areas almost in the shadow of the giant metropolitan dailies. At first glance the looming presence of these "mets" might suggest that the cause of the suburban daily is discouraging. This is far from the case. In fact the reverse is true in many instances. The existence of several "fringe' dailies within 25 miles of its own publishing plant can make dangerous inroads into a metropolitan paper's circulation and advertising.

These suburban dailies are usually afternoon papers, often with Sunday editions. They flourish because they provide the average reader with as much, or nearly as much, press association and feature material as he desires, and in addition they give him the news of his local community.

Density of population in these suburban areas is sufficient to provide a strong circulation potential. Not only do the papers have local merchants as sources for advertising, but many downtown department stores have joined the flight to the suburbs by opening branch stores at several points in the urban region. In Los Angeles, for example, one leading department store has 16 large branches in suburban areas. Most of these place advertising in the suburban papers—advertising revenue which might previously have gone to the metropolitan papers. Thus the metropolitan daily must compete for circulation and advertising not only against its downtown rivals, but against a dozen or more smaller competitors within its general circulation zone.

The standards of these suburban dailies in content, policies, and personnel are quite high, in many respects as high as those of their metropolitan neighbors. Located as they are, they have access to a supply of able manpower, and they pay salaries almost equal to those of the downtown papers. Often they receive both press association wires plus supplemental background services and give their readers many of the same syndicated features to be found in the metropolitan papers. Their Sunday editions are usually covered by colored comic sections "just like downtown."

These suburban dailies have made spectacular circulation gains in the past decade as the population of the large cities has overflowed into the outskirts. The well-edited tabloid, *Newsday,* published in Nassau County outside New York City, has a circulation approaching 400,000, placing it among the top ten of all evening newspapers in the country and ahead of three of the city's six dailies. The nearby *Long Island Daily Press* ranks in the top 20 of evening newspapers with 300,000 circulation. Similar success stories on a smaller scale can be found in other American urban areas, especially Los Angeles. The growth of evening dailies in many communities surrounding the metropolis may well lead to the eventual elimination of afternoon papers published in the big city in favor of all-day newspapers with a primary morning field of operation.

Editors of these suburban dailies keep a keen eye on the news "play" by their metropolitan rivals. Frequently they give their readers later news than the big city papers do because the latter have the problem of delivery time to get their papers out to the suburbs through traffic. By establishing a later deadline, the fringe daily can take advantage of the quick delivery time to its nearby area and thus beat the downtown rivals on the latest news.

THE METROPOLITAN PRESS

The newspaper as a mass communications medium reaches its highest development in our great metropolitan centers. Here the publishers and editors think of readers not in terms of thousands but of millions. Figuring three readers to each copy of the paper printed, which is a common rule of thumb in the profession, a big city newspaper with a Sunday circulation of a million copies is read by 3,000,000 people. The impact of a single news story flowing from the typewriter of one reporter, and published in such a huge edition, is easy to conceive.

Many newspapermen in editorial, advertising, and circulation departments look upon a metropolitan newspaper job as the goal of their careers, the ultimate whose achievement is the sign of professional success. Ironically, quite a few big-city newsmen in their quiet "bull" sessions between editions talk longingly of escaping the scramble of metropolitan journalism for what they envision as the calmer, more orderly and satisfying life on smaller papers. Given an opportunity to break away from metropolitan work, however, many of this wistful brigade either refuse to do so or drift back to the so-called "big time" within a few years. The tempo, adventure, and prestige of the metropolitan newspaper are alluring.

Few if any stories in a metropolitan paper are read by all who purchase the paper. Every reader is selective in the stories he chooses, picking a limited number of items from the huge tray of reading delicacies on the basis of his needs, interests, and even his whims. Even so, every story in a metropolitan paper, no matter how insignificantly it is displayed, is seen by thousands of readers.

Thus the reporter on a large newspaper assumes with good reason that his work is being absorbed by a very large number of persons. Yet the very size of the metropolitan region in which his paper circulates makes it impossible for him to have direct contact with his audience. Except for personal acquaintances and the handful of readers who are either irate or thoughtful enough to report their reactions to an individual story, the metropolitan reporter has little opportunity to determine how his stories are being received. This is one of the most striking differences between big-city and small-town newspaper work: the larger the city and the paper's circulation, the less personal contact there is between the newspaper's creators and its readers.

The young man or woman looking toward metropolitan newspapers as a place to work discovers two major differences from smaller dailies: greater speed and greater specialization.

Most small dailies have one basic edition a day, designed primarily for delivery to homes. Some may supplement this with a street sale edition in which the front page is remade with larger, flashier headlines and late sports results for sale to casual purchasers. Or they may have an early, skimpily organized edition for distribution to rural areas. In contrast, many metropolitan papers publish at least five editions within a period of eight hours. Afternoon papers are especially burdened with numerous editions because of the fast-changing nature of news during the daytime hours. This means high-speed work by the editorial staff, which must be constantly alert for last-minute news developments, and equally fast work by the circulation department in distributing papers to locations where crowds are gathered temporarily, such as homeward-bound commuter crowds. The edition schedule is an almost sacred document, whose stated deadlines govern the work of several hundred employees. If the press run of a big newspaper starts 15 minutes late, the recriminations can be heard all over the building and often precipitate a blunt-spoken post mortem in the publisher's office to determine the blame.

The final minutes before the deadline in each newspaper department are a-tingle with concentrated work. When the deadline has passed, and each department in the complicated process knows that it no longer can call back anything it has done or push something more into the paper, there comes a period of relaxation and waiting for the fresh edition copies to be brought up from the pressroom. Then the buildup process for the next edition begins.

A typical metropolitan deadline sheet has minute-by-minute rules telling when the final story must cross the city desk and move from the copy desk to the composing room; when the last photograph must leave the editorial art department for the engraving room; when the final page must move off the composing stone; when the last plate must be cast in the stereotype department; and finally what minute the press must start. For the system to work successfully the pages must flow smoothly through the complex assembly line at a designated pace. In a huge newspaper plant the production of a daily newspaper is a coordinated effort rarely exceeded in manufacturing, especially when we remember that the primary product fed into this conveyor belt system, news, is an intangible raw material difficult to find and hard to define. Few readers realize the immensity of effort and planning behind the daily newspaper tossed upon their doorsteps. Partly this is because newspapers have failed to tell their own exciting story well enough.

The young reporter who obtains a metropolitan job right out of school usually considers himself extremely lucky, believing that he is starting his career a big jump ahead of his classmates who go to work on weeklies or small dailies. Unfortunately for him, this is not necessarily the case.

He finds stimulation in associating with skilled veteran reporters and watching exciting stories move through the big paper's production line, on some of which he may do part of the work himself. But too often he finds himself shunted into a minor reporting job, like covering the overnight police beat, where he is unable to get the all-around experience his classmates are absorbing on smaller papers. Years may pass before he gets an opportunity to work on the copy desk, if, indeed, he ever does. Seniority plays an important part in assignments on metropolitan staffs, and unless he is fortunate or shows exceptional talent for writing, the young reporter on a large daily advances rather slowly.

Many editors and personnel managers of metropolitan papers advise beginners to work on small papers for from three to five years before trying the metropolitan field. Often a young man coming to a metropolitan staff with three or four years of smaller city work to his credit will advance faster than one of similar age who has spent those same years on the big-city paper. The all-around experience of a smaller paper prepares the young reporter to fill many different jobs as they become available.

How a metropolitan news staff functions. The key figure in the local newsgathering activities of a big-city paper is the city editor. He may have a staff of as many as 50 reporters, even more in a few cases, who are deployed at the most productive news sources or held in reserve as general assignment reporters to be dispatched as important stories break. The reporters who are placed on specific beats, such as the police department or city hall, are responsible for gathering all news that occurs in their territory and turning it in to the city desk. When time permits they write the stories themselves. But the urgency of deadlines often makes this impossible, so they telephone their facts to a rewrite man. These men are veterans, swift in their writing and quick at organizing a mass of facts into a story which reads smoothly and concisely.

When the story has been written, either by the reporter who covered it or by a rewrite man, it is turned in to the city desk. There the editor or an assistant reads it to catch errors, to be sure that it is easily understood and to look for "angles" which need further development. Writers and editors alike concentrate on finding a good "lead" for the story, an opening paragraph which summarizes the situation or entices the reader to continue further into the article.

Much reporting is done by telephone. The man assigned to a story calls as many sources as possible to cross-check his facts for accuracy and to make sure that he presents the best-rounded story he can. If he went in person to see each of these sources he would never get his job done in time for the next edition. Some metropolitan beat reporters, or "legmen," especially those on the police beats, may not write a story a week, even though they have worked on dozens of them by telephone.

While the city editor and his staff are gathering the local news, other groups are putting together the other parts of the paper. News from the rest of the country and the world clatters into the office over the wire service teleprinters and from special staff correspondents. This is edited and coordinated on the telegraph desk.

City news and telegraph stories pass across the news desk, where they are weighed for importance and general interest by the news editor. He assigns them appropriate size headlines and marks them into position on dummy sheets; it is these sheets that tell the printers how to assemble the mass of stories into the proper pages. The stories move along to the copy desk, usually semicircular with the supervisor or "slot man" in the middle. He is also known as the "dealer," because of the way he hands stories around to the "rim men" for editing. These language experts give the stories a final polishing and write the headlines. From the copy desk the stories are sent by pneumatic tubes to the composing room, where the process of turning them into type begins.

The sports department, woman's section, financial editors, and other specialist groups are also at work filling the pages allotted to them in a similar manner.

The man in charge of the entire editorial department is the managing editor, just as on the very small daily we discussed earlier. Only instead of doing the detailed work himself, he supervises the dozens of men and women who do it under his direction. The managing editor's post on a metropolitan newspaper is one of the most demanding and responsible jobs in all journalism.

SUNDAY PAPERS—WORLD'S LARGEST

By far the bulkiest newspapers published anywhere are the Sunday editions of American metropolitan newspapers. These mammoth publications wrapped in sections of colored comics often contain more than 300 pages, nearly 4 pounds of reading matter covering everything from the current world crisis to interior decorating advice, theatrical notices, baseball scores, and weekly television logs.

There are two dozen such Sunday newspapers in the United States with 500,000 or more circulation, and five with more than a million. Even these mammoth figures, however, are greatly exceeded by the circulation of several English Sunday papers, printed in London and distributed throughout the British Isles.

The Sunday paper is designed for family reading and is distinguished from the daily editions by two elements: a huge feature "package" and bulk retail advertising. As a medium for late spot news, the Sunday paper is less important than the daily editions because relatively less news occurs on Saturday (which it is covering) than on weekdays. Much of the material in the news sections is of a feature and background nature, stories for which there is no space in the smaller daily editions. Many newspapers print part of their Sunday editions well in advance because of the difficulties of printing such huge issues on the available press equipment on publication date. Stripped-down, predate versions of the New York Sunday tabloid, containing the colored comics and magazine features, are distributed to rural areas across the United States several days before publication day.

The Sunday editions of most newspapers have substantially larger circulation than the daily editions and sell for a higher price, sometimes more than double. Publishing a Sunday paper is a very expensive operation because of the heavy costs involved in buying the colored comics and nationally syndicated magazine inserts and in preparing the abundance of locally created feature material, such as the weekly television log and the staff-edited local magazine feature section. Newsprint costs on bulky papers are very high. Many smaller newspapers find such a publishing effort unprofitable, especially since they must compete against the metropolitan editions which are distributed over very wide circulation zones. As a result the Sunday field is dominated by the big-city newspapers which can afford to enter it; for most of them it is very lucrative, providing a substantial share of their annual profits.

Department stores have found Sunday editions to be one of their most effective selling tools. The paper is read at home in leisurely surroundings, and almost every member of the family peruses at least one part of the edition as it is scattered around the living room floor. So the stores put a heavy share of their advertising budget into the Sunday edition, often taking multiple pages or even entire eight-page sections to publicize their wares.

SUMMARY

The newspaper in all its forms from the tiny weekly to the enormous metropolitan daily is the basic medium of mass communication in the world today. Its stories and advertisements have the lasting power of the printed word and the advantage of distribution in some form to almost every community.

Although rising costs, changing population patterns, and the development of radio and television have complicated the business of newspaper publishing, the newspaper industry as a whole is in a relatively healthy condition. Consolidation of rival newspapers because of economic problems has given the United States more one-paper cities than ever before. Yet as a group the "monopoly" publishers have shown a moderately strong sense of public responsibility in the material they publish. Competitive pressure from the other news media contributes to this balanced presentation.

There are approximately 8500 weekly and semiweekly newspapers published in the United States and 1750 dailies. The dailies appear in 1470 cities, 50 of which have competitive papers published by separate owners. Daily newspaper circulation totals 59,000,000 circulation. Half of the American dailies have circulations of 10,000 or less; another quarter range in circulation from 10,000 to 25,000. These are known as the small dailies; other categories are the suburbans and the metropolitans.

Newspapers have five major departments: editorial, advertising, circulation, production, and business. The amount of specialization varies according to the size of the newspaper; on the smaller weeklies the editor-publisher may perform several of these tasks. Specialization within a single department also increases with the size of the organization; some of the areas are reporting, copy editing, photography, departmental work (such as woman's page, sports, or business news), editorial page work, retail advertising sales, national advertising sales, promotion, and research.

Simplicity of writing style has been a trend in recent years, as has been greater emphasis on the "why" of news stories and a larger attention to interpretation of the news.

As a field for the young man or woman building a career, newspaper work offers many opportunities. Jobs for beginners are relatively easy to find, especially on smaller dailies and weeklies. Salaries have improved sharply in the past quarter-century and are now comparable and in some cases superior to those in other fields carrying similar responsibilities. For anyone interested in communicating the actions and thoughts of human beings to each other, a newspaper career is stimulating and rewarding.

STUDY QUESTION

What significant changes are taking place in the newspaper field?

PROJECTS

1. Bring to class, properly identified, clippings that illustrate each of the functions of a newspaper.

2. In a 500-word essay describe the contents of a weekly newspaper (rural or suburban) and show how those contents fulfill its special function.

3. Read a recent issue of *Editor & Publisher* or the *Publishers' Auxiliary* and write a brief report of an article that pertains to one of the points made in this chapter.

4. Find an offset newspaper in your school library or elsewhere. In 500 words or more contrast and compare it with a newspaper produced by the letterpress method of printing. Consider such elements as reproduction of photographs, typography, and general appearance.

CHAPTER 10

TELEVISION
AND RADIO

BROADCASTING AND THE FUTURE

Television and radio are the electronic magic carpets that transport millions of persons each day to faraway places. They are the twentieth-century creations of the technological revolution that has been transforming much of the world for almost two centuries, and their impact on our social, political, and cultural life has been profound.

As relatively new media, radio and television have only begun to make their mark on world civilization. Shortwave radio has linked the nations for years, and now television is bouncing its signals off space satellites and using oceanic telephone cables to transmit live telecasts to and from peoples the world over. Scarcely a country, even in Asia and Africa, fails to receive and transmit television programs. Despite the headstart which the United States got in telecasting in the late 1940's, families in this country today own fewer than half the sets in the world. The impending cultural, economic, and political impact of a worldwide exchange of programs, including virtually instantaneous coverage of important events in many countries, will be profound.

In the United States, the growth of community antenna television systems (CATV) is bringing a choice of commercial programs to millions in communities beyond the reach of big-city broadcasts. A Federal Communications Commission 1964 requirement that all new sets must be equipped to receive both the regular Very High Frequency (VHF) signals and Ultra High Frequency (UHF) signals was aimed at increasing the number of UHF stations and thus providing a greater choice of programs for Americans. A four-month tryout of pay television in Los Angeles and San Francisco in 1964 collapsed in the face of a referendum disapproval by California voters, but its supporters had not given up hope of its eventual success elsewhere.

Miniaturization and amplification of light soon will revolutionize our home-communication center, in the opinion of Richard A. R. Pinkham, a senior vice president of the advertising firm of Ted Bates & Co., Inc. The equipment will get smaller and the results larger, he wrote in a *Printers' Ink* article. Said Pinkham:

In the 1970's—or maybe earlier—your picture will be received on a set the size of a cigar box and projected on a curved wall for 3-D effect. Full color, of course, and you can make the picture any size you want from eight inches to eight feet. You will show your home movies on your television set, and no developing needed. It will all be on tape and your set can transmit what your camera recorded. . . .

Following pay-TV, and probably supplanting it in turn—with the exception of the big event-type programs—will be the video tape cartridge. Then will the minority be served, because it will be possible to go to the corner drug store and buy a cartridge of video tape containing a Leontyne Price "Aida," if you wish; or an Olivier's "Hamlet"; or golf lessons by Palmer; or bridge lessons by Goren—insert them into your home set and watch what you will on your television screen.

But just as phonograph records did not wipe out radio, video cartridges will not wipe out commercial television. With automation "doubling" our leisure time, we will have plenty of opportunity to enjoy both. And we will be tuning in Paris, Moscow, Elizabethville, Tokyo, and Little America with scarcely any memory of the days when the line, "Live from Hollywood," seemed charged with electronic wizardry. None of this is pie-in-the-sky. It's all invented now. Just needs further miniaturization. In the words of Al Jolson: "We ain't seen nuthin' yet."

THE SCOPE OF BROADCASTING

In the United States. The stations' claim that "radio is your constant companion" is literally true. Every community in America is served by its own or a nearby station. Car radios, portable transistor radios, and multiple-set and intercommunication-wired homes provide constant contact with the unseen world of the wave lengths. Even television, despite its shorter range and fewer stations, is viewed in almost every part of the country, and community antenna systems soon will carry TV to virtually every hamlet.

Radio listening, after a temporary eclipse by television in the 1950's, came back strong with news, music, and programs designed for Americans' leisure habits. By 1965 approximately 54,000,000 homes, or 98 per cent of all those in the United States, were equipped with one or more radio sets. The Radio Advertising Bureau estimated that 228,000,-000 radio sets were in operation. Of these, 160,000,000 were in homes, 57,000,000 in automobiles, and 11,000,000 in public places.

Even FM (frequency modulation) stations, whose development had been limited through the national preoccupation with television, could boast of 25,000,000 sets in operation. Because of good music programming, stereophonic sound, virtually static-free reception, and the capability of attracting loyal specialized audiences, FM was growing rapidly. A Harvard study predicted that FM would pass AM broadcasting by 1975.

In all, almost 40,000,000 United States homes tuned in radio during the average week. Radio listening in each home averaged one hour and 32 minutes a day, with morning audiences generally exceeding those of television. Portable and automobile radios added uncounted millions of other listeners.

The number of television sets in use had climbed to 61,000,000. More than nine out of ten American families (93 per cent) had TV, and nearly 7,000,000 of them had more than one set. At any one average minute of any one evening, 7,500,000 homes were watching network shows, according to the Advertising Research Bureau. Of the well over 150,000,000 Americans watching TV for an average of six hours and 48 minutes each day, 98 per cent could choose from two or more stations; 85 per cent from at least three; 50 per cent from four or more; and 15 per cent from seven.

In 1965 approximately 1,300,000 homes were wired to receive television on a paid subscription basis through 1400 community antenna television (CATV) systems. Community antenna homes were increasing at a rate of about 15,000 per month. Started about 15 years ago to pep up weak signals in fringe areas and extend them to nonservice areas, CATV was exerting such pressure that some regular TV broadcasters were fighting to survive. The Federal Communications Commission assumed regulatory power over systems using microwave relays. CATV owners were required not to duplicate a TV station's programs in a community for 15 days before or after their presentation on the local station.

However, about 25 per cent of the CATV systems were originating programs of their own and in some areas were selling time to advertisers.

There were 4046 AM and 1280 FM radio stations on the air at the start of 1965, and 588 commercial and 114 noncommercial educational television stations. Authorized but not yet on the air were 71 AM stations, 217 FM stations, and 85 television stations. Including authorized stations, there were 568 Very High Frequency (VHF) television stations (510 commercial and 58 noncommercial), received on channels 2 through 13, and 219 Ultra High Frequency (UHF) stations (163 commercial and 56 noncommercial), received on channels 14 through 83—a total of 787. Many independent television and radio stations were affiliated, by two-year contracts, with the National Broadcasting Company, Columbia Broadcasting System, and American Broadcasting Company. Others were served by the Mutual Broadcasting System and several smaller networks. The networks themselves owned 19 radio stations and 15 television stations. There were 58 regional radio networks and 10 regional television networks. Newspapers and magazines were associated in common ownership with 9.8 per cent of the AM stations, 13 per cent of FM stations, and 31 per cent of television stations.

Television stations and networks grossed $1,394,000,000 and radio stations and networks $711,700,000 in 1963 time sales, a National Association of Broadcasters survey revealed, and the industry as a whole was adjudged healthy indeed.

Broadcast stations and networks employed 71,728 persons, according to a study by *Broadcasting Yearbook*. Although there were almost seven times as many radio as television stations, 40 per cent of the total broadcast personnel were employed at TV stations. The figures: 42,523 in radio and 29,205 in television. The typical television station employed more than five times as many full-time executives and staff members as the typical AM radio station (51 to 10). Most radio stations (1706) employed from 5 to 10 persons; 386 hired fewer than 5 persons; 758 had 16 or more; 223 had 25 or more; and 4 hired in excess of 100. Eighty TV stations employed 25 or fewer; 237 employed 50 or fewer; 258 employed 51 or more; and 58 employed more than 100. One TV station reported a full-time staff of 220. The 14,620 full-time executives and employees of national radio and TV networks were broken down as follows: ABC, 2525; CBS, 6327; MBS, 168; and NBC, 5600.

Although they are small in comparison with some United States "industries," television and radio are responsible for the livelihood of thousands of persons in related businesses. The 1965 *Broadcasting Yearbook* reported that 70 talent agents and managers represented radio-TV artists, 724 companies supplied program services, 56 firms provided research services, 48 unions represented workers and performers, 496 attorneys specialized in Federal Communications Commission practice, 242 consulting engineers served broadcasting, and 66 consultants aided with management, personnel, and similar problems. Also serving the broadcast world were 37 news services; 66 firms offering public relations, publicity, and promotion assistance; 28 station brokers; 147 station representatives; and 16 station finance companies. Not estimated were the tens of thousands of firms selling and servicing television and radio sets throughout the nation.

International broadcasting. The world is being wired for sight and sound. In the words of LeRoy Collins, former president of the National Association of Broadcasters: "Communications systems now circle the earth like the threads of a ball of yarn and bind this world together with invisible but nonetheless real threads. Events in the remotest part of the earth can be instantaneously and fully reported by the men who use them—broadcast men."

The United States Information Agency reported that on January 1, 1964, there were 80,329,000 TV sets and 3444 stations outside of the United States and Canada. Another USIA survey revealed 267,490,000 radio sets, exclusive of wired speakers, in these other countries.

More than 40 free-world countries offer some sort of commercial television. Of these, Canada, Great Britain, and Japan have attained the greatest development, outside of the United States, in numbers of stations and sets. In Great Britain both radio and TV use is rising, with two out of every three persons watching television every day. Italy has more than 550 stations. Television is just gaining a foothold in the emerging nations, such as those in Africa.

A *Broadcasting* magazine study disclosed that many U.S. investors have purchased stock in stations in 25 countries on all of the continents except Antarctica. Most of these were minority holdings, representing generally from 10 to 20 per cent of total investment. The biggest investors have been the three TV networks and, more recently, Time Inc.'s Time-Life Broadcast International. The field also included such others as Screen Gems and Bartell Broadcasting (MacFadden-Bartell Corporation), both of which owned stations outside of the United States; former NBC executive Al Capstaff, who had a community antenna setup in operation in the Virgin Islands; and Warner Bros. The latter company was among the owners of ABC Television, the British programming contractor, which also operated stations in 17 countries.

United States companies have competed vigorously in selling filmed, sometimes taped, programs to overseas broadcasters. Sales of U.S. programs to some 300 overseas clients exceeded $50,000,000 in 1962 and the figure was increasing rapidly. These overseas sales have accounted for 40 to 50 per cent or more of the total net income of U.S. companies from all sources.

As reported in Chapter 15, United States advertising agencies were rushing to open branches overseas and U.S. advertisers were expanding their foreign operations. All were buying foreign television and radio time.

The National Association of Broadcasters appointed a committee on international broadcasting in 1964 to provide leadership for America's role in worldwide television and radio. The NAB study was expected to develop opportunities for expanded business advantages to American broadcasters, to discover ways to enhance the American image abroad, and to aid countries everywhere in achieving greater broadcast competence and better understanding of free institutions.

As a succession of space satellites provided the capabilities of world telecasting, the United States government entered into international conferences to make vital decisions leading to maximum, coordinated development. Congress in 1962 established the Communications Satellite Corporation as a private, profit-making corporation to own and operate the U.S. segment of the projected space communications system. Portions of the worldwide Vatican City conference in 1963, the funeral of President Kennedy in 1963 and of Winston Churchill in 1965, and shots of the 1964 Olympic Games in Japan were relayed via satellites to television audiences across oceans, as Comsat prepared to institute regularly scheduled commercial programs.

RISE OF THE BROADCAST MEDIA

Radio enjoyed only a quarter-century of commercial development in the United States before its electronic fellow, television, emerged as still another of the major mass communications media. Various inventions during the nineteenth century paved the way for the perfecting of radio in the twentieth. Guglielmo Marconi's development of wireless telegraphy was followed by an improvement made by Dr. Lee De Forest in 1906 in the vacuum tube that made voice transmission possible. There was little interest in the possibility of mass radio listening, however, and Congress in 1912 empowered the Department of Commerce to issue licenses to private broadcasters and assign wave lengths for commercial operators primarily to prevent interference with government point-to-point message communication.

Many amateur enthusiasts built their own receivers and transmitters and finally Westinghouse, sensing a new sales market, applied for the first full commercial license for standard broadcasting. Its station, KDKA in Pittsburgh, began operating on November 2, 1920, by broadcasting returns from the Harding-Cox presidential election. An experimental station, 8MK, had begun daily operations from the Detroit *News* building on August 20, 1920, and in October, 1921, the *News* obtained its full commercial license for what became station WWJ.

The number of stations increased from 30 in January, 1922, to 556 in March, 1923. At the same time the number of receiving sets rose from about 50,000 in 1921 to more than 600,000 in 1922. National interest was heightened by the broadcasting of such events as the Dempsey-Carpentier fight in 1921 and the Army-Notre Dame football game and the World Series in 1923. Listeners delicately ran the "cat's whisker" across the crystals of their sets, trying to bring in a station on the earphones; many such sets were homemade. On certain nights local stations would remain silent so listeners could tune in out-of-town stations, and the excitement of picking up KDKA in Pittsburgh, or WBAP in Fort Worth, or WLS in Chicago, was a conversation piece the next day. The introduction of sets with loudspeakers increased the nation's pleasure.

At first, stations in scattered cities were hooked together to broadcast special shows with such stars as Paul Whiteman, Vincent Lopez, Ed Wynn, and Roxy and His Gang. Twenty-one stations from New York to California joined to broadcast Coolidge's second inauguration in 1925. The National Broadcasting Company, a subsidiary of the Radio Corporation of America, was formed late in 1926, and extended programming "coast to coast" in 1927. WEAF was the originating station for NBC's Red network and WJZ was the flagship for its Blue network. The

Columbia Broadcasting System came into being in 1927. By 1934 CBS had 97 affiliated stations compared with 127 for the two NBC networks. The Mutual Broadcasting System was organized that year, primarily to provide network-caliber programs to smaller stations. Regional chains also developed. In 1943 an order by the Federal Communications Commission led to the sale of the Blue network and its renaming in 1945 as the American Broadcasting Company. The four networks continued to complete vigorously for outlets until by 1964 ABC-Radio had 424 affiliated stations; ABC-TV, 244; CBS-Radio, 225; CBS-TV, 200; NBC-Radio, 192; NBC-TV, 201; and MBS-Radio, 510.

Under the First Amendment to the Constitution, government is restrained from interfering with the freedom of the press or the freedom of speech. But while anyone with enough money is free to found a newspaper anywhere at any time, there are only a limited number of broadcast channels. The theory is that these channels belong to the people and since they are limited the people must allocate them through Congress. Thus, when stations jumped from one wave length to another to avoid interference, Congress in 1927 established a five-man Federal Radio Commission, empowered to regulate all forms of radio communication. The Communications Act of 1934 established a seven-member Federal Communications Commission to regulate the airwaves in the interest of the public. It has been in efforts by the FCC to define "public service" that controversy has arisen, such as Congress' requirement that equal time be provided for rival candidates for public office. The newspaper can publish what it desires in such matters, whether in the news, editorial, or advertising columns, subject only to public opinion and the laws of libel and obscenity. Broadcasting, however, because of its peculiar physical structure, must be regulated.

Many newspaper publishers began to view radio with some alarm as they noted the growing advertising revenue of the new medium since they were fearful that radio news might reduce the circulation of newspapers. A press-radio battle continued for nearly a decade, with the newspapers attempting to prevent the major press associations from selling their news reports to radio stations. It was a losing fight, however, and in 1933 a Press-Radio Bureau was established to provide the stations with two daily news reports and bulletins of "transcendent importance." The public demand for news by radio grew, and Trans-Radio Press, a unique newsgathering organization catering mainly to radio clients, came into being. In 1935 the United Press and International News Service began to service radio networks and stations with news that could be sponsored. The Associated Press soon followed suit, and the war was over.

By 1965, voices decrying the continuation of sales of press association reports to broadcasting stations were so few as to be almost inarticulate. Indeed, such a turnabout had occurred that both of the existing wire service organizations had more radio-TV station customers than newspaper customers. By 1965 the Associated Press was sending its reports to 2500 stations and 1750 publications, whereas United Press International was serving 2300 stations and 1600 publications.

Radio developed its own stars, including such attractions of the 1920's as the A&P Gypsies, the Gold Dust Twins, Goodrich's Silver Masked Tenor, and Billy Jones & Ernie Haire ("We're the Interwoven pair"). The networks were on the air from 9 a.m. to 11 p.m., Eastern Standard Time, with a melange of humor, kiddie stories, soap operas, variety shows, interviews, poetry, dance bands, and symphony orchestras. The disk jockeys of affiliated stations were morning announcers, and local live talent generally was heard from 7 to 9 a.m. or so.

During the depression years of the 1930's radio provided inexpensive home entertainment. President Franklin D. Roosevelt's "fireside chats" helped allay fears that the nation's future was seriously threatened and, psychologically, bound the country together. In the field of entertainment, such personages as Will Rogers, the cowboy comedian-philosopher, with alarm clock at his elbow to clang when his time was up, and Eddie Cantor, banjo-eyed comedian singing "Potatoes are cheaper, tomatoes are cheaper, now's the time to fall in love," did their bit to bring their fellow countrymen out of the economic doldrums.

Radio was a part of almost everyone's life, and each program had its theme song. As one observer has written, "Five times a week, Kate Smith's moon came over the mountain—Bing Crosby's gold of the day met the blue of the night." Millions of listeners thrilled to "Gang Busters," "The Lone Ranger," and "Sherlock Holmes." They awaited the daily or weekly visits of Amos 'n Andy, Myrt and Marge, the Boswell Sisters, Boake Carter, Graham McNamee, Fibber McGee and Molly, Walter Winchell, Jack Benny, and Bob Hope.

In 1939 the almost hysterical tirades of Adolf Hitler formed an ominous backdrop to news of the march into the Low Countries and Poland, and the advent of World War II. Then, on an otherwise peaceful

Sunday, December 7, 1941, radio brought the catastrophic news of the Japanese attack on Pearl Harbor. Millions remained close to their radio sets during the eventful years of America's counterattack, invasions, A-bomb dropping, and eventual victory over both Nazis and Japanese in 1945. Commentators such as Elmer Davis, Eric Sevareid, Edward R. Murrow, and H. V. Kaltenborn gained immense followings with their daily quarter-hour interpretations of the news.

On June 8, 1948, comedian Milton Berle produced his first program for the young NBC-TV network. There were fewer than 1,000,000 sets in homes and bars, and the show was viewed in only 13 NBC-outlet cities. But almost the entire nation suddenly became aware of television and its potential, and the rush to build stations and buy sets was on. Radio was eclipsed. A year later TV was viewed in 2,500,000, or 6 per cent, of the nation's homes. The percentage rose to 19 in 1950, 70 in 1955, 87 in 1960, and 93 in 1965. Radio shifted patterns of operation and recovered to remain a prime U.S. necessity. Newspaper and magazine advertising and circulation also sagged, but recovered as a rapidly growing population continued its strong demand for all the media.

The story of television's development has largely been that of NBC, CBS, and ABC, which have spun electronic webs across the continent and dominated the stations because they provide most of the programming. It is also the story of the major advertisers and advertising agencies, which have influenced the nature of the programming so as to attract the most viewers. It is the story of the audience measurement agencies, such as the A. C. Nielsen Company, whose ratings have determined which programs shall continue to be broadcast.

The dominant figure in the industry has been General David Sarnoff, chairman of the board of the Radio Corporation of America, which owns NBC. Sarnoff, sometimes termed Mr. Electronics, dominated much of the development of radio and as early as 1938 predicted the role that television would play. William S. Paley, chairman of the board, and Frank Stanton, president, have sparked the rise of CBS. And a Harvard lawyer, Leonard Goldenson, and Robert Kintner, later president of NBC, rescued ABC from near-oblivion, largely because of a 1953 merger with Paramount Theatres, Inc., and heavy programming in Westerns.

Sylvester L. (Pat) Weaver, Jr., went from an advertising agency, Young & Rubicam, in 1949 to the presidency of NBC, where his imaginative programming, including "Monitor," "Today," "Tonight," and the

90-minute "Spectaculars," marked him as a broadcasting genius. When Sarnoff promoted his son, Robert, to run NBC as executive vice president, Weaver became head of the international division of the huge McCann-Erickson advertising complex.

Weaver went to California in 1963 to head Subscription Television, Inc., the first nonexperimental pay TV venture in the U.S. The company began operating in Los Angeles in mid-1964 and quickly spread its operations to San Francisco. Subscribers paid $5 each and let the company run a three-channel coaxial cable into their homes and attach a small box to their sets. Then, for prices ranging from 50 cents to $2 per show, they had their choice of such programs as the Los Angeles Dodgers' or the San Francisco Giants' baseball games, a Laurence Olivier play, Carol Channing in "Show Girl," an off-Broadway play, foreign movies, and concerts by Artur Rubinstein and Van Cliburn—in color and uninterrupted by commercials.

An electronic device known as the "Interrogator and Responser," capable of checking the programs being viewed on as many as 712,000 television sets every six minutes, handled the bookkeeping, feeding the information into an IBM computer by tape. Each customer had a choice among three programs, or he could choose none, and he received his bill once a month.

Motion picture theatre owners and commercial television operators bitterly attacked the venture. Many TV viewers feared that free television eventually would carry only mediocre programs or that, ultimately, viewers would have to pay for *all* TV programs, including advertisements as well. By a margin of more than 1,500,000 votes, California voters in November, 1964, approved a referendum banning subscription television in the state. The company ceased operations and planned to test the verdict in the courts. At the same time, the company revealed that only $1,600,000 remained of its original $20,000,000 investment. The cause of pay TV was set back indefinitely and, perhaps, irretrievably.

Commercial television entered 1965 faced with the growth of CATV systems, a pending rash of new UHF stations, the spread of international TV via satellite and cable, the possible future rebirth of pay television, and innumerable criticisms and threats of further governmental control over program content, advertising, and ownership (see Chapter 8). In response, the industry prepared to put teeth into its Radio and Television Code and to take such corrective steps as the formation of a

Broadcast Rating Council, which was developing accrediting and auditing procedures to ensure the accuracy and reliability of rating services. On the whole, the industry relied upon its own immense store of capital and imaginative business and political enterprise to solve its many problems and meet the challenges of the volatile and changing broadcast world.

THE NEWS FUNCTION

The area of news and information is an important, aggressive, and prestige-building division of the television-radio programming structure. When there's big news breaking, such as during a national political convention or a crisis in world affairs, regular commercial programs are dispensed with to permit a complete news service to the American public. Documentaries, such as the NBC White Papers, CBS Reports, and ABC Close-ups, often are given prime evening time on the networks. Commercial programs are always interrupted to convey news bulletins of high importance.

In the area of news and information there are three types of programs for which the journalist's talents are suited. One is the newscast, giving generally a 5- or 15-minute summary of happenings throughout the community, nation, and the world. Another is the program that provides background information or interpretation. It may be simply a straight presentation of facts by a veteran newscaster, or it may be a panel discussion, an interview, or an elaborate documentary. In the third category are programs that provide information to groups with both general and special interests. These concentrate on one or more areas of information, such as sports events, child care, home decorating, medical first aid, or spring planting. They have their counterparts in the departments, columns, and feature stories that appear in every newspaper.

Television has made its greatest contribution in the field of information by bringing to the people the major events of government, such as the inauguration of a president and the coverage of a political convention. In this area it has excelled and has no equal. It has forced the good newspaper to be even better in a field in which it now leads, that of presenting intelligent interpretation of an event after the people have seen it.

A prime example was provided by the assassination of President John F. Kennedy and the quick-moving events that followed. Within an hour after the slaying, the tragic word had been transmitted to every corner of the earth. The news went farthest and fastest by TV and radio. Words and pictures reached all the way to Japan, by television signals bounced off the U.S. satellite Relay I. For four days the television networks cancelled all programs to carry the momentous events as the late President was buried and Lyndon B. Johnson assumed the reins of government. The most dramatic and unexpected moment occurred when network cameras focused on Jack Ruby as he fatally shot the alleged assassin, Lee Oswald, in what was beyond all doubt history's most public crime.

Television and radio alike spend a great deal of time and money to keep their audiences abreast of the news of the day. Stations quite early discovered that news programs rank exceptionally high in public interest. Robert K. Richards, former administrative vice president of the National Association of Broadcasters, has pointed out that surveys show radio news programs are "the most listenable, listened to, and salable programs on the air."

Thorough local coverage and accurate, impartial handling of the news not only build listener and viewer loyalty, but also produce station revenue that almost always exceeds the costs involved. One manager estimated that his news department produced 20 per cent of the station's net revenue while using only 15 per cent of its total program time. In a slide-film presentation, the Associated Press pointed out that radio news has the highest percentage of men, women, and children listeners of any type of program. News programs were described as the best possible means of rendering public service and as the best audience-builder for stations. It was further noted that newscasts are a steady source of revenue.

During television's pioneer decade, many veteran journalists (including the much-revered interpreter of trends at home and overseas, Elmer Davis) concluded that the electronic infant would never amount to much as a conveyor of spot news. It was too slow, they said, compared to radio; it had too many limitations. By the time production techniques were completed for a TV news report, it would be entering the realm of history. Film coverage of necessity was restricted to planned events. Hence the medium threatened to give viewers a grossly distorted picture of the goings-on in the world. It would forever accent the trivial—bathing beauty contests, Paris fashions, new arrivals at the zoo. It would forever eliminate the significant—Communist witchcraft in the Middle East, recommendations of the Hoover commission on reorganization of the federal government, actions taken at last night's meeting of the local school board.

Happily, the spectacles of the early seers proved to be dust-covered. Television news was saved from a fate worse than death by simultaneous improvements that have nearly solved the problems of slowness and mediocre coverage. The development of film of exceptionally high speed, eliminating the necessity for complicated lighting equipment in shooting a story, was a major breakthrough. The perfection of television tape was another. Refinements in both motion and still picture cameras contributed immensely to the common goal, as did the coming of age of TV mobile units. Faster transmission of films and pictures from the scene of an event to the network or station also played a part. Perhaps equally important was the improved training given newsmen and stringers in the use of camera equipment.

As succinctly stated by Jim Bormann, chief of the WCCO (Minneapolis-St. Paul) news department and a past president of the Radio-Television News Directors Association, television news directors "haven't licked *all* their problems yet, but the remaining problems in TV news seem to be more budgetary than journalistic in nature." By the 1960's television newscasts were virtually as up to date and reflected the same careful selection and editing of news as did the better radio newscasts. A survey by Motivation Analysis, Inc., brought out the fact that TV news has a much greater impact than it is generally thought to have. Half of the people interviewed (in the study of audience reaction to TV for Corinthian Broadcasting Corporation, which operates KHOU-TV, Houston) wanted more TV news than they were getting, although 18 per cent wanted fewer newscasts.

The president of the research firm, Dr. Phillip Eisenberg, stated that "the TV news experience is the most real in comparison with any other medium, if it is presented properly. It is the closest thing to the actual experience itself." Furthermore, he noted, "one of the medium's great strengths is its ability to expose us directly to the personalities in the news. We see them and form opinions of them as people. The names in the news are no longer just names, they take on an immediate reality." Who can forget the jolting spectacle of Lee Oswald's murder on live television in the Dallas, Texas, municipal building basement?

The clicking, rumbling teleprinters of the Associated Press or United Press International (and sometimes both) play a staccato rhythm night and day in the newsrooms of every television and radio station in the country. These newsgathering organizations provide the state, national, and foreign news reports that can be relayed almost instantaneously to the public. Regrettably, a considerable number of stations depend almost altogether upon giant press associations for their newscasts; in the lingo of the broadcast world their announcers simply "rip and read" these stories, frequently against a recorded background of wire machine cacophony and preceded by whistles, the ringing of bells, and other attention-compelling sounds. Many small stations also provide poor local news coverage, depending upon publicity handouts and upon rewriting the newspapers because they cannot or will not meet the cost of main-taining a news staff. By contrast, the quality stations rewrite wire dis-patches, working in as much interpretative (not opinion) material as possible; their newscasts are presented in a more dignified manner; and they maintain staffs of varying talent and size in order to keep abreast of local news developments.

The most common types of radio newscasts are the 5- and 15-minute sponsored programs. The former provides about 3½ minutes of news and the latter about 12 minutes. The networks recently began using the 5-minute, hourly newscast technique, a service that would have been impossible in the old days of the half-hour sponsored network music, comedy, or drama show, because of programming difficulties. The hourly 5-minute newscast is also a basic ingredient in what is known as "formula" radio. This is high-tension programming, with all announce-ments read at least 10 per cent faster than ordinary, much playing of "survey" records—"the week's top 40 pop tunes"—and often double- or even triple-spotting of commercials between records.

Stations with larger staffs tend to produce 15-minute newscasts for airing early in the morning, at noon, in the late afternoon, and around 10:00 or 11:00 at night. The material for these newscasts is gathered in much the same manner as the newspaper employs. Reporters contact officials in such information-collecting centers as police departments; city, county, and federal offices; courts; chambers of commerce; industries and labor union headquarters. They either telephone accounts to a rewrite man or return to their newsrooms to write the stories themselves. Mean-while, other developing stories are obtained by telephone from such sources as hospitals, funeral homes, weather bureaus, airports, and civic organizations. Many stations are staffed by men who have not only been trained to gather and write news but also to deliver it on the air. At other stations news scripts are prepared by trained journalists but the station's regular announcers broadcast the news. This system proves most effective when one writer, or set of writers, prepares copy regularly for the same announcer. Those writing the copy get to know the peculiar style, cadence, and microphone personality of the announcer, and they prepare their stories to fit the type of interpretation which they know will be given to the copy.

Reports direct from the scene of a news happening, radioed to the station from a mobile unit, frequently enliven newscasts. Often these reports are recorded earlier and interspersed into the regular newscasts. Reporters for stations which do not have a mobile unit frequently telephone their accounts; their narrations are recorded and may be placed on the air almost immediately.

Newspapers appeal to the sense of sight and radio appeals to the sense of hearing, but television caters to both and offers the additional factor of motion. To capitalize upon its advantages, journalists who prepare news programs for television not only must write copy but also must use every available visual aid, such as newsreel-type film clips, still photographs, maps, charts, and drawings (as well as the man on camera) for an effective presentation. There is great variety in types of television news programs. Some stations project still photographs to illustrate what the newscaster is talking about. Others combine films and stills, perhaps with charts and drawings as well. Whatever the technique, television news programs call for a maximum of cooperation among the director, camera crew, newscaster, announcer (for the commercials), and the artists, who prepare displays for the advertisements. Each portion of the presentation must be carefully cued and timed for a smoothly produced show.

The production of television and radio newscasts for the networks requires the cooperation not only of large staffs, centered in New York City and Washington, D. C., but also of trained personnel scattered throughout the world. Events in other countries are filmed and the footage dispatched by plane to the United States for immediate network use. Radio "pickups" can be made almost anywhere in the world and transmitted instantaneously to the American public, although these accounts often are recorded for rebroadcast at program time. Affiliated television stations throughout the United States provide man-on-camera narration and film clips which are interspersed into newscasts otherwise emanating from the principal network studios. Almost all of the highly skilled personnel required for network news programming consist of men who have obtained their basic training with local stations throughout the country or who have been engaged in competitive newspaper or press association reporting.

At one time there were great differences between the styles of radio-TV writing and newspaper writing, chiefly because broadcast copy was written for the ear and newspaper copy for the eye. Today, however, primarily as a result of the numerous readability studies of the 1940's and 1950's, much newspaper copy has been simplified to the point where it is just about as easy to comprehend as copy prepared for newscasts. With certain style exceptions, news that is easy to follow when it comes from the loudspeaker is also easily understood when read in a newspaper.

There are, of course, logical reasons for certain differences in the styles of writing news for the three media. Since many newspaper readers are inclined to be "skimmers" and to pay less than undivided attention to what they read as they ride on buses, planes, or commuter trains or while they sit at home absorbing the outpourings of television and radio sets and record players, newspaper stories must present their most important facts first—and fast. However, the newspaper reader has headlines and bold-faced paragraphs or subheads to help him grasp the significance of an array of facts. And if he doesn't get it the first time, he has a physical account to which he can refer again and again until it all becomes clear. So a newspaper account begins with the crux of a story and continues with facts ranked according to their importance; transitional phrases are dispensed with so that paragraphs may be rearranged or cut to fit allotted space.

The radio listener, on the other hand, must be prepared for the story with a clear and attention-arousing statement of what it concerns. He has none of the orientation aids the newspaper reader has—no headlines, no bold-faced matter, no printed page to refer to. So copy must be written with extreme simplicity to get the message across to him: if he doesn't get it the first time, he doesn't get it. Furthermore, key ideas (not words or phrases, but ideas) must be repeated in radio copy at times to put over a complex point. Such repetition would be both deadly and unnecessary in newspaper copy.

The television viewer ordinarily, though not always, gives his full attention to the televised news report. He doesn't have the newspaper's type guides to assist him in understanding the day's happenings; nor does he need them. Instead, he has a completely different set of tools—films, still pictures, symbolic art work, and background music—to help him follow what the newscaster is saying.

Yet a television news script often reaches the zenith of "tight" writing, for many stories must be completely covered while film is being shown and the running time for a news clip ranges from about 50 to 83½ seconds (for 30 to 50 feet of film). This would be about 125 to 209 words in terms of radio copy, but it is far less than that for a television news script because the man on camera usually must coordinate certain remarks with the action in a given scene, and he dare not be so glued to his script that he can't watch the action on the studio monitor. Average film scenes run from 2 to 6 feet (enough time for about 6–18 words). Action scenes average out to about 18–30 feet each (allowing approximately 54–90 words).

Hence the heavy emphasis on "rapid" sentences in TV news, sentences of four or five words which may not be complete in the sense of having all the elements—subject, verb, and object. Physically, the TV script reveals another difference from those for newspapers and radio: news which is to be read occupies no more than two-thirds of the space from left to right on a sheet. The remaining one-third, usually on the left side, is used to write in instructions for cueing film, music, sound effects, commercials, etc.

These differences stem mainly from the fact that a newspaper is a physical thing, whereas radio and TV programs are ephemeral (sure, they could be taped and replayed, but how many persons would go to all that bother?). Other major differences have to do with the fact that the newscaster has a rather strong contact with members of his audience at the time they expose themselves to the news, whereas the newspaper reporter does not have such a contact. To take advantage of this, broadcast news attempts to be conversational and highly informal. It is intended to sound like a story told by one good friend to another. It makes greater use of active voice and present tense than newspaper copy does; it rarely departs from simple, direct sentence structure; and it occasionally goes overboard in the use of colloquial and idiomatic expressions.

THE EDITORIAL FUNCTION

Approximately one-third of the broadcast media by the mid-1960's were exercising their rights and privileges to present informed opinion. Individual news analysts such as H. V. Kaltenborn, Clifton Utley, Elmer Davis, John W. Vandercook, and Bill Henry had performed notable public service during the quarter-century when radio controlled the airwaves. Gradually, as television lured multitudes from their radio sets, these commentators lost their grip on the populace. TV, with its unique ability to bring the sights and sounds of live action into the home, soon found it had no place for the type of analyst who just sat and talked, except during events of transcendent news importance when, for example, the nation was nominating or electing its top executives and legislators.

In the field of the documentary, the versatility of films and remote pickups enabled television to score successes that its sightless partner could scarcely match, although radio continued to produce superb "actuality" shows—using the voices of participants instead of those of actors—and occasionally excelled in the presentation of public affairs programs.

From the long view, the only trouble with such outstanding TV originals as "See It Now" and "Wide, Wide World" was that they were expensive—and, hence, expendable. This resulted in their rather spasmodic appearance and disappearance. Sponsors felt a detectable reluctance to put on such programs for an appreciably smaller audience than that which could be attracted to low-budget westerns—despite the fact that one forum of enlightenment, CBS' "Twentieth Century," successfully bumped a horse opera competitor off of home screens. A satisfactory solution to the problem has yet to be found. The progress of the documentary has been indeed notable, but it has been closely akin to that of the track star who broke all world's records while running around his living room.

The area of the opinion function in which the media are making continuous advances is presentation of owner viewpoints. Editorializing (the word most often used) consists of the advocacy of opinion that is clearly identified as the view of a broadcasting organization—as opposed to "commentating" in which the opinions expressed are those of an individual.

In 1941 the Federal Communications Commission decreed in its famed "Mayflower Decision" that licensees should not air their own editorial opinions. The decision concerned a Boston station held to be in violation of the Federal Communications Act because of its political broadcasting. In its opinion, the commission expressed concern that only one side of an issue might be placed before the public in one-station communities and in those in which the only newspaper and the only station were owned by the same persons. In 1949, however, the FCC reversed itself, declaring that it would be in the public interest for stations to "editorialize with fairness." In other words, the FCC decided that if a broadcast licensee undertakes to present programming dealing with controversial issues of public importance, he must make reasonable efforts to present conflicting points of view on such issues.

For some years after the FCC reversed its decision, station managements made only limited attempts to offer their own "editorials of the air." There was no tradition to spur them on. Besides, effective editorials require careful research and expert writing. Since an editorial itself brings in no direct income, stations were reluctant to employ the extra manpower needed to do the job well. The first station to offer a daily editorial on television was WTVJ (Miami, Fla.) in September, 1957. Since then this station has achieved distinction in the field of the broadcast editorial, under the leadership of News Director Ralph Renick. WMCA, New York, became the first radio station to endorse a candidate for the Presidency with its editorial support of John F. Kennedy in 1960, and the station is a recognized leader in broadcast editorializing.

A strong movement toward the airing of editorials began in 1958, reached a peak a few years later, then subsided somewhat. A *Broadcasting Yearbook* survey revealed that 47 per cent of AM radio stations editorialized daily, weekly, or occasionally in 1959. By 1963, however, only 32.6 per cent of all stations broadcast opinions. The sharp decline might be attributed, in part, to the fact that 365 new stations went on the air during the four-year period and most of them undoubtedly had not acquired the maturity and staff necessary for effective editorializing.

Of 576 television stations on the air, 189, or 32.8 per cent, reported that they broadcast editorials with some regularity in 1963. This compared with 30.1 per cent in 1959, when 15 fewer TV stations were in operation. A Television Information Office study in 1963 indicated that 87 per cent of TV editorials dealt with local subjects. Twenty-six stations reported that they sometimes editorialized on international matters and 41 per cent sometimes dealt with national affairs. About half of the stations discussed political issues, but only 6 per cent took sides for or against candidates. It required an average of 5.3 hours for special editorial personnel or news staff members to prepare each editorial. The station manager most often delivered the message, usually in two to three minutes of air time.

Many broadcasters who have failed to air editorials, or whose expressions have represented bland, "middle-of-the-road" points of view, have complained that the FCC's fairness doctrine is to blame. Why, they argue, should the station be forced to grant valuable air time for reply even if a reasonable determination can be made as to who should reply and on what specific issues? General Counsel Douglas Anello of the National Association of Broadcasters asked: "If a broadcaster can be forced to give time for the expression of a contrary point of view, isn't this comparable to the levy of damages for saying what you think?" Both actions, he declared, are equally inhibiting to free and open discussion. Fairness, he contended, should remain always a moral obligation, never a legal one. Furthermore, broadcasters are fearful that the FCC, which has power to revoke their licenses, may disagree with the stations' handling of certain controversial cases.

FCC Chairman E. William Henry has replied that it isn't the commission's fairness doctrine that is to blame for bland broadcast editorials and commentaries that lack a point of view—it's the broadcaster who is more concerned with his ratings than with winning a Peabody or Sigma Delta Chi Award. "The real difficulty," Henry said, "lies with broadcasters who aren't seriously committed to the journalistic function or to the exposure of controversy." Such broadcasters, he said, follow this rule: "Controversy may sell newspapers, but in this business it's the funny page that counts. Mr. Average Viewer will not consider buying your brand or Brand X when an editorial has just made him apoplectic."

Henry said the FCC has enunciated only the most general principles— "that the basic right to be protected is the public's right to hear both sides of a controversy, that a broadcaster has an obligation to respect that right, that he must make an affirmative effort to discharge this obligation over and above making his facilities available to contrasting points of view on demand. . . ." He added that the FCC has often upheld the broadcaster's judgment against the complaints of those whose ideas of fairness differed.

Dr. Frank Stanton, president of CBS, Inc., said in 1964 that he and his fellow broadcasters must "use our editorial strength boldly, imaginatively, and with insight and wisdom." He said broadcasters should participate more fully in stimulating public opinion through stronger, more skillful, and more eloquent editorials on urgent matters, such as civil rights. In the past 10 years, he reported, CBS-owned radio and TV stations had carried 2675 editorials. He added that although some of these were "powerful and persuasive," he did not consider it reassuring that only about one in 10 provoked a rebuttal.

OPERATING STANDARDS

The National Association of Broadcasters in an operational guide, "Broadcasting the News," pointed out that "the better news operations":

1. Maintain staff reporters to provide original coverage of local news.

2. Write or rewrite all local copy for newscasts.

3. Carefully edit and frequently rewrite national-international wire copy.

4. Make wide use of tape recorded interviews and telephone "beeper" reports, keeping such pickups to 1–2 minutes on newscasts and 3–4 minutes for special shows and roundups.

5. Use mobile units for fast, flexible coverage and direct broadcasts from the scene via two-way radio.

6. Train their news staffs to contribute new ideas and to be aware that radio and television are new and flexible media for news coverage and suitable to imaginative and unusual treatment of the news.

7. Exercise, in cooperation with the program director, control over staff announcers who are reading news copy.

8. Make wide use of local film and local stories.

"The prime requisite in radio-TV news is to provide listeners and viewers with news with which they may make some personal identification, which they understand, and which, because they understand, they find absorbing and exciting," the association booklet declared. "Good news operations, however, do not create false values through use of production or electronic devices."

In this latter statement the association referred to certain undesirable trends in the treatment of television and radio news that tend to deceive audiences. RTNDA directors likewise deplored these practices which, they asserted, "are basically misrepresentation and include false claims of exclusivity, false claims of wire service by-liners, false pretension of men on the spot, etc. This board condemns any style of news presentation which, in its writing or broadcast, gives a distorted or incomplete report. Attempts at sensationalism serve only to create possible hysteria."

The RTNDA board also "frowns upon gimmickery in newscasts, upon the sirens and whistles heralding the coming of news periods, upon the use of filter mikes or phony reports allegedly from the scene. News is not vaudeville; its purpose is to keep the public well informed." At the same time the board praised "the hundreds of quality stations, both small and large, both radio and television, which are making an earnest and honest effort toward public service in electronic journalism."

The association repeatedly has expressed the conviction of its membership that newscasts must serve only the public, and never a private, interest. The news director or the newsman on duty, it is asserted, should have the opportunity to determine the content of newscasts and the treatment of the news. In matters of policy he should be responsible only to the station manager and should have complete supervision over the handling of the news. Material selected for newscasts should be judged on news merit alone and presented accurately, factually, in good taste, and without bias or sensationalism.

ADVERTISING AND PROMOTION

Network advertising, national "spot" advertising, and local advertising provide the bulk of operating revenue for television and radio stations. Large stations may also receive income from such services as producing programs for clients, making transcriptions, and handling talent.

The advertising staffs of the national networks solicit advertising from companies whose products or services are marketed throughout the country. They provide a continuing flow of fresh, up-to-date information about the markets served by their affiliates, making contacts both directly with big companies and with the agencies that represent them.

National firms with large staffs of trained solicitors represent individual stations in calling on agencies and companies for business. They sell spot advertising, which may range from a series of brief announcements to full programs originating in the local studios and from filmed commercials to filmed 15- or 30- minute programs. These firms, located strategically in the major cities, make sales presentations for any or all the stations on their lists.

This leaves local advertising to be handled by the station itself. The commercial manager must build a staff of highly trained solicitors who often have a triple job to do: sell advertising in general, television and radio in particular, and their own station specifically. This is true because the local merchant may not be fully aware of the advantages of advertising and he may have practically no knowledge of what a carefully conceived television or radio advertising campaign may do for his business.

The salesman first learns all he can about his prospective client's business. In consultation with the local sales manager and station program director, he then prepares a suggested plan, involving possibly a regular program and a series of commercial announcements. If the plan is accepted, he oversees the necessary arrangements to ensure the effectiveness of the campaign. Skilled writers prepare the copy and continuity. After the advertiser is convinced that his campaign is selling his goods or services, the salesman seeks gradually to sell the sponsor additional broadcasting.

An important adjunct to sales is the promotion department. The promotion manager may be a staff member with no other responsibilities or he may be the general manager, the commercial manager, a copywriter, or a salesman. In order to attract both audiences and advertisers, the promotion manager prepares station advertisements and publicity stories for the local newspapers, for trade publications read by agency and company advertising men, and for use over the station's own facilities. In addition, he develops ideas for posters and other outdoor advertising; engages in such public relations activities as delivering speeches, answering station mail, and handling telephone inquiries; and attracts attention to the station and its individual programs through such devices as parades, stunts, and personal appearances by star performers. Journalistic training is almost imperative for successful performance in this capacity.

PROGRAMMING

Television and radio programs are planned, prepared, and produced by the programming department. On small stations, only a few persons may be employed to make commercial announcements, read news and sports summaries, select and play recordings, and introduce network programs. Large stations, however, may employ 75 or more persons to handle a variety of specialized jobs.

The programming policy and scheduling for a large station are handled by the program director. The traffic manager prepares daily schedules of programs and keeps a record of broadcast time available for advertising. The writing and editing of all scripts are the responsibility of the continuity director. Assisting him is the continuity writer, who prepares announcers' books containing the script and commercials for each program together with their sequence and length.

The director supervises individual programs. He may work under the supervision of a producer, who handles the selection of scripts, financial matters, and other production problems. At times these functions are combined in the job of producer-director. Program assistants obtain props, film slides, art work, and makeup service; assist in timing the program; and prepare cue cards. Some stations employ education and public affairs directors, who supervise most noncommercial programs such as those presented by churches, schools, and civic groups.

Television and radio staff announcers present news and live commercial messages, identify stations, conduct interviews, describe sports events, and act as masters of ceremonies. On the smaller stations they may also operate the control board, sell time, and write scripts and news copy. Announcers on small stations often obtain FCC licenses in order that they also may operate transmitters.

Large television and radio stations may employ a librarian to handle the music files, and also a musical director to supervise rehearsals and broadcasts. Television stations have film editors, who prepare films and video tape recordings for on-the-air presentation. The stations' files of films and tape are maintained by a film librarian.

Television performances which are aired either live or on tape require the services of a studio supervisor, who arranges scenery and other equipment; a floor or stage manager, who directs the movement of actors on the set and relays stage directions, station breaks, and cues; floormen, who set up props, hold cue cards, and perform other such chores; makeup artists, who prepare personnel for broadcasts; scenic designers, who plan and design settings and backgrounds; and sound effects technicians, who coordinate special sounds.

Working with all of these programming personnel are the engineers and broadcast technicians, who use their highly specialized knowledge to convert the sounds and pictures into electronic impulses that can be received by the public.

OPPORTUNITIES AND SALARIES

There are hundreds of openings in television and radio news departments each year (and a few in the radio departments of press associations and in newsreel companies). To fill them, the news director or station manager usually turns to his file of job applicants, many of whom are seeking to advance from a smaller operation. Some small stations may employ a local high school graduate who has displayed an interest in "learning by doing." A number of quality stations, as well as others, recruit newsmen directly from departments and schools of journalism and communications. The most sought-after graduates are those trained at schools which have highly developed programs in television and radio news instruction. These graduates not only have learned to gather, write, and edit news but they have also been introduced to newsroom equipment and techniques and thus are enabled to perform specified chores almost immediately.

Because of the relative scarcity of instructional programs in television and radio news, however, many stations must seek out the graduates of print-oriented schools and departments of journalism and convert them into broadcast personnel.

If the recruit is employed by a radio station, he will be assigned to established news beats or given a rewrite job in the newsroom; if he doesn't already know how to operate a tape recorder, he will be taught how to do this and how to conduct a telephone interview to be placed on the air, or how to report from the scene of a news happening. If a television station employs him, he will be assigned to rewriting wire copy or will be handed a camera, either motion picture or still, and, if necessary, given minimum training in its operation. He then will be expected to report the news with both pencil and camera.

Many women write and edit television and radio news copy, although only a relatively few become widely known news personalities such as Pauline Frederick, NBC reporter who specializes in covering the United Nations. Countless women become local celebrities of a sort, particularly with feminine audiences, in preparing and narrating interview and demonstration programs relating to the news of fashions, foods, and other such fields. A knowledge of home economics, as well as journalism, is a tremendous asset for this work.

According to their abilities, both men and women may advance from beginning jobs to become news directors, commentators, program directors, announcers, directors of public affairs and special events, and station managers. University speech and radio-TV departments provide training for most of the performing and production jobs in broadcasting.

Stations also are constantly in the market for competent advertising solicitors and continuity writers. Writing commercials requires a knowledge of selling, and more often than not such a job is filled by a woman. Salaries in these fields compare favorably with those requiring similar talents with the other media. Good promotion men for the larger stations commonly earn $8000 or more.

Beginning salaries for television and radio news personnel are comparable to, or slightly higher than, those paid newspaper reporters and editors. By 1965 these starting salaries were around $4000 to $5000, depending upon the size of the station, regional competitive factors, and the training of the applicant. After three to five years, salaries for radio news writers range from $5500 to $7500, while television news writers may reach the $10,000 level on large stations. Talent fees for those with on-mike and on-camera assignments push their incomes even higher.

Wage scales in effect at the National Broadcasting Company and the American Broadcasting Company ranged between $153 and $200 a week, considerably above the scale won by the American Newspaper Guild. Additional $5 per day fees were paid to so-called "desk men," who act as TV and radio assignment editors or "produce" TV net shows. Additional fees also were paid for network news "cut-ins." Newswriters at network originating points and at stations owned and operated by the two networks are represented by the National Association of Broadcast Employees and Technicians. The union's news jurisdiction includes all writing, editing, processing, collecting, and collating of news, including film. The bargaining agent for Columbia Broadcasting System writers is the Radio Writers Guild.

Newsmen under individual contract to the networks to write and deliver their own news programs are members of the American Federation of Television and Radio Artists, the union that covers all on-the-air performers. AFTRA members may either prepare their own copy or read copy written by NABET members. AFTRA members are sometimes used as on-the-street reporters. They work under a fee system of talent payments for newscasts and air work toward a guaranteed wage. Individual contracts call for guarantees of $250 a week and higher. It is estimated that Chet Huntley and David Brinkley, both veteran newsmen with large national followings, have reached total annual incomes well in excess of $100,000.

Approximate salaries earned by broadcast personnel in the mid-1960's may be deduced from a *Printers' Ink* nationwide survey and biennial studies undertaken by the National Association of Broadcasters. Generally, the gross volume of business is the single most important factor which determines the salaries paid to television and radio station personnel.

The median salaries paid to executives of television stations grossing below $500,000 per year have been computed as follows: General manager, $15,250; station manager, $11,800; commercial manager, $9200; program manager, $7500; promotion manager, $5400; chief engineer, $7500. By contrast, the median salaries paid by stations grossing in excess of $2,000,000 annually was as follows: General manager, $39,000; station manager, $29,275; commercial manager, $20,700; program manager, $13,800; promotion manager, $11,500; chief engineer, $14,950.

Radio stations grossing less than $50,000 annually paid the following median salaries: General manager, $6820; station manager, $6600; commercial manager, $6820; program manager, $4485; chief engineer, $4400. Those grossing more than $1,000,000 paid the following median salaries: General manager, $35,200; commercial manager, $21,450; program manager, $11,000; promotion manager, $8000; chief engineer, $12,100.

The salaries of television station news directors, although not reported in the *Printers' Ink* study, ranged from $6000 to $15,000 and upward, other surveys indicate. The salaries of radio station news directors ranged generally from $5200 to $10,000.

These salaries included fees and commissions, but not fringe benefits. It was evident that compensation varied widely according to geographic location, station and market size, and other factors.

Competent college graduates could expect to receive beginning salaries ranging from $4160 to $5200 per year for most non-news broadcast jobs, with annual raises of $10 to $15 per week the customary pattern.

The earnings of employees in television and radio broadcasting ranked second highest in the entire industrial economy, a Department of Commerce survey of current business disclosed in 1962. The average annual earnings in broadcasting during the previous year were $7477. This was exceeded only by the average annual earnings of $9607 for employees of security and commodity brokers, dealers, and exchanges.

QUALIFICATIONS

Sound training in reporting and editing is essential for success in television and radio newsrooms. A knowledge of photography is desirable for those who aspire to positions in television. The successful newsman or newswoman must have curiosity, persistence, an interest in people, a good educational background and a knowledge of current events, an ability to write clearly and speedily, poise under pressure, and, if he is expected to read news copy, a voice of acceptable quality, inflection, and diction.

One of the most comprehensive lists of the qualifications radio newsmen should possess is that prepared by the Accrediting Committee of the American Council on Education for Journalism. The checklist was part of the Employee Appraisal Form sent to employers of graduates of schools or departments of journalism seeking accreditation. The committee asked employers to appraise the graduates on the basis of poor, below average, average, above average, and outstanding. Although prepared for radio news personnel, the list of qualifications is equally applicable to those working in television newsrooms. Some of the points covered follow.

The newsman must be able to gather and write news quickly and under pressure. He must be able to edit the stories of others, including wire copy. He must have the ability to find local angles in national stories and to simplify complex matters and make them meaningful. He should quickly recognize feature angles in routine stories. If he reads his own copy on the air, he must do so with an acceptable voice.

Responsibility is a prime characteristic of the good newsman. He must be familiar with all laws applicable to broadcasting, including copyright, libel, and slander. In the handling of news, he must be well aware of broadcasting's responsibilities to the public and exercise judgment and good taste in selecting news items.

His must be a well-rounded knowledge that includes familiarity with general broadcast operations, including mechanical problems, and interest in current electronic developments and research methods. He must be familiar with the various techniques of newscasting, including first-person reporting, wire recordings, on-the-scene live broadcasts, and interviews. And he should know all about production matters such as the timing of a script, the placing of commercials, rehearsal, and coordination of the efforts of the newscaster, commercial announcer, and engineer.

An announcer must possess many of these same qualifications. In addition, he should have a pleasant and well-controlled voice, a good sense of timing, and excellent pronunciation. His English usage must be correct, and he should keep abreast of sports, music, current events, and the like. In television, high standards of personal appearance must be met. An announcer should be a convincing salesman in presenting commercials and he should have a flair for showmanship. The ability to react quickly and imaginatively in unusual situations is important.

The television program director must have a comprehensive knowledge of all of the production techniques entailed in staging a performance before cameras and microphones, such as sets, graphics, script, makeup, lighting, music, and the like. He must be a master of detail and know how to work with all kinds of people.

The film director must have the same broad background as the director in TV, but he must also be acquainted with the special characteristics of film, including types of emulsions, camera limitations, special sound recording problems, and lab processing techniques. Often he must be both a writer and director.

The ideal advertising salesman is an enthusiastic, personable extrovert with a knack for making friends and a keen business mind that enables him to evaluate the needs of a particular firm and come up with a carefully planned program of television or radio advertising that will sell goods and services. He must be well trained in the basic functioning of advertising and must keep abreast of general business as well as media developments.

The copy and continuity writer, of course, must be a word craftsman, able to set a mood or epitomize a situation with a paucity of expression. He too must be well informed about the entire business of television or radio advertising.

The best promotion manager is an experienced journalist and an idea man. He can write news and advertising copy or dream up a publicity gimmick. He can design a highly complex campaign to project a favorable image for his station. He should know typography, layout, writing, editing, and public speaking and have a full awareness of public relations principles and practices.

SUMMARY

Television and radio stations virtually blanket the United States. Audience surveys repeatedly confirm the strong appeal of the broadcast media. More than 228,000,000 radio sets are in operation in homes, public places, and automobiles, and the number of television sets in use has climbed almost to 61,000,000. It's truly big business, for television stations and networks annually gross close to $1,400,000,000 and radio stations and networks gross well over $700,000,000 from time sales.

The broadcast media have made these spectacular advances, altering the basic pattern of American living, within only the last half-century or so. The development of radio from the first general public broadcasts about 1920 has been characterized by the growth of four large networks and numerous regional chains, extensive ownership of stations by newspapers, a prolonged battle with newspapers for the right to broadcast news, and the establishment of strong controls by the Federal Communications Commission.

Television has made equally impressive advances within only a decade or so. Recent developments, including global telecasting via space satellites, the spread of broadcasting in other countries, the introduction of pay television, the growth of community antenna TV systems, and the pending increase in the number of Ultra High Frequency stations, threaten to revolutionize television's already volatile world.

Both television and radio provide functions that are of an informational, entertainment, educational, advertising, and propaganda value. News is one of the chief commodities of the media; hundreds of stations have developed staffs skilled in the gathering, writing, and broadcasting of news programs.

The airing of station editorials developed largely in the late 1950's after the FCC reversed an earlier ruling that the broadcast media could not exercise the opinion function historically filled by the press.

The National Association of Broadcasters and the Radio-Television News Directors Association have outlined standards of operation to which they hope all stations will aspire. Frowned upon are practices that tend to distort the news and deceive audiences. Both groups have expressed pleasure that the majority of stations broadcast factual, objective, and timely news and in so doing perform a high public service.

The hundreds of job openings that occur each year within the industry are filled largely by men and women educated in schools and departments of speech, journalism, and communications. Salary scales have been advancing so that production and performing personnel earn from $5200 to $9000 or more, with station managers averaging from $19,000 to $39,000 annually.

Almost all of the jobs in broadcasting are so highly specialized that specific personal attributes as well as particularized training are required for each duty assignment. A broad liberal education, however, is equally as essential as special training for advancement to the top positions.

STUDY QUESTION

In what ways have television and radio affected (a) other media and (b) American life in general?

PROJECTS

1. Tune in three television or radio newscasts and write a 300-word comparison of their content and method of presentation.

2. Write a 500-word comparison of the techniques of newsgathering and writing employed by television and radio stations, newspapers, and news magazines.

3. Read a recent issue of *Broadcasting* and write a brief report of an article that pertains to one of the points made in this chapter.

CHAPTER 11

MAGAZINES

THE ROLE OF MAGAZINES

Much communication of ideas, information, and attitudes among the American people is carried on through magazines. Hundreds of periodicals fall within this category, ranging from the slick paper picture weekly with circulation in the millions down to the small special interest quarterly which, though virtually unknown to the general public, may have very strong influence within its field.

The magazine exists to inform, entertain, and influence its readers editorially and to put before them the advertising messages of national or regional commercial organizations. With a few exceptions, its outlook is national in scope rather than local. Magazines never appear more frequently than once a week; thus they have more time to dig into issues and situations than the daily newspaper, and consequently they have a better opportunity to bring events into focus and interpret their meaning.

So many different types of magazines exist that making broad statements about their functions and goals may lead to inconsistencies. Some are published solely for their entertainment value and are loaded with material of little consequence. Others deal entirely with a serious investigation of contemporary problems, and many combine entertainment and service material with reporting and interpretation. It is valid to state that magazines have a much better opportunity than newspapers to serve as thoughtful interpreters and analysts of events and trends.

The men who create and write for magazines stand back a little further from the tumbling immediacy of events than do newspaper reporters and editors. Often the magazine writer moves into a situation as the spot news reporter hastens on to something new.

In the case of a mine disaster, for example, the newspaper stories tell of men trapped, the rescue efforts, and the emotional scenes above ground as the families await word of survivors. If at some later date there is an official investigation of the causes of the disaster, the newspaper will cover that, too, but by this time the urgency of the story has dimmed and the headlines go to some new event. The magazine writer, with more time at his disposal and more space in which to develop background information, may spend weeks investigating all aspects of the disaster and gathering much information the newspaper reporter had no time to search out. The result may be a magazine article that brings the entire mine situation into focus and perhaps leads to reforms in mine safety procedures.

Each man has done his job equally well, but they are different jobs. The magazine writer probes the "why" of a situation and is an interpreter of events far more than a newspaperman can be. Occasionally, of course, a newspaper reporter is given the same amount of time to do his research.

The magazine with its more durable cover and bound pages has a semipermanence which the newspaper lacks. Magazines such as the *National Geographic* often are kept around a home for years, or passed from hand to hand. They are halfway between newspapers and books in this regard and also in content. Broadly speaking, the magazine examines a situation from the middle distance, and the book examines it from the higher ground of historical perspective.

There is another basic difference between newspapers and magazines. A newspaper must appeal to an entire community and have a little of everything for almost everybody. With a few exceptions, like the *Wall Street Journal*, a newspaper cannot be aimed at a single special interest group and survive. Yet hundreds of successful magazines are designed for reading by such limited-interest groups as gasoline station operators, dentists, poultry farmers, and model railroad fans. Therein lies the richness of diversity that makes the magazine field so attractive to many editorial workers. The possibilities for the specialist editor and writer are greater than on newspapers, although the total number of editorial jobs on magazines is less.

TYPES OF MAGAZINES

Generalizations about content, style, and appearance of American magazines are dangerous because so many variations exist among the approximately 8000 periodicals now being published. That is the number given in Ayer's *Directory,* as distinguished from listings of newspapers with general circulations. Not all of the 8000 appear in magazine format, however; quite a few are tabloid or regular newspaper size. No more than 600 can be classified as general interest magazines. In contrast, there are 2500 specialized business and trade publications, 1500 in the field of religion, and about 800 agricultural periodicals, to list three major subfields. Not included in these figures are some 9000 industrial, or company, publications designed for employees, customers, stockholders, dealers, and others. Many of these are issued in magazine format. Although all magazines share certain basic problems of production and distribution, their editorial content and advertising are of a hundred hues. Even trying to group them into categories becomes difficult because inevitably there is overlapping, and a few magazines almost defy classification.

A glance at the magazine rack in the corner drugstore shows what a kaleidoscopic outpouring of periodicals is being offered to the public. These are only a fraction of the magazines being published today. In fact, judging the magazine field by the publications available on general newsstands would be a grave error. The preponderance on the racks of so-called men's, fan, and "girlie" magazines, which survive only by sex-ridden headlines and other sensational newsstand-sale techniques, gives the casual observer the impression that magazines are a shoddy lot of trivia. This is untrue. Fortunately what appears on the stands is only a small segment of American magazine publishing. Many of the best and most significant ones are difficult to find on public racks because they are sold primarily by subscription or are distributed to special audiences.

Most magazines fall into these general categories:

General interest. Four mass circulation magazines which sell 6,000,000 or more copies per issue dominate this group. They are aimed at the entire population and are edited to appeal to the interests of everyone, man and woman alike. One, the *Saturday Evening Post,* contains both fiction and nonfiction. The largest in circulation of the four, the *Reader's Digest,* concentrates on informative and entertaining nonfiction. The other two are the heavily pictorial periodicals, *Life* and *Look,* which blend textual material with elaborate photographic layouts. Closest competitor to these four is *Redbook,* which has a circulation of about 4,000,000 copies. When someone mentions the word magazine, these mass circulation mixtures of information and entertainment with their heavy volume of colorful advertising usually are the first to come to mind.

News Magazines. These weekly publications are designed to summarize the news and provide background, adding depth and interpretation that most newspapers cannot give. They publish articles on news situations, examine headline personalities, and discuss trends in such diverse fields as religion, labor, sports, and art. Atop this potpourri they sprinkle a spice of predictions about things to come and give "inside" tips.

The present group of news magazines got its start with the appearance of *Time* under the direction of Henry Luce and Briton Hadden in 1923. *Time* introduced a bright, flippant narrative style of news reporting, which includes a strong editorial viewpoint in its coverage. A more staid and conservative predecessor, the *Literary Digest,* was once an American household word. It ceased publication after a long slump that was climaxed by the monumental mishap of publishing a supposedly accurate national straw poll on the 1936 presidential campaign, predicting the election of Alfred Landon to the White House. Landon was overwhelmingly defeated by Franklin D. Roosevelt, winning only 2 of 48 states, and the magazine never recovered from this blow to its accuracy.

Leaders in the news magazine field are *Time,* with a circulation close to 3,000,000, *Newsweek* at 1,750,000, and *U.S. News & World Report,* above 1,300,000.

Quality magazines. Although their circulations do not approach those of the mass appeal periodicals, a group of serious-minded publications offers high-level reporting, opinion, or fiction to the general public. Such magazines as *Atlantic, Harper's, Saturday Review,* and the *New Yorker* explore subjects in a thoughtful manner with emphasis upon literary, ethical, social, and political problems. Those which include fiction choose stories primarily for their literary merit rather than for entertainment and romantic value. Their circulations are substantial, ranging from 465,000 for the *New Yorker* and 375,000 for *Saturday Review* to 275,000 each for *Atlantic* and *Harper's.*

There also are smaller, more combative magazines of opinion, like the *Reporter* and the older *Nation* and *New Republic,* which were once more famous than they now are. Periodicals of this type, important in the United States at the turn of the century, have not maintained the influence that they have in Great Britain and the European countries.

Women's interest. Many of the largest, most successful magazines are aimed straight at the woman reader. Men who happen to pick up the *Ladies' Home Journal, McCall's,* or *Good Housekeeping,* to mention a few of the long-time leaders in the feminine field, feel as though they have accidentally opened the wrong door. The inside of a woman's magazine is a world of fashions, food, beauty hints, homemaking advice, inspiration, frank talks about personal problems, and emotional fiction. By the mid-1960's *McCall's* passed the 8,000,000 circulation point and *Ladies' Home Journal* exceeded 7,000,000.

At a time when most women's pages of newspapers were filled with stereotyped "society" news, the editors of women's magazines began to experiment. They quit publishing stilted love stories and flattering articles about the activities of social queens and used their space to serve the personal interests of women as a whole. They found that women in every category of life were interested in much the same things—how to improve themselves physically and emotionally and how to be better homemakers and career women. On this formula some of the country's greatest magazine successes have been built.

Another group of women's magazines, edited on a lower level, is aimed at the feminine desire to escape the humdrum of everyday life. These are the publications of romantic fiction, some of them published under the guise of "real life" stories. The movie and TV fan magazines, with their purported "inside" stories about the lives and loves of popular entertainment figures, are designed for the same market. Although these publications draw sneers from the critics and many better-educated readers, some of them have huge circulations. Their brand of glamorized escapism fills a need in the lives of many women.

Still a third group of women's magazines concentrates on special categories of feminine interest and age groups, such as *Vogue* and *Harper's Bazaar* in fashions and *Seventeen*.

Men's interest. Some magazines are aimed just as firmly at masculine readership. None of them reaches the circulation level of the most popular women's magazines. Men's magazines fall into two major categories: those concerned primarily with sports and he-man adventure and those which emphasize urbane sophistication, liberally illustrated with pictures of girls wearing as little as postal regulations permit. Among the leaders in sports are *Sports Illustrated, Sports Afield,* and *Field and Stream;* in the rugged masculine category, the leading magazines are *True* and *Argosy.* For many years *Esquire* set the pace in the sophisticated field, offering a mixture of high-quality articles and fiction, men's fashions and sexy drawings. More recently it has become more conservative—the metamorphosis that frequently follows success in the mass media field—and has come closer to the quality group in editorial tone. Its place in the barber shop magazine rack has been taken by the more uninhibited *Playboy* and its rash of imitators. *Playboy* has been a phenomenon of the 1960's, a mixture of nude photographs, articles and stories, and rather pompous editorials based on a hedonistic philosophy. Even on newsstands which carry no other "girlie" magazines, *Playboy* always seems to have a prominent place.

Also important in the men's field are the mechanical and how-to-do-it magazines such as the perennial favorites *Popular Mechanics* and *Popular Science,* each with a circulation well above a million. Science fiction magazines also had a vogue for some years.

Special interest magazines. The hundreds of periodicals aimed at special audiences form a very large segment of the magazine industry. Some are little known to the general public because they are infrequently displayed on the newsstands; others fall in major circulation categories.

The latter type includes the "shelter" magazines about family living, headed by *Better Homes and Gardens* and *American Home;* farm magazines like *Farm Journal* and *Successful Farming;* and such diverse-interest publications as *National Geographic, Scientific American* and *Science Digest,* and the Negro magazines, *Ebony* and *Jet.* In the world of business and trade publications, issued often by specialized publishing houses, there are such leaders as McGraw-Hill's *Business Week* and *Electrical World;* Fairchild's *Women's Wear Daily;* Chilton's *Iron Age;* and *Advertising Age* and *Modern Medicine.* Others include trade and technical journals, professional and scientific publications, and publications aimed at readers with hobbies such as boating, model railroading, or stamp collecting. Religious magazine publishing is an influential and important field. There are both denominational and nondenominational publications, the largest of which—*Presbyterian Life, Catholic Digest,* and the *Christian Herald*—circulate to hundreds of thousands of readers.

Although the "glamour" names of the magazine world get the most public attention, the size and influence of some less commonly mentioned periodicals are large. The rise of the supermarket as a magazine sales outlet has led to development of such periodicals as *Everywoman's Family Circle Magazine,* with a guaranteed circulation of 7,000,000 over grocery counters, and *Woman's Day* with more than 6,000,000 copies. *Boy's Life,* sponsored by the Boy Scouts of America, has a circulation of

2,000,000 and *Parents' Magazine* has about the same. *TV Guide,* designed to help the average viewer choose his programs, circulates more than 9,000,000 copies. The staid *National Geographic* has risen to the 4,000,000 mark.

Hardly a form of human endeavor or recreational interest exists without at least one magazine entering it. As a small sample of the fields covered, there are magazines published weekly or monthly on bowling, industrial photography, motel management, skiing, office procedures, hot-rod racing, newspaper editing, trailer living, architecture, the desert, antique collecting, and dentistry. Many of these specialized magazines are edited and produced with the same high professional polish to be found in the better-known consumer periodicals.

Sunday supplement magazines. Among the magazines with the greatest circulation are those distributed as part of the Sunday newspapers in many large American cities. *This Week* reports a circulation of more than 13,000,000; *Parade,* above 12,000,000; and *Family Weekly,* 4,500,000.

These magazines are edited for the entire family with a mixture of humor, self-improvement, human interest, entertaining short fiction, and inspiration. They are sold to the subscribing newspapers on a bulk wholesale rate and have been instrumental in building the sales figures of the newspapers which use them. The magazines have enjoyed growing success and influence in recent years, partly because they have kept their editorial content in step with the upsurge in suburban living.

Company publications. These are magazines published by corporations for distribution to their employees and customers, usually without charge. Their purpose is to present the company's policy and products in a favorable light and to promote a better sense of teamwork and "belonging" among the employees. They are known also as individual magazines; the term "house organ" which once was widely used for them has fallen into disfavor.

This field of industrial publishing has made large advances as corporations have become more conscious of their public relations. Many of these company publications are edited by men widely experienced in general magazine work, who have been given ample funds to produce magazines of sophisticated appearance and high-grade editorial content. More and more companies are coming to the realization that they must hire professional people and set their standards to compare with general magazines on a broad basis. As one leading industrial editor, himself a veteran of general magazine staffs, expressed it, "No longer can the mail clerk or the personnel manager be regarded as an authority in the field of industrial editing. The emphasis definitely is on editing—and on journalism." When hiring staff members, the editors of the better industrial magazines give particular attention to men and women who have strong newspaper writing and editing backgrounds. As the field of industrial editing grows, it can be expected to draw with increasing frequency upon well-trained newspaper people who wish to move on into another related field. Some journalism graduates move directly into industrial editing.   In many such publications articles of general interest, unrelated to the company's products, are included, and company "propaganda" is kept at a very subdued level. Some large corporations, in fact, publish a number of magazines aimed variously at customers, stockholders, and employees. For example, the International Harvester Company of Chicago has 23 employee magazines at different plants; the Ford Motor Company publishes 21. Some of the more elaborate company publications, intended to reach the public as well as employees, have circulations above a million.

Company publications are of many sizes and shapes, and it is difficult to say at any given time how many of them qualify as magazines. Many appear in newspaper format. One recent estimate put the combined circulation of major company periodicals above 100,000,000. American business and industry invests more than $500,000,000 a year in these publications.

HOW MAGAZINES ARE MARKETED

The magazine industry rests upon twin foundations, circulation and advertising. General practice is for the publisher to sell each copy to the reader for less money than it costs to produce it. He closes this gap and makes his profit through the sale of national advertising. Failure of the magazine to attract and hold advertising is fatal and accounts for the disappearance of several well-known magazines during the past quarter-century.

Since hundreds of magazines, plus other media, are competing for the advertiser's dollars, the successful publisher must convince the advertiser that purchase of space in his pages is a good investment. This proof is based largely upon his circulation figures. Either he must show very large mass distribution figures among a general readership or a firmly established circulation among the special interest group to which his publication appeals editorially.

These economic principles have a powerful influence on the entire shape of the magazine industry. A magazine either must be designed for appeal to a well-defined segment of the population, such as outboard boating enthusiasts or members of a fraternal order, or it must be of such broad interest that it will attract huge numbers of general readers. In the latter category, the circulation figures of the leading magazines run high into the millions.

Reader's Digest, founded and long directed by DeWitt Wallace, is among the most fabulously successful magazine ventures of the twentieth century with a circulation of 15,000,000 copies for its basic domestic monthly edition plus another 11,000,000 for its overseas editions. *Reader's Digest* started the trend toward pocket-size magazines. For many years it was published without advertising, almost alone in this respect among consumer magazines. But the rising costs of production that have plagued all publishers eventually caught up even with this giant, and it now sells advertising space. Many lesser magazines are created in just the opposite way: the publisher sees a field of special interest in which he judges that sufficient advertising support can be developed and so brings out a magazine aimed at that audience.

Recent studies show about 50 magazines with circulations of more than 1,000,000. *McCall's, Look,* and *Life* are in the 7–8,000,000 bracket; *Saturday Evening Post, Ladies' Home Journal,* and *Better Homes and Gardens* in the 6–7,000,000 class. *Good Housekeeping* is at the 5,000,000 level, and *Redbook* and *National Geographic* at 4,000,000. The *Farm Journal, American Home,* and *Time* are in the 3,000,000 group. Rising population in the United States makes the big publishers hopeful of even greater circulation figures in the next decade. They constantly seek to increase their circulation by costly sales promotion devices and editorial and advertising research programs in which students with advanced degrees in mass communications are finding significant and lucrative careers.

The death of several mass circulation magazines such as *Collier's, Coronet,* and *American* in recent years has created the false impression in some quarters that hard times have hit the big magazine field. The figures just quoted and other evidence, such as all-time record revenues, show that this is not the case. Individual magazines have suffered because of changing public tastes and marketing conditions, but the general interest magazine field as a whole is in healthy condition. Editors have had to make major changes in content to counteract the element of fictional entertainment brought into the lives of their readers by the television screen. Extremely heavy production and distribution costs mean that when a major magazine gets out of step with the reading public's tastes, it either dies or, like the *Saturday Evening Post,* goes through many vicissitudes in trying to solidify its audience.

Hundreds of smaller magazines operate profitably year after year by concentrating in their special fields. Since advertising rates are based largely upon circulation, many advertisers cannot afford to buy space in magazines with circulations in the millions, where the rate for a single black-and-white advertising page sometimes exceeds $20,000. Instead they spend their money in publications they can afford and which offer them an audience especially adapted to their products. To counteract this, some of the mass circulation giants are offering advertising space on a regional split-run basis (*Reader's Digest,* for example, now carries advertising for just the copies sold in the New York area) or on a fractional-run basis (*Saturday Evening Post,* for example, will carry an ad in every third copy of its entire circulation). But the competition among types of magazines is intense.

These marketing conditions encourage group publication of magazines. Rather than put its financial eggs in a single basket, a publishing firm brings out magazines in several fields, using common management facilities for all. This has created several extremely powerful magazine empires, of which the largest are Time Inc., the Curtis Publishing Company, and the Hearst chain.

The Curtis Publishing Company's wealth and prestige were built around its two periodicals with circulations in the millions, *Saturday Evening Post* and *Ladies' Home Journal.* For many years this company was the dominant one in the consumer magazine field, leading both in circulation and advertising. As it lost momentum it disposed of *Country Gentleman* and added *Holiday,* a luxurious travel magazine; *Jack and Jill* for children, and *American Home.* But management difficulties and competitive pressures turned its once large profits into losses in the early 1960's despite the still great circulations of the *Post* and *Journal* and its problems still remained intense at the start of 1965. Curtis recorded losses of nearly $40,000,000 in the years 1961 to 1964, with the *Post* losing some seven of the nine millions deficit for 1964, and in desperation the company ordered the *Post* cut to a biweekly (26 issues) in 1965. It also looked toward diversification, by entering the broadcasting field, as a means of saving the magazine empire.

For a long time a leading rival in the general magazine field was the Crowell-Collier Co., whose list of publications was headed by *Collier's, Woman's Home Companion,* and the *American Magazine.* However, Crowell-Collier encountered financial difficulties after World War II and closed all its magazines, to the dismay of millions of readers who had looked upon them as household friends.

Biggest of all magazine publishers today, in terms of total income, is Time Inc. Started in the early 1920's, when *Time* made its shaky appearance with a new style of news magazine, this corporation has grown spectacularly. Its picture weekly, *Life,* has held top place among all magazines in gross advertising revenue since the 1950's, and *Time* now ranks third (behind *Look*). The firm also publishes *Fortune,* devoted to the business world, and *Sports Illustrated.*

The Hearst magazine group is affiliated with that newspaper publishing family's empire. The chain includes such large and profitable properties as *Good Housekeeping, Cosmopolitan, Harper's Bazaar, Popular Mechanics, Sports Afield,* and *House Beautiful.* Its group of more than a dozen publications also lists magazines in the motoring, medical, and leisure fields.

Other major groups include the McGraw-Hill trade publications, headed by *Business Week;* the McCall Corporation, with *McCall's* and *Redbook;* Meredith Publishing Company, with *Better Homes and Gardens* and *Successful Farming;* Cowles Magazines, with *Look, Family Circle,* and *Venture;* and Condé Nast publications, led by *Glamour, Vogue, Mademoiselle,* and *House and Garden.*

In some of the smaller group publishing operations, the same man will edit two or more magazines. Sometimes a company will publish three or four periodicals in the same field, such as crime or confessions, diverting manuscripts from one to another to fill its formula requirements.

Magazines are sold by two principal methods, single copy sales on newsstands and mail delivery of copies to subscribers. Mass circulation magazines consider newsstand sales more important than subscriptions. Some trade publications are distributed free of charge to controlled lists in order to give the advertiser a large audience for his product. Circulation is one of the most costly and complex problems a magazine publisher faces. Copies of each issue must be distributed nationwide and must be on sale by fixed dates each week or month. Copies unsold when the publication date for the next issue comes around must be discarded at heavy loss.

Newsstand sales of magazines are handled through news wholesalers. Intricate arrangements and "deals" are made to assure good display at outlets, since many sales are made on the buyer's impulse as he walks past the colorful array on the racks. This makes attractive cover design and provocative, attention-getting titles and sales catchlines on the covers extremely important. Even the conservative quality magazines have entered the battle for newsstand sales with brighter colors and more compelling headlines. Out of this scramble for attention came that American phenomenon, the cover girl, whose voluptuous charms are credited with selling millions of magazines. Some periodicals operate entirely on street sales whereas others, especially among the trade and professional fields, are sold predominantly by subscription. Consumer magazines as a whole probably get slightly more than half their sales from subscriptions. Across the United States there are more than 110,000 retail magazine sales outlets, many of them in supermarkets.

Unlike newspapers, a large majority of magazines do not own their own printing facilities. The editors and advertising staffs prepare each issue in their office and then send the material to a commercial printer who holds a contract to produce the magazine. In fact, a few large printing houses with high-speed color presses do the printing for most of the major national magazines. This freedom from the heavy initial investment in printing equipment enables new publishers to start magazines with limited capital; however, unless the new venture embodies an attractive basic idea or "angle," and is well edited, the printing and circulation bills can soon eat up the adventurous newcomer's capital. Although there are notable examples of successful magazines starting on small sums, even in these days of high costs, the odds against success with a national magazine by a new publisher are great. New publications created by established publishers are always preceded by detailed research of the market possibilities and extensive promotion.

Because of the necessity for quick nationwide delivery, some magazines are printed and distributed regionally. The plates are prepared at a central plant and then flown to presses in several parts of the country for simultaneous printing. Thus identical copies can be delivered to sub-scribers in New York and Los Angeles on Tuesday morning, although they came off presses situated 3000 miles apart. Some magazines handle overseas editions similarly.

ADVERTISING AND PROMOTION

Magazine advertising has played a significant role in the growth of the American economy and the distribution of consumer goods. Many manu-facturers have concentrated their advertising budgets in the magazines for two reasons: the periodicals have nationwide distribution, thus carry-ing the story of an advertiser's product from coast to coast, and by use of color printing processes on smooth paper stock magazines are able to present more alluring advertisements than newspapers can on their coarser, uncoated paper.

Use of selected newspapers enables an advertiser to pinpoint his market areas across the country, whereas magazine advertising gives him a general nationwide audience. A major corporation introducing a new product frequently uses both media, providing different copy and layouts to fit each; television programs and radio spot announcements are used simultaneously with the printed advertisements if the company can afford such a mammoth expenditure. This technique is used by automobile manufacturers to introduce their new models.

The other important advantage of magazines as advertising outlets is their ability to provide the advertiser with special interest audiences. The other media cannot do this, except in a very limited way.

For those who desire to build a career on the business side of publish-ing, magazines provide job opportunities in advertising selling and circu-lation, as well as in sales promotion. The promotion department utilizes the findings of the commercial research department to exploit the maga-zine as an advertising medium and handles major promotion and pub-licity campaigns. Salaries for jobs in these business departments are very attractive.

EDITORIAL CONTENT AND OPERATION

The editorial content of American magazines is predominantly nonfiction. About three-fourths of the material printed in consumer periodicals is factual, and the percentage is even higher in the trade and professional journals. Many magazines carry no fiction at all.

From decade to decade the public's mood and tastes change. Through readership studies, magazine editors try to keep abreast of this shifting interest and to alter the content of their publications accordingly. A study of nine major general interest magazines reported by Jerome Ellison and Franklin T. Gosser in *Journalism Quarterly* shows that in the decade from 1947 to 1957 a pronounced increase occurred in the number of articles on personal management, both physical and spiritual. Several of the magazines showed an increase in the number of first-person experience stories published. Cultural subjects and personality sketches were also popular throughout the period examined. The style of writing in the magazines is predominantly narrative.

Editorial operation of magazines varies greatly, depending upon the size, type, and frequency of the publication. Generally, editorial staffs are relatively small. As an example, *This Week* with more than 13,000,000 circulation has an editorial staff of 50. A magazine selling 4,000,000 copies can be prepared editorially by a smaller staff than the one needed to put out a newspaper which sells a half-million copies. This is possible because much of the material published in many magazines is written by free-lance writers, either on speculation or on order from the editors. These writers are paid fees for their work and do not function as members of the staff.

The magazine editor's job is to decide what kind of material he wants to publish, arrange to obtain it, and then present it in his "book" in a manner pleasing to the reader's eye. Most editors work from a formula; that is, each issue contains specified types of material in predetermined amounts, arranged to give a desired effect. Articles and stories are selected for publication not only on their merit but for the way they fit the formula.

The editor has a staff of assistants to screen free-lance material, work with writers, think up ideas, and edit the material chosen for publication. An art director arranges attractive layouts and chooses the covers. A cartoon editor selects such drawings if the periodical carries them. On many magazines a substantial portion of each issue is written by staff members.

The skillful, imaginative use of photojournalism has contributed heavily to the acceptance gained by many magazines in recent years.

Combining technical efficiency with an appreciation of the aesthetic and the dramatic, the photojournalist is an able communicator with a camera. He performs his art as powerfully for the advertiser as for the editor. His work is best exemplified by the sequence of well-planned pictures that, combined with the correct proportion of textual material, tells a story with unified effectiveness. Most magazines have their own staffs of professional photojournalists, but free-lance photographers, often working through agents, provide many striking pictures. Rates range in excess of $300 per page for black-and-white pictures, $400 for color pages, and $500 for cover shots. Charges may be assessed for time taken in shooting the pictures at rates in excess of $100 per day. Picture editors make assignments and select the photos wanted for publication.

A key part of most magazine operations is the editorial conference, a session in which the editors discuss the forthcoming issue, make decisions on the material to be used, examine proposed layouts, and agree upon projects for future issues. Magazine projects frequently are planned months in advance of publication. On some staffs one editor makes the decisions on nonfiction ideas and articles and another is responsible for the selection of fiction. Details of editorial procedure vary from one magazine to another, depending upon the type of contents, size of the staff, and personality of the chief editor.

The news magazines operate somewhat differently. All their content is written by staff members, who are responsible for designated categories of material and for specific assignments, somewhat like a newspaper. Bureaus around the country submit material as ordered from the home office, which then is rewritten and condensed to fit the available space. The magazines also lean heavily upon press association material. News magazines operate on a rigid schedule in order to put the latest information on the newsstands throughout the United States.

A problem that news magazine editors and writers face is "writing around" the time lag between the closing of the editorial forms and actual distribution of the magazines to the public. There is constant danger that a late development on a major story will make part of the magazine's contents look outdated, even ridiculous. Regional printing his reduced this time lag considerably.

Most magazines have at their command large amounts of free-lance material submitted by writers who hope to "strike it lucky" and sell their work for a substantial sum. As most editors will testify, a relatively small amount of the unsolicited material unloaded on their desks by the mail-man each day ever reaches print. Not that most of it necessarily is badly written or devoid of fresh ideas, but much of it does not fit the magazine's formula. Either it covers a subject the editor does not regard as suitable for his audience, is not written in the style he seeks in order to give his publication "character," or is about a subject similar to something the magazine has run recently. An article rejected for publication in one magazine may be purchased immediately by another. The problem for the free-lance writer is to have the right manuscript in the right editorial office at the right moment—not an easy task. Professional writers usually submit their articles in outline form or just a brief writeup of the idea.

Since editors have found that they cannot depend upon unsolicited free-lance material to fit their individual needs, they go in search of what they want. They assign article ideas to writers they know, and then work with them until the manuscripts have the desired flavor and approach. Or the idea might be assigned to a member of the staff and developed in the same manner.

The volume of unsolicited manuscripts submitted to the large consumer magazines like the *Saturday Evening Post* is immense, and many editorial man-hours are required to screen it. The mass of free-lance material is at once the burden and the salvation of the magazine editor: it is the raw material which must be examined and reported upon quickly, and from which he occasionally draws fresh stories and new talent. The *Post* receives nearly 100,000 free-lance manuscripts a year; other consumer magazines receive from 5000 such unsolicited manuscripts upward.

Very few men in the United States, perhaps only 250 or 300, make a living as full-time, free-lance magazine writers. Probably fewer than a hundred of them earn $10,000 a year. Although an established writer may be paid from $1000 upward per article, the uncertainties of the craft are many and the number of big money markets is relatively few. Most of these full-time magazine writers work largely on assignment, being commissioned by editors who know and like their work to prepare articles on ideas proposed by the editors or ideas approved by them. In many cases the free-lance writers use agents to sell their output to editors on a commission basis. Almost all fiction in big magazines is sold by agents, and many professional article writers use their services. The agent functions to a degree as an adjunct of the editorial staff; he screens the output of his clients, channeling the worth-while stories to appropriate magazines. The better-known agents are quite selective in the authors they will handle, and having a well-known agent is a helpful endorsement for a writer.

Even an assignment from an editor, faithfully carried out, does not assure that the article will be printed. It may be rejected at the last moment as "not quite what we had in mind" or the editor who ordered it may be replaced by someone who doesn't care for the idea. The vicissitudes are many in the life of a free-lance writer. It is normal practice for the magazine to pay for an article or a piece of fiction upon acceptance of the final draft.

Much of the contributed material published in magazines is written by men and women who do free-lance work on a part-time basis as a sideline to their regular occupation. Newspapermen, members of other mass media, teachers, attorneys and other professional men, even housewives with a flair for writing try their hands at free lancing with varying degrees of success.

There are hundreds of places where magazine material can be sold. Competition to place articles and fiction in the mass circulation magazines is intense, and the material purchased must be excellently written and extensively researched. Preparation of a major magazine article requires so much skill and time that the work for the top dozen magazines is done largely by the small group of full-time professionals and staff members. However, the part-time free lancer can hit even the biggest magazines with short material, such as anecdotes, personal experiences, and humor. With a little luck and a large amount of perseverance, a writer can sell numerous articles to smaller magazines and specialized periodicals. However, the pay in these smaller markets is not large, ranging from $50 for a 2500-word article or short story up to about $500. Rates of payment for the confession-type magazines are three to five cents a word. At the upper end of the scale, where the competition is intense, the mass circulation magazines pay from $1000 to $3000 or higher for an article. The rates are flexible because the editors will pay extra if they consider that the material is exactly right for them or if the writer has a well-known name worth publicizing on the cover. One of the best ways for the newcomer to break into the market is to submit short-item filler material for which many magazines pay $10 or more.

A successful magazine writer must do more than conceive fresh ideas and write good articles based on them; he also must be a close student of his market. "Study the magazine; see what type of material we use and how we present it," is the advice of editors to those who would write for them. It would be a waste of time and postage to send an article on fishing to a women's magazine, unless perhaps the writer could think up a feminine angle such as how a woman should behave if her husband invites her along on a fishing trip. The usual procedure on major articles is for the writer to query a magazine with his idea; then if the editor indicates interest, the author either submits a detailed outline or the complete article.

There also is a market for the sale of pictures by free-lance photographers to company and trade magazines.

JOB OPPORTUNITIES

The magazine industry provides interesting, stimulating, and generally well-paid jobs for thousands of men and women. On some periodicals the editorial staff members do extensive writing, handling special departments and articles, whereas on others the editors are engaged largely in selection and editing of submitted material.

Magazines offer larger opportunities for the woman editorial worker than newspapers do. The percentage of staff positions held by women is greater and the opportunity for advancement to high editorial positions is much brighter. Feminine associate editors, managing editors, and even editors-in-chief are not uncommon.

Although there is no certain formula for the man or woman college graduate to use in seeking a magazine job, the surest way to draw attention to yourself is to sell the magazine some articles or stories. The very fact that the editor buys the material shows that he approves of the writer's work. Personal contacts developed in this editor-writer relationship sometimes lead to staff positions. In some of the large magazines young men and women get their start in the research department and other jobs around the fringe of the editorial staff.

Large magazines draw many of their staff members from the trade magazines and company publications, much as metropolitan newspapers hire reporters who have had training on smaller dailies. The mechanical techniques of magazine editing and design are complex and can best be learned by experience on smaller publications.

Industrial magazines are among the finest training grounds for magazine workers. This is a rapidly expanding field, as more and more corporations realize the value of issuing a periodical for customers, employees, salesmen, stockholders, and other groups the management wishes to impress. These are divided into internal publications, for distribution within a company, and external ones, which go to nonemployee readers. Many are combinations of these approaches. The type of distribution influences the kind of editorial matter used and to some extent the size of the staff. The best available estimate puts the number of editorial employees on company publications around 15,000. Although many of these publications are prepared by a single editor, with clerical help, the more elaborate ones have a staff of six or eight editors. They use the same technique of design, multicolored art work, and editorial presentation as those employed by the better-known consumer magazines.

External publications usually are published by manufacturers who hope for repeat sales of their products of relatively high price. The automobile manufacturers are among the most lavish publishers in this field; magazines like the *Ford Times* and *Dodge News* are widely circulated to maintain contact with users and to promote sales and service.

Many fraternal and nonprofit organizations publish magazines, too, in order to maintain the bond with their members or supporters. Such periodicals as *American Legion* and the *Rotarian* publish a rather broad range of general articles which their editors consider of interest to their readers and interweave promotional and fraternal material about the sponsoring organization.

A college degree, or at least a partial college education, is almost essential for the editorial job applicant in the magazine field. Although quite a few industrial editors have moved into that work from other corporation departments, a recent survey shows that three out of four editors of these industrial magazines are college graduates. The percentage in consumer magazines is probably even higher.

Work on specialized magazines, both of the industrial magazine and trade varieties, sometimes requires technical knowledge in such fields as engineering, electronics, and chemistry. It is natural for a young man or woman seeking a job to enter whatever trade field holds particular interest for him or her. No matter what technical knowledge may be necessary, however, the fundamental requirement in all magazine work is a sound training in English. With this foundation and a willingness to work hard at learning the rudiments of a specialized field, the aspiring trade journal or industrial editor can progress steadily. A knack for simplifying technical material for the layman reader is a desirable asset. College courses in economics are valuable in almost any kind of magazine work because so much of the material printed in magazines deals in some way with the operations of American business. Many schools offer industrial and technical curricula to help their students prepare for industrial journalism.

Pay scales on magazines are generally attractive and rise to high figures for a small number of men and women in the top editorial positions of the mass circulation magazines. The chief editor of a major consumer magazine may receive a salary of at least $25,000 a year, going to more than $100,000, if he is a veteran with a proven "touch" or if he directs the work of a magazine group.

These high salaries carry with them a substantial amount of job uncertainty. If a magazine begins to lose circulation or advertising, frequently one of the first corrective moves is to change editors, even though the fault may not lie in the editorial department at all. When a magazine is struggling to work out a new formula to regain readership, it may try several editors before finding one who can do the job. The pay offered to college graduates as beginners is in line with that offered by other media.

Salaries in the trade and industrial magazine fields are somewhat lower but still good, and the job security is better. A recent survey by the International Council of Industrial Editors shows that about half of the company editors surveyed earn more than $500 a month. Salaries for industrial editors range to $15,000 a year or somewhat higher. The salaries received by editors of large farm publications range from $15,000 to $22,000.

Editorial and business offices of most large national magazines are in New York and other eastern cities. Trade publication headquarters are situated throughout the United States, depending in part upon the market being served. There are numerous editorial links between magazine and book publishing, since much magazine material eventually finds its way into book form. This leads to some movement of editorial workers from magazines to book publishing firms and occasionally back in the other direction. Many writers and editors move into magazine work from positions on newspapers; in fact, most magazine staff writers and editors have a background of newspaper work.

SUMMARY

Periodicals published weekly, monthly, or quarterly are a major channel of communication in American society. They give a more comprehensive interpretation of the world both in its contemporary aspects and in historical perspective than newspapers do, since their basic objectives are different.

Within the world of magazines there are many types of publications— those aimed at the mass general audience, those designed for special segments of the population such as trade, fraternal, religious, and professional groups, and the publications issued by commercial organizations to influence employees, customers, and other business associates.

Magazine publishers generally follow the practice of selling copies for less than it costs to produce them. Some trade periodicals even give away their copies to controlled circulation lists. The better a magazine's circulation, either in mass quantities or in coverage of a specialized market, the better chance it has to attract the national advertising that enables the publisher to operate at a profit.

The multiplicity of magazine types leads to large variations in editing procedures. Editorial material is drawn from two main sources, staff writers and free-lance contributors; despite the hundreds of articles, short stories, and serials published every month, only a few men and women make their living as free-lance magazine writers because of the uncertainties of the trade. The magazine writer must be a marketing expert for his wares as well as a literary craftsman.

Magazines provide an attractive field of employment for college graduates who have a flair for writing and editing, a knack for divining the public taste, and technical knowledge of the complex machinery of magazine production. The hundreds of specialized magazines and company magazines serve as a training ground for young men and women who later join the staffs of the large national periodicals.

Magazine publishing is an expanding field which has overcome the inroads of television and moved on to greater advertising and circulation records in the past decade. With an eye on the boom in the country's population and the rising level of education, publishers are optimistic about even more spectacular gains for the magazine industry in the coming decade.

STUDY QUESTION

How do magazines fit into the total scheme of things among the mass media? What are their advantages and disadvantages as compared with the other media?

PROJECTS

1. Examine a special-interest magazine and in a 300-word report discuss the type of reader for whom, judging by its articles and advertisements, the magazine apparently is intended.

2. Examine *Writer's Market* or another reference listing magazines in the United States and write a 300-word report describing the scope of the magazine field.

CHAPTER 12

BOOK PUBLISHING

THE ROLE OF BOOKS

Books are a medium of mass communication that deeply affect the lives of all of us. They convey much of the heritage of the past, help us understand ourselves and the world we live in, and enable us to plan better for the future. Books are a significant tool of our educational process. And they provide entertainment for people of every age.

The nation's educational, business, professional, and social life could not survive long without books. Judges and attorneys must examine law tomes continually; doctors constantly refer to the repositories of medical wisdom and experience; governmental officials must remain aware of all the ramifications of legislative fiat. Teachers and pupils alike find in textbooks the vast knowledge of history, philosophy, the sciences, literature, and the social sciences accumulated throughout the ages. Men and women in every walk of life read to keep abreast of a fast-changing world; to find inspiration, relaxation, and pleasure; and to gain knowledge. Books, without doubt, explain and interpret virtually every activity.

Creative writing has been one of the principal hallmarks by which each succeeding world civilization has been measured; the works of Plato and Aristotle, for example, both reflected and refined the quality of early Greek life. Social historians long have examined the creative literature as well as the factual records of a civilization in their efforts to reconstruct the life of the people of a particular time and place. In the United States today the finest published fiction has a reverberating impact upon our society; the ideas and the techniques employed have an enormous effect on the theater, movies, television scripts, and magazine pieces. Many outstanding productions result from the book publisher's enterprise in encouraging and promoting new as well as established authors. Creative writing enhances most of the art forms by which our civilization will one day be judged.

Books printed on quality paper with long-lasting ink and bound in hard covers provide a permanence that is characteristic of no other communications medium. The newspaperman and the radio-television commentator write and speak in the main to an ephemeral audience. Those who write for magazines may anticipate longer life for their messages. Books, however, such as the superb copies of the Bible produced by Gutenberg in the fifteenth century, have an almost endless existence.

Clarence Day put it so aptly: "The world of books is the most remarkable creation of man. Nothing else that he builds ever lasts. Monuments fall, nations perish, civilizations grow old and die out and, after an era of darkness, new races build others. But in the world of books are volumes that have seen this happen again and again and yet live on, still young, still as fresh as the day they were written, still telling men's hearts of the hearts of men centuries dead."

For the mass communicator, books and book publishing provide several important functions. They not only serve as well-springs of knowledge for him as for all men, but through translation and reprinting book publishing may convey his own ideas to billions of people throughout the world. And in the publishing trade itself the journalist may find a rewarding outlet for his skills in editing and promoting the distribution of books.

In the writing of books, journalists such as Lincoln Steffens, Vincent Sheean, Walter Lippmann, John Gunther, John Hersey, and William Allen White, to name only a few, have vastly increased the size of the audience for their reporting efforts and each has produced an impact in the world of ideas that almost invariably accompanies the creation of a widely read book.

Because of the relative slowness of writing, editing, and publishing a manuscript, books lack the characteristic of immediacy possessed by other media in conveying messages to the public. What may be lost in timeliness, however, is often more than compensated for by the extreme care possible in checking facts, attaining perspective, and rewriting copy for maximum effectiveness. This sustained, systematic exposition of a story or of an idea (with the reader's concomitant opportunity to reread, underscore, and study at leisure) is afforded only by books among all the media of communication.

Unlike most newspapers, but like many magazines, books may have a highly selective audience that makes it not only unnecessary but also undesirable to aim the communication at a fairly low common denominator of reading or listening ability. Nevertheless, authors and publishers definitely are engaged in mass communication, even though their efforts at times may be directed toward only a very small segment of the public.

A COMMON HERITAGE

Newspapers, magazines, and books had a common beginning and the paths to the attainment of their present central roles in civilization were beset by mutual problems pertaining to printing and distribution. The art of writing itself has been traced well beyond 4500 B.C. when the ancient Egyptians carved hieroglyphic, or pictograph, messages in stone and the Babylonians formed their wedge-shaped, or cuneiform, letters in clay tablets. In China scholars used ink made from tree sap to write on slips of bamboo or wood. The first books may possibly have consisted of a number of these bamboo slips, each about 9 inches long, tied together by a thong. When learned men such as the philosopher Me T had to load their bamboo books into several carts to transport them from place to place, it was apparent that a new writing material was needed. The Chinese are credited with the invention of paper, and Egypt later developed the first cheap writing material, made from papyrus plants growing along the Nile.

Europeans, however, did not begin making paper until the fourteenth century. Their books had been hand-written and illustrated on vellum or parchment, usually by the monks. Gutenberg's invention of movable type opened the door to the printing of books on paper, of which his famous Bible of 1456 is an example. Several million volumes came off European presses by 1500; this printing of books in large quantities paved the way for the religious reformation and made possible popular education.

Both books and newspapers, which developed as news books and broadsides, were considered threats to the authority of church and state. In England Henry VIII started the control of the press with a list of prohibited books in 1529. The censorship restrictions which continued until 1694 were aimed as much at books and pamphlets as at newspapers. The human target often was the same, for the occupations of bookselling and journalism were closely allied throughout the early period. The bookshop was the center of literary culture; the printer was often also the bookseller; it was he who got out the news broadsides and news books.

The heavy emphasis upon book advertising in early newspapers also testifies to the link.

Book and newspaper publishing were also closely identified in early United States history. The first book published in the American colonies came off the Puritans' Cambridge printing press in 1640. Early book publishing in each colony often was of a religious tone, but local histories were also produced. Then, as the journalists took over, the horizons widened. Benjamin Harris, who got out one issue of his *Publick Occurrences* in Boston in 1690, was a bookseller importing from London. Editors such as James and Benjamin Franklin had sizable libraries and reprinted literary material in their papers—including Daniel Defoe's *Robinson Crusoe*. The patriot journalist Isaiah Thomas was also an important book publisher; his shop at Worcester produced the first American novel, the first American dictionary, more than 400 technical books, and 100 children's books. Thomas was the first American to publish Blackstone's *Commentaries,* Bunyan's *Pilgrim's Progress,* and Defoe's *Robinson Crusoe* in book form. He himself wrote a two-volume history of American printing.

By 1820 more than 50,000 titles, including books, magazines, and newspapers, were listed as American. Readers were still buying 70 per cent of their books from European publishers even though American book publishing was increasing 10 per cent in a decade. Names such as Emerson, Thoreau, Poe, Cooper, and Whitman emerged in the realm of American literature, giving both books and magazines a great lift, even though English writers such as Dickens remained favorites. By 1850 and later some publishing houses, including Harper's and Scribner's, were active in both the book and magazine fields. Book publishing, however, came to require distinctively specialized equipment and editing knowledge, and the two areas of book publishing and journalism gradually became separate.

The great cultural stirring following the Civil War brought a sharp expansion of both scholarly book publishing and publication of literary and popular books. Works in science, history, and philosophy came from the presses along with millions of encyclopedias and even more dime novels. Free public libraries, spreading across the country after 1880, played an important part in stimulating book publishing and reading. Henry James, Mark Twain, and William Dean Howells became leading names in American literature. At the turn of the century the "muckrakers" produced books as well as countless newspaper and magazine articles to expose instances of corruption and greed in American life— among them were Lincoln Steffens, Jack London, Frank Norris, and Upton Sinclair. Thus the print media continued to share a common background in their use by American writers to discuss the social, political, and economic problems of each generation. Social historians must examine all the print media to gain a full understanding of the development of our civilization.

THE SCOPE OF BOOK PUBLISHING

Today, book publishing is a pygmy among American industrial giants; it represents only a tiny fraction of the country's more than $600 billion economy. Yet some 1,200,000,000 books and approximately 20,000 new titles are now produced each year by more than 1500 publishing firms. Actually, some 300 publishers bring out 90 per cent of these titles, with no more than two dozen firms accounting for two-thirds of the grand total. In general (trade) publishing, fewer than 5 per cent of hardbound books sell more than 5000 copies in the life of the particular title.

Because of the availability of all types of specialized services, most publishing companies are concentrated in the eastern seaboard cities of New York, Boston, and Philadelphia.

Textbook publishing produces almost one-third of the industry's annual gross income of almost $1,700,000,000. It is estimated that 275,000,000 new textbooks are sold each year. About 290,000,000 copies of hard-cover adult general trade books are sold annually through bookstores and book clubs, and by direct mail. Children's books sell close to 140,000,000 copies.

Book publishing offers a number of intriguing specialties. Many publishers concentrate successfully in special areas. Medical, religious, garden, law, music, and art books, mystery stories, westerns—all may constitute special departments of publishing firms. University press publishing, concerned largely with professional monographs and materials, attracts many interested in embarking on a publishing career. Subscription-reference book publishing is one of the largest and most remunerative special areas with sales of almost $400,000,000.

Approximately 7 per cent of the total volume of books, largely texts, scholarly works, and paper-bound reprints, are exported to overseas markets for a revenue in excess of $125,000,000 a year.

There are some 9000 outlets for hard-cover books in the United States, including more than 800 bookstores and between 600 and 700 book divisions of department stores. Around 75 book clubs dispose of more than 150,000,000 copies a year and publishers themselves mail another several million direct to readers. More than 70,000 libraries acquire books. Among them are about 5800 public library systems and more than 4000 branches; 2200 university, college, and junior college libraries; 4000 "special" libraries such as law and medical collections; and around 55,000 libraries in elementary and secondary schools.

The inexpensive paper-bound book today probably constitutes the most widely discussed phenomenon of publishing. Yet historically paperbacks have been with us both here and in Europe since the early 1800's with a major splurge here taking place in the 1870's and 1880's. In 1885 about one-third of all titles published were bound in paper.

Since World War II the sale of paper-backs, in drug stores, supermarkets, airports, regular bookstores, and elsewhere (there are more than 85,000 outlets at present), has cut deeply into the sale of magazines as well as of hard-cover books. Whereas in 1960 more than 300,000,000 copies were sold annually at a gross income in excess of $100,000,000, today the number has increased to more than 400,000,000 copies, grossing about $300,000,000. The sale of paper-backs to elementary and secondary schools and to colleges and universities has increased dramatically, and these books now greatly exceed the mass market of "wholesaled" paper-bounds in quantities sold and money received. Printed from rubber plates on high-speed rotary presses, these volumes are almost without exception books that have previously succeeded in the conventional format. The prices of all paper-backs have risen markedly, and there is less of a price gap now between them and the cloth-bound books that existed formerly. Publishers are pleased that the huge sales of paperbacks have increased reading, proliferated the use of books, and, as a result, made all forms of publishing more profitable.

Most leading book publishing firms that started 100 or more years ago began as either printers or booksellers. Today, with the exception of Houghton Mifflin; Doubleday; and World Publishing, book publishers have removed themselves from the printing field. The temptation to feed the hungry presses and pressroom gangs by taking on inferior and unsalable manuscripts was one of the principal contributing reasons.

And only Scribner's; Harcourt, Brace & World; Doubleday; and Mc-Graw-Hill operate bookstores of their own. A recent merger trend has resulted in the disappearance of such strong, separate entities as Macmillan; Appleton-Century-Crofts; Row; Rinehart; and World Book. These consolidations mainly occurred after Wall Street "discovered" the publishing field despite its relatively small size. From 1959 to 1962, the owners of publishing houses were offered the chance to "go public," that is, to convert their proprietorship into shares that would be traded, and priced, on the stock market. Some firms responded to this opportunity. The interest of Wall Street in publishing has now subsided somewhat, however, and further mergers appear to be less likely in prospect.

Only about 1000 to 1500 booksellers are deemed worth calling on by the regular salesmen from general trade publishing firms. As George Gallup has pointed out, Denmark, a nation with a population smaller than the state of New Jersey, has 650 bookstores. If the United States had the same number in proportion to population, we would have in the neighborhood of 23,000 bookstores. This same Gallup survey showed, too, that fewer books are read in America than in any other major English-speaking country. In England, for example, where the typical citizen has far less schooling than has the typical citizen here, about three times as many people were found to be reading books at any given time, and in Canada almost twice as many people read books as in this country. The statement is sometimes made, in defense of American readers, that both fiction and non-fiction, later to appear in book form, are first read in the popular magazines and that Americans do as much *reading* as other nations when newspapers and periodicals are also taken into account. But we are concerned here more with a qualitative than a quantitative judgment. Relatively little first-class fiction or non-fiction, other than material written primarily to entertain, is issued and read except in book form—hard-bound or, later, paperback.

THE CHALLENGE OF PUBLISHING

Is book publishing a business or a profession? What strong attraction does it hold for the thousands who have made it their life's work? Chandler B. Grannis, in his Columbia University Press book entitled, *What Happens in Book Publishing,* has the following to say about the basic nature of publishing:

Book publishers may be overheard referring to their work, loftily, as a profession; realistically, as a business; ruefully, as a gamble. It is essentially a business, of course. It is something of a gamble, too, in that it involves considerable risks, even when its effort is directed towards educational or specialized audiences that can pretty well be estimated in advance. But it is a business that has strong professional overtones; it serves all the professions and it has room for a remarkable number of professional skills and non-publishing professional backgrounds. Moreover, it faces a responsibility to society akin to the responsibility faced by educators.

The fascination of book publishing may lie in the undercurrent of excitement that accompanies the discovery of new authors and the sparking of ideas in them. Or perhaps the fascination stems from the very diversity of the industry, for a wholly different batch of new products must be promoted and sold each season. (What other manufacturer of physical entities can make such a claim?) The gambling aspect to which Grannis refers may account for part of the interest: who knows whether a book will flop financially or will sell a half-million copies? A strong appeal also undoubtedly lies in the highly individualistic, non-scientific nature of book publishing, with important decisions often based on intuition as well as on analysis.

Vice Admiral H. G. Rickover, U.S. Navy, emphasized the professional nature of book publishing in an address in 1965 before the Publishers' Lunch Club in New York City. He complimented the publishers for printing books "on any subject under the sun" and for publishing controversial books and books that appeal to limited audiences, "though you know full well they may bring you no profit." He likened this concept of professional service to that of "good physicians whose practice habitually includes patients too poor to pay their medical bills."

Warning that technology is undermining human liberty by creating giant, bureaucratic organizations that often are oblivious to human needs, Admiral Rickover said that book publishing, because of its professional, individualistic spirit, is one of the few remaining strongholds of free men against huge enterprises that tend to consider only economic rights. Said Rickover:

Your business is conducted more nearly as a profession than any other business I know. I assume this is due, in part, to the kind of work you do; in part, to the human scale of your enterprises. So far, you have avoided the organizational giantism that is so prominent a feature of American life.

Huge organizations have difficulty maintaining a professional viewpoint;

chiefly because, in our country at least, such organizations are customarily run not by the people who do the productive work but by a special category of career men whose particular *metier* is to rule large-scale enterprises—the "pure" administrators. To them, the decisive consideration is the good of the organization, by which they nearly always mean whatever enhances its power and profit. Administrators are rarely receptive to the professional viewpoint which has an ethic of its own; an ethic that, to professional people, supersedes material considerations.

It is then perhaps not surprising that when communications enterprises grow overlarge, and therefore succumb to the rule of "pure" administrators, they tend to interpret freedom of speech and the press as an *economic* right, the right of communications media to decide what to say or print and, conversely, what to play down or omit entirely. All too often, the determining factor will be profit, not principle. In contrast, *you* see more clearly that freedom of speech and of the press is a great constitutional right and has as its correlative the obligation to give the public the truth in all matters—all of the truth, no matter how controversial, how distasteful to powerful pressure groups. Book publishing is today the main bulwark of freedom of speech and the press, in the original sense of the expression which meant not an *economic* but a *human* right—the right to be informed and the right to be heard. I hope you will never grow so large that you lose your basic professionalism.

William Jovanovich, president of Harcourt, Brace & World, has called attention to the creative craftsmanship that must be displayed by all persons engaged in the production of books. Addressing a conference of editors, designers, and production men, he declared:

The essence of our work is that the skill and imagination of writers and artists and publishing people are eventually transpired into learning and insight by readers of books. As an end in itself, you and I would wish to seek new forms of communication and to fashion words and lines into aesthetic and meaningful patterns. We are compelled to this, beyond the goads of the market place, because we are dealing with a noble thing: the book.

Is it not a wonder to watch an idea nurtured, made viable? Is it not a sustenance to be so engaged that an idea is made whole and visible by words and lines and is given permanence by ink and paper and cloth so that at last there is a book that will stand in welcome readiness on a shelf, will be carried to and from in a hurried young hand, and will perhaps bring to old eyes of an afternoon the picture of bright mornings in the beginning?

STEPS IN PUBLISHING

All books begin with an idea, germinated usually by the author or by an editor employed by a publishing concern. If the author has the idea, he generally prepares a précis and perhaps several sample chapters and submits them to a literary agent or publisher. If it is the editor's idea, he seeks out the writer who he believes can best develop the book he has in mind. Publishing firms vary in the number of editors employed and the duties with which they are charged. In general, however, the editor works closely with an author in the preparation of a manuscript, and he also may shepherd the work through various business and production stages. The editor must keep abreast of matters of public taste and interest and be able to anticipate insofar as possible the types of books that will find markets in the months ahead. Reference, technical, and textbook editors, having specialized subject matter, often employ professional readers, but trade editors, especially in fiction, are less likely to employ outside advice.

A common fallacy held by each summer's crop of job applicants in book publishing is that a publisher, or an editor, is simply a person of taste who sits with his feet on his desk waiting for hungry authors to seek him out with best-selling manuscripts. Book publishing, however, is like an iceberg. The part that shows, namely books that are reviewed in mass media journals and magazines and that are sold in the general bookstores, constitutes only about 8 per cent of the over-all dollar volume in books. For every editor who breaks bread with a J. D. Salinger or an Arnold Toynbee, there are hundreds who are editing reference works or working with college and school textbook authors. For most publishing houses, the over-the-transom manuscript is almost never publishable. The beginning reader of these voluntary contributions soon becomes appalled with his screening operation.

Accepted manuscripts are turned over to copy editors, who search for grammatical, spelling, and punctuation errors; corroborate facts; correct discrepancies in style (such as writing 20th Century in one chapter and twentieth century in another); perhaps cut the copy to a predetermined length (despite the author's probable scream of anguish: "Sir, would you cut the Bible?!"). The copy editor must also coordinate entries in the bibliography with the citations in footnotes (if the book has them); insure that chapter headings correspond with tables of contents; relate pictures, tables, charts, and the like with the text; query the author if necessary; read the galley proofs including indexes; check corrections made by the author in the proofs; and in general satisfy himself that the text is as accurate as possible.

The production department, which may consist of from three or four to two dozen or more persons, normally serves as the book publisher's liaison with the printer. Highly specialized employees oversee the designing of the book, obtain art work if necessary, estimate length, select the type and paper, and order the typesetting, printing, binding, and preparation of the cover and the jacket. Every book presents an individual problem and every stage of production must be worked out carefully in advance.

Long before the book has been produced, plans are under way for its distribution. The sales department studies possible markets and lays its campaign plans in cooperation with advertising, promotion, and publicity personnel. The "travelers" who visit bookstore buyers throughout the country are called in for conferences concerning the entire list of books being prepared for sale. In accordance with the advertising budget established for the book, based on anticipated sales, media are selected and dealer aids such as posters, circulars, or mail enclosures are prepared.

The publicity department writes and mails news releases, arranges author interviews and other appearances, sends copies to reviewers, announces the book in trade magazines, arranges for exhibits at conventions attended by book sellers, and works on other "angles" to promote the sale of the book. The primary responsibility of the promotion department is to establish a climate of acceptance for the new title, employing every possible means at hand.

The larger accounts may be called on by the publisher's salesmen 15 or 20 times per year. The men work normally on salary or commission or a combination of the two, and frequently carry the lines of two or more houses. There are more than 700 men currently so employed. In addition, of course, many salesmen call on book sellers in behalf of jobbers and other outlet accounts.

There are today about 1000 college travelers and these men perform a distinctly different function. Calling on the nation's college professors, they make certain that their clients are acquainted with or have complimentary copies of textbooks appropriate to the courses they teach. Travelers seldom if ever write up bookstore orders themselves. They must hope that the professors they visit, who usually have freedom of textbook selection, will give them their share of business via the local college bookstore. The college traveler also acts as a manuscript scout for his firm since all of its college textbooks are, of course, written by college professors.

The more than 2000 school book agents work through state, county, and city adoption systems in selling their wares except where local boards of education, teachers, or superintendents are involved. School textbooks are largely written by staff members of a publishing house working in active collaboration with professional teachers.

Many other ramifications involved in producing and selling books are not covered in this sketch of the principal steps in publishing. It is an intricate business, and many years are required to learn the ground rules.

HOW THE JOURNALIST FITS IN

The kinship of book publishing to other mass media activities should be apparent. There are writing and editing to be done; copy editing and proofreading; illustrating and designing; and advertising, publicity and other forms of promotion, printing, and distribution. There must be shrewd insight into what the public is interested in, and why; the newspaper city editor's sense of rapport with his readers finds its counterpart in the identification of the book editor with the tastes of various segments of the book-buying population.

It is true, as pointed out earlier in this chapter, that book publishing is a step removed from the operations of the other media that have a genuinely mass audience to deal with continually; books often are read by highly selective groups. Yet, reporting and editing and preparing advertisements for any of the other media can provide an ideal background for the performance of those duties in the book publishing field. The writer for newspapers, magazines, and radio-television, for example, inevitably gains insights into human life that can be drawn upon to advantage at the book editor's desk. As a student as well as a practitioner of effective writing, he can recognize craftsmanship in others and can quickly spot good or poor writing in the manuscript he is reading. The editor's experience in rewriting the work of others can enable him to shore up the weak spots he finds. As a journalist, he has learned to respect facts and documentation and will insist upon high standards in the materials that cross his desk in the book publishing offices. He knows the principles of style and grammar; he can supervise the work of copy editors, as well as proofreaders. His experience in having worked with printers and with other high-priced craftsmen, including photographers, artists, engravers, and pressmen, will assist him well in the all-important area of reducing job costs. As a reporter or editor for a newspaper, magazine, or radio or television station, he has drawn paychecks from a profit-making organization and has gained an appreciation of sound business methods that serves him well in dealing with authors who may never have earned bread and butter in the ordinary business world.

The knowledge of typography that the mass communicator learns in journalism school or on the job will be of use to him in the ordering of printing for a book and the production of its cover and jacket. The advertising staff man or woman can draw upon this same knowledge of typography, as well as other journalistic techniques, in the preparation of direct mail folders, posters, and advertisements for newspapers and magazines. He will find that the same principles of copy, layout, illustration, color, and selection of paper and ink apply in the preparation of advertisements for new books.

The man or woman writing news releases and other publicity materials, and contacting the various media, will likely be a former newspaper editorial employee. There is no substitute for such experience in fitting a person for effective promotion, publicity, and general public relations duties. The cliché, "I was a newspaperman once myself," can truthfully be voiced by most employees in these departments.

RUNGS ON THE JOB LADDER

Horace Greeley's celebrated admonition, "Go west, young man!," still applies to beginners in the book publishing trade. Even the publisher's son "hits the road" west—or north or south, as the case may be—to learn the business from bottom up. Traveling to the cultural oases of the nation—wherever books are bought, sold, and read—is the normal beginning pursuit for men who seek careers in book publishing. The theory (and it has been proved a thousand times) is: You can't become a good editor sitting in a New York or Boston office; you can learn the facts of bookselling life only by prolonged and intimate acquaintance with a constantly changing market, finding out what will sell, and what won't, and getting a pretty good idea of "why" in both cases.

It's a rigorous, timetabled sort of life, but after three to seven years the traveler, now well seasoned, may wish to swap his suitcase for a swivel chair in the home office, qualified to serve as an editor or in some other specialized capacity.

Scores of men, however, make lifelong careers as travelers. They enjoy being their own bosses and being free from office routine. Although traveling is the best way to enter publishing, it also may serve as an end in itself.

Most travelers are personable, college-trained lovers of books whose starting salaries generally range upwards from $4500, depending on their age, experience, and potential. All their expenses while on the road are paid, of course. An experienced traveler may earn between $10,000 and $15,000 or even more annually.

Moving in to the main publishing offices, he most likely will put his road experience to work in textbook, general trade, or the editorial, sales, or advertising department. Or he may elect to enter the production department. Eventually, he may become a department head, later perhaps an officer and director of the company. The creativity and business knowledge that could propel him to such heights merit accompanying salary boosts to the $20,000, $30,000, or maybe even the $50,000 range.

That's the male route to the top. The women skip the road work, but frequently have an equally humble beginning as typists who earn $3000 a year. With a toehold thus established, they become secretaries earning $5000 to $6000 per year. Indirectly and gradually, they display an interest in subject matter, tackling the pile of unsolicited manuscripts that almost every mail delivery augments. They make brief reports of the value of these manuscripts; as their judgment is corroborated by an editor, they are given more creative tasks. Some demonstrate an admirable ability at correcting grammatical errors and punctuation faults and become copy and proof editors. Others prove they can rewrite portions of manuscripts with distinction. Those with an even more scholarly bent may exhibit proficiency in researching facts in encyclopedias and other reference works.

Hundreds of women free-lance as copy editors, taking manuscripts home with them to earn $2.50 to $3.50 per hour. Those who read galley proofs generally work at the printer's plant.

There is a fairly definite ceiling for opportunity at this point in their development, but some ascend the publishing ladder as editors. More women find success in editing or producing children's books than in any other field of book publishing. Countless others, however, move into well-paying advertising and publicity jobs. They write news and feature copy, prepare advertising materials, compose jacket blurbs, engineer radio and television personal appearances and lecture tours, and otherwise exhibit ingenuity in promoting the sale of books. For these services they may be paid from $6000 to as high as $15,000 annually.

Both men and women may find employment, including an apprenticeship while they are still in college, with the more than 40 university presses in the United States. These presses bring out from 15 to 25 per cent of the new titles each year and gross in the neighborhood of $8,000,000, so opportunities are ample. Hundreds of smaller printing shops do some book work but also much commercial printing. Students interested in the graphic arts may serve as printing salesmen, typographers, layout men, or editorial advisers for large-size printing plants which seek magazine, pamphlet, and book publishing jobs from businesses and other organizations. Those who demonstrate a real ability in the graphic arts area are well rewarded financially in such commercial enterprises.

QUALIFICATIONS

A good education, high intelligence, a love of books, and an ability to keep abreast of the latest trends and developments in all phases of human life but particularly in the area of one's specialization are prime characteristics of a good editor. He need not be a creative writer; in fact, there is little place in book publishing for the varying temperament that frequently afflicts (or aids) authorship. Persons with highly individual ideas and taste are sometimes less willing to remain anonymous and to play second fiddle to authors with quixotic personalities. The good editor has the capacity to deal in calm, unruffled fashion with the prima donnas whose genius or near-genius often spells the difference between profit and loss in a publishing year. ("Sir, don't you dare change a word of this manuscript!" "I insist on an advertisement on every book review page in the country!")

The ideal copy editor is a perfectionist who can detect the slightest deviations in style and form. He has the forbearance to leave original writing alone; yet his necessary alterations are so skillfully done that no author objects. He has a mania for the exact word and can verify a fact with expedition.

Whether he wishes to become a general editor, a copy or proof editor, an advertising specialist, or a publicity or promotion man, the young college man who aspires to a career in book publishing will profit by an education, as well as experience, in mass communications. He will seek to acquire a sound background in literature, history, languages, the natural and social sciences, philosophy—in fact, in all areas of knowledge that comprise a liberal education. He will not overlook his professional education, for the insights, skills, and fundamental knowledge gained in the classrooms and laboratories of a school of communications should prove of inestimable value throughout his career.

SUMMARY

Books are the most lasting products of mass communicators. Their comparative slowness of manufacture is compensated for by the great care that may be taken to insure accuracy, historical perspective, and writing effectiveness. Books undergird nearly every profession, occupation, or other activity.

Books share the beginnings and the struggle against censorship common to all the print media. The publishing industry itself represents only a tiny part of the country's $600 billion economy; yet some 20,000 new titles and 1,200,000,000 books are produced in the United States each year. The companies mainly are centered in the Northeast.

Editors work closely with authors in preparing manuscripts and employ readers to look over the hundreds submitted each year without request. Copy editors correct errors in style and grammar and otherwise prepare manuscripts for the printer. Production department employees oversee details connected with art work, typesetting, printing, binding, the cover, and the jacket. The sales force handles the marketing, aided by advertising, publicity, promotion, and public relations personnel.

The challenge of creating, selling, and promoting an ever-changing product and the excitement of discovering new authors combine with other factors to make book publishing a fascinating career for many. Men generally begin their careers in book publishing as travelers. Women often move from typing or secretarial jobs to the evaluation of manuscripts and to copy and proof editing responsibilities. Some attain success as editors of children's books and in key advertising and promotion roles.

The trained journalist, with his insights into human nature and what interests people, his experience in writing and editing copy, his recognition of good and poor craftsmanship, his respect for facts, and his knowledge of printing techniques and sound business practices, may well find book publishing an exciting as well as a lucrative career.

STUDY QUESTION

What role or roles do books play in undergirding and transforming American life?

PROJECTS

1. Examine at least two issues of the Sunday book review magazine of the New York *Times* or *Book Week* in the New York *Herald Tribune,* Washington *Post,* or San Francisco *Examiner,* or your local newspaper book section, or *The New York Review of Books.* Write a 300-word essay describing your interpretation of the principal objectives of the editor of the magazine. Are the books reviewed as news or as literature?

2. Read a recent issue of *Publishers' Weekly* or *Library Journal* and write a brief report of an article that pertains to one of the points made in this chapter.

CHAPTER 13

THE FILM

THE ROLE OF MOTION PICTURES

Of all the mass communications media, the motion picture has the most universal impact. Properly conceived, a film can rise above language barriers through the power of its visual images and convey the same message to a sophisticated audience in New York, a crowd of French peasants, and a gathering of natives in the African jungle.

Shortly after the advent of sound pictures more than three decades ago, this appeal was enhanced by having the performers talk. When American-made films are sent abroad, as scores of them are every year, other voices substituting for those of the English-speaking performers deliver the dialogue in a wide range of foreign languages. But motion pictures are essentially visual and often can put across their message without a word being spoken—or at least being understood by the viewers. Use of color makes the visual power even greater.

The stimulation of working with such a medium of communication is alluring to many young people. Not only does the motion picture have high audience attention, because a crowd gathered in a darkened room applies undivided concentration to the lighted screen before it, but there is such a highly developed network of film outlets here and abroad that almost any commercial film will be seen by hundreds of thousands. The total audience for a major entertainment film runs into the millions.

When we mention films, everyone's mind turns automatically to the "movies"; that is, the entertainment films produced or distributed by the huge Hollywood studios. They are the most spectacular, best publicized, costliest, and most-viewed of all film productions. However, it would be a mistake to assume that Hollywood's output (and that of its foreign entertainment rivals) constitutes the whole of contemporary film-making. Just as newspapers range in size and function from the husband-and-wife weekly to the huge metropolitan dailies, and the term magazine is applied equally to the small trade periodical and the pictorial weekly with a multimillion circulation, the field of film-making covers a very wide range. In recent years, with the arrival of television and its dependence upon motion pictures for much of its programming, the range of film production has grown even broader than it was before World War II.

THE ENTERTAINMENT FILM

"Going to the movies" has been an American social custom for nearly half a century. Actually, the history of motion pictures goes back to the start of the twentieth century. But mass movie-going reached the proportions of a major phenomenon about the end of World War I. During the 1920's Hollywood became the symbol of glamour, fame, and sophistication; the silent films its studios produced were viewed around the world. Development of the star system, with its calculated buildup and clever publicity campaigns, turned previously unknown young men and women into figures of world acclaim and made many of their films extremely lucrative productions.

Just before the United States entered the period of grave economic depression in 1929, the Hollywood films were changed from silent pictures to talking ones. A revolution of shattering dimensions struck the film industry. Within a few months the "talkies" had taken over, creating new stars and greater profits. Almost overnight some of Hollywood's most famous performers disappeared from the screen, the unfortunate victims of squeaky voices or heavy accents.

During the 1930's and early 1940's the producers of entertainment films issued motion pictures of growing technical excellence; from a creative standpoint, every year a few pictures of exceptionally meritorious content were released, along with hundreds of routine ones.

The second revolution to erupt in the film kingdom was the arrival of television after World War II. As explained earlier in Chapter 6, television forced the motion picture producers into making fewer and more spectacular films and employing the new wide-screen processes.

Despite these blows from television, the production of American entertainment films remains a massive business. The average weekly attendance at motion pictures in the United States is about 45,000,000, down heavily from the pretelevision peak. The gross income of movie theaters in this country is about $1,500,000,000 a year. There are some 17,000 theaters, a fourth of them drive-ins. The 12 major national film distributors release between 250 and 300 films annually. Of these about one-third are wide-screen productions and about one-third are filmed in color. During the 1960's employment in the American motion picture industry fell below 175,000; however, the production of motion pictures and television films in Hollywood has become so interlocked that there inevitably is an overlap in the employment figures between these two mass communications media.

Although most American movie-goers do not realize it, the Hollywood producers receive much of their income from the showing of their motion pictures in foreign countries. Often, in fact, foreign box office receipts make the difference between profit and loss on a film. The foreign market's needs and desires have a strong influence on the decisions of the producers about the pictures they will make. Major distributors receive more than $300,000,000 a year from overseas sales outlets. In turn, foreign films gross less than $100,000,000 in U.S. theaters despite their exciting qualities and impact upon film-making techniques, although their take increased rapidly in the 1960's with improved distribution.

Despite the vastness of the Hollywood film industry, the number of jobs available for writers and other journalistically minded communicators is rather small. There is no established path for young people of such inclinations to follow in getting themselves established in motion picture making, no clearly defined apprenticeship system or starting point. For the creative person, the Hollywood film studios provide an uncertain and often frustrating life, with relatively little credit but often with surprisingly high weekly salaries—while they last. There is less security in the motion picture industry for creative talent than in any of the other mass communications media.

Writers are creative by nature; the ideas they conceive and develop are brought to the screen by actors and directors who interpret the material they are given. Behind these two relatively small groups, the creators and the interpreters, stand the vast mass of Hollywood workers —the technicians who operate the complex machinery of cameras, sound equipment, editing, stage setting, costuming, and other processes essential to making a motion picture.

As an example, a major Hollywood studio made a film which included a scene in a newspaper office. This consisted merely of an office boy tearing a bulletin off a press association teleprinter and rushing across the city room to hand it to the managing editor. The action required less than a minute on the screen and filled barely a page in the shooting script.

For authenticity, the film producers arranged to shoot this brief scene in the city room of a Los Angeles metropolitan newspaper, after the last afternoon edition. Technicians and stage hands brought in lights, sound equipment, and cameras. Lighting experts put masking tape over all shiny articles in the city room to reduce the glare. Desks were moved to make an easier path for the actor playing the office boy role. Clerical assistants, supervisors, and actors arrived. By the time the little episode had been shot, nearly one hundred people had been involved and several hours were consumed.

This kind of procedure is what makes Hollywood films so expensive to produce, and also so technically expert. One reason for the huge overhead is the high degree of unionization among motion picture personnel. Few industries are so intensively organized; rigid limitations are enforced upon the duties each worker can perform and the kinds of physical properties he can touch. The creative and interpretative talent also have banded together in unions and guilds to create working standards and protect themselves against exploitation. The American Federation of Motion Picture Artists is a major force in the film field.

Most screen writers get their jobs, not by working up through the ranks within the industry, but by being invited in from the outside after they have won prominence as the authors of popular books or successful plays. Frequently an author is brought to Hollywood by a producer on special assignment to help adapt his own book for filming. Such assignments are for only a few months, at very high pay. Sometimes, however, the writer finds that he has a special flair for screen writing and stays on indefinitely in Hollywood. He may hold a staff writing job for one of the large studios, or work on special assignment, somewhat as actors do.

Two recent examples of men with journalism school, newspaper, and writing backgrounds who arrived in Hollywood on such special assignments are Max Shulman and Norman Katkov. Some motion picture writers are recruited from television.

The motion picture studios also have jobs for men with a journalistic background in their publicity departments. Salaries for this work are high, compared to those paid to reporters and editors on metropolitan newspapers, but not spectacularly so in the way that screen writers' salaries are. Also, there are related jobs for reporters and writers on film trade journals and in independent publicity firms which handle promotion of films and actors on a fee basis.

For the young men and women interested in the production aspects of motion pictures, a background in camera work, staging, and costuming is required. Some universities give courses in motion picture and television production.

Although the Hollywood entertainment films get the giant's share of public attention, there are several other less glamorous but highly important fields of film-making. In many respects these offer greater opportunities and a stronger feeling of significant achievement for the mass communicator.

DOCUMENTARY FILMS

These motion pictures frequently are major productions, using Hollywood's excellent technical facilities. They bear much the same relation to the entertainment picture as a nonfiction article does to a short story. Sometimes they have a strong strain of social and economic consciousness, as for example those notable documentary films in the New Deal era of the 1930's, *The Plow That Broke the Plains,* made by Pare Lorentz, *The River,* and *The City.* Others turn to nature for subject matter: Walt Disney's outdoor films, such as *White Wilderness,* are outstanding examples. During World War II the British caught the spirit of their war effort with telling effect in such documentary pictures as *Desert Victory.* These played in major theaters around the world, drawing the same audiences which normally attend entertainment films. UNESCO carried on this documentary tradition with a series of productions about economic and social reforms around the world, including typically Paul Rotha's and Basil Wright's *World Without End.*

Opportunities for journalistically minded people in the documentary field are limited, but for those who do find places in it there is a feeling of accomplishment in capturing facts and moods for a mass audience.

NEWSREELS

Before television, the newsreel was a basic ingredient of every motion picture theater's program. Newsreel cameramen went everywhere, bringing visual reports of the day's news to theater audiences. The newsreel fell into decline when TV audiences began to get much the same material on their home screens, and many theaters abandoned it. However, some experts believe that it can make a comeback as a semidocumentary vehicle, rather than as a straight presentation of news events and frothy features.

FILMS FOR EDUCATION AND INDUSTRY

This is a mushrooming industry in which an estimated 1200 firms are at work in the United States, producing pictures on a multiplicity of topics for showing to community organizations, schools, industrial and sales groups, the armed forces, and professional and religious bodies. These firms might be compared to the hundreds of small trade journals in the magazine field. Few of them are major organizations but in the mass they form an influential channel for communicating information and ideas.

Nontheatrical film-making is heavily financed by American industry, which has found in this type of motion picture a highly effective means for presenting its purposes, methods, and achievements. By 1965, non-theatrical film production was approaching 10,000 a year. Most were produced on 16 millimeter film, the standard size for projection by small and portable machines. A few of the more elaborate were made on 35 millimeter, some even for wide-screen projection. This total included some 5500 business and industrial pictures, 1700 government films, 1200 educational films, 300 for medical use, and 200 religious films. More than $350,000,000 was being spent annually to produce these films and for other audio-visual aids, such as filmstrips and slides and equipment.

The price of making and distributing a good company film averages nearly $90,000, with some major productions running close to a half-million dollars. As many as 200 prints are made for some of these films to satisfy the demand for them. The average total audience for such a film is estimated to be 1,250,000. Many educational and instructional films are produced on far smaller budgets, some of them only a few thousand dollars, and are shown to more limited audiences.

Production of educational and informational films began with the development of the 16 millimeter portable projector in 1923. By now it is estimated that there are 750,000 projectors in use in the United States, most of them in schools and businesses, but others in clubs, libraries, homes, and churches. Another half-million filmstrip projectors are in use.

A large proportion of these nontheatrical films are available for use by organizations and private citizens free of charge. The cost is under-written by business organizations as part of their institutional public relations budget, by the government, by social or economic organizations which seek to present educational material in their particular fields, or by tax-supported institutions such as public libraries or adult education schools. There are 2600 film libraries in the United States distributing 16 millimeter films. The H. W. Wilson Educational Film Guide lists 20,000 films which can be borrowed.

Some idea of the diversity and purpose of these free films is to be found in the catalog of the Modern Talking Picture Service, the largest distributor in the field. Typical of the films it offers to loan without charge are these:

One Hoe for Kalaboe, a 27-minute production in color telling the story of modern tool building and its effects on economies and civiliza-tions. The film is produced by the National Machine Tool Builders Association.

Adventures in Dairyland, a Technicolor picture prepared by the American Dairy Association in which two city youngsters visit a Wiscon-sin farm and learn the methods of modern daily farming.

Working Dollars, a 13-minute color cartoon story explaining how the stock market works and the advantages of the monthly investment plan. The film is financed by members of the New York Stock Exchange.

The Clean Look, a half-hour color film in which experts give the secrets of good grooming, such as posture, care of hair and complexion. The film is made by Armour and Company.

In addition to these industrial films, there are straightforward educa-tional pictures without an overt or implied commercial message. Ex-amples of these are the Encyclopaedia Britannica Films, sponsored by the University of Chicago, which include such projects as a chemistry course of 160 half-hour films and a history course with Arnold Toynbee as instructor. Medical films are used to demonstrate operations, to show to those within the medical profession, and to inform general audiences about diseases and public health problems. Church organizations present religious films to dramatize the teachings of the Bible and to generate support for their missionary and welfare activities.

From this brief survey the diversity and potential of the nontheatrical film is apparent. It is a growing field, well-financed in many instances, in which there is need for creative thinking. There are jobs available in it in many cities for young men and women who have the ability to tell a story in visual form and to convey facts and ideas in pictures. The creative person in nontheatrical work must be able to plan films (a journalistic job of determining what the story is and what can be filmed), write a script knitting the facts into an interesting narrative, and plan production so that the story can be filmed economically and effectively. Filmstrip making is another journalistic job of these commercial firms.

One obvious opportunity is to work on film production for a large company. Many corporations have staffs in their public relations departments in charge of audio-visual materials and film work; however, most of them assign the actual shooting of the pictures to film production companies, which work with materials provided by the corporation public relations department.

SUMMARY

Mass communication through use of film has many facets, of which the entertainment motion pictures produced in Hollywood are the best known and most expensive. Television has forced major changes in motion picture production, causing a reduction in the number of pictures produced and the introduction of new filming processes and outlets. Job opportunities for writers and other idea-creators are relatively few and open mostly to men who have made names in other fields of writing. The rewards are high but uncertain. The production of documentary films and newsreels for commercial release is a challenging but small offshoot of the entertainment business.

The creation and production of nontheatrical films and other audio-visual material for educational, sales, training, and inspirational purposes is an expanding business in which 1200 companies are engaged. Much of this film production is financed by American industry, which uses these pictures for institutional public relations and direct sales purposes. Other nontheatrical films are made by educational, social, medical, and religious organizations for the purpose of distributing knowledge. Stimulating and satisfying job opportunities exist in nontheatrical film-making for communicators who can create ideas and present them visually.

STUDY QUESTION

What advantages do films have in transmitting information and ideas to audiences?

PROJECTS

1. Write a 300-word essay about the documentary film as an opinion-making force, using references available in your library.

2. Make a brief report on an educational or company film you have seen, explaining its purpose.

CHAPTER 14

PRESS ASSOCIATIONS AND FEATURE SYNDICATES

THE ROLE OF PRESS ASSOCIATIONS

Without the services of the two huge American newsgathering agencies, the Associated Press and United Press International, only a handful of American newspapers could give their readers a comprehensive report of the world. In fact, it is doubtful whether many could carry on daily publication if they did not have the wire services.

These gigantic organizations are the eyes and ears of most daily newspapers for coverage of news outside their home communities. They take over where the local and area coverage of the city desk ends. Even the largest dailies with extensive staffs of their own correspondents in Washington and abroad, such as the New York *Times,* are heavily dependent upon the press associations for domestic and foreign dispatches.

An understanding of the American press is impossible without knowledge of the press associations and their role. They are the mass production factor which, for better or worse, brings a strong degree of uniformity to the news content of daily newspapers situated across 3000 miles of the North American continent. Because of them readers in Boston and San Francisco, Chicago and Dallas, read identical reports of events in Washington and foreign capitals.

The United Press International and Associated Press, commonly known as the UPI and AP, are highly competitive. They are in a daily race to be first with the news. There is an intense rivalry to deliver to their newspaper customers dispatches that are comprehensive, accurate, objective, and written in a manner sufficiently simple and interesting to be absorbed by a mass audience.

This competitive urge is one of the attractions of press association work, especially for younger reporters and editors; it adds a zest to news-gathering which has disappeared to some degree from the local news staffs in many cities where only one newspaper now exists. Commercially, this competition to be faster and better than your rival has great impor-tance, because the AP and UPI are in constant battle to take away cus-tomers from each other. (The AP calls them members; the UPI refers to them as clients.)

Although the services they deliver to newspapers, television, and radio stations here and abroad are similar, the two press associations are organ-ized quite differently. The Associated Press, which is much older, is a cooperative newsgathering association. Each American newspaper which purchases its service becomes a member of the cooperative and has a voice in setting the association's newsgathering and financial policies; also, it is obligated to turn over its local news coverage to the cooperative. Television and radio stations taking AP service become associate mem-bers without voting rights; the total now exceeds that of newspaper members. The Associated Press was founded in 1848 by six New York publishers, primarily to cooperate in the gathering of news from ships arriving in eastern harbors from Europe. It has been in continuous exist-ence ever since, having gone through several major reorganizations includ-ing one in 1900 which established it in its present form.

United Press International is a privately owned company, dealing on a contract basis with newspapers, television and radio stations, and other organizations which have need for a news report. Its individual clients influence the shape of the UPI news report only through their suggestions and criticisms, solicited by the UPI management, or through their ulti-mate power to cancel the service. An Associated Press member can with-draw on two years' notice; the usual United Press International contract with a client runs five years. The United Press was founded in 1907 by E. W. Scripps, the owner of a large group of newspapers, with the pur-pose of supplying news to papers which could not obtain Associated Press membership under the then-existing rules. In 1958 the United Press absorbed the International News Service, which had operated as a relatively weak third American competitor in the field since William Randolph Hearst founded it in 1909. The combined service became known as United Press International.

The Associated Press and United Press International are now comparable in strength, the UPI having improved its position by the merger with INS.

The Associated Press reported that in the mid-1960's it was serving approximately 8500 newspapers and television and radio stations around the world; the United Press International reported it had approximately 6000 clients for its news and picture services. The UPI was operating in 114 countries and territories, the AP in 104. To provide this global news service, the UPI had 264 news and picture bureaus, while the AP listed 169 for news (the AP was slower to organize its own foreign bureau network than the UPI, which operates in some 30 more foreign points, and did not differentiate its picture bureaus). Both press associations leased more than 400,000 miles of telephone wires in the United States for transmission of news and pictures, and both used globe-girdling radio teletype circuits and underwater cables to carry their news reports to and from Europe and Asia. For the United States alone, the two associations reported these figures: AP, service to 1750 publications and 2500 television and radio stations; UPI, 1600 publications and 2300 television and radio stations. For both it was a big business; the AP annual budget had reached $44,000,000 and UPI's $43,500,000.

Regardless of whether it is called a member or a client, the net result for each daily newspaper is much the same. It receives the UPI or AP news report by teleprinter for a specified number of hours each day, for which it pays a fee based upon its circulation and the amount of news received. Prices range from roughly $100 a week for a paper of 10,000 circulation up to $2000 or more a week for the metropolitan dailies. Both news agencies offer supplemental sports and financial and other specialized services at additional fees.

Most small dailies, and even some very large ones, operate successfully with only one of the two major wire services. Of the 1750 American daily newspapers, approximately 45 per cent subscribe only to AP, 30 per cent only to UPI, and 25 per cent to both services. This means only some 450 dailies purchase both news reports to have a wider choice of news stories to publish. When both services provide stories on the same news events, as they do scores of times daily, the telegraph editor of the two-service newspaper selects the dispatch which arrives first, if an urgent news break is involved, or which seems to him more complete, concise, and interesting. Sometimes the two dispatches are combined to provide a more well-rounded and complete story.

The rival agencies keep close watch on selected lists of these two-service papers to determine the "play" their respective stories receive. Bad "play" on a big story—or worse, being badly beaten by the rival agency on a news break—brings sharp backstage criticism from the New York home office down upon the head of the offending bureau involved.

HOW PRESS ASSOCIATIONS FUNCTION

The news reports of each press association are carried to newspapers by leased telegraph circuits from offices scattered across the United States. The stories arrive in the newspaper office on a continuous role of paper in a teleprinter, a machine resembling an automatic typewriter whose keys are activated by impulses transmitted over the telegraphic circuit from a press association office. This paper is cut into segments by the telegraph editor, who selects from it the stories he will publish in his newspaper that day. Originally transmission was on Morse dot-and-dash circuits, but these have been replaced everywhere by automatic teleprinters. An elaborate system of traffic controls allows the various press association offices on each circuit to transmit their stories in turn and to make inquiries about stories already sent or those possibly overlooked by a busy office. When a major news break develops, the first portion of it is marked "bulletin" and transmitted along the circuit on a priority basis.

Each press association divides its flow of news into P.M. and A.M. reports, or cycles, the former for afternoon newspapers and the latter for morning papers. These reports always begin with a "budget," or checklist, of the most important stories that are to be transmitted. The budget represents a summary of the basic stories then available, or known to be forthcoming during the next few hours, plus sports and feature highlights. Usually it contains 10 or 12 items. The news editor is thus enabled to plan his make-up to ensure space for stories that he most likely will want to run. Since the large majority of American newspapers are published in the afternoon, and most news occurs during daytime hours, the P.M. reports are generally handled with a greater sense of urgency.

Basic stories on major news situations are transmitted early in each cycle. If later developments occur on a story, a new "lead" is moved on the wire. This reports the latest news on the situation and ends with a transitional paragraph which blends into the earlier dispatch at a specified place. On big, fast-breaking stories a press association may carry half a dozen leads in a cycle; these are edited so compactly that the dispatch which ultimately appears in a client newspaper reads with smooth continuity, even though it may contain segments of several leads.

Such methods are necessary because press association clients are constantly going to press and must print what is available on a given situation at press time. To use a phrase popular with United Press International, somewhere there is a deadline every minute. This is a major difference between press association and ordinary newspaper writing: the press association correspondent must keep feeding latest developments onto the news wires immediately, even when their meaning and ramifications are not fully disclosed; the newspaper staff correspondent (called a "special" by wire service men) usually has more time before his deadline to digest and consolidate his information. Press association men always work under time pressure. When we consider this, the amount of background and interpretation an experienced press association man can weave into a fast-breaking story is remarkable.

The press associations have main trunk teletype circuits running across the country, serving the major metropolitan newspapers. The largest bureaus are also cut in on these circuits with the power to transmit stories on them. From these main trunks, regional and state circuits strike off at relay bureaus to serve the smaller papers in different areas of the country. The editors who control the flow of news onto these secondary wires, known as "wire filers," must see that the newspapers on each receive a balanced menu of regional news along with the most important national and foreign dispatches. Thus an Associated Press member in Arizona will receive some stories of interest only to readers in the Southwest which will not be delivered to another member in Florida. These members will receive identical dispatches on the day's major news from Washington and London, however. Proper channeling of the daily news report, so that each newspaper gets the largest possible number of stories pertinent to its needs, is a basic problem for press association editors. Many stories are shortened when relayed on secondary circuits, because smaller newspapers do not have the space to publish them in full. Dispatches from the press association bureaus abroad are sent to the New York home offices for processing and filing on the domestic circuits.

As an example of the press association wire operation, a story originating in a small bureau may be distributed around the world, if various wire service editors along the way consider it sufficiently interesting; or it may never go farther than the circuit serving the newspapers in a nearby region. The bureau of origin transmits it on the state or regional wire. The editors at the control point for this circuit may consider the item to have national appeal and relay it on the transcontinental trunk wire. By this method it reaches the New York general office, where an editor may put it on circuits serving newspapers in other parts of the country. The foreign desk editor may see in the dispatch something of interest to newspapers abroad and relay it overseas by radio. Every wire service story undergoes this selective screening process, by which the editors tailor the news report on each circuit to fit the needs and interests of its client newspapers.

As discussed earlier in this book, the creation of teletypesetter circuits is a major development in press association work. On these circuits the news is delivered to client newspapers on a teleprinter roll, but typed in capitals and lower case with the lines justified to fit a newspaper column width for quick typesetting. In addition, the newspaper receives the story in perforated tape for automatic typesetting.

SPECIAL WRITING TECHNIQUES

It is evident that a news story which goes through all these vicissitudes of editing en route from reporter to each client editor's desk requires special writing techniques. It may be published 500 words long in one newspaper and only 100 words in another. Thus the writer must keep his fundamental information near the top of the story so the dispatch can be trimmed from the end upward without having any key facts omitted. He must write concisely, in simple sentences. Because his dispatches will be printed in newspapers of differing political persuasions and social viewpoints, he must be carefully objective in handling stories, even the complicated, controversial ones which require background and interpretation. The primary goal of press association writing is clear and swift communication of ideas and events, and the staff man's stock in trade is straight news, well written. More distinctive forms of creative self-expression find their way onto the wires, but those who wish to specialize in this type of writing usually choose other outlets.

Press association editors have been experimenting with methods to inject background interpretation into spot-breaking news stories, especially those from abroad. One method is insertion of parenthetical paragraphs. The aim is to give the dispatches proper significance without changing them into interpretative "think pieces." The more complicated the world becomes, the more difficult it is for press associations to find a proper balance between quick-breaking facts and interpretation that gives them perspective without distortion. This calls for highly skilled reporting and editing.

OTHER PRESS ASSOCIATION ACTIVITIES

Both the United Press International and Associated Press were founded to provide news for American newspapers. That remains their primary functions, but they have branched out into several additional services. Each now delivers its news to newspapers and broadcasting stations in many foreign countries. A constant flow of overseas news comes to this country while news originating here is being dispatched throughout the world. Much of this global two-way news flow is accomplished by radio transmission, but because it is sometimes subject to interruption, both agencies also operate leased cable circuits under the Atlantic to London.

From New York radio teletype circuits operating around the clock transmit news both east and west for both the AP and UPI. In either operation, a transmitter on Long Island beams the signal by radio to Tangiers, where a relay station boosts the signal and beams it to Europe, the Middle East, South Asia, and South Africa. In London, the incoming beam is fed into teletype circuits covering more than 20,000 miles in Europe. In each country, the news is translated into that country's language and then put onto a separate national teletype network (translation into Spanish for Latin-American countries is largely done in the New York offices). The file to Asia is beamed by radio from San Francisco to booster relay stations at Manila and other points. Thus an important bulletin news story can flash by teletype within a minute or two on a Rome-London-New York-San Francisco-Tokyo transmission network. Pictures likewise are transmitted throughout the world by radio facilities.

The foreign bureaus of the American press associations usually are headed by an American, but they also employ local nationals in substantial numbers as reporters, editors, and translators. The number of foreign correspondent jobs available to Americans on the press associations is thus smaller than many people may believe.

A survey by John Wilhelm published in *Journalism Quarterly* (Spring 1963) showed 515 U.S. citizens serving as overseas correspondents for U.S. media. The great majority of these work for the press associations.

Others are employed by the TV-radio networks, individual newspapers, and magazines. Many of these "special" correspondents went abroad originally as press association men and later switched to their present jobs because of better salaries or less rigid working conditions. The survey listed 718 other correspondents of non-U.S. citizenship working abroad for U.S. media. The total of correspondents around the world reporting for U.S. news media was placed at 1233, including 291 UPI staff members and 268 AP correspondents. Thus it is apparent that the commonly held and commendable desire of young newsmen to become foreign correspondents is not easily fulfilled. By far the largest single delegation of U.S. news representatives abroad is stationed in London because of its central location for communications and transportation. In the Far East, Tokyo is the focal point.

At many points around the world the American organizations are in sharp competition, in both newsgathering and sales, with such foreign news agencies as Reuters of Great Britain and Agence France-Presse. The impact of these foreign agencies upon the American press is negligible, however, since only a very few metropolitan papers purchase any of their material.

The American press associations have become important transmission belts for presenting a picture of life in America to foreigners. The hunger in many countries for news about the United States has been growing in proportion to this country's increasingly dominant role in world affairs. The Associated Press and United Press International carry a heavy responsibility in their selection and writing of news for the overseas audience, so that a well-balanced picture is presented. This does not imply censorship, the hiding of unpleasant news, or peddling of propaganda, but a judicious budget of stories to provide a multifaceted view of American life. For a great many citizens of foreign countries, press association dispatches provide the chief source of information about life, political policies, and attitudes in the United States.

Special news service for television and radio stations is a major part of the agencies' operations. This is transmitted on different teletype circuits from the newspaper service and is rewritten from the stories in the basic report to please the ear rather than the eye. The style is more conversational, with simpler sentence structure and less detail. Distribution of this specially processed radio report was inaugurated by the United Press in 1935. The Associated Press followed reluctantly five years later.

Another important service provided to newspapers by both wire agencies is news picture coverage. Both AP and UPI operate coast-to-coast circuits for rapid transmission of news photographs. The larger newspapers are connected with these circuits and receive photographs, about 80 a day, instantaneously as they are transmitted. Smaller newspapers receive selected airmailed packages of glossy prints or mats processed from the wire photo circuit by regional control points. The news agencies supply pictures to foreign clients by radio-photo, leased circuits, and mail.

Some newspapers purchasing the nationwide direct service receive the news photos in their offices over facsimile machines, which translate the electrical impulses of the transmission circuit into black-and-white photographs by means of a scanning device; these pictures are ready for immediate engraving and printing. Other newspapers obtain glossy black-and-white photographs from negatives activated by the transmission circuit on equipment in their own plants. Both UPI and AP have staffs of photographers, who are assigned to stories much as are reporters. In addition the Associated Press distributes many pictures taken by photographers on the staffs of member papers. UPI also supplements its staff picture coverage with photos from newspaper sources. In addition, United Press International operates a daily motion picture newsfilm service for use on television news programs, an audio news service for radio station voice pickups on news events, and an Ocean Press radio news report to 160 passenger liners at sea.

On still another front, the Associated Press and United Press International, the latter through its subsidiary United Feature Syndicate, provide comic strips, women's features, political columns, and a host of other syndicated material for newspaper publication.

Thus the two organizations have journeyed far afield from their original purpose of providing dispatches for newspapers. However, the daily newspaper report continues to be the core of each agency's operations. The UPI and AP now serve not one but three of our mass communications media—newspapers, television, and radio, plus special services to magazines.

CRITICAL VIEWS OF AGENCIES

Students of the American press sometimes are critical of the heavy dependence of newspapers upon the press associations; this criticism is aimed more at the role of the wire services than at their daily performance. There is an undercurrent of uneasiness among these critics because more than 1700 daily newspapers look to these two organizations for the great bulk of their nonlocal news. Anyone who listens to a succession of radio newscasts and hears the identical words from the radio news wires spoken to him repeatedly on different wave lengths realizes the dependence of radio stations in particular upon the press associations. In fact, an overwhelming percentage of the American people are largely dependent upon the two organizations, through their various newspaper and TV-radio ramifications, for knowledge of what is happening in the world. In the eyes of the critics this constitutes a danger involving conformity of reporting and thought.

The argument is more philosophic than practical. The economics of newspaper publishing makes it impossible for even the largest, richest newspapers to have staff reporters stationed around the world in sufficient numbers to give them exclusive reports, for the costs would be prohibitive. Therefore some form of cooperative newsgathering is necessary.

So long as the United Press International and Associated Press remain free of governmental control or subsidy, operate in a highly competitive manner, and hold to their principles of objective news coverage, the perils of undue conformity are relatively small. The efficiency and far-reaching news lines of the press associations contribute greatly to the mammoth amount of information about the world available to readers and listeners throughout the United States.

The editors of client and member newspapers, and wire service executives themselves, subject the press association news reports to a constant scrutiny for accuracy and completeness. When instances of insufficient or inaccurate coverage come to light, such as failure by an agency to anticipate the victory of the Cuban rebels under Fidel Castro, steps are taken quickly to remedy the weakness. The competitive factor is a very wholesome one.

The press associations are scolded at times by critics because they must depend upon the reporting services of part-time local "string" correspondents in some parts of the world. When a major story breaks in a normally quiet and remote area, they must use the sometimes inadequate services of these men until an American-trained correspondent can reach the scene. Press association executives answer by pointing out that it is economically impossible for them to keep highly qualified men in every country.

Another criticism of the press associations is shared by the newspapers themselves—an alleged preoccupation with "crisis" reporting. That means trying to find conflict and excitement in every situation, to the point of distorting the news. In particular this charge has been made concerning the handling of political and legislative news. It is stated that too much emphasis is placed upon the routine partisan postures of the two major parties. This allegation results from the striving of each association to find sharp "angles" that induce telegraph editors to print its stories instead of its competitor's. Recently, however, both wire services have been broadening their coverage by offering more thoughtful, interpretative articles in such fields as religion, education, labor, and social problems. The news services are also criticized for not carrying enough foreign news, to which criticism they reply that their newspapers will print only a limited amount of such news, and there is no use in taking wire transmission time to give them what they won't use.

Actually, the conformity in presentation of national and foreign news by newspapers is somewhat less than might be expected. Checks of representative groups of newspapers receiving the same wire service show a surprisingly wide variation in the stories chosen from the telegraphed news report by editors for publication in their newspapers. Stories selected for prominent front page play by some editors may be dismissed by others with brief mention on inside pages, or omitted entirely. This is not surprising when we realize that the press association wire delivers far more dispatches than most newspapers can use, and the pressures of local news vary from city to city. So do the news judgments of the individual editors.

JOB OPPORTUNITIES

The press associations are among the finest training grounds in the entire field of mass communications for young men and women interested in a career of working with news. The work is challenging. It puts a premium upon speed, conciseness, and judgment. Moreover, these organizations have a tradition of hiring young newsmen of limited professional experience and training them. Since the turnover in press association personnel is relatively high, this means that there are quite a few job openings each year.

The beginner in press association work is usually given routine stories to rewrite from the local newspapers, items to check by telephone, and similar simple duties while he is getting the "feel." He must learn to look outward from his local community, to weigh each story for its interest to readers in other cities. He may have a period of wire filing, determining the order in which dispatches are to move on a state or regional wire, under the watchful supervision of his bureau chief. And at quite an early age, he may be named night manager of a small bureau, his first opportunity to exercise a limited amount of administrative responsibility. Because of the nature of press association work, wire service staff members do more editing and less original reporting than newspaper staffs do.

Those who stay with the press associations for a number of years, as many do, usually become managers of small or middle-sized bureaus or are transferred into such large offices as Chicago, Washington, or the New York general headquarters. After training in New York, a few are sent abroad to become foreign correspondents in the wire service offices overseas.

Salaries for press association work are approximately in line with those on large daily newspapers. Both the Associated Press and United Press International have contracts with the American Newspaper Guild, under which the employees advance through a well-defined series of pay levels based upon experience. There are supplemental payments for night work, and pay levels rise higher in the metropolitan bureaus. Salary increases above these specified experience levels are obtained on individual merit through negotiation with the management. The top minimum scale in 1964 for both men and women ranged from $8000 annually in smaller bureaus to $9400 in key bureaus. Salaries of $12,000 to $18,000 were paid a considerable number of top correspondents, desk editors, and news and business managers; executive salaries ranged from $20,000 to $40,000.

Although quite a few men and a few women spend virtually their entire careers in the press associations, there is a fairly heavy turnover in personnel. Some wire service men grow tired of the time pressures and the writing restrictions. They believe that while advancement is relatively fast when they are starting, it slows down as they mature.

They may find better salary opportunities in special reporting jobs and editorships on newspapers or in public relations, radio, television, and other related fields of mass communications. Many of the country's best-known reporters, writers, television commentators, and editors worked for the press associations in their younger years; almost unanimously they are grateful for the experience, especially for the writing discipline it taught them.

NEWSPAPER FEATURE SYNDICATES

The other major source of editorial material used by daily newspapers from coast to coast, and tending to bring uniformity to the American press, is the feature syndicates. These sell to the newspapers a multitude of material for the entertainment and education of their readers, edited and ready for publication upon delivery. Comic strips and some other features are provided in mat form; other text features are supplied in mimeographed form, in type galley proofs or in prepunched TTS tape.

An editor can load his paper as heavily with such syndicated material as his budget and his conscience will allow. The larger the feature "package" in a paper, the less space there is to be filled with locally created news and press association dispatches. A publication too full of such "canned" features gets a reputation of being more an entertainment medium than a newspaper and of being deficient in editorial enterprise. Readership polls show, however, that there is a very strong desire among readers for certain syndicated features, especially the better-known comic strips.

So the newspaper editor tries to strike a suitable balance. There is no firm rule of thumb about this; one good newspaper of substantial circulation and a reasonably large editorial "hole" (the space left in a newspaper after the advertisements have been inserted) will publish 16 comic strips daily while a comparable one runs only 10 or 12. The same is true of political columns and other material offered by the syndicates.

Examination of a typical well-edited newspaper with 50,000 daily circulation shows this material purchased ready-made from national feature syndicates: 12 comic strips, 12 cartoon panels, 5 political columns, medical column, personal advice column, crossword puzzle, astrological forecast, political cartoon, 2 entertainment columns, and juvenile information feature.

Some features, especially comic strips, have run in newspapers so many years that they have become household words, a commonplace in contemporary American life. Millions of readers every day look to see how Dick Tracy is getting along in his pursuit of a clever criminal, how the hillbilly Li'l Abner is faring in Dogpatch, and how Dagwood, the ordinary family man, is dealing with his domestic problems. The political opinions of columnists Drew Pearson and Walter Lippmann cause discussion among businessmen at lunch. And such free-swinging personal advice columns as "Dear Abby" are the predinner fare of many housewives.

Approximately a dozen major syndicates provide the bulk of the features appearing in American newspapers, although there are more than a hundred smaller companies, some of which operate in specialized fields like boating and book serializations. The major syndicates have from 25 to more than a hundred different features in the lists they offer for sale to editors. These include illustrated or text features on such diverse subjects as bridge, teen-age advice, beauty, Biblical tales, inspirational verse, automobile repairs, fashions, Hollywood gossip, Little League baseball, and handwriting analysis.

An editor who has trouble saying "no" to the sales talk of the syndicate salesmen soon finds himself overloaded with material for which the total weekly fee can run uncomfortably high. But an editor who can't say "no" is a contradiction in terms. On comics especially, many editors make a habit of dropping one feature whenever they buy a new one. Papers make occasional readership surveys to determine which comics and daily features are most popular. So attached do readers become to individual comic strips that the dropping of any single one almost always provokes a torrent of complaints; consequently, fewer changes are made than many editors desire.

Features are sold to newspapers for prices scaled to the paper's circulation. A famous comic strip that costs a metropolitan paper $50 or more a week may cost a paper with less than 10,000 circulation only $3. Although some features are sold for specific contract periods, many are on a "t.f." basis—the abbreviation for the phrase "till forbid"—meaning that the feature runs until the editor sends in a cancellation, usually on 30- to 90-day notice.

Competition among the syndicates to sell their features is intense. There are more than 250 daily comic strips on the market, many of which are also issued in color for Sunday comic sections; about 40 health columns; nearly 70 religious features; and a dozen competing columns on stamp collecting. Although many well-established "name" features go on year after year, a new group of comic strips, panels, and text columns is brought onto the market annually. Features which lose popular appeal are dropped by the syndicates.

As a rule an editor organizing a comic page for his paper tries to offer readers a mixture of adventure continuity, serial stories similar to radio's soap opera drama with strong feminine appeal, children's interest, a strip slanted to teen-agers, and gag-a-day strips without continuity except in the characters themselves. Until a few years ago, most comic strips ran five columns wide; now almost all are in four columns. Closely connected with the comic strip is the cartoon panel, usually two columns wide, in which some familiar characters, such as Dennis the Menace, are involved in daily humorous misadventures; there is no continuity of action in these panels, which resemble those published in magazines. Several exceptionally popular comic strip and cartoon characters have been transformed into "live" versions on television, with uneven success.

The feature syndicates do not offer a very large potential for the young man or woman seeking a job. Their editorial and sales staffs are small and mostly drawn from professional journalists with several years of editorial or business-side experience. Most of the artists and writers whose material is distributed by these organizations do their work outside the syndicate offices and send or bring it in for editing and approval. Usually they work on a percentage arrangement with the syndicate, receiving a portion of the fees paid by the newspapers. Syndicate editing requires knowledge of the public taste, as well as the space problems, buying habits, and idiosyncracies of the various newspaper editors who are the customers for the syndicate products.

SUMMARY

The United Press International and the Associated Press, the two American press associations, provide essential news of state, national, and world affairs for the daily newspapers and radio and television stations of this country. They also distribute specially edited news reports to media in more than 100 foreign countries. Television and radio stations are served by specially written wires. The two agencies also distribute news pictures, special sports and financial reports, and other news features.

Founded in 1848, the AP is a cooperative organization controlled by its American daily newspaper members. The UPI is a privately owned company; it represents a 1958 merger of the Scripps-owned United Press (founded in 1907) and the Hearst-owned International News Service (founded in 1909). By the mid-1960's the AP was serving approximately 8500 newspapers and TV-radio stations throughout the world; the UPI approximately 6000. Among American daily papers, some 45 per cent used only AP news and 30 per cent only UPI news; 25 per cent used both services. The AP was leading in serving American television and radio stations, 2500 to 2300. News is distributed on more than 400,000 miles of leased wires in the United States by each of the agencies, and overseas by radio teletype circuits which activate teleprinters abroad just as they run in American newsrooms.

The press associations are splendid training grounds for young reporters and editors. They put a premium upon speed and accuracy and enforce a valuable writing and reporting discipline. Newsmen and newswomen often move from the press associations to the specialized writing media, and into television and radio.

The other major source of nonlocal editorial material for American newspapers is the syndicates. These sell comic strips, opinion and advice columns, and other popular features to newspapers, thus tending to bring a degree of uniformity to the contents of publications situated in far distant parts of the country. Syndicate staffs are small and offer only limited opportunities for newcomers.

STUDY QUESTION

What effects have the press associations and feature syndicates had upon the content of newspapers throughout the United States?

PROJECTS

1. Clip from newspapers, and compare in a brief written report, accounts of a single event as reported by both the Associated Press and United Press International.

2. List, in order, what you consider to be the three most popular syndicated features in your local newspaper. Prepare to explain in class why you think so. Check your selections against a readership study if one is available in your library.

CHAPTER 15

ADVERTISING

ADVERTISING AND THE FUTURE

Advertising has come to play a unique and central role in the functioning of the American economic system. Our skills in producing goods and services have grown so great that *production* no longer is our primary concern, as is still the case in most countries. Instead, *distribution* has the principal task of maintaining a high level of employment and general prosperity. And the distribution of goods and services depends largely upon the effective use of advertising in the media.

As Frederick R. Gamble, former president of the American Association of Advertising Agencies, has pointed out:

Advertising is the counterpart in distribution of the machine in production. By the use of machines, our production of goods and services has been multiplied. By the use of mass media, advertising multiples the selling effort. Advertising is the great accelerating force in distribution. Reaching many people rapidly at low cost, advertising speeds up sales, turns prospects into customers in large numbers and at high speed. Hence, in a mass-production and high-consumption economy, advertising has the greatest opportunity and the greatest responsibility for finding customers.

Advertising men are a creative and resourceful lot, but even they have not been able to find the proper words to describe adequately the tremendous rise of advertising since World War II. In 1947 American business spent slightly over $4,000,000,000 to cry its wares. By 1965 advertising exceeded $13,000,000,000 a year, and it was said that every person in the country was exposed to no fewer than 1600 advertisements each day. Predictions were that advertising expenditures would reach $22,000,000,000 and possibly even $25,000,000,000 by 1970. By that time a person might see or hear 2000 advertisements each day!

Another $12,000,000,000 spent at present in the packaging of products also is certain to increase substantially. This function has more and more become a responsibility of advertising as thousands of retail stores have converted to self-service.

In the United States advertising is serving a population predicted to reach 260,000,000 by 1980. There are 11,500 or so babies born every day. The 5-to-17-year school census, now listing well over 50,000,000 youngsters, is rising at a pace double that of the population as a whole. And medical science is helping to swell the ranks of the middle-aged and the elderly. The production of goods and services inevitably must expand tremendously, and advertising will expand right along with them.

An historic surge of research and development by American industry, education, and government has produced more efficient manufacturing as well as countless new products. Research expenditures now exceeding $13,000,000,000 each year have revolutionized much of American business. For example, in only a decade we have increased the production of plastics by 300 per cent, electronics 240 per cent, and aluminum products 200 per cent. The manufacturing and marketing of semiconductors alone is a half-billion-dollar per year business. Approximately 6000 new products account for 10 per cent of all sales each year, and the volume of new products is expected to double in five years, triple in ten! Advertising, along with its marketing aids of sales promotion, product design, packaging, point-of-purchase displays, product publicity, and public relations, has its work cut out for it.

J. Davis Danforth, formerly executive vice president of one of the largest advertising agencies, Batten, Barton, Durstine & Osborn, Inc., took a look at the future in a speech before an advertising group, and declared:

If our national productivity increases, as most economists predict, advertising will have to grow to move the mountain of goods which will be produced. New color television sets, fuel injection automobiles, hundreds of new appliances that are in laboratory stages now, millions of new homes with advanced radiant heating and cooling equipment, and the astonishing new furnishings that will go into them . . . and we'll have to help sell them all!

We will be selling windows that close themselves when it rains, and food that will be practically non-perishable, irradiated by electronic rays to keep it fresh almost indefinitely. Perhaps you will shop by TV by just sitting at home and dialing a number, color TV will hang in a picture frame on your wall, phones will come equipped with viewing screens so you will be able to see as well as hear (is that good?). Already we can dial long distance almost anywhere in the country without ever contacting an operator. We will have doubledeck streets in the high traffic centers, daily newspapers may be printed in color, and perhaps you will have a unit in your house so that your morning newspaper will be printed right in your own home while you are sleeping. With the new science of geriatrics, everybody is going to live longer—maybe even advertising men! . . .

Advertising men almost certainly will want to live longer, for they will be caught up in the key roles of helping to bring about the dazzling pattern of living for the future. Hundreds will find their opportunities overseas, for American business has truly gone international. Every one of the 100 leading corporations in the United States is involved with international trade, and most of them have their own manufacturing facilities overseas. Well over 50 American advertising agencies are represented abroad, involving 62 cities around the world. As more and more countries become industrialized and personal incomes increase, American business and American advertising men will explore new frontiers of worldwide expansion and opportunity. These pioneers of the future will be paid well, in both money and satisfaction, for their abilities to help move the products of a new age into the hands of people everywhere. Small wonder that advertising as a career is appealing to an increasing number of the most mentally alert and imaginative of today's youth.

THE LURE OF ADVERTISING

Few careers provide the day-by-day job satisfactions inherent in advertising. Each sales problem that must be solved and each advertisement that must be conceived, produced, and presented to the public challenge the creativity and the skill of the men and women so engaged. The industry richly rewards those people with imagination, those with the ability to think for themselves. It brings a sense of fulfillment to those who have cultivated the "whole man"—who have achieved a liberal education through delving into philosophy, foreign languages, literature, art, music, astronomy, and other such fields. It enables them to call upon their own inner resources, to test new ideas and new approaches, and to seek results through subtle means as well as directly. Like fiction writers, they have the opportunity to *create* the mental images they want to evoke in the minds of the public.

There's an intensely satisfying thrill in seeing one's ideas assume form and substance in an advertisement that actually produces the intended response. There's an accompanying thrill in viewing the creativity of others. "It's probably terrible to say this, but I buy the *New Yorker* to read the ads," exclaimed a young advertising career woman. The advertisements, she explained, excited her aesthetic sense and produced the same stimulation that a young voice student must experience upon hearing a famous operatic singer.

Since most advertising has a positive social value in bringing a higher standard of living to America and in helping to satisfy people's desires and needs, many engaged in the industry tend to identify their own efforts with these larger objectives and thus find increased satisfaction in what they are doing. Bruce Barton, who with two partners in 1919 formed an advertising agency which has since become one of the largest in the world, recalls an incident that illustrates this point. He wrote an advertisement for a life insurance company, addressing it to young husbands and fathers. From Rio de Janeiro came a reply from a 38-year-old New Jersey man, married, and the father of three children. He wanted, and obtained, a policy that would guarantee his family an income of $3000 a year in the event of his death. A few days after the policy was written, the man had a wisdom tooth extracted; the cavity became infected and he died. "That incident made a deep impression on me," Barton later wrote. "Many times in the intervening years I have been reminded that somewhere in New Jersey there are a mother and three children, now grown up, who, without the slightest suspicion of my existence, have had their whole lives changed by the fact that one day I put together some words that were printed in a magazine, and read in a faraway country by their husband and father, who was influenced to do what I suggested."

HOW ADVERTISING DEVELOPED

Until the advent of mass selling in the nineteenth century advertising played only a minor role in the conduct of business. In early Greek and Roman days signboards were placed above the doors of business establishments and town criers proclaimed that merchants had certain wares for sale. These were merely means to attract customers to a shop, however; in contrast with modern advertising and sales techniques, the display of merchandise and personal selling were depended upon to make the sale.

After the invention of movable type accelerated printing in the mid-fifteenth century, handbills, posters, and then newspapers were used in increasing quantities to advertise products. Advertisements appeared in early American newspapers, but the volume did not grow to sizable proportions until trade began to flourish in the metropolitan centers in the early days of the republic. Almost all selling was local until about 1840, when the development of railroad transportation enabled industry to send its products to consumers far from the manufacturing plants. National advertising resulted as businessmen used both magazines and newspapers to broaden their markets. The first advertising agency in the United States was organized by Volney B. Palmer in 1840 or 1841. His agency, and those which followed his, did not prepare copy but served primarily as publishers' representatives. They contracted for space in various publications and then sold it at higher prices to advertisers. Some 30 agencies were selling space for more than 4000 American publications by 1860. Since there were no public lists of these publications and no way of substantiating circulation claims, the agents could manipulate their buying and selling of space to substantial personal advantage.

In 1869, however, George P. Rowell began publishing his *American Newspaper Directory,* a rather complete list of newspapers together with careful estimates of circulation. The same year F. Wayland Ayer founded N. W. Ayer & Son, Inc. (with his father) to buy space in the interest of his clients rather than to sell it for newspapers, and his agency began its continuing directory of all periodicals in 1880. Soon other agencies were started along professional lines of providing planning and space-buying services for their clients. There was an upsurge in the use of pictorial art in advertisements, and the nation began to be conscious of the first widely quoted slogans such as Ivory Soap's "99 $44/100$ Per Cent Pure" and "It Floats," Eastman Kodak's "You Press the Button—We Do the Rest," and "Good Morning, Have You Used Pear's Soap?"

As newspaper and magazine circulations increased and new technological advances were made, advertising at the turn of the century developed new slogans, better copywriters and artists, and a greater analysis of products, media, and markets. A crusade was begun in 1911 against the gross exaggerations and misleading claims of some advertisers, notably those selling patent medicines. Various advertising organizations were formed which helped elevate the ethics of the business. To promote truth in advertising many states adopted a model statute proposed by *Printers' Ink,* magazine for advertising people, at the behest of the Association of Advertising Clubs. The first Better Business Bureau was formed in 1913, and the next year saw the establishment of the Audit Bureau of Circulations, a nonprofit organization making unbiased periodical audits and statements concerning a publication's circulation.

The advent of radio and a steady improvement in the techniques of advertising, such as copy-testing, the study of psychological appeals, and plans for integrated campaigns, characterized the 1920's. Advertising fought to hold its own during the depression years of the 1930's against both the near-paralysis of business and the organized objections of consumers to what they considered to be improper practices in advertising. In 1938 the Wheeler-Lea Act was passed to protect the consumer against false advertising by business firms, mainly in selling foods, drugs, and cosmetics.

During World War II the War Advertising Council was established by advertising agencies, media, and advertisers as a voluntary contribution to the total war effort. So successful was the council in promoting the sale of war bonds, donation of blood, rationing, and the like, that it has been continued in peacetime as the Advertising Council to promote America's welfare. Advertising had demonstrated that it could "sell" ideas as well as merchandise and services.

Our booming economy after World War II produced rapid growth in all areas of advertising. Staffs were enlarged, branch offices of advertising agencies proliferated, and small agencies formed networks to provide reciprocal services for their clients in cities across the country. The development of television as an advertising medium accelerated the trend to larger agencies, however, because it increased the complexities of advertising. Television arrived at a most opportune time, for advertisers were introducing hundreds of new products and consumers were eager to learn their merits. The older media, also growing, soon adjusted to television, although radio and the national magazines felt the new competition most keenly. Advertisers turned increasingly to research to provide facts about their products and to discover the motivations of consumer markets.

Advertising surged past the mid-1960's confronted with the staggering task of helping to move into the hands of consumers an unprecedented volume of manufactured goods. More money was entrusted to advertising personnel, and their responsibilities mounted. Management demanded more efficient methods of measuring the effectiveness of advertising as distinguished from other marketing functions. The computer, in wide use for such housekeeping chores as accounting, billing, and reports, still awaited full development by the industry. Some agencies, including Leo

Burnett Company, Young & Rubicam, and Batten, Barton, Durstine & Osborn, placed media data in storage on their computers. This trend toward what one observer termed "a mechanized handling of raw facts" was countered by an equally strong movement emphasizing creativity in advertising, although some viewed research and creativity as complementary rather than conflicting forces. As American business rapidly increased its operations overseas, new patterns of diversification were introduced into agencies. An example is Interpublic, Inc., comprising a group of components active in producing various marketing-communications services on a farflung scale. The new technology, coupled with a dynamic, fluctuating world economy, was rapidly sweeping advertising into uncharted, troubled, but rewarding waters.

Curiously, as the demands mounted that advertising help keep our economy sound and advance our standard of living, the number and the vociferousness of the critics of advertising also increased. On top of the suspicions aroused by consumer group allegations in previous decades, numerous anti-advertising novels, articles, and movies continued to depict advertising men as "hucksters" and Madison Avenue as the sinister locale of powerful, hidden persuaders determined to control the thoughts and actions of the entire nation. The more objectionable forms of television advertising, intruding into almost every living room, gave the critics even more complaints, as were detailed in Chapter 8 and discussed there.

The world of advertising thus felt an urgent need to intensify its efforts at self-improvement and to explain more successfully the constructive contributions of advertising to the economy. Hostile public opinion could add to the problems advertising men have always faced in preventing passage of injurious tax laws and restrictions on advertising by federal and local units of government; the Advertising Federation of America moved its headquarters to Washington to give advertising a voice in the national capital. Business managements generally were exhibiting concern and were adding their voices to those of advertising's leaders as they set out to present their case and to launch a vigorous counterattack against their critics.

THE SIZE OF THE ADVERTISING FIELD

In the United States. The number of persons engaged in advertising activities in the United States has never been determined exactly. The 1952 edition of the Statistical Abstract of the United States indicates

72,975. The American Association of Advertising Agencies, in a recent booklet, estimates a conservative 90,000. *Printers' Ink* figures, however, that as many as 375,000 are employed in the field. A close look at the trade weekly's informed estimate will reveal to the beginning student of mass communications the wide range of business firms that employ advertising specialists. The estimate includes those who "create or sell advertising for an advertiser, medium, or service, but not the thousands behind the scenes such as printers, sign painters, and clerical help."

Those who handle advertising for the nation's radio and television stations, including 700 sales representatives, total 33,900. Employed by daily newspapers, including 1500 representatives' salesmen, are 14,268. Nondailies add another 14,194. Approximately 8000 periodicals other than newspapers, including 2000 business publications and 44 mass circulation magazines, add 28,490.

About 2500 are employed by 1200 outdoor and transportation advertising companies. Advertising agencies themselves add 50,000.

Estimating that 22,000 of the country's 300,000 manufacturing and service companies have formal advertising departments, *Printers' Ink* adds 110,000. Only 10 per cent of some 265,000 wholesalers are believed to have advertising departments, but they contribute another 26,500.

If only half of the country's 100,000 retail establishments with four or more store units have a formal advertising function, 50,000 workers can be added. Another 5000 likely can be found in the 50,000 retail companies that operate two or more stores. There are a million and a half single-unit retail establishments; estimating that only 1 per cent have an advertising department adds 15,000.

A miscellaneous group, including specialty suppliers, point-of-sale creators, commercial film producers, association staffs, consultants, artists, and others not mentioned specifically, contributes a final 25,000. The total: 374,852.

Thus it appears, surprisingly perhaps, that the nation's manufacturing and service concerns employ the largest number of advertising workers. Much of their effort, of course, goes into advertising directed to consumers which increased 77 per cent during the 1950's. An important reason that manufacturers' advertising staffs have increased, however, lies in the fact that industrial advertising, as measured by the McGraw-Hill Company, increased 145 per cent during the same period. A recent study by the Industrial Advertising Research Institute, research arm of the

National Industrial Advertisers Association, disclosed that the internal advertising departments of about half of the nation's industrial companies had five or fewer staff members, but that 24 per cent of the biggest industrial advertisers (those billing over $500,000 annually) had at least 30 staff members in their advertising departments.

Following manufacturing and service companies, in order of the number of advertising employees, are the mass media (newspapers, radio-television, magazines, outdoor and transportation advertising, totaling 93,352), retail establishments, advertising agencies, wholesalers, and miscellaneous specialty companies.

International advertising. United States advertisers, agencies, and advertising personnel have been engaged in international advertising for nearly two-thirds of a century. Today our participation is steadily and dramatically increasing. Standards of living in Europe, the Far East, Latin America, and other heretofore untapped marketing areas are constantly improving. The literacy rates have been rising, and the growth of both print and broadcast media in many countries has provided a larger audience for advertising. American wares are in great demand. We are exporting some $30,000,000,000 worth of products each year. These join the flow of goods produced by overseas plants in which Americans have invested more than $30,000,000,000.

As a consequence, giant corporations such as IBM World Trade, Standard Oil (New Jersey), Coca-Cola Export, General Motors, and Monsanto, long in the international field, are being joined by countless other companies seeking their share of the world market. IBM World Trade alone, according to *Printers' Ink,* has more than 300 sales locations in 94 countries, 194 data processing centers, and 45,000 non-U.S. employees. Its gross earnings abroad measure well over $500,000,000.

The J. Walter Thompson Company and McCann-Erickson (International) have about two-thirds of all the advertising business handled by the ten largest "international agencies." The clients of these two agencies total almost 1000. Since its first foreign office was opened in London in 1899, the J. Walter Thompson Company has sent hundreds of its American employees abroad to staff them. Today more than 4000 employees work in 37 offices in 22 countries. McCann-Erickson (International) staffs its more than 50 foreign offices largely with nationals of the 22 countries in which they are located. The firm is a part of Interpublic, Inc., the parent company of ten such corporations and divisions.

Both the J. Walter Thompson Company and McCann-Erickson (International) handle more than $125,000,000 a year in billings outside the United States. Five other U.S. agencies have overseas billings in excess of $20,000,000 annually.

The smaller domestic agencies operate overseas in four ways: through subsidiaries, of which they own part or all of the stock; through "exclusive" affiliations; through "account" affiliations with overseas agencies which may also work with other U.S. agencies; and through "export" media, such as *Life International, Reader's Digest International,* and *Vision.* The fourth method often is used along with any of the other three.

The total number of advertising employees serving overseas with U.S. companies and agencies has never been estimated. Despite automation, or partly perhaps because of it, the number is certain to increase. In a *Printers' Ink* article, L. T. Steele, executive vice president of Benton & Bowles, Inc., sums up the opportunities in this fashion:

Young people coming into advertising in the 1960's will discover, in the international scope of the business, a whole world of opportunities. Advertising men and women of our generation are rightfully proud of their contributions to the American economy. The new, young breed will extend these contributions to many other economies in other countries. If we, in our time, have found excitement, stimulation, and rich rewards in our careers in advertising, think how much greater their achievements can be!

It is they who will truly be co-architects of the world of tomorrow.

WHAT ADVERTISING PEOPLE DO

Advertising may be defined as the dissemination of sales messages through purchased space, time, or other media to identify, inform, or persuade. What people do to accomplish this objective can be described by examining briefly the roles they play in advertising agencies, in advertising departments of the mass media, in retail store and company advertising departments, and, finally, in the planning of a national advertising campaign.

Advertising agencies. A booklet issued by the American Association of Advertising Agencies provides us with an outline of typical agency functions. The agency first studies its client's product or service to learn the advantages and disadvantages of the product itself in relation to its competition. It then analyzes the present and potential market for which the product or service is intended. Taken into consideration next are the distribution and sales plans of the client, which are studied with a view to determining the best selection of media. A definite plan is then formulated and presented to the client.

Once the plan is approved the agency staff writes, designs, and illustrates the proposed advertisements; contracts for space or time with the media; produces the advertisements and sends them to the media with instructions; checks and verifies the use of the ads; pays for the services rendered and bills the client; and cooperates in such merchandising efforts as point-of-purchase displays.

Who are the persons who perform these services? The answer varies, since advertising agencies range in size from the so-called "one-man" agency with an owner and one or two assistants to organizations employing a thousand persons or more. The executive heads of an agency are usually people who have proved they can produce sales for their clients through print and broadcasting and who are capable of procuring new business for the agency. They may be organized as a plans board, giving general direction to departments of research, planning, media, copy, art and layout, production, traffic, merchandising, checking, and accounting.

The key man in "servicing an account," that is, in providing liaison between the agency and the client, is called the account executive. He must have a general knowledge of all phases of advertising, merchandising, and general business practices, as well as an ability to aid creatively in solving a client's special advertising problems and in planning campaigns. The account executive calls upon the agency's various departments for assistance and correlates their efforts in behalf of his particular client.

The research department carries on market research (consumer surveys to determine present and potential markets, dealer and trade-channel studies, product testing on consumers, studies of effectiveness of brand names and package designs) and copy research (analysis of advertisement readership studies, pretesting of printed ads and commercials, studies of typographical and layout effectiveness, analyses of campaign results). Its findings help guide the work of those in planning and of the account executives. Closely allied are the space and time buyers, known as media men, who help decide to what extent a particular client's advertising will be carried in newspapers, magazines, on radio or television, or be handled in other ways, and who study constantly the relative merits of the various media as advertising vehicles and comparative costs of reaching consumer audiences.

Copy and art chiefs are responsible for the actual creation of advertisements. The copywriter, working with the layout man, artist, and photographer, prepares the ads. The production department orders engravings and printing. Making certain that all the many schedules of copy preparation and distribution to the media are being maintained is the important but prosaic job of the traffic department. Merchandising personnel work with the client in coordinating point-of-purchase displays in retail stores and other promotional campaigns.

Other employees check to determine that the advertisements have been used by the media as planned and compute the agency's commission. This is generally 15 per cent of the medium's published rate; if the advertising space or time cost $100, the agency collects that amount from the client and pays the medium $85. Most agencies today operate under the commission system because the bulk of their compensation comes from commissions allowed by media. This averages about 75 per cent of income. The remaining 25 per cent compensation to these agencies is from clients. It consists of fees, plus out-of-pocket expenditures, for special services and collateral work performed at the client's request, and service charges, or commissions as they are more commonly called, added to the cost of materials and services purchased in the preparation of advertising. The suppliers of materials and services used in preparing advertising, typography, plates, filmed commercials, artwork, printing, etc., do not allow a commission to the agencies as do the media. When these charges are billed to the advertiser, commission generally is added. Until recent years commission was usually 15 per cent on the net bill, but it is becoming more standard to make the commission 17.65 per cent in order to receive 15 per cent on the gross bill.

After all expenses have been met, the agencies generally wind up with 3 to 4 per cent net profit on their gross income each year.

Advertising departments of mass media. As detailed in earlier chapters, all the media employ space or time salesmen and almost all engage national sales representatives to obtain advertising for them. The principal function of the time or space salesman is to show how the medium can assist in the sale and marketing of the product or service to be advertised. He provides fresh, up-to-date information about the markets that his newspaper, magazine, or station covers and about the medium itself. This information comes from the research men in his advertising department. His calls are not limited to the advertising agencies that generally represent the largest accounts; he also makes certain that the advertiser himself is aware of the particular advantages of his medium in selling his product or service.

Each salesman can provide general information about newspaper and magazine readership and the ratings accorded radio and television programs. These facts are coordinated by his own research and promotion departments and by national trade associations or bureaus representing each medium. Formerly, the salesman worked on a commission basis; the trend today, however, is to place him on a salary, with perhaps a bonus arrangement as well. He thus is less apt to "oversell" an account and drive away future business.

Informing and persuading generally are his chief functions in the offices of advertising agencies and in the advertising departments of large companies, since trained personnel there usually plan campaigns and prepare copy. Managers of smaller firms, however, may ask him and other media staff members, such as artists and copywriters, to carry out these latter functions. In addition, the medium provides promotion, market research, and merchandising services.

The newspaper advertising salesman often works first in the classified department, where he solicits and writes copy for the large variety of advertisements that are "classified" according to category (for rent, for sale, jobs wanted, etc.) He may move to the local retail display department, handling larger accounts, or to the general advertising staff, which cooperates with national advertising representatives in servicing nationwide accounts. Or he may be hired by an agency that wants an advanced-level staff man who has worked with the media.

Television obtains roughly 80 per cent of its income from network and national spot advertising; the rest comes from local advertising. Radio, on the other hand, gets approximately 60 per cent of its income from local advertising. Major advertising agencies contract for the network time, dealing directly with the networks themselves, which pay the individual stations at a specified rate for the time used. National sales representatives solicit agencies to obtain nonnetwork, or spot, advertising, which may range from a brief announcement to an entire program originating in the studios of the station. Local advertising is sold by time solicitors and prepared usually by copywriters employed by the station. Many advance to the position of commercial manager and eventually to that of general manager of the station.

Most magazines deal directly with national advertisers or indirectly through national representatives. As is true with the other media, copywriters, artists, and production, promotion, and merchandising personnel supplement the sales force. And there is a similar ladder of promotion to executive positions.

Retail store advertising. As noted earlier in this chapter, retail firms employ some 70,000 persons in their advertising departments. These range from one-man staffs to those employing dozens of persons. In a large store the advertising manager works closely with sales promotion and marketing specialists and also usually with an advertising agency. In one large Chicago department store, the staff consists of a copy chief, production manager, and proofreader; an art director and assistant art director, together with six layout artists, five "finish" artists, and two apprentices; and five copywriters, mostly women with a high degree of creativeness who specialize in women's and children's apparel, men's apparel and accessories, and home furnishings. In addition, two copywriters are assigned to the basement store and the suburban store. Other journalistic personnel may be found in the public relations and publicity office and in the radio-television division preparing special product demonstrations.

Industrial advertising. The public is well aware of the large quantity of consumer goods advertising: we see and hear advertisements almost every moment of the waking day, and often advertising jingles course through our brains even as we sleep. Not so with industrial advertisements. And yet advertising agencies receive more than $154,000,000 annually with which to service industrial accounts. And total industrial advertising volume reached a new high of $1,329,700,000 in 1963, according to a McGraw-Hill Publishing Company estimate. These figures include not only business publication advertising, but also direct mail, catalogs, exhibits, films, and other advertising expenditures. Here, industries are selling their products and services to other industries, and to wholesalers and retailers, not directly to the general public.

The industrial advertising department may employ only one man, the advertising manager, or as many as 400 or more persons. The typical department, however, employs about seven persons. These are likely to include the advertising manager, secretarial help, a writer, perhaps an artist, and one or two persons engaged in marketing research, media evaluation, or production work.

The department handles inquiries and prepares catalogs and technical data sheets, direct mail, exhibits, and sales promotion materials such as slide films, movies, and props for sales meeting. It likely will engage in market research, but most departments obtain market data through business paper research services, without charge.

Almost all industrial advertising departments employ outside agencies to handle trade advertisements. More than half the advertising placed in business publications comes from general agencies. Others identify themselves as industrial advertising agencies, although most of them also handle consumer goods advertising. They specialize in industrial, technical, scientific, commercial, and merchandising products and services. A few agencies confine themselves to such fields as financial or pharmaceutical advertising.

The industrial agency is most likely to emphasize the services of account executives who work directly with the client, write copy, and make media-buying analyses and decisions largely on their own. There is a minimum of creative direction by an over-all planning board. Between 20 and 50 per cent, or more, of industrial agency income is derived from fees rather than media commissions. This is caused by the fact that commissions are limited, generally amounting to only $150, often even $25 or $50, per insertion. And an agency may be called upon to prepare between 50 and 100 different advertisements each year per $100,000 in annual space expenditures. With costs for research, layout, merchandising, and public relations running high and commissions low, the charging of supplemental fees for these services is a necessity.

Planning a national campaign. Selecting appropriate media for a particular advertising campaign demands great business acumen and reliance on research studies. If an advertiser decides to use magazines as his vehicle, for example, he must next decide which class or group, such as women's magazines, to choose, and then must select the specific publication, such as *McCall's*. The size of the advertisement and the frequency of publication also must be determined. Similar choices must be made for all the media to be employed.

In introducing its 1964 Mustang automobile, the Ford Motor Company combined thorough market research with an advertising, sales promotion, and public relations campaign that achieved spectacular results. Ford's market researchers accurately gauged the impact of two trends—the tremendous increase of the teen-age population and the equally large increase in the number of two- and three-car families—and uncovered a market looking for a product. Engineers produced the automobile, and national advertising and national promotion, coupled with local follow-ups, produced the sales.

Ford bought simultaneous prime time on all three major television networks. Three commercial minutes on the "Perry Mason" and "Jimmy Dean" shows, as well as on Ford's "Hazel" program, reached an audience of some 28,000,000. In all, 46 minutes of network commercial time was carried from mid-April to mid-May. In addition, 315 TV stations used film clips, with both sound track and script, on news programs. Radio disc jockeys were given Mustangs to test-drive and were sent back to local stations with orders for spot paid commercials which the disc jockeys themselves wrote or ad-libbed.

On introduction day, advertisements appeared in 2612 newspapers in 2219 markets, covering 75 per cent of all households. A special ad, tailored to women, stressed the Mustang's Tiffany Award for excellence in design. Followup newspaper advertising appeared for weeks.

Twenty-four national magazines carried advertisements. There were four-page, four-color layouts in *Life, Look, Saturday Evening Post,* and *Reader's Digest.* Two-page, four-color layouts ran in *Sports Illustrated, Esquire,* and other magazines. As a bonus, both *Time* and *Newsweek* printed simultaneous cover stories, and there was extensive photo coverage in other national magazines.

Mustangs were displayed in airport terminals, bank lobbies, shopping centers, the New York World's Fair, and other high-traffic locations, including 100 Holiday Inns. Mustang ads ran on the cover of 7,000,000 Holiday Inn directories, on the cover of the motel chain's magazine, and in its travel and safety films and other materials.

The car was advertised on 15,500 outdoor boards in 170 markets.

Business and professional men, college newspaper editors, automotive editors, and others were given Mustangs to test-drive for a week. There were numerous tie-ins with national TV programs, point-of-purchase displays, advertisements, and contests sponsored by a hair dressing company, hobby shops, and other firms. Local promotions were varied, including the mailing of thousands of picture post cards by local dealers.

The result? Within the first five months the Mustang sold more units than any other U.S. car in history in a similar span. The company attributed its success to thorough market research *before* the product was made and thorough promotional penetration of that market *after* the product was made.

Few advertising and promotional budgets can be this extensive. The procedure, however, is the same in each: The judicious expenditure of an allotted sum in a carefully coordinated campaign utilizing every medium necessary to accomplish the specified sales objective.

SALARIES

The over-all trend in advertising agency salaries is up, surveys made by *Printers' Ink* have disclosed. These advances include across-the-board increases, partly to take care of cost-of-living hikes. The main reason for the raises, however, lies in the fact that most agencies today are handling far more business than they did before and immediately after World War II.

Agencies in metropolitan areas (New York, Chicago, Los Angeles, Detroit, and Boston were those surveyed) pay from 10 to 15 per cent higher salaries than those in smaller cities. In both metropolitan and non-metropolitan areas, respectively, salaries now vary little from one section of the country to the other. In both large and small cities, however, one fact stands out: the heavier the gross billings by an agency, the greater the salary scale. There are agencies that gross less than $250,000 a year, whereas those in the giant category take in $10,000,000 and more with the largest going above $200,000,000.

Suppose the young advertising graduate goes to work for an agency grossing between $1,000,000 and $2,000,000 in a *nonmetropolitan* area; what may he expect in pay? If he avoids, as he should, an apprenticeship at a discouragingly low wage, he may be made a junior copywriter at $4000 or $4500. Junior copywriters for agencies this size average $5700, and earn up to $10,000. When he advances to senior copywriter, he will find a minimum of $5200, an average salary of $8000, and a top of $12,800. As an account executive in an agency this size, he may expect an annual salary varying from the $10,500 average to as much as $16,500. If he becomes a part- or full-time owner, he will be in the $20,000 to $50,000 bracket.

At the level of the agency grossing $10,000,000 or more a year, our advertising graduate will find higher pay scales. Here the minimum for junior copywriters is likely to be $5500 a year, with an average of $7800 and a top of $14,000. For senior copywriters, the minimum figure is $10,000, the average $13,700, and the top $16,000. Account executives average $16,000, and the more experienced ones join department chiefs in the $20,000 and more bracket. Top executives and senior partners take home pay checks ranging up to $90,000 a year. In key metropolitan areas, pay scales beyond the beginning levels may be even higher.

As his skills and experience increase, the advertising specialist will find that he possesses knowledge for which there is a great demand. In moving from one agency to another, often taking accounts with him, he will naturally move into higher pay brackets.

A somewhat similar promotion situation is true in media and company advertising departments. The top advertising executives in the offices of newspapers, magazines, and other media, and in client companies, likely will earn only about two-thirds of what their counterparts with the agencies receive. Other factors, however, such as security and fringe benefits, often more than make up for the lower salaries.

In the general magazine field, advertising directors earn from $6500 to $40,000, depending largely upon circulation. Business paper advertising managers may earn from $5000 to $25,000. Advertising managers for newspapers will be paid about the same. And commercial managers for radio and television stations may be paid from $4000 to $21,000.

Salaries paid beginners in advertising departments of both print and broadcast media generally exceed those for beginning news personnel, whose starting salaries by 1965 were varying widely from $3500 to $5200 a year. Starting salaries of $4500 to $5500 were not uncommon for trained advertising personnel. Manufacturing companies were making similar offers to advertising graduates in many cases; retail store salaries for copywriters ranged lower, however, with women receiving perhaps $3500 and men $4000 to start.

Those who rise to the position of advertising manager of an individual company may expect salaries ranging from $5000 to $70,000 a year, depending on the size of the business and the responsibilities involved. By contrast, a decade ago the advertising director of even the largest company received only about $30,000 a year.

Men and women who join the advertising staffs of these companies have excellent opportunities to advance to high positions regardless of the types of power echelon jobs they fill. Jumps directly to the position of advertising manager have been made by copywriters, account executives, salesmen, sales promotion people, merchandising managers, and advertising production managers.

QUALIFICATIONS

Successful advertising people are constructive, adaptable, and eternally curious, according to a booklet prepared by the American Association of Advertising Agencies.

Advertising people, it is pointed out, must be constructively optimistic because they are called on to originate ideas and to initiate action—to visualize in full operation something that has not yet been started. They must be adaptable because of the infinitely varied problems and the different types of persons that they meet almost daily. And they must have an unceasing interest in people and things and the operation of business in general and the industry they serve in particular. They must keep abreast of developments in advertising and remain keen and interested students in many fields throughout their careers.

Imagination, foresight in sensing trends, the ability to reason analytically, and a sense of form are other characteristics frequently cited. Also emphasized is a broad general education in the liberal arts along with professional training in schools of communication or commerce.

Some beginning students mistakenly believe that they must know how to draw in order to succeed in advertising. An ability to do the rough layout work required to project an idea onto paper is useful, but the finished drawing can always be prepared by a professional artist.

It's equally true that not all people in advertising must know how to write advertising copy. Numerous jobs, such as those of the artist, production man, researcher, salesman, and media analyst, do not demand proficiency in copywriting, although such a skill would be a definite advantage at times.

Along this same line, men and women who feel that they are not "cut out" to be advertising solicitors should observe that there are many jobs in advertising in which soliciting is not necessary. Those who are called upon to sell time or space should realize that they are not asking favors but are offering the prospective customer an opportunity to build his business.

Possessing the proper attitude of a learner cannot be over-emphasized, since the man or woman interested in advertising almost invariably undergoes an apprenticeship which can be genuinely trying to the person bursting with ambition to undertake greater responsibilities and command a higher salary.

Many women graduates go to work immediately as copywriters for department stores and other companies and for the agencies. A few sell space and time for the media or enter the classified advertising departments of newspapers. When a creative job opening of the sort they want and in the city of their choice is not immediately available, some women accept "foot-in-the-door" employment as typists, clerks, and secretaries before moving into jobs for which their education has qualified them.

A number of national advertising campaigns have been masterminded by women, functioning as account executives. The advertising directors of some of the largest department stores are women, and women also have achieved success as media buyers for agencies as well as in almost all other advertising capacities. A typical success story is that of Harriet Raymond, advertising manager of the plastics division of Celanese Corporation of America. She began in the sales department at the age of 14, then won recognition in the advertising department. Honored recently as "Advertising Woman of the Year" by the Council on Women's Advertising Clubs, an affiliate of the Advertising Federation of America, she was cited for her pioneering work in coordinating advertising with sales and sales promotion. She and thousands of other successful career women have proved that advertising is not merely a man's world.

RECRUITMENT PROGRAMS

Advertising associations, as well as individual agencies and departments, for years have been aware of the necessity of insuring a continuing flow of qualified young men and women into the field. The American Association of Advertising Agencies conducted an annual examination, administered throughout the country, to test prospective advertising men and women for various kinds of work in the industry. More than 300 advertising executives cooperated in the preparation and administration of the examination each year.

Beginning employees likely will find themselves in organized training programs designed for the orientation of potential top account executives and creative personnel. Some firms use the traffic department as a proving ground. Others have a program of eight months to a year of indoctrination, with men moving from one department to another. Still others conduct evening classes, addressed by department heads and agency executives.

One of the nation's leading advertising agencies, Campbell-Ewald Company of Detroit, provided a two-phase program designed to help young promising talent grow from students, graduates, or trainees into capable staff personnel. The first was a trainee program designed for about 20 persons and extending not longer than 24 months. After a 90-day period the trainee's performance was reviewed and he was continued in his preferred departmental function, transferred to another department where his potential could be developed to better advantage, or released as unsuited to the business.

The second phase of the company's program was a "creative internship" affording two months' summer employment to picked groups of eight university students.

Other agencies have developed trainee programs of their own since widespread concern has been expressed that an even greater shortage of trained advertising craftsmen will likely occur in the future. Raiding each other's staffs for high-priced talent is the only alternative.

The man or woman who wants a job in advertising and who is willing to work hard to achieve his ambition will find many helping hands.

SUMMARY

Its volume having trebled since World War II, advertising passed the mid-1960's faced with the enormous task of helping to move a steadily growing volume of goods flowing from technologically improved plants throughout the nation.

With distribution rather than production now the chief concern of the American economy, business was spending more than $13,000,000,000 a year for advertising, and there were predictions that these expenditures would reach $22,000,000,000 and possibly $25,000,000,000 by the end of the decade.

Advertising indeed has come a long way from its crude beginnings in Greek and Roman days. It has taken its present form only in the last 50 to 75 years as business itself became big and refinements in advertising techniques and ethics became necessary.

As many as 375,000 persons, it is estimated, are employed in all branches of advertising—the agencies; the media; the advertising departments of manufacturing, service, and retail companies; and miscellaneous related firms. They perform a variety of functions.

Salaries generally are increasing, largely as a result of the steadily rising volume of business being handled. Beginners usually work in training positions while they demonstrate their abilities. It is not uncommon, however, for those with talent and determination to begin in better jobs and to move quickly up the promotion ladder to responsible and well-paying positions. This is true for women as well as for men.

For years advertising associations, as well as the individual agencies, the media, and the client companies, have been aware of the necessity of insuring a continuing flow of qualified personnel for jobs in advertising. These needs have been increasing, and as a result advertising executives have looked to the universities and some firms have developed their own in-service training programs.

Besides the opportunity to share in the total increasing profits of advertising, the field is attracting men and women with imagination, curiosity, and creativity—writers and artists and others who enjoy tremendously the challenge of solving new problems, of conceiving and executing campaigns to achieve desired results, and of sharing the job satisfactions inherent in an industry that is helping to elevate living standards and is performing other essential services for the American public as well as people around the world.

STUDY QUESTION

What role does advertising play in the distribution process of the American economy?

PROJECTS

1. Read a recent issue of *Printers' Ink* or *Advertising Age* and write a brief description of a current research undertaking in the industry.

2. Check the current offerings of the various communications media and write a brief description of the advertising campaign of a company or institution that is employing more than one medium to reach the public.

CHAPTER 16

PUBLIC RELATIONS
AND INFORMATION
WRITING

WHAT IS PUBLIC RELATIONS?

One of the most rapidly growing and attention-exciting fields in mass communications is that loosely identified by the term "public relations." Some 100,000 men and women are engaged in some form of public relations work for thousands of institutions of every conceivable type—business firms, trade associations, civic organizations, colleges, social work groups, churches, trade unions, government bureaus, and schools. More often than not, they had worked previously for one of the mass media.

Probably no term which became so commonly used in the past few decades has been more misunderstood than "public relations." Many a businessman assumed that a skillful publicity writer who could concoct interesting stories for the papers was a public relations man, not realizing that publicity writing needs to be done with purposeful planning as a "tool" operation in an over-all public relations program. Groups ranging from church congregations to tavern owners' associations decided that they had better do something about their "public relations," and they debated exactly what they meant. Few understood the social science theory, stemming from a study of public opinion processes, which should guide a proper and beneficial public relations program.

The public relations function is defined as the planned effort to influence and maintain favorable opinion through acceptable performance, honestly presented, and with reliance on two-way communication. It necessarily must be a "management" function; that is, the planned effort must be based on established and agreed-upon policy statements which reflect the operating principles and the working practices of the company, organization, or group. In this aspect, public relations is one of the operating concepts, or business philosophies, of management.

But public relations is also a specialized staff function in management, drawing heavily on journalistic skills and upon social science techniques. The professional practitioner must ascertain and evaluate the opinions of various "publics" or groups (e.g., employees, stockholders, dealers, customers, residents of a given community) which collectively make up an institution's total public if communication is really going to be "two-way." He must counsel management on ways of dealing with public opinion as it exists at a particular time and suggest points at which the policies and procedures of the company should be revised if the management wants to earn an "acceptable performance" rating from groups it seeks to influence. Finally, he plans and executes a program of action to develop effective two-way communication which will result in mutual responsiveness, understanding, and acceptance. The staff function is to represent the public to the management and the management to the public so that there will be a two-way flow of both information and attitudes.

At this, the highest level of public relations work, the public relations executive is a top-level management man. He deals directly with the president, board of directors, and chief operating officers of a company. Basic principles of operation are fashioned which will guide everyday working practices, and no major decision is made without considering its public relations effects. The public relations staff acts as a balance wheel to protect, insofar as possible, the conflicting interests of the company's various publics: the shareholders who want the best possible return on their investment, the employees who want the best possible wages, the customers who want good service or products at the lowest possible cost. The public relations staff must act, too, as a constant guardian of the program's integrity, since other people do the actual "acceptable performing" in direct communicative contact with employees, customers, and others with whom the company deals. It is the public relations staff, of course, which maps out the ways of reaching the company's various publics through formal communications—printed materials, films, meetings and talks, and through use of the mass media: newspapers, radio, television, magazines.

Historically, this concept of public relations developed only recently. The term "public relations counsel" was first used by Edward L. Bernays, one of the pioneers in the field, in 1923. At the same moment an influential literature of public opinion theory was appearing in response to a growing realization of the important role of public opinion in modern society. The experiences of Bernays, Ivy Lee, T. J. Ross, and other pioneers had taught them that publicity in itself was not enough; there needed to be a counseling operation. The need for a company or institution to have such counseling, and to make a planned effort to influence and maintain favorable opinion, was slowly accepted as the professional public relations practitioners translated the theories of public opinion scholars into practical arguments and programs for their clients.

Long before the term "public relations" was invented men had performed the communicating functions, because they had a general understanding of the importance of public opinion. Much of the communicating, however, was what is called *casual publicity;* age-old, this is publicity without any planned objective or social purpose. *Informational publicity,* through which an organization tells its story to the public, is a second or midway level of activity. Bernays, Lee, Carl Byoir, and other early public relations counselors had been educated to the importance of basing an opinion-forming campaign upon full dissemination of information during World War I, when George Creel developed an admirable informational program for the government (the work of the Committee on Public Information). It was only one more step to the two-way aspect and the organized policy-level planning of *public relations counseling.* Development of market research and of customer opinion surveys came during the 1920's, followed by the working out of sound opinion measurement methods in the 1930's and 1940's—the now-familiar Gallup and Roper polls. The use of scientifically determined samples of a total population or public has enabled researchers to find out what the general public thinks about a given issue or what it knows about a given subject. Such a study of an employee group, for example, can be followed by depth interviews with individuals which probe to find out why attitudes are held or how facts have been learned.

Political and social pressures arising out of the modern environment accounted for this growth of public relations activity. The country had become industrialized, and society was more and more complex and interdependent. The public interest and the private interest had to be more nearly reconciled; individuals and institutions found the amount of their activity which could be termed strictly private in its effects was steadly declining. Government was called upon to intervene in economic and social affairs—social security, labor relations, and other areas. In the realm of business, the idea that the public had a stake in how owners and managers conducted their affairs came to be accepted, if only because pressures of public opinion threatened to bring (or brought) governmental regulation of business activity in increasing volume. Gradually some businesses and other organized groups—educators, doctors, banks, stockbrokers—came to see the values of two-way responsiveness, of seeking to reconcile private and public interests in behalf of the general welfare.

But such transitions occur slowly, and only a portion of the converts to public relations planning have known how to fashion proper programs. Today all the historical levels of publicity and public relations activity are still represented. There are thousands of casual or opportunistic publicists who were once called press agents but who now prefer the more elegant "public relations" label. There are thousands more who are information writers who do creditable enough jobs but who have no share in policymaking and so likewise should not assume the full "public relations" label. There are thousands of men and women who operate behind a façade of a public relations program—complete with everything except the integrity of the operating concept of the management. Finally, there are effective public relations directors and staffs operating to the best of their abilities under the basic concept as described and public relations counselors who offer sound advice and programs of benefit both to the client and to society, not merely publicity gimmicks.

It is important that persons interested in service to society, as journalists are, see and understand these various levels of what is loosely called "public relations" work. As either news media people or potential public relations people, they should understand the theoretical bases of a proper public relations philosophy and be able to differentiate between the useful and the useless and even dangerous activities.

A man who undertakes community relations work in behalf of an industrial firm or public utility that is anxious to contribute to the welfare of the city in which it is located, as a "corporate citizen," can make effective contributions to civic progress. A woman who develops a working statement of the objectives of a social work organization, such as Family Service, and who interprets the work of that group to the community with two-way communication as a goal, likewise has a satisfying job. A public relations counsel who persuades a company to undertake a comprehensive scientific sample of employee attitudes, as a basis for developing better programs of work supervision and promotion standards, has contributed to cooperative good will within that company.

On the other hand, the seven press agents who each received $50 a week to get the name of one New York restaurant mentioned in the gossip columns scarcely are doing work of benefit to society. Nor are the hundreds of publicity bureaus which flood the mails with press releases of the horn-blowing or inconsequential type prized by some clients. It should be perfectly obvious that the so-called public relations staffs employed by some companies and organizations to manipulate public opinion, or to apologize as best they can for the group's antisocial activities, are detrimental to society. The activities of the press agents are less obviously detrimental, but they can be so if they clog the avenues of mass communication. Information writers should strive to give newspapers and other media material of interest and value to readers; they should not, as one California publicity firm did, brag publicly how they obtained 650 inches of space in Los Angeles papers which would have cost $8775 in advertising money in behalf of a client's real estate promotional activity. Such stupidity on the part of men who call themselves public relations experts merely infuriates conscientious newspaper editors who hate being made to look like suckers.

TYPES OF PUBLIC RELATIONS WORK

The largest single area of public relations work is in corporate public relations. Thousands of United States industrial firms, banks, trade associations, cooperatives, stores, and other businesses have organized their own public relations departments. The public relations director and his staff work as employees of the organization. About 85 per cent of the companies which have public relations programs have company public relations departments. These often may be combined in the organizational structure with advertising, or with personnel.

Similarly, staff positions within the organization are maintained by chambers of commerce, federal government bureaus, state government offices, universities and colleges, community chests and social work organizations, labor unions, farm organizations, medical associations, bar associations, and countless other groups. These may be fully planned public relations efforts or middle-level information-writing assignments.

Smaller numbers of public relations men and women work as independent counselors, or members of an advertising agency staff with public relations specialization. The public relations counsel, studying the client firm from an independent outside role, offers program planning and management-policy advice to the firm's executives. He is paid on a fee basis, as a consultant. About 30 per cent of United States companies having public relations programs utilize the services of a public relations counseling firm; about 40 per cent use the services of public relations workers in advertising agencies. But only 15 per cent rely exclusively on these types of public relations direction. Some 40 per cent of company public relations departments buy the services of a counselor or an advertising agency in addition to their own activities.

There are large public relations firms, such as Carl Byoir & Associates or Hill & Knowlton, in which staff members do specialized assignments (information writing, radio and television contacts, magazine article preparation) as well as client counseling. There are individual public relations counselors, with only a one-secretary staff, who handle all aspects of a client's needs. Public relations specialists working within an advertising agency may give advice at a policymaking level, may help prepare a publicity campaign, or may handle the stories about company products for trade journals. But whether they are doing counseling work or tool-type operations, they likely will be described as "public relations men." Here lies the difficulty of nomenclature which confuses the picture of what public relations work is.

VARIOUS PUBLIC RELATIONS ASSIGNMENTS

Let us consider, for example, a university journalism graduate who goes to work for a public utility, such as the telephone company, after spending a few years in newspaper, broadcast, or advertising work. He joins the staff of one of the Bell operating companies, perhaps as a member of the three-man employee magazine staff. His next assignment is in the company news bureau, preparing news stories for the home-town newspapers in cities where the company operates—stories about personnel changes and promotions in the local telephone office, about retirements of old-time employees, about additional services or improvements in long-distance dialing, and so on. He is working at the "tool" level, using his journalistic skills. He is not immediately making policy, although he attends staff meetings in the public relations department at which policy is argued. He is being indoctrinated in company policy and procedures, and he is beginning to understand the total nature of the company operation.

Next he may be sent to the community relations section, where he is more of an "idea" man. He consults with the local office manager in a town where customer attitude survey studies have shown dissatisfaction with service or misunderstanding of billing procedures and rates. They decide they need better employee communication and arrange for foremen to hold group meetings; they check to see if the local managers are making effective use of the company's films which can be shown to civic groups; they plan an institutional advertising series in the local newspaper which will explain the company's costs and the needs for revenue if the town is to have the best possible telephone service; they check through various ways in which the company can show responsiveness to the community.

Now he returns to employee relations work, perhaps as editor of the magazine, or as an information specialist who develops manuals and programs for the use of supervisory management. He attends employee meetings as a consultant to the operating programs. He suggests ways in which employees can be made more interested in the company's financial problems. He may help run "indoctrination sessions" for higher supervisory personnel in which the public relations objectives of the company are explained. Why should a local manager spend time working with the local newspaper editor? How should he go about it to be welcome as a news source? Why should the manager belong to the Lions or Kiwanis Club and spend time "doing good"? The employee relations specialist tries to relate the facets of the total public relations program to the personal interests of employees.

There are other assignments—if he has had advertising experience, our public relations man may be placed in charge of institutional advertising or of the product news bureau in a manufacturing firm. If he has training in sampling procedures and statistical method, he may take charge of the customer attitude survey and its interpretation. He may become director of the company's radio and television programs. He may head the audio-visual section, handling films, slides, and pictures. He may return to the news bureau as director in charge of the major company stories. He may edit the company's annual report for a time and do shareholder-relations work. He may become a "policy thinker"—preparing speeches for the company president, writing a manual explaining the public relations policies of the company, working with various executives on long-range planning. He might in time become assistant director of the department. And he might finally become vice president in charge of public relations, and a member of the key company management group. Or, he might move on to the central public relations staff of the parent company, American Telephone & Telegraph. More likely he will remain in a median-level assignment, rounding out a comfortable and satisfying career as a telephone company employee who serves the community and other employees in a specialized staff role demanding technical journalistic skills and policymaking ability.

Another example might be of a young woman journalism graduate who is not convinced she wishes to do newspaper work, but who has acquired some understanding of newspaper routines through her classes and a vacation stint on a small paper. She is more interested in magazine writing and layout and begins as assistant editor of a company employee magazine. A year later she becomes editor. After she has married, she has time to do some work at home, on a part-time basis, and finds a local hospital needs a woman to edit its informal staff bulletin, handle the printing of occasional brochures and reports, and represent the hospital with the local newspaper when newsworthy events take place. She is able to advise the hospital administrator on both printing matters and news policy and develops some interesting stories of value both to him and to readers.

A third example might be a five-year veteran of metropolitan newspaper work who is offered a position with a major automotive company. He starts in information work, quickly moves into employee relations, and becomes assistant director for a major branch plant. Three years later he is shifted to Detroit, where he becomes assistant manager of the company's public relations department. He decides he would prefer to enter a counseling firm and becomes an account executive for one specializing in automotive clients. At 35 he is a vice president of the firm and receives as much pay as a major executive of the largest metropolitan dailies. When he visits his old newspaper shop, he feels a little "tug" for having left the main stream of news work, but his work and pay satisfactions are far more than enough to keep him satisfied with his career choice. In a counseling firm he is freer to carry out his own plans and ideas than in a company staff role. But he also needs to be more daring, for he has less personal security.

Technical writing for agricultural organizations, aviation firms, manufacturing companies serving scientific audiences, and other groups proves interesting to some journalists. The United States Information Service overseas, other federal government agencies, state tourist bureaus and industrial development departments, and some city school systems employ information writers. Colleges and universities, state health departments, the Red Cross, and many other service organizations do likewise. These usually are writing and editing assignments, but sometimes there is opportunity for making policy suggestions, and always there is a chance to do an effective job of working with the news media.

There are those who like to handle what might be called "promotional publicity"—building a story in behalf of a client, creating frothy feature stories, publicizing a queen contest, and otherwise earning a fee without too much effort or any serious thinking. This can be a pleasant enough career if the press agent—for that is what he is—stays in the good graces of the newsmen upon whom he depends and does not drop into the habit of handling dubious stories. But in middle age, the press agent might find himself outwritten by younger and fresher competitors and earning less money than his college classmates who chose more productive and serious roles in mass communications.

OPPORTUNITIES AND SALARIES

Several thousand United States companies and firms maintain fairly well-developed public relations departments—the number employing at least some public relations personnel has never been accurately determined. Best estimates are that 100,000 are employed in the field in the 1960's, at all levels, and that the number may double by the 1970's as businesses grow with the sharp demands of population increases. Firms which in 1945 had but a single public relations man had full-blown departments of 25 or more employees by 1960. Companies which did not organize their departments until the late 1950's—and there were many of them—still were in this growing stage. Men hired as information writers by smaller organizations, and who advanced to policy levels, were able to employ younger men and women to do writing and editing work, employee communication assignments, and similar jobs. The best estimate for public relations counseling firms is that there were nearly 2000 in 1965, and several hundred advertising agencies offered public relations services.

A survey of 166 manufacturing corporations made by the Public Relations Society of America showed that companies with more than a billion dollars of annual sales had public relations staffs averaging 65 in number. Those at the hundred million to half-billion sales level had a dozen or so staff members. Smaller companies averaged four public relations workers. Such large counseling firms as Carl Byoir and Hill & Knowlton employ more than 300 persons; but many independent firms are essentially one or two-man operations. A survey of advertising agencies showed those which had public relations sections employed from 3 to 10 persons, although the Young & Rubicam agency had more than 100 in its public relations department.

Salary levels of corporate public relations men and women tend to be equated more with general levels of business salaries than with those in the news media. As a result, the average veteran public relations man in a major company probably earns from half to two-thirds again as much as an average newspaperman, at the time each has reached his peak and has leveled off. A salary of $10,000 to $15,000 might be expected by a moderately successful public relations man in a large company after perhaps 15 years of service; a moderately successful newsman who stayed close to the established minimum salary for large metropolitan newspapers might range from $7000 to $9000 in peak pay. His superior colleague on the newspaper staff probably would receive five-figure pay and might be happier doing his chosen work than shifting to public relations. So might a moderately successful newsman, despite the pay differential. For public relations work requires differing personal outlooks and abilities than news work, despite the many common basic qualifications.

Should the corporate public relations man advance to executive levels he will earn a salary ranging from $15,000 to $35,000 a year. Independent counselors report incomes of from $7500 a year to $35,000, depending upon their success in attracting clients and their firm's size. Those who remain at the employee magazine, information writing, and technical writing level earn from $6000 to $15,000 a year, with a few rising to $20,000. Those who stay in public relations work for smaller companies and noncorporate organizations also tend to remain in this more average salary bracket. Many a young newsman who was attracted to public relations work by a $7000 salary (well in excess of his third-year newspaper salary scale, for example) offered by a smaller organization has found that it was a top salary as well as a beginning salary. He then has found it difficult either to return to newspaper work or to join a larger company's public relations staff. For although the larger companies have openings at advanced levels, they prefer to fill them with persons with media training—newspapers, radio and television, magazines, advertising—or with persons specially trained in such areas as speech, film, and communication research. Public relations does not have the turnover and exchange of personnel prevalent in the advertising agency field.

Beginning salaries in public relations departments and information writing posts tend to equal or exceed those in the mass media. A woman offered a magazine editing job by an industrial company might receive $4500 a year to start and advance to $6000. Her classmate who began in newspaper work might start at slightly less, but on a metropolitan newspaper she might expect to receive $6500 to $7000 after four or five years of service. Men journalism graduates are offered $5500 or more as starting salaries by such large employers as General Electric Company— well in excess of starting newspaper pay. For those who are convinced their futures lie in corporate firms this is a tempting offer, particularly if they feel they lack the zeal for news work. But 15 or so years later the company may give a prized promotion of executive level to a staff member who was well seasoned in the mass media and pass by the man who came to it directly, on the theory that the ex-newsman had plus values and more rounded abilities to direct all phases of the public relations program. A student interested in a public relations career may be advised to avoid immediate entry into the field, particularly in well-paying but "go-nowhere" jobs with smaller organizations at the "tool" level, and instead to gain the invaluable experiences of work in one of the mass media. Reporting on the news side and sales on the advertising side are the best training grounds for higher levels in any of the communications industries, including the associated field of public relations.

TALENTS AND EDUCATIONAL PREPARATION

Anyone who aspires to the executive level of public relations work, involving policymaking for management, obviously must have excellent preparation. He should have a good grasp of the communications skills and an understanding of the mass media. He should be well grounded in the social sciences: economics, psychology, political science, sociology, history. He will have to know how to deal with people, as well as with facts.

Writing ability is mentioned more often than any other by public relations men asked by the Public Relations Society of America in a representative sample survey to rank skills needed in their work. Seven out of ten listed writing ability as one of four or five most important skills. Tact in dealing with people and creative ability ranked next. Speaking ability also was ranked high. General intelligence and good general background came next.

More than 90 per cent of this sample of public relations men had attended college and 29 per cent had taken graduate work. The three leading major subjects in college were journalism, 32 per cent; English, 28 per cent; business administration, 24 per cent. Slightly more than half, 53 per cent, had been in newspaper work; 43 per cent had been in advertising or merchandising; 10 per cent had been in magazine work; 6 per cent had been in radio, television, or movies. Only 43 per cent had been in full-time public relations work prior to the job they then held.

Some basic courses a future public relations worker should include in a college program would be newspaper reporting and editing, broadcasting, principles of advertising, marketing, public opinion, public speaking, principles of economics, American government and history, general psychology. The public relations prospect cannot overspecialize in his educational training, by the very nature of his chosen field. He must be careful to select a broad band of social science courses, in addition to his communications concentration. If he is in the news-editorial or advertising area, he will include basic courses in the other area. If he is in business administration, he will want to include several basic journalism courses, and vice versa. If courses in public relations theory and methods are offered (and they are more commonly offered by journalism schools than by business schools), he will of course take them. In a few instances, he will find a major offered in his field.

College graduates who prepare themselves both in communications skills and in general background knowledge are in demand even though they may be inexperienced. A survey of public relations departments and firms by the Public Relations Society of America showed that one out of every three persons hired is a college graduate without experience. Entry is easiest in advertising agencies, industries, and institutions; it is less easy in public relations firms, welfare organizations, and governmental units. These employers, having typically smaller staffs, are more likely to demand previous media experience.

Although writing skill ranks highest in the minds of public relations men, there are openings on large company staffs for those who write adequately but who prefer other types of work. Specialists in survey and statistical work, good speakers who have organizational ability and training in group discussion, radio-television and film specialists, persons who have specialized in corporate organization or labor relations—these are some who can find a place in the public relations field and advance to high levels.

SUMMARY

The fields of public relations and information writing attract many persons, the majority of whom have had previous experience with news organizations. True public relations work is based upon social science theory, stemming from the study of public opinion processes. It is a management function which evaluates public attitudes, identifies the policies and procedures of the company or organization with the public interest, and executes a program of action to earn public understanding and acceptance. Publicity thus becomes a tool which the company uses to explain itself in the two-way communications process.

Some 100,000 men and women were employed in this rapidly growing field in the 1960's by several thousand United States companies, by some 2000 public relations firms and several hundred advertising agencies, and by many trade associations, civic organizations, colleges, churches, social work organizations, schools, trade unions, and governmental units. The majority work in staff positions within their organization; others are outside counselors in public relations firms or advertising agencies. Information writing, technical writing, and employee magazine editing are important areas of employment.

The major sections of a corporate public relations department are the news bureau, the employee relations section including the employee publication, the community relations division, shareholder relations and the annual report, audio-visual section, radio and television, informational advertising, speakers' bureau, and attitude surveys and statistical section. Employee relations and community relations are two of the rapidly growing and crucial areas. Many corporate public relations departments are allied with advertising or personnel departments. Professional staffs range from one or two in small organizations to 65 or more in major companies.

Salaries for beginning workers equal or exceed those in the mass media and range substantially higher for successful public relations men. Salaries in smaller organizations and for writers and editors who do essentially tool operations rather than policy making are not much higher, if any, than in news work. Beginning salaries range from $4000 to $5200 for college graduates, men or women, and public relations executives rise to pay levels of from $15,000 to $35,000.

Writing ability is the most frequently demanded skill, but public relations work requires a broad band of training in communications skills and in the social sciences. Although companies and firms employ college graduates without experience, promotion to higher levels often goes to those who have worked on newspapers or magazines, in radio or television, or in advertising before entering upon public relations careers. More than half of established public relations men have had newspaper experience.

STUDY QUESTION

In what ways can public relations play (a) a socially valuable role and (b) a socially harmful role?

PROJECTS

1. Clip three newspaper or magazine advertisements in which a company or institution is seeking to influence the public in favor of an *idea* rather than a product or service. Compare the effects of the three advertisements.

2. Clip three newspaper stories that apparently originated in the office of a publicity writer for a company or institution. Identify the probable sources.

CHAPTER 17

MASS COMMUNICATIONS RESEARCH

THE NEED FOR RESEARCH

The rocket-like growth of the various forms of mass communications in the mid-twentieth century has resulted in an increasing need for better knowledge of the processes and effects of mass communications. A core of specially trained research men and women has arisen to search for and supply this knowledge to working communicators.

Take the magazine or newspaper editor, for example. He needs to know such things as these:

How many persons read my publication? (Typically, each copy has several readers so the total audience may be something quite different from the total circulation.)

What kinds of persons read my publication? (The New York *Times*, for example, is aimed at a different audience than is the *Daily News;* the audience of *Holiday* is almost completely different from that of *Jack and Jill.*)

How am I doing as an editor? Am I printing the kinds of things my audience wants to read about? Are my stories easy to read or hard to read?

How can I improve the content of my publication? How can I improve the presentation of this content in terms of layout and typography?

The broadcaster, the advertising man, and other communicators have similar questions to ask.

Time was when an editor could know many of these things pretty well by personal contact with the people of his community or area. By informal means, through his experience, he developed a rough idea of the composition of his audience and how they liked his publication. This unsystematic, informal "intuitive" method is no longer adequate for the modern communicator for several reasons:

1. *The increasing number of communications media:* In the present-day community, the average person has access to many media—local and out-of-town newspapers, several television and radio stations, and hundreds of magazines, books, and films.

2. *Increasing competition among the media for the attention of the public:* Since no individual has enough time to read or listen to all the media, or even to pay attention to all the output of just one medium, this means he must select a small fraction of the available output and ignore the rest. This leads to intense competition among the different media to capture as much of the public's time and attention as possible—obviously, the newspaper or magazine or station which succeeds in satisfying the needs of the public, whose messages are interesting and easy to absorb, will get a good share of public attention. Those which do not succeed in doing this will eventually fall by the wayside.

3. *The increasing number of people in the audience:* An editor or broadcaster has from several thousand to several million people in his audience, and the tendency is constantly toward larger audiences. No communicator can possibly have personal contact with everyone in his audience and knowledge of all their varying needs, likes, dislikes, and opinions.

4. *The changing tastes of the public:* People are becoming better educated and more sophisticated; they travel more, know more about the rest of the world, and are constantly developing broader interests through exposure to more communications from outside their immediate environment. Any communicator's audience is in a constant state of turnover and interest change. He cannot base his decisions on what he knew to be true ten years or five years or even one year ago. It is a "fickle public" in the sense that it is constantly changing in taste and mood.

These are all good reasons why the effective communicator—whether he be advertising copywriter, editor, or broadcaster—can no longer rely on "hunch" and "intuition" alone to capture and hold the attention of the public. As Harry Henry says in *Motivation Research:* "There are examples, of course, of 'hunch-merchants' who hit on successful ideas with enormous success, and finish up as classic case-histories. But no case-histories are written up of the 99 equally self-confident but not so lucky venturers whose only spell of glory is in a brief trip to the bankruptcy courts."

In the face of all these changing requirements, then, just how does the modern mass communicator get the precise information he needs to make his medium a successful one? He turns to communications research, a specialty which has grown up in the past two decades to help answer some of the questions which he doesn't have the time or training to answer for himself. The communications researcher is just one member of the team of writers, editors, artists, advertising men, and others working together to help a medium do its job, which is to transmit information, opinion, and entertainment to a mass public. Or again, he may be a scholar in a university setting whose main objective is that of adding to our general knowledge of the communication process.

WHAT IS COMMUNICATIONS RESEARCH?

A broad definition of research is simply "careful investigation" or a diligent inquiry into any subject. This broad term would include almost any kind of study—the literary scholar who reads through all of Shakespeare's works, the biographer who finds out all he can about a famous man, or the historian who compiles a history of American newspapers.

Mass communications research has taken on a somewhat more specialized meaning, however. First of all, it is usually (though not always) considered as *behavioral* research—the study of human beings (rather than inanimate or nonhuman objects). It is a branch of the behavioral sciences such as psychology, sociology, and anthropology.

Thus we see it is also *interdisciplinary* research. That is, it borrows the tools and knowledge of various other fields of study which will help in the understanding of mass communications problems. It does not confine itself to any particular point of view or theory or subject matter. It may borrow from linguistics, general semantics, philosophy, economics, or any other discipline which might help communications effectiveness.

It is *scientific research,* since it uses scientific methodology in solving communications problems. As in any science, its aim is to explain, predict, and control. In achieving this end, its methods must be objective (as opposed to subjective) and systematic (as opposed to unsystematic). Although most mass communications research is done on specific problems, the goal—as in any scientific field—is to formulate general principles and theories which can bring about more effective communication.

Being scientific, it is, of course, *quantitative research.* Random sampling methods, the laws of probability, and mathematical statistical techniques all help to make more precise and meaningful the findings from any particular investigation.

It is generally *primary* research rather than secondary. That is, the mass communications researcher customarily gathers new and original information rather than relying on printed source material. This is not always the case, however, since one may, for example, have to consult year-by-year statistical figures gathered in the past by other researchers in order to spot a trend over a period of time.

And, of course, the subject matter of communications research is *communication.* More specifically, it is concerned with *mass* communications, the communications behavior of large numbers of people, particularly those who make up the *audiences* for the different media. But other groups can be studied, too, of course—newspaper reporters, news sources, magazine editors, or public relations men, for example. In order to understand the behavior of groups, however, it is usually necessary first to understand individual behavior.

To summarize the definition of mass communications research: It is generally the scientific study of the mass communications behavior of human beings, usually in current situations requiring the gathering of primary quantitative information. It also includes the study of the communicators, their media, and the content of their messages.

This is not the only definition that might be legitimately applied. It leaves out other kinds of research done in the field of journalism and mass communications (e.g., historical, literary, biographical, legal, economic, international aspects), which are discussed in Chapter 19 on journalism teaching, and editorial research of the "fact-checking" variety. It also includes some topics which might be claimed by other disciplines. It is, however, a reasonably comprehensive definition of the specialized type of mass communications research which has grown up recently.

KINDS OF COMMUNICATIONS RESEARCH

Research can be, and has been, used by every kind of communicator—newspaper and magazine editors and writers, television and radio broadcasters, advertising men, public relations men, government information specialists, book publishers, and film producers. Some examples will show the usefulness of this kind of research in practical situations.

Readership studies. Sometimes called "reader traffic" studies, these tell the editor how many and what kinds of people have read *each item* in his publication. For example, story A had 40 per cent readership whereas story B had 10 per cent, picture A had 37 per cent readership whereas picture B had 12 per cent. Such information, gathered by trained personnel in personal interviews with representative samples of readers, provides a check on editorial judgment. It is useful to the editor in following trends of audience interest, in evaluating effects of typographical make-up and display of stories on readership, in deciding which of several syndicated features he wants to retain or drop, and so on. Effectiveness of various types of advertising also can be studied.

Audience studies. These are somewhat broader in scope. Knowing the number and description of people in a medium's audience is especially useful to advertisers to help them reach the right kind of person for their products. A baby-food manufacturer, for example, may want to know which of two magazines of equal circulations is better for him to advertise in; if magazine A has primarily an elderly audience and B has primarily young married women, he can easily decide which is better for his purpose. Such studies are also useful to editors in the selection of editorial content; a farm journal audience may change in reading interests due to shifts in composition and in living standards, for example. In another area, the reading likes of young newspaper readers are quite different from those of older folk, and some editors have recognized this by including specially edited "teen-age" pages.

Similar research is conducted on television and radio programs. The various "rating" services can determine how many sets were tuned in to each of a number of programs, how many people were listening to each set, and what kinds of people they were. One TV-radio research service gets its information from an electronic device permanently attached to the television or radio sets of a sample of households. Another "rating" service makes personal telephone calls to homes while programs are on the air. Another method is to have listeners keep diaries.

Graphics research. Typography, layout, and make-up fall within the area generally called "graphics" by the print media. By experimentation with different methods of presentation, the researcher can tell the editor the most effective means of presentation of a given item. A book publisher or magazine or newspaper editor may choose to test, say, audience preference for one kind of typeface as compared with another; the use of one large illustration instead of several smaller pictures; or the effectiveness of a news item published in an area two columns wide and 5 inches deep, as contrasted with the same item set in one column 10 inches deep. Much research has been done on the legibility of typefaces and aesthetic preferences for them.

Advertising men, too, are strongly interested in graphics research. Which ad gets across the most information—an ad with a big picture and a little text, or a little picture and a lot of text? Such research may be done by "split-runs" in the publication, so that the alternatives are presented to two different samples of readers whose reactions then can be compared after a readership survey, or by experimentation with a relatively small group of persons before publication.

Graphics research has its parallel in the broadcasting media. Research can tell whether three minutes of commercial time are most effective at the beginning of a program, at the end, or spread through it. Or it can tell whether, on a radio newscast, a summary of "headlines" at the start of the program will increase interest in the news items which follow.

Advertising research. The various media and almost all advertising agencies conduct advertising research to help them in their job of persuading people to buy. *Market research* has been carried on since the start of the century and was the forerunner of other public opinion research. It includes consumer surveys on potential markets for new products, dealer studies, customer attitude surveys, and studies of effectiveness of brand names and package designs. Media use by advertisers is determined in part by market research results, and various media seek to point out their usefulness by undertaking market research studies for particular advertisers' products. *Copy research* includes analysis of advertisement readership studies, pretesting of advertisements, evaluation of printed advertisement campaign effectiveness, and graphics. In broadcasting, commercials and programs may be tried out on small samples of listeners by use of response recording devices. The same is true of films.

Public opinion research. Every communicator is interested in knowing the state of public opinion about himself or his medium. The publisher wants to know how the public "feels" about his newspaper, magazine, or books. The broadcaster and film producer are equally sensitive to public approval. Public relations and advertising men want to know if they have succeeded in creating a favorable "image" for their companies or products in the public mind. Surveys of attitudes held by specific customer groups, and by the public generally, give them some answers.

Communicators are interested in public opinion from an additional viewpoint—that is, public attitudes toward social and economic issues, government officials and their policies, and important events. The familiar national polls conducted by George Gallup, Elmo Roper, and others offer a check on prevailing opinion. And since public opinion is news in itself, the polls are sold to many newspapers; in addition, some newspapers conduct their own polls and report the outcomes as news stories. Large companies subscribe to opinion-survey services as a part of their public relations programs. Government also uses public opinion research —the United States Information Agency has a survey research division whose sole function is to measure public opinion toward the United States in other countries, and the effects of our various foreign information programs including the Voice of America. Politicians are increasingly using public opinion surveys to gauge campaign progress and important issues.

Content analysis. Much can be learned about a publication merely by studying its contents. (This falls somewhat outside the definition of "behavioral" research.) Content analysis provides a clue to an editor's or writer's intentions and to the kind of audience which a publication or broadcast attracts. Combined with readership studies, it gives clues to what people want to read about. This form of research can be especially valuable when more precise kinds of research are inappropriate or unavailable. For example, a content analysis of German wartime broadcasts gave the Allies useful clues as to the enemy's war strategy. An analysis of Soviet "cold war" propaganda helps the U.S. Information Agency in the formulation of its own propaganda, since it reveals the themes which are currently being stressed and enables us to combat them.

Communications "effects" research. As mentioned before, every communicator is interested in the effect he achieves on an audience with his message. Did people pay attention to the message? Did they understand it? Did it change their opinions or add to their store of useful information? Did they take any action as a result? Various research tools are used in answering these questions in a more precise way than any communicator can do intuitively, no matter how astute he is. This is the most rapidly growing area of the communications research field.

Research on the communicator. In addition to studying the audiences, the messages, and the media, the researcher also studies the communicator himself. It is logical that one way to improve communications is to find out what kinds of people are best suited for the job. What are the essential characteristics of good reporters or editors or advertising men? What "blocks" to effective communications exist in the ranks of existing job holders, as the result of lack of capacity or training, and what training can best be offered to future professionals? By finding out these essentials, better selection and training of communications personnel can take place.

Creative research. Most of the research enumerated thus far deals with familiar and continuing problems, using fairly standardized research techniques from job to job. However, one of the most satisfying aspects of communications research is in doing original, imaginative thinking and investigation. The creative researcher tries to think of different ways to do a particular communications job and then tests the alternatives to see which is the most effective. He critically analyzes the long-standing traditions and accepted practices of the media and then tests these "tricks of the trade" to see if they are really the most effective ways to communicate. He devises new and original research techniques and methods to solve particular problems. He keeps abreast of developments in related disciplines such as psychology and sociology, applying the findings and theories from those fields to communications problems. Creative communications researchers also make valuable contributions to theory and practice in those related disciplines. They both borrow from and contribute to other areas of knowledge.

These are just a few general classifications of the wide variety of activity that goes on under the name of mass communications research. They are not mutually exclusive—a readership study, for example, is just one form of audience research. All of these mentioned are concerned, directly or indirectly, with "effects" research. Most of them could be classed under public opinion research. They all overlap and interact.

A glance through a few issues of the *Journalism Quarterly* and *Public Opinion Quarterly* will reveal in more detail some of the directions that mass communications research now takes. Although the questions or problems explored do not differ greatly from those explored 20 years ago, the emphasis now is on the use of more scientific methods of studying those questions. Earlier expressions of subjective opinion by communications experts are being subjected to scientific scrutiny and the "folklore" of the media are being validated or disproved.

OPPORTUNITIES IN RESEARCH

Research is being conducted in every kind of communications and business enterprise today. All of the media are engaged in research to some degree: newspapers, magazines, radio, television, publishing houses, film producers. So are the supporting agencies: press associations, advertising agencies, public relations firms, specialized commercial research firms. So are manufacturers of consumer and industrial products, retail and wholesale business firms, the federal government, and colleges and universities.

A survey made in 1957 showed that 79 per cent of all United States companies had a department (one man or more) engaged in market research, which almost always includes some form of communications or opinion research in its activities. Even among the smaller firms—those with sales under $5,000,000 annually—58 per cent had a research department.

Advertising agencies are the most avid users of research; 90 per cent of all United States agencies have a research department. Publishing and broadcasting organizations are close behind with 86 per cent employing researchers.

Naturally, the larger the firm, the more likely it is to have a research department. However, both it and the smaller firm frequently turn to commercial research firms, whose sole business it is to conduct research for outside business clients. Most medium and large cities in the country today have at least one commercial research firm, and the number of such firms is increasing yearly. Many of these firms serve clients on a national basis and a few conduct research in foreign countries. Some of the largest are the Opinion Research Corporation of Princeton, New Jersey; International Research Associates and Alfred Politz Research of New York City; A. C. Nielsen Company in Chicago; and Field Research on the west coast.

Advertising agencies tend to have larger research staffs than other kinds of businesses; the largest agencies employ an average of 50 persons in their research departments. Large publishing and broadcasting firms average four research employees, but a few have departments more the size of those in the agencies.

How is the pay for the worker in communications research? Because of the extensive amount of advanced training and specialized knowledge required, researchers are well paid compared with other mass communications personnel. The holder of a master's degree who has specialized in research may expect a starting salary of $6000 to $8000 a year. The more advanced student in communications research—who has completed most or all of his doctoral training—can initially command $8000 to $10,000 a year. These figures vary, of course, with location and size of firm. With the gaining of experience, communications research specialists rise above the $10,000 level in salary, with some progressing to $20,000 or higher. Research directors average that figure. Research analysts reach a $10,000 level, on the average. Women are frequently employed in analyst positions, less often in the top research posts. Their pay tends to be 10 or 15 per cent lower than that quoted for men.

Opportunities for advancement in mass communications research are good, because of the expansion taking place in the field. Not only can research be a rewarding and satisfying vocation in itself, but it also serves as a stepping stone to other kinds of work, both in the creative and business aspects of communications. One example is Dr. Frank Stanton, who started in research and became head of the Columbia Broadcasting System. Two others are A. Edward Miller, who became publisher of *McCall's,* and Marion Harper, Jr., who became head of McCann-Erickson advertising agency.

Another excellent opportunity for researchers exists in schools of journalism and mass communications. More and more universities are adding communications researchers to their staffs, both to do research and to teach and train students in the skills involved. In addition, such schools often contract to do research for the media or for civic and governmental agencies. A doctoral degree is generally considered a requirement for such a faculty position.

TRAINING FOR RESEARCH POSITIONS

Until just after World War II, most scientifically trained researchers on mass communications problems came from psychology and sociology.

The importance of research as a specialty has since led some of the nation's leading schools of journalism and mass communications to set up graduate programs in quantitative scientific research methods.

In some of these schools, mass communications research is offered as just one of several communications fields which a graduate student may elect in his course of study; in others, the entire graduate program is devoted to courses in behavioral research theory and methodology with a minimum of emphasis on the "communications" aspect. In almost all of them, however, the research specialization requires a sampling of appropriate courses drawn from several different disciplines and a heavy emphasis on statistics and scientific method courses.

A typical graduate program calls for a major in mass communications or journalism with a minor in psychology, sociology, or statistics. Various other departments—anthropology, philosophy, economics, political science, marketing, to name a few—may also figure in the program to a lesser extent, depending on the individual interests of the student. Some individuals prefer to major in social psychology or sociology, and minor in communications or journalism.

It is generally considered desirable—though not necessary—for graduate students in communications research to have professional experience in one or more of the mass media. The first wave of communications research Ph.D.'s—those receiving degrees in the 1950's—almost without exception had practical journalism experience, as newspaper reporters and editors, radio newsmen, and so on. The value of a practical journalism background lies in the greater awareness of crucial communications problems, a better knowledge of the questionable assumptions of the trade, and a generally better critical perspective based on an understanding of journalistic processes and folkways.

However, it should be emphasized that prior journalistic experience is not a requirement, but merely helpful, for the person interested in mass communications research. He or she can acquire knowledge of the media and of journalistic techniques in journalism courses and in post-degree professional work. It should be noted, too, that the only distinction between the graduate program of a mass communications researcher and that of the less-specialized behavioral scientist is the former's preoccupation with mass communications as the subject matter of his research; in practice, he is qualified to do almost any kind of social research he wishes.

SUMMARY

Mass communications research is defined here as primarily the scientific study of the mass communications behavior of human beings, usually in current situations requiring the gathering of primary quantitative information. It also includes the study of the communicators, their media, and the content of their messages. This definition of a specialized type of research, interdisciplinary in character and centered in the behavioral sciences area, leaves out other highly important types of research in journalism and mass communications: historical, literary, biographical, legal, economic, international journalism (discussed in Chapter 19).

The growth of specialized scientific research as an aid to the communicator was made necessary by the increasing number of communications media, by increasing competition among the media for attention of the public, by the increasing number of people in the audience, and by the changing tastes of the public.

Mass communications researchers do readership studies, audience studies, graphics research, market research and copy research in the field of advertising, public opinion research, content analysis, communications "effects" research, research on the communicator, and creative research. They work for all of the mass media, advertising agencies, public relations firms, specialized commercial research firms, manufacturers and business firms, government, and universities. Their pay is commensurate with the amount of advanced training and specialized knowledge required.

Preparation for a career in mass communications research involves graduate work in mass communications or journalism, usually with a minor in psychology, sociology, or statistics. The student may also draw from several different disciplines—anthropology, marketing, economics, philosophy, political science. He studies statistics and scientific method intensively. Mass communications research borrows the tools and knowledge of various other fields of study which will help in the understanding of mass communications problems; the goal—as in any scientific field—is to formulate general principles and theories which can bring about more effective communication.

STUDY QUESTION

What research aids are available to the mass media in their efforts to communicate effective messages to their audiences?

PROJECTS

1. Write a 300-word essay describing research techniques used in advertising, after consulting references available in your library.

2. Examine the summary of the *Continuing Study of Newspaper Reading,* or another readership study made available to you, and comment on differences in readership preferences between men and women.

3. Examine recent issues of the *Journalism Quarterly, Public Opinion Quarterly,* or *Journal of Marketing,* and report briefly on three examples of mass communications research of the behavioral variety.

PART V

EDUCATION FOR
MASS
COMMUNICATIONS

CHAPTER 18

EDUCATION FOR PROFESSIONAL CAREERS

THE ROLE OF EDUCATION

Informing and enlightening the public is a difficult task. Few can succeed as practitioners in mass communications without mastering the principles and practices of broad areas of knowledge that comprise the basic ingredients of a college education. Society has become so complex, its specialties so numerous, and its varying relationships so involved that only a person with a sure intelligence and a comprehension of many facets of human activity can understand the meaning of events. And without understanding, any attempt at reporting or interpreting is not only superficial but actually dangerous to the security of a democratic nation.

It is true that the exceptional individual can acquire a broad education without entering the portals of an institution of higher learning. A number of men and women with limited academic backgrounds are exerting genuine leadership in the editorial offices of the country today. But for most of us the only certain path to the acquiring of knowledge about our world lies in formal courses of instruction in the social sciences, the natural sciences, and the humanities. Here we discover the precise methodology of the researcher and the scientist and the skills of the writer or artist; we have guided access to the accumulated wisdom of the ages; we learn what men have considered to be the good, the true, and the beautiful; and we study the behavior of man, both as an individual and in his relationships with others.

Acquiring such a basic education has special importance to the future journalist. For one thing he is exposed to areas of thought and criticism that give him the opportunity to become a cultured person of discrimination and taste in his own right. From these experiences he should be able to acquire a sound working knowledge of society and a sensitivity to its many problems that will enable him to exercise the type of forthright citizenship so essential in our democracy. If his exposure to the processes of education has been productive, he will be enabled, in the words of Newman, "to see things as they are, to go right to the point, to disentangle a skein of thought, to detect what is sophistical, and to discard what is irrelevant."

Education, however, assumes an even greater importance to the future newsman or newswoman: almost every bit of knowledge and every insight that he acquires in college, from a study of the love life of the oyster to Thorstein Veblen's views on "conspicuous consumption," eventually seem to become grist for the mill as he reports and interprets the kaleidoscopic nature of life in the most practical of working assignments.

For example, in covering a state legislative hearing concerning a new sales tax proposal, the reporter should be aware of the various types of taxation and how they operate; assigned to interview an Oak Ridge physicist, he should know something about atomic power and its uses; reporting a discovery in the field of medicine, he may put his knowledge of biology or chemistry to work; an interview with a famous author may call forth his familiarity with the methods of literary criticism or a knowledge of current trends in writing; in handling a story about Saudi Arabian oil operation he must recall his studies in history, geography, and possibly geology; interpreting the new city budget will demand a knowledge of economics and accounting; covering a musical concert, a dramatic production, or the opening of an art exhibition, he will be grateful for any background which he may have acquired in those fields; and on and on. The journalist eventually puts all his education to use, and fervently wishes he knew more.

CHANNELS OF EDUCATION FOR MASS COMMUNICATIONS

Men and women desiring to equip themselves for journalistic careers in mass communications may follow several avenues in reaching their goal. The most common method is to enroll in a school or department of journalism or communications offering a four-year program leading to a degree in journalism. Approximately 200 colleges and universities in the United States provide such courses of study. Some of these institutions have provided separate administrative units (colleges, schools, divisions) for their journalism or communications instruction. The majority have located the school or department of journalism or communications within the liberal arts college. In either case, a student typically takes no more than 25 to 30 per cent of his course work in journalism or communications; the remainder is spread through the social sciences, humanities, and natural sciences, as well as physical education or military fields, in accordance with the university's requirements for both breadth and depth of study in the various areas of learning. In effect, the student elects a major specialization in professional studies which give him instruction in basic communication skills and in social science-oriented courses which relate journalism and communications to society. He does this just as other students elect a major concentration in geology, physics, political science, or English—and he is no more "specialized" in one subject than are they.

Many practitioners in mass communications are college graduates who have pursued noncommunications majors in liberal arts colleges. Seldom, however, does such a student consciously plan a mass communications career when he embarks on his college studies; almost always he acquires this goal late in his college career or he turns to a communications career after his graduation. Some employers among the mass media seek out such students, in the belief that their background in a general liberal arts study best equips them for full development within their organizations. It seems more reasonable, however, that the men and women who acquired both professional and general liberal arts education while enrolled in schools and departments of journalism, television-radio, speech, or communications would be better prepared for professional work and would be employed more readily. Such is the case.

This fact has been corroborated by numerous surveys. One, for example, was a poll of a cross-section of newspaper managing editors, undertaken in 1958 by Alvin E. Austin of the University of North Dakota as part of an intensive study sponsored by Dow Jones & Company, publisher of the *Wall Street Journal*, and by the Dow Jones Foundation. Already, by that year, of 128 managing editors who replied, 91 definitely would employ journalism graduates ahead of general college graduates;

29 preferred the latter over the former; 8 had no preference. Similarly, broadcast executives have shown a decided preference for graduates who already have acquired some educational background in television and radio functions.

Journalism educators knew about this increasing reliance by newspapers upon their graduates through the operations of their placement offices. The placement service is one of the most important functions of a journalism school as far as the prospective graduate is concerned. Employers rely upon the schools to recommend applicants for both beginning and advanced positions and make calls directly to the journalism offices rather than to the college's general placement service. Surveys taken each year by *Journalism Quarterly* show that the schools receive far more requests than they can fill, particularly for beginning men and women workers. A large journalism or communications school will handle several hundred requests each year, the majority coming from newspapers. During the 1950's and 1960's no journalism graduate went without a starting job if he or she really wished to apply for work, and most had choices of alternative offers. There has been steadily increasing use of the journalism school placement services by press associations, television and radio stations, magazines, advertising agencies, major industrial companies seeking advertising and public relations personnel, and others wishing to employ graduates with communications skills.

The diversity of career goals of journalism majors is reflected in a 1963 poll of juniors and seniors in 46 accredited schools and departments. Of the 4679 who replied, 2020, or almost one-half, said they intended to become newspaper reporters. Advertising ranked second with 1111 replies. The other preferences, in order, were television-radio news, 550; public relations, 434; magazine writing, 194; agricultural and home economics reporting, 103; science and technical writing, 41; photography, 31; community journalism, 24; and others and undecided, 171. There were, by the way, almost two men for every woman in this embryo journalist group.

Many students are introduced to the mass communications field through study at the more than 400 four-year institutions in the United States that offer some journalism courses but not a full major. High schools and junior colleges provide the beginning courses for thousands of other students. Some work on campus newspaper, yearbook, and television or radio staffs, or find part-time employment with local newspapers and broadcast stations while still in school. Since the nation's journalism schools graduate only about 2400 students each year, far fewer than the number required by the media, many students from these non-journalism-major institutions and from the junior colleges and even high schools find jobs in communications.

Students desiring careers in advertising and communications management frequently find the courses of study they want under the professional and liberal arts listings of schools and departments of journalism, speech, radio-television, and communications. Much of this training for jobs in the nonmechanical and noneditorial aspects of the media, however, also is offered through schools of business. In many universities a cooperative arrangement exists so that, regardless of the type of degree sought, such students obtain their specialized courses in both business and communications areas. The business major must become familiar with the peculiar problems and structure of the branch of the communications industry he proposes to enter; the communications major must learn principles of sound business practice. Along this same line, the future advertising man, whether enrolled in business or communications, must learn writing and editing while at the same time mastering the principles of marketing and retailing, and such business "core" subjects as accounting, business law, finance, management principles, and statistics.

With the tremendous expansion of industry since World War II, public relations has risen to prominence as a career sought by thousands. Most schools and departments of journalism offer one or two orientation courses in combination with preparation in basic journalistic training; they and those schools with more fully developed curricula suggest programs emphasizing electives in economics, psychology, sociology, and other social sciences. Few schools of business offer separate courses in public relations although they incorporate course units emphasizing the theory and over-all knowledge of public relations essential to successful management. Journalism school courses seek to offer the student both this background and the instruction necessary for becoming an actual practitioner in public relations.

In the broadcast area, students desiring careers in performance and production generally concentrate on courses in speech and radio-television. Those desiring to become radio and television newscasters and writers combine journalism, speech, and radio-television courses. Those headed for sales, promotion, public relations, and management positions may choose to major in business with allied instruction in journalism and radio-television. Those entering educational broadcasting frequently obtain teaching certificates while also acquiring a background in radio-television and speech. Television production students likely will take as much work in theater and dramatic literature as possible. The possible variations in these emphases are almost endless, depending upon the students' objectives. Common to all of these career paths, however, is a strong background in the liberal arts. The interlocking nature of broadcast instruction is a factor in the recent development of schools or colleges of communications, linking speech, radio-television, advertising and journalism.

Combination programs have been developed at many universities to enable the student interested in a career as a communications specialist in such areas as agriculture, home economics, medicine, or science to obtain basic proficiency through courses made available in two or more departments, schools, or colleges.

A relatively new development in education for journalism has been the establishment of in-service training programs by newspapers and magazines themselves. A Dow Jones Foundation study revealed that 35 newspapers in 28 states and the District of Columbia had instituted such programs or were planning to do so. Hard hit by the shortage of qualified applicants for newspaper editorial jobs, these newspapers sought both journalism and nonjournalism graduates. One of the most elaborate of these programs, which primarily involved indoctrination into actual working conditions, was a 21-week, on-the-job study course provided by the Gannett Newspapers. The Copley Newspapers had a similar, extensive training program for new employees.

Summer internship programs with dailies and weeklies supplement classroom and laboratory instruction in many states. A Newspaper Fund survey revealed that in 1963 internship programs provided newspaper jobs for 795 journalism students. An additional 117 liberal arts students gained reporting experience through the Newspaper Fund internship plan. Typical of these programs is that of the Texas Daily Newspaper Association, originated in 1948. During the summer preceding their senior year students serve internships for 10 weeks or longer in editorial or advertising capacities. The newspapers pay their living expenses and most of the interns also receive college credit. The Texas Press Association began a similar program for weeklies in 1958. In a few states, including West Virginia, both prejuniors and preseniors are provided this indoctrination into newspaper work. Some magazines, television and radio stations, and advertising agencies also offer summer training for college students, as well as "refresher" experiences for instructors. Many work part-time at journalistic jobs throughout the year, some even accepting jobs with their home-town newspapers while in high school. Working on a high-quality college newspaper is also an internship, with the added value of being tied closely to a parallel course work program.

HOW JOURNALISM EDUCATION DEVELOPED

Journalism, a comparative fledgling among university disciplines, gained its foothold on college campuses about a half-century ago. Formal education for journalism was inevitable in the face of the steadily increasing complexities of the twentieth century which demanded better-trained personnel on American newspaper staffs. None other than General Robert E. Lee first proposed a special college education for printer-editors. That was in 1869 when the general was president of Washington College, now Washington and Lee University, in Virginia. Little came of his proposal. Other early attention was given to printing instruction, such as that beginning at Kansas State College in 1873. It was 1893 before the first definitely organized curriculum in journalism was established in the Wharton School of Business at the University of Pennsylvania, an effort which languished in 1901.

In 1904 the first four-year curriculum for journalism students was organized at the University of Illinois, and journalism instruction began the same year at the University of Wisconsin. Four years later the first separate school of journalism was founded at the University of Missouri by an experienced journalist, Dean Walter Williams. In 1912 the Columbia University School of Journalism, endowed with $2,000,000 from Joseph Pulitzer, opened its doors. A survey disclosed that more than 30 colleges and universities were then offering courses in journalism.

The first courses were largely vocational in nature as pioneer teachers in the field endeavored to prepare college students for careers on newspapers, then the unrivalled medium of mass communication. During the 1920's, however, emphasis on technique lessened and curricula began to reflect an increasing interest in the social, ethical, and cultural aspects of journalism. Dr. Willard G. Bleyer, director of the University of Wisconsin School of Journalism until his death in 1935, is credited with leading the movement away from a preoccupation with techniques. Also influential was the exposure to methods of teaching the social sciences that journalism instructors were receiving in graduate programs. Courses in the history and the ethics of journalism became popular, and they were followed by studies of the newspaper as a social institution, of the interpretation of current affairs, and of public opinion.

These courses, together with those dealing with foreign news channels and legal aspects of the press, heightened respect for journalism as a discipline among other college teachers. At the same time products of journalism departments were earning a grudging acceptance from curmudgeons of the editorial offices who, as Horace Greeley put it, learned their journalism through eating ink and sleeping on the exchanges. Teachers began to offer courses to prepare students for careers in newspaper management, advertising, photography, and other such specialized fields. And while recognizing the importance of the humanities and the natural sciences in the total educational program of their students, teachers came to achieve the closest working relationships with the social sciences.

As both the breadth and depth of subject matter in journalism increased, master's degrees were offered. In 1935 the Pulitzer School at Columbia restricted its year's course to holders of a bachelor's degree, and the Medill School of Northwestern University established a five-year plan for professional training in 1938. Graduate study for journalism majors developed at a rapid pace after World War II, as the schools themselves and some of the media units began to urge advanced study in both journalism and the social sciences. Many of those who obtained master's degrees entered journalism teaching, but increasing numbers spent five years of study in preparation for professional journalism careers.

At the doctoral level, most graduate schools which recognized journalism instruction followed the lead of the University of Wisconsin in providing a minor or a double minor in journalism for candidates who generally majored in such fields as history or political science. The University of Missouri, however, awarded the first degree of Doctor of Philosophy in journalism in 1934. Also now offering the Ph.D. in journalism are Minnesota and Northwestern, with a strong supporting emphasis in the social sciences. Other universities elected to offer doctorates in mass communications in which journalism study was related to psychology and sociology as a behavioral science. The first such program was announced at the State University of Iowa in 1944. It has been followed by those at Illinois, Stanford, Wisconsin, Syracuse, Michigan State, Southern Illinois, and North Carolina. Minnesota also offers the behavioral emphasis as one of its fields of study.

Some Ph.D. degree holders entered the communications industry, but most joined journalism faculties of colleges and universities. The number of journalism professors holding doctorates rose from 25 in 1945 to 117 in 1954 and was well over 200 by 1965. The great majority of other journalism teachers in colleges held master's degrees, in addition to several years of professional experience in the media generally required by the schools.

It has been pointed out that early journalism instructors concerned themselves almost entirely with effective teaching and curricula development. Soon, however, the service obligations of journalism training units became apparent. As a result, there developed seminars and workshops for all branches of mass communications personnel, conferences for high school teachers and pupils, and other assorted projects.

Research, the third obligation of the university, developed somewhat slowly. For many years journalism scholars applied themselves largely to a study of the history of mass communications media. A development of the last two decades has led to the amassing of a substantial body of literature in communications research. Journalism scholars adapted the techniques of the behavioral sciences and joined sociologists, psychologists, statisticians, and other such investigators in unearthing a wealth of insights into the problems that face the communicator and his audiences and the effects of the communicated symbols on attitude and behavior. To many, the world of the statistician's chi square and variance and multiple regression seemed far-removed from the usual paths of journalism instruction, but research scholars are slowly penetrating hitherto unknown areas of communications and achieving a new respect for journalism as a scholarly discipline that can be a science as well as an art.

Important communications findings are also being developed by research personnel who are not required to use precise quantitative measurement tools; examples are studies in the broad realm of American civilization and in such areas as economic and political history and cultural anthropology.

Research personnel are sought after by both industry and the teaching profession, and salaries for men and women who have mastered the techniques required frequently range in the $10,000 to $20,000 realm.

The growth of the philosophy that journalism schools should develop research scholars capable of critical analysis of the media and their social environment coincided with television's rise and the increased importance of departments of speech and radio-television in providing study for broadcast careers. New, integrated instructional units in communications emerged, a few merely for administrative convenience, but most of them prepared for serious study of communication as the common denominator linking several academic departments.

Michigan State University brought its speech, journalism, advertising, and TV-radio instruction together into a College of Communication Arts, with a research unit at its center. The University of Texas similarly combined its speech, radio-television-film, and journalism programs into a School of Communication. Other universities at which "Communications" or "Communication" became the identifying part of the title of a teaching unit concerned with journalism and broadcasting included Illinois, Stanford, Washington, Florida, Arizona State, Brigham Young, Washington State, Houston, and Boston. Kent State University linked a number of departments into its College of Fine and Professional Arts. Educators with a background in speech, as well as in journalism, assumed leadership of units at Colorado State University and University of Houston. Other journalism schools with a longtime interest in broadcasting instruction have included Georgia, Indiana, Iowa, Kansas, Minnesota, Missouri, Montana State, Northwestern, Ohio, and Pennsylvania State.

ORGANIZING FOR HIGHER STANDARDS

The beginning student in mass communications soon may find himself as confused about the organizational structure of journalism education as were newspaper readers during the 1930's. Then a plethora of New Deal agencies known principally by their initials—NRA, HOLC, FERA, WPA, CCC—sprang into being. When the student hears reference to AEJ, ACEJ, AASDJ, or ASJSA, he should know that these are the alphabetized symbols for the four leading organizations in journalism education today.

A desire to exchange information and raise teaching standards prompted the organization in 1912 of the American Association of Teachers of Journalism. Five years later the American Association of

Schools and Departments of Journalism was created. By establishing certain standards for institutional membership, the AASDJ acted as a recognizing agency in the field. Eight schools and departments were approved by AASDJ at the time of its organization; by 1965 membership numbered 46. In 1924 the two associations jointly established the *Journalism Bulletin,* devoted to investigative studies in journalism; in 1928 the name was changed to *Journalism Quarterly.*

Efforts by AASDJ to work more closely with the press and to improve teaching standards culminated in January, 1939, with the organization of what is now known as the American Council on Education for Journalism. Present at the historic Chicago meeting were five journalism educators and representatives of five associations: the American Society of Newspaper Editors, American Newspaper Publishers Association, Southern Newspaper Publishers Association, National Editorial Association, and Inland Daily Press Association. Subsequently, the National Association of Radio and Television Broadcasters (later renamed the National Association of Broadcasters) and the Magazine Publishers Association became full members. As industry support broadened, seven other organizations were admitted as associate members: the Newspaper Advertising Executives Association, International Council of Industrial Editors, National Conference of Editorial Writers, National Press Photographers Association, Radio-Television News Directors Association, and Associated Business Publications and National Business Publications (later merged as the American Business Press, Inc.).

ACEJ works for the improvement of education for journalism and conducts a program of evaluation in accredited universities and colleges throughout the United States. In this program, ACEJ cooperates with the National Commission on Accrediting and other national and regional accrediting organizations and collects and makes available information about journalism education programs that are of value to schools and departments of journalism. Other activities include the distribution of career booklets for high school students throughout the United States. In 1965 the council consisted of seven educator and seven industry representatives.

A second administrators' organization, the American Society of Journalism School Administrators, was established in 1944, partly in protest to what its members considered a trend toward monopoly of journalism education among the schools that comprised AASDJ. The expressed purpose of ASJSA was to encourage the exchange of ideas and information about journalism administrative and teaching problems. Its primary interest lay in undergraduate teaching, its secondary concern in research and advanced-degree guidance. Members represented schools or departments in accredited colleges and universities that offered four-year programs leading to a degree in journalism.

Emphasizing service to all its members, ASJSA established a mimeographed publication, the *Roundtable,* to exchange "how we do it" ideas. The chief publication was the *Bulletin,* a semi-annual printed publication which became a quarterly when its name was changed in 1958 to the *Journalism Educator.* The organization also sponsored a summer intern program for journalism teachers in cooperation with industry. ASJSA membership had reached 70 by 1965 and included one Canadian administrator.

Major structural changes in 1949 and 1950 welded all journalism teacher and administrator groups into one organization. The American Association of Teachers of Journalism in 1949 adopted a new constitution and voted to change its name to the Association for Education in Journalism. In 1950 AASDJ and ASJSA agreed to become coordinate bodies within AEJ. The educator group serving on ACEJ was reconstituted to consist of two (later three) representatives from AEJ and two each from AASDJ and ASJSA. The merger of the several organizations into AEJ was hailed as an action giving greater recognition to the individual teacher and uniting schools, administrators, and teachers of journalism into one cooperative group. AEJ in 1965 had a membership of 950 teachers and administrators.

Two separate organizations for education in specialized fields are the American Academy of Advertising, with headquarters at Syracuse University, and the Association for Professional Broadcasting Education, sponsored by the National Association of Broadcasters, with the *Journal of Broadcasting* as its publication.

INDUSTRY ATTITUDES AND COOPERATION

Journalism as an educational discipline has engaged in a half-century struggle toward full acceptance and recognition. Many hard-bitten newspaper executives who had learned their craft the difficult way, without benefit of higher education, would have none of "those college-educated fellows." In the first few decades of the twentieth century, journalism teachers were forced to demonstrate their ability to duplicate actual newspaper conditions on the campus and to produce graduates who could report and edit well soon after joining a newspaper staff.

The pendulum then swung the other way, and the cry went up: "Give us men and women with a strong liberal arts background; we'll teach them the techniques." The educational world responded by emphasizing what it already had learned: that every valid journalism education program had to permit its students to take at least two-thirds—and preferably three-fourths—of their work in liberal arts areas, with the remaining journalism courses enabling students to bring those materials and insights into sharp focus as effective communicators of news and opinion. A 3-1 ratio between nonjournalism and journalism subjects now is considered by most news executives and educators to provide the best preparation for careers in mass communications, and it is the stated goal of the American Council on Education for Journalism.

Today a college education is the minimum requirement for most newspaper editorial positions, particularly those on large newspapers. Here are some typical comments obtained in a recent poll of newspaper editors: "A college education is an absolute essential in editorial work, that is if any degree of success is to be attained." "We are now hiring only college graduates for our news department." "A college degree has become an accepted part of newspaper hiring standards and I do not think there can be any argument about the wisdom of that generally accepted policy." "I believe a college education is extremely valuable, but in many cases not completely necessary." "College men are more valuable, as a class, than non-college."

There is less unanimity when the question is asked whether journalism graduates are preferred above those who have obtained other degrees. The majority of newspaper editors definitely prefer the journalism graduate. Some papers, however, find that men and women who have majored in history, political science, English, or some other field are equally acceptable as, if not more desirable than, journalism graduates. The crux of the matter appears to be the individual; if he demonstrates maturity, ability, and industry he may find a place for himself in mass communications regardless of his college major field of study. By far the greatest supply of newsroom talent, however, is issuing from journalism schools and departments because young people who seriously contemplate careers in mass communications almost invariably are drawn to journalism training programs.

The cocksure, "know-it-all" attitudes of a small minority of graduates have soured some news executives on journalism schools and departments. One editor complained that "journalism graduates seem to think they're finished products when in reality they're just ready to start." Remarked another: "Too many college men consider themselves above performing routine reportorial tasks. They're pundits." Some editors feel that journalism graduates place too much emphasis on beginning salary and too little on the necessity of proving their worth on the job. Lack of initiative and industry in digging for facts is another complaint. Other editors have decried a lack of education in depth in such areas as economics and science. A complaint heard probably more frequently than others is that newspaper tyros make too many mistakes in spelling and grammar.

"In examining job application letters, I always watch for two things: good spelling and grammar, and a proper attitude," one newspaper executive has declared. "It is surprising how many applicants just out of school, or with very brief experience, virtually set forth a set of conditions under which they will work for a paper. Some of them are as concerned with asking about working conditions, salary, hours, etc., in the initial letter as they are in setting forth their own qualifications. This does not make a good impression. I suppose the same situation may exist in other business fields, too. If I were coaching a young job applicant on how to apply for a newspaper job, I would urge him to emphasize what he might contribute to the paper, not what he wants from it."

Although a few broadcast executives urge that radio-television instruction be made more practical and that students learn techniques so as to be immediately useful in their job assignments, most station managers recommend that students be given a broad general background and that any high degree of specialization be left for development on the job. Polls have indicated that most station managers regard the liberal education courses in the broadcast curriculum to be of indispensable value to the student. One such executive declared: "Training beyond the fundamentals is not as important as a liberal education. We promote from within, which means that we are looking at the potential man, not the technician." Another stated: "A liberal arts background is something we look for. If the applicant knows only TV, speech, and allied subjects, he doesn't have the depth of background to continue day-by-day doing a creative job. He should know art, music, languages—and, incidentally, TV."

Broadcast executives generally search out speech, radio-television, and drama graduates for their performing and production positions. For news jobs, they tend to prefer journalism graduates.

Some of the reasons why newspaper executives generally prefer journalism graduates to nonjournalism applicants were advanced in a poll. One managing editor declared that the journalism graduate "had a better foundation on which to build." Another cited his "greater ability to recognize the newsworthiness of a situation." Other comments: "Possesses wide fundamental knowledge of newspaper craft and requires less training to acquire skill." "J-school grads move up much faster if they show they can out-produce non-J-school grads, which they usually do." "General preference based on the fact that his choice of journalism indicates a more avid interest in newspaper work." "Usually better equipped to tackle major assignments, more worldly wise, aims at jobs requiring more education, such as editorial writing, business editing, etc."

Although some negative industry attitudes are based upon performance records of beginning newsmen, others spring from a lack of knowledge by busy executives of the objectives and curricula of journalism departments and schools. In a field in which communication is integral, it is ironic that communication between journalist (educator) and journalist (practicing) should have broken down as much as it has. As veteran editor Carl E. Lindstrom declared, "In those newspaper shops where journalism graduates are now welcomed, there still remains a disposition to regard 'professor' as a bad word—especially journalism professor—this only because most editors don't know most professors."

In recent years an increasing number of print and broadcast executives, particularly since the nationwide shortage of skilled craftsmen became so acute, have discovered what actually is included in modern journalism or communications education. For many their prior notion that schools were preoccupied with teaching *techniques* has been dissipated. They have found that the emphasis in schools today is on the development of clearthinking men and women well versed in national and world affairs and able to report as well as to interpret them for the public and on the training of research personnel to investigate aspects of the art and science of communication. As one university president declared, upon examining the curricula of a school of journalism, "This is heretical. Imagine turning out a professional man who also is well educated!" Administrators hope that more industry executives, as well as college presidents, will investigate what journalism and communications departments and schools are teaching.

Although the legal, medical, and dentistry professions support their schools more fully than journalism schools are backed by the media, journalism educators and media personnel have developed a multiplicity of programs of mutual support, and cooperation by the industry is improving steadily. After the media for the most part failed to assume the responsibility of providing recruits for employment, the schools took on this function. The media have accepted virtually all these young men and women, and have wanted more. Educators needed new or modernized buildings and better equipment; in many states the media both individually and through their associations have given money and other support for these undertakings. A number of schools and some media groups wanted to raise the standards of journalism education; the American Council on Education for Journalism was established, with media associations underwriting most of the expense of operation. Educators saw the value of summer internship programs both for themselves and for their students; such plans to provide realistic training with newspapers, magazines, radio-television units, and other media groups have been operating in some areas well over a decade.

Some schools have felt a need to employ nearby practitioners of journalism as part-time teachers; the media almost invariably have cooperated. Educators asked that the number of scholarships, fellowships, and loan funds be increased; in a number of states media groups have responded wholeheartedly. Educators in some states wanted to establish foundations to aid journalism education; in North Carolina tax-deductible funds thus contributed by newspapers by 1965 exceeded $200,000 and the School of Journalism at The University of North Carolina at Chapel Hill had received more than $85,000 in income from the School of Journalism Foundation of North Carolina, Inc.

Many schools regularly conduct seminars, conferences, and other such gatherings so that professional men and women may exchange ideas and learn of new advances in their fields; these meetings almost always are well attended by personnel from the newspaper, press association, magazine, radio-television, advertising, public relations, and related fields. Virtually every institution calls on practitioners in mass communications to speak for classes, convocations, and other student gatherings; numerous organizations have established national bureaus to provide speakers, audio-visual materials, and printed literature for college students, and local and regional media personnel are always available for campus appearances.

The Association of Advertising Men and Women and the Advertising Club of New York established in 1950 a program known as "Inside Advertising Week." Its purpose was to show the nation's leading advertising students, enrolled in colleges and universities, a glimpse of the advertising business, its aims and ideals, in an attempt to explain the why and wherefore of the industry. Each year advertising and marketing seniors have participated in a five-day program of activities in New York City.

Other advertising groups have provided guest speakers and films for college career days and clinics, arranged scholarships and loans, donated advertising libraries, invited students to professional meetings, arranged tours, helped place graduates in jobs, sent agency executives on "task force" visits to campuses, and provided summer work opportunities for both the students and their teachers. One advertising agency has had as many as 15 students with it in a single summer. Various councils of the American Association of Advertising Agencies sponsor scholarships, as do at least 16 agencies that are Four A members.

Summer internships for teachers with general magazines and with radio and television stations have been provided by the Magazine Publishers Association and the National Association of Broadcasters. Daily newspapers also have accepted teachers for summer intern spots.

The National Association of Broadcasters provides the Harold E. Fellows Memorial Scholarship for students of broadcasting in member schools of the Association for Professional Broadcasting Education. Named for the NAB's president and chairman from 1951 to 1960, the fund provides two annual scholarships in the amount of $1100 each.

The most important of all these significant evidences of continuing support of journalism schools by the mass media lies in the realm of employment. Journalism school records across the country show that graduating seniors go directly into responsible work for the various media with substantial success. Two of the co-authors of this book (Phillip Ault and Edwin Emery) described the employment process in their Dodd, Mead & Company text, *Reporting the News:*

The largest single group enters reporting. Many who later make the finest records get their start on small dailies or weeklies, where they must handle many aspects of reporting and editing, and where they have the greatest opportunity for personal self-development and overcoming any natural tendency toward shyness. Those who go directly from school into large metropolitan papers face the danger of being restricted indefinitely to a limited job, such as overnight police reporter, without the opportunity to experience the broader aspects of news work.

Other journalism graduates fan out in small numbers into a variety of starting jobs. Some sell advertising for newspapers, a basic experience for advertising careers; some become newsmen or production men for radio and television stations; some join magazine staffs or edit a small publication; some become advertising copywriters for companies or stores; some join news desks of newspapers or become press association writers; some become news photographers.

Ten to fifteen years later some have become key persons in journalism. Our beginner now works as a science news writer, a city editor, a press association bureau chief, a magazine managing editor, a weekly newspaper owner, an advertising agency vice-president, a television news director, a Washington correspondent, a foreign correspondent, a newspaper advertising manager. These are not idle fancies; they are examples taken from journalism school records.

Major companies such as General Electric, Procter & Gamble, Sears, Roebuck & Company, Curtis Publishing Company, Meredith Publishing Company, Time-Life, and Eastman Kodak regularly recruit journalism graduates to fill positions ranging from advertising and promotion to news reporting. Partly because of the broad education of the journalist and the expanding nature of journalistic occupations, schools and departments of journalism and communications have been unable, for the last decade or so, to produce enough graduates to meet demand.

A JOURNALISM EDUCATION NEVER ENDS

It's a truism, of course, to point out that a college diploma, or its equivalent in individual attainment, is only the beginning of a lifetime of education. For no other group does this fact hold greater validity than for those who embark on careers in mass communications. Every aspect of human experience and emotion can become their concern; the world changes and so must their ability to understand and interpret those changes.

The man or woman who wants to develop his fullest potential in the field of mass communications cannot neglect his reading, both fiction and nonfiction. Aside from sheer enjoyment and enrichment of the inner self, books and magazines of high quality provide information and insights that surely will improve his performance as a mass communicator. The reading of trade and professional publications is essential to this process of continuous educational development. Just as the physician peruses similar periodicals to keep abreast of advances of knowledge in medicine, so the journalist must examine on a systematic, continuing basis such research journals as *Journalism Quarterly, Public Opinion Quarterly,* and *Journal of Marketing;* newspaper trade journals such as *Editor & Publisher* and *Publishers' Auxiliary;* other trade journals such as *Broadcasting, Printers' Ink, Advertising Age,* and *Public Relations Journal;* and general interest professional journals such as *Nieman Reports, Quill,* and *Columbia Journalism Review.*

In the trade and professional periodicals he finds the latest developments in many areas of continuing concern for which there are no fixed answers: What is the social justification for printing or refusing to publish the names of juveniles involved in crimes? What are the rights of the individual in connection with pretrial news stories and newscasts? How far should government supervise the conduct of television and radio stations? What advertising procedures are unethical? What is the meaning of the latest research developments in communication? No journalist can be truly professional and remain ignorant of changing attitudes and legal actions that affect any of the mass media.

The journalist also can remain well informed of developments in communication through maintaining active membership in organizations that are engaged in programs of self-study. According to his particular field or position, he may find highly stimulating the conferences and literature of such organizations as the American Society of Newspaper Editors, the National Conference of Editorial Writers, state press associations, the Associated Press and United Press International, the Association for Education in Journalism, the American Association of Advertising Agencies, Sigma Delta Chi, Theta Sigma Phi, and the National Association of Broadcasters.

With society becoming increasingly complex and new knowledge appearing in almost every sector, many media people have returned to college for regular courses as well as for such adult education activities as residential workshops, summer laboratories, short courses, educational camps, community development projects, seminars, forum series, and televised discussions. For example, Columbia University has initiated a study program for science writers; Northwestern University has sponsored periodic seminars for crime news reporters; Pennsylvania State University has provided forums bringing together newspaper and broadcast men, public officials, and community leaders and opinion makers for a critical examination of key communication issues. Other universities are offering similar refresher experiences for communicators.

The *Wall Street Journal's* Newspaper Fund, Inc., has sent more than 3000 high school journalism teachers back to college during the summer months for special training. Sigma Delta Chi has cosponsored seminars for such specialized groups as business news writers from over the nation, and the professional journalism society's eleven annual regional conferences are planned as forums for the exploration of pressing news problems. At least one of the society's professional chapters pays half the tuition when its members elect to enroll in college enrichment courses.

Several hundred newspapermen have been selected by the Nieman Foundation for a year of study at Harvard University under a million dollar endowment left in 1936 by the widow of Lucius W. Nieman, founder of the Milwaukee *Journal*. A dozen highly qualified newspapermen are selected annually as Nieman Fellows; they spend the year pursuing any course of study they desire. Louis M. Lyons, emeritus curator of the foundation, established a quarterly magazine, *Nieman Reports,* in 1947.

Another opportunity for intensive study and discussion of problems is provided through the American Press Institute seminars conducted at Columbia University in New York for managing editors, city editors, circulation managers, and similar identical-interest groups. Press associations in some states sponsor similar seminars; an example is the Texas Daily Newspaper Association seminar program established in the early 1950's by Walter R. Humphrey, editor of the Fort Worth *Press*.

SUMMARY

A college education or its equivalent is an essential for any young man or woman who plans a career in mass communications. Most persons seeking to qualify for careers in this demanding field enroll in schools or departments of journalism, radio-TV, and communications that provide, as a minimum, four-year programs leading to the bachelor's degree. Graduates of straight liberal arts programs also are employed by the mass media, but most executives prefer persons who have had print and broadcast training along with their liberal arts studies. Schools of business provide part of the training required by those entering noneditorial branches of mass communications, and speech departments prepare many of those employed in broadcast journalism.

During the last half-century education for mass communications has passed from its early preoccupation with techniques to an emphasis upon the study of the press as a social institution and, in its integration with the social sciences, to research in the field of communications as a whole. Educators and communications executives alike are insisting upon an education involving about three-fourths background liberal arts and one-fourth professional study. Graduate programs have assumed an increasing importance, and significant research activities are being undertaken along both quantitative and qualitative lines.

Efforts to improve the standards of education for mass communications, and of professional journalism itself, are being made by organizations of journalism teachers and administrators. Foremost is the Association for Education in Journalism with approximately 950 teachers and administrators listed in its membership.

News executives have praised journalism graduates for the basic educational foundation they have acquired, for their knowledge of what is news and how to report and edit it, and for their avid interest in newspaper work. Others have complained that some journalism graduates can't spell, that they lack initiative and industry, that they assume incorrectly that they are finished products when they are graduated, and that they place an undue emphasis upon beginning salary.

Few criticisms of journalism or communications schools are being voiced by executives who have taken the time to investigate the underlying philosophy and form of professional education. And industry and education have developed innumerable programs of mutual support.

Journalistic craftsmen who are truly professional are continuing their education through constant reading of books and periodicals, membership in professional and trade organizations, attendance at conferences and seminars, and postgraduate enrollment in college courses and other continuing education activities. For the student of mass communications, learning can never cease.

STUDY QUESTION

What evidence is there that the mass communications industries are cooperating with educators in recruiting new young talent for the media?

PROJECTS

1. Write a 300-word report on an article in *Journalism Quarterly* concerning communications education, or on the information contained in the American Council on Education for Journalism's brochure, "Choosing a Career in Journalism" (see bibliography).

2. Examine the newspapers in your school library and find an article, or series of articles, that apparently was written by a reporter who has continued his studies beyond his earlier formal education. Why do you think so?

CHAPTER 19

JOURNALISM
TEACHING
AS A CAREER

JOURNALISM TEACHING IN THE SECONDARY SCHOOL

There are more potential openings for teachers of journalism in the secondary schools of the United States than in any other field for which journalism training provides preparation. The best estimates are that approximately 45,000 senior and junior high school publications—newspapers, magazines, and yearbooks—are being issued regularly. More than 1,000,000 students work on these publications, which cost collectively around $36,000,000 a year.

Expert instruction should be provided for these undertakings and for the journalism classes that usually produce them, both for credit and as an extracurricular activity. So severe, however, is the shortage of qualified instructors that frequently a teacher of language arts, business education, or social studies—with no background whatever in journalism—is assigned to provide a measure of guidance. This happens, too, when a principal fails to realize the importance of providing qualified instruction in the high school journalism field.

The first known high school paper, the *Literary Journal,* appeared in the Boston Latin Grammar School in 1829. Other publications were founded by New England high schools in the 1850's and 1860's. It was not until 1912, however, that the first known class in high school journalism was started in Salina, Kansas. The movement became widespread in the 1920's, apparently in an effort to motivate students in English composition and to broaden the curriculum beyond the traditional classical subjects. A number of local, state, and national organizations were founded in the mid-1920's. Among them were three of the current national organizations: Quill and Scroll, the honorary society of high school journalists, now housed at the State University of Iowa; the Columbia Scholastic Press Association at Columbia University; and the National Scholastic Press Association, with headquarters at the University of Minnesota. Their national magazines, begun at this time, are *Quill and Scroll, School Press Review,* and *Scholastic Editor,* respectively. The Catholic School Press Association, founded at Marquette University in 1931, publishes *Catholic School Editor.*

High school journalism matured during the 1930's and 1940's as school boards, superintendents, and principals noted its educational value. The objectives outlined for the Baltimore, Maryland, secondary school course in journalism exemplify those elsewhere: To teach the functions of a school paper; to foster an understanding of the role of the newspaper in a democracy; to encourage the development of qualities essential to a competent school journalist; to develop a working knowledge of newspaper ethics; to promote the critical selection and reading of newspapers and periodicals; to develop skill in accurate, clear, and forceful journalistic writing; to provide experiences in the technical processes in producing a school newspaper; and to give practice in the use of the correct mechanics of English.

Those who have taught high school journalism over the years speak with genuine enthusiasm about the satisfactions they have found in handling journalism classes and advising school publications. For one thing, they enjoy having many of their school's most brilliant students on their publications staffs; frequently the highest ranking group of students in the English placement tests is assigned to the teacher producing the school paper. These imaginative and creative youngsters are stimulated by actually writing for print. Many of them go on to other fields of study at the universities, but some become the prize students of journalism or communications schools and eventually take their places in professional work. Many an editor or reporter can trace his interest in journalism back to a high school journalism teacher or publications adviser who transmitted some of the enthusiasm of the craft to his or her students. The school paper and the annual are major activities at the high school level; this gives their adviser additional prestige as a teacher. He or she also is brought into close contact with school administrators, and quite a number of able journalism teachers have moved into administrative work.

The most substantial support accorded to high school journalism teachers has come from the Newspaper Fund, Inc. At the end of the summer school session in 1964, more than 3000 teachers had received grants for summer journalism study from the Fund. More than $1,000,-000 had been invested in these teachers by the Fund, which is fully supported by the *Wall Street Journal*. The number of annual grants had grown from 131 in 1959 to about 750 in 1964, and the number of special programs for teachers sponsored by the Fund had increased from four in 1959 to 31 in 1964. The special studies increased the capabilities of the teachers and also their enthusiasm for journalism as a socially important career field. In addition, the national grants were credited with improving their prestige as teachers of journalism.

Men and women entering journalism teaching at the junior and senior high school levels also have the support of such organizations as the National Scholastic Press Association and the Columbia Scholastic Press Association, which issue publications and guidebooks for teachers and students and conduct critical services providing professional evaluation and ratings of school newspapers, annuals, and magazines. The National School Yearbook Association, located at the University of Missouri, offers a critical service for annuals and publishes *Photolith*. There are also regional associations, like the Pacific Slope School Press which has its headquarters at the University of Washington. The associations and many schools and departments of journalism hold conventions for high school journalists. The teachers themselves are organized as the Journalism Education Association. Newsmen and educators also cooperate in organizing high school chapters of the Future Journalists of America, founded at the University of Oklahoma.

The educational preparation necessary to teach secondary school journalism varies widely from state to state, a study by an Association for Education in Journalism committee revealed. Some states, including Florida, Kansas, Louisiana, and South Dakota, require up to 12 semester hours of college journalism study for teachers of credit courses in journalism. Colorado and Oregon, however, report "standards," though no requirements, of seven to nine hours in the larger schools. Teaching minors, ranging from 12 to 24 semester hours, are established in California, Illinois, Indiana, Louisiana, Montana, Washington, and Wisconsin.

Some prospective teachers major in journalism and minor in an area such as English or the social sciences, meanwhile acquiring sufficient hours in education courses to qualify for certificates. Others major in education and take first and second minors in journalism and some other field. Still others major in English or language arts and take as many journalism courses as they can work into a four-year program that often is crowded because of the double professional preparation required. All realize that they likely will be teaching only one or two courses in journalism, with the balance of their instructional load in another subject.

Salary levels, which also vary widely throughout the country, have risen considerably in recent years because of the shortage of teachers and increased public awareness of the necessity for better supporting the schools. Many teachers, after acquiring some experience in the classrooms, return to seek a master's degree both for increased proficiency and for higher pay. Summer work on newspapers and other media can provide both additional pay and professional experience that makes a teacher better qualified to teach journalism. With the dearth of adequately prepared teachers in the field, those who take at least a substantial minor in journalism or who return for graduate work are sought after by those school systems which place some real emphasis on high school journalism and publications work.

JOURNALISM TEACHING IN THE JUNIOR COLLEGE

Countless other opportunities for teaching journalism are available in junior colleges throughout the United States, which are growing steadily in enrollment and importance as the population increases.

Surveys have indicated that most of these two-year colleges favor a program aimed at preparing their graduates for a major in journalism or communications at four-year colleges and universities. A number of junior college educators state that their primary purpose is to acquaint students with the mass media and to teach them to become discerning "consumers" of news and opinion so they will be better able to discharge their responsibilities as citizens. Others organize courses around the publication of newspapers and yearbooks. Some seek to prepare students to take jobs with the media immediately after the completion of their two-year studies; the teaching of occupational journalism, however, is frowned upon both by a majority of the junior college instructors surveyed and by almost all the journalism administrators in four-year colleges and universities.

Whatever their purposes, these junior college journalism programs abound in opportunities for the young man or woman who desires to teach on the college level. Some schools will accept an applicant with the bachelor's degree, preferably in journalism, and some media experience; others insist upon the master's degree. In many junior colleges, as in some four-year schools, the journalism teacher directs publicity in addition to supervising school publications.

THE COLLEGE AND UNIVERSITY LEVEL

The story of the rise of journalism and communications as a teaching and research discipline in American colleges and universities was related briefly in the preceding chapter. During the past half-century approximately 200 institutions have established four-year programs leading to a degree in journalism or mass communications; more than 400 others offer some instruction in the study. As college enrollments continue to rise, many newly established state colleges and expanding liberal arts colleges will join in the teaching of journalism and communications. And some (for example, the rapidly growing state colleges in California) will recruit sizable new faculties to meet the professional interests of those among the thousands of their students who wish to study in preparation for careers in the mass media. The older established schools and departments likewise will be seeking new faculty members.

Journalism and communications faculty members at the university or college level are engaged in three major activities: teaching, research, and service. They have one or more specialties in the journalistic techniques, acquired through their own professional experience with the mass media: reporting, news editing, magazine writing, radio and television news, typography and graphic arts processes, advertising, public relations, news photography, critical writing, broadcast programming and production, and editorial writing are among these technique fields. The young teacher usually starts at this techniques level, but he is well advised to be equipped for teaching and research in one or more of the scholarly fields of interest: history of journalism, literary journalism, the press and society, economics of mass communications, legal aspects of communications, international communications and foreign journalism, public opinion and propaganda, mass communication theory, and the advanced fields of advertising research. He should be interested, too, in performing services for the mass media with which the school or department is in close contact and in spending long hours offering advice and counsel to students who turn to him for guidance and stimulation.

Those who aspire to the top ranks of university or college teaching in journalism and mass communications usually seek master's degrees in the field. They then undertake study toward the Ph.D. degree in the graduate school of a college or university which offers either a major or a minor in the subject and which has a journalism and communications faculty of graduate school caliber. Some prefer to minor in journalism or communications and to do their major doctoral work in political science, history, psychology, economics, drama, American studies, or another related field; others enter the relatively small number of universities which award Ph.D. degrees in journalism or in communications. In either case, there is a blending of study and research in journalism or communications with study and research in the social sciences, behavioral sciences, or the humanities. One major school of journalism, for example, has on its staff eight men with Ph.D. degrees: two in political science, three in mass communications, one in history, one in American studies, and one in psychology. Four of its other seven staff members hold M.A. degrees in journalism, the other three in economics, English, and history.

Not all college journalism or communications faculty members need undertake doctoral work; some with sound professional experience and specialized abilities in such fields as graphic arts, news photography, weekly journalism, or radio and television writing, production, and programming find their services amply rewarded at the M.A. level. There have been shortages of qualified teachers in the advertising and broadcast media fields, particularly. As the size of the institution or of the journalism or communications teaching staff decreases, there is additional emphasis upon the teaching function and the all-around ability of faculty members to handle technical work. The amount of emphasis placed upon the research function, for which the discipline of doctoral study is highly important, varies from campus to campus.

Opportunities for research and publication in the mass communications field are almost unlimited. Many aspects of the history of communications remain to be explored, despite the fact that this area traditionally has been a favorite one for journalism professors. Biographies and histories of individual newspapers, broadcast facilities, and magazines remain to be written in virtually every section of the country; for example, there are no really good and recent biographies of such newspaper greats as Joseph Pulitzer and E. W. Scripps, let alone many other capable editors and publishers of regional importance. Nor are there adequate histories of more than a score of the country's many newspapers, broadcast stations, and magazines. The literary aspects of journalism constitute another little-plowed field. Important studies of the relationships between the press and society, and of the conflicts between press and government, await future scholars. Only a start has been made on penetrating studies of the economics of the mass media. Advertising offers wide opportunities for advanced study and research projects of both basic and applied character. As explained in Chapter 17, the fields of mass communications theory and research, of public opinion and propaganda, and of other studies allied to the behavioral sciences have barely been opened by scholars. Particularly, there is a need for interpretative analysis of scientific findings and quantitative data by men who can relate what the researchers have found to the everyday problems of the mass media. The processes of international communications and the study of foreign journalism have become more important in recent years, also, with few faculty members qualified to do advanced teaching and research in the field.

At the level of the 400 or more institutions offering nondegree study in journalism, there are at least 150 colleges which offer more than 18 semester hours (or 27 quarter hours) in journalism, including 30 or more which offer a journalism minor. Another 75 offer up to 12 semester hours; the remainder provide one or two courses, usually connected with the college student publications. About three-fourths of these institutions house their journalism instruction within the English department; the others list it separately. Men and women with M.A. degrees, at least, in journalism can find beginning teaching positions in these colleges, and sometimes they are able to carve out satisfying professional careers in them; this is true particularly of those who also are interested in the teaching of English and writing. They may become publications and broadcast advisers, as well, and sometimes also serve in the college's public relations and publicity offices.

Offering assistance to the publications adviser at the junior college and college level are the Associated Collegiate Press, companion organization of the National Scholastic Press Association, and the National Council of College Publications Advisers. The ACP issues guidebooks and other publications for college publications staffs and maintains critical services for newspapers, annuals, and magazines.

Salaries for communications teachers in colleges and universities run somewhat above the averages for other disciplines, because of the competitive bidding from the mass media for the services of those who are preparing for teaching careers. University and college salaries have improved substantially in recent years, and those who reach professorial status can look forward to nine-month salaries running from $10,000 to as high as $20,000 a year. There also are opportunities for additional income from summer teaching, summer "refresher" work in the media, consultantships to advertising agencies and other groups, research projects, and book publication and other writing.

SUMMARY

There is a great shortage of qualified teachers of journalism at the secondary school level and of advisers for the more than 45,000 senior and junior high school newspapers, magazines, and yearbooks. Those who teach in high school find many rewards, including the opportunity to stimulate many of the best student minds. National and regional scholastic press organizations and the country's schools of journalism aid the high school teacher in his or her work. Prospective teachers can either major or minor in journalism; many major in the language arts or in education. In school systems where principals desire to employ well-prepared journalism teachers and publications advisers, salary levels and professional opportunities can be quite attractive. Salary levels for teachers have also been increasing generally.

The rapidly expanding junior colleges offer another teaching opportunity, often in combination with advisory positions on publications or publicity work for the college. At the college level, there are more than 400 institutions offering nondegree course work in journalism or communications, many of them as an adjunct to their curriculum in English.

Four-year programs leading to a bachelor's degree in journalism and communications have been established in some 200 colleges and universities, and the area has won recognition as a teaching and research discipline. Journalism and communications faculty members at this level are engaged in three major activities: teaching, research, and service. They have one or more specialties in the journalistic and broadcast programming and production techniques, stemming from their own professional media experience; they are equipped for teaching and research in a field of scholarly interest; and they are interested in performing services for the mass media and for their students. They have either M.A. or Ph.D. degrees, depending upon their desire to contribute in the field of research. Opportunities for research and publication in the mass communications field are almost unlimited, and society needs more competent teachers of journalism and communications who also will investigate the problems of the mass media.

STUDY QUESTION

What are the social contributions of a career in journalism or communications teaching and research as compared to a career with one of the media?

PROJECTS

1. Examine the contents of a year's issues (four) of *Journalism Quarterly* and write a 500-word report on the *variety* of research being carried on in mass communications.

2. Study the curriculum of a good-sized school or department of journalism or communications (your own or one listed in a catalog for another university available in your library or registrar's office). Analyze the division of journalism or communications course offerings between (a) those developing technical competence and (b) those giving students background knowledge about mass communications. How many of the latter type qualify as being essentially liberal arts courses in character?

BIBLIOGRAPHY

This is a selected, annotated bibliography of books dealing with mass communications and journalism. It is organized to correspond with the five principal sections and 19 chapters of this book.

It is the authors' aim to introduce the reader to some of the basic books which, if he has the time and interest to explore them, will take him beyond the necessarily limited syntheses of an introductory survey of mass communications. If a student reader has the interest and opportunity to elect further studies in the field, he will meet many of these books again in advanced courses; if he goes no further, this bibliography will give him a personal reading list for more detailed examination of various facets of the field. It is in no sense an all-inclusive bibliography; for that purpose the reader is referred to Warren C. Price's *The Literature of Journalism: An Annotated Bibliography* (Minneapolis: University of Minnesota Press, 1959), with its more than 3000 entries covering all aspects of mass communications except book publishing and the film. Those areas, and others, are covered in Eleanor Blum's *Reference Books in the Mass Media* (Urbana: University of Illinois Press, 1962). Another excellent aid is a 24-page guide, *Organizations, Publications and Directories in the Mass Media of Communications,* compiled by Wilbur Peterson (Iowa City: State University of Iowa School of Journalism, 1964).

This bibliography also lists the principal journals and trade publications with which students of mass communications should be familiar, and in a few instances makes references to articles in them. In cases where books have gone through revised editions, the date given is for the most recent revision. In subsequent listings of a book, place and date of publication are not repeated.

PERIODICALS, ANNUAL PUBLICATIONS, AND DIRECTORIES

Research journals

Journalism Quarterly—published by the Association for Education in Journalism, devoted to research articles in journalism and mass communications. Contains extensive book reviews, bibliographies of articles in American and foreign journals, news of journalism education.

Public Opinion Quarterly—emphasizes political and psychological phases of communication. Book reviews and summaries of public opinion polls.

Journal of Marketing—articles and book reviews in the fields of marketing and advertising.

Gazette—international journal, published in Amsterdam, devoted to research in mass communications.

Audio Visual Communication Review—reports on research activities and findings in the communication area.

Newspaper area

Professional journals with general interest articles on press problems: *Nieman Reports,* published by the Nieman Foundation; *Columbia Journalism Review* (Columbia University Graduate School of Journalism); *Quill* (Sigma Delta Chi); *Masthead* (National Conference of Editorial Writers); *ASNE Bulletin* (American Society of Newspaper Editors); *IPI Report* (International Press Institute); *Matrix* (Theta Sigma Phi); *Journalism Educator* (American Society of Journalism School Administrators).

Trade journals: *Editor & Publisher,* whose focus is on the daily newspaper and general industry problems, but which reports on advertising, marketing, and public relations areas; *Publishers' Auxiliary, American Press,* and *National Publisher* (National Editorial Association), for weeklies and small dailies, with the first named being the widest in scope; *National Press Photographer* (National Press Photographers Association); *Guild Reporter* (American Newspaper Guild); *Circulation Management; Inland Printer,* for the printing industry.

Annual publications: *APME Red Book,* containing the record of the annual meeting and the reports of the Continuing Studies Committee of the Associated Press Managing Editors Association; *Problems of Journalism,* covering the annual meeting of the American Society of Newspaper Editors.

Directories: *Editor & Publisher International Year Book,* source for statistics and information about dailies; N. W. Ayer and Son, *Directory of Newspapers and Periodicals,* covering all newspapers and magazines.

Radio, television, and films

Professional journals: *Film Quarterly; Journal of Broadcasting; RTNDA Bulletin* (Radio-Television News Directors Association); *Television Quarterly* (National Academy of Television Arts and Sciences).

Trade journals: *Broadcasting,* the spokesman for that industry; *Television Age; Television; Variety,* voice of the entertainment world; *Billboard.*

Directories: *Broadcasting Yearbook,* source for statistics and information about radio and television; *Television Factbook.*

Magazines and book publishing

Trade journals: *Publishers' Weekly*, for the book publishing industry, whose focus is largely on general and children's books with limited attention to textbooks, technical books, and reference works; *The Retail Bookseller; Bookbinding and Book Production; Author and Journalist, Writer,* and *Writer's Digest*, for free-lance magazine writers; *Reporting for People in Industrial Communications* (International Council of Industrial Editors).

Directories: *Literary Market Place*, for book publishing; N. W. Ayer and Son, *Directory of Newspapers and Periodicals*, for magazine statistics and information; *Writer's Market* and *Writer's Year Book*, guides for magazine article writers; Gebbie Press, *House Magazine Directory*.

Advertising and public relations

Professional journals: *Journal of Marketing; Public Relations Journal* (Public Relations Society of America); *Public Relations News* (newsletter).

Trade journals: *Printers' Ink* and *Advertising Age* are the major spokesmen for the advertising industry; *Media/scope; Advertising Agency; Advertising Requirements; Sponsor*, for buyers of broadcast advertising; *Industrial Marketing; Sales Management*.

Directories: Standard Rate and Data Service, *Consumer Markets; Editor & Publisher Market Guide; Broadcasting Marketbook; Printers' Ink Advertisers' Guide to Marketing*.

Part One

THE ROLE OF MASS COMMUNICATIONS

Perhaps no book better illustrates the importance which society attaches to the mass communicator and the mass media than the brief *A Free and Responsible Press* (Chicago: University of Chicago Press, 1947). It summarizes the opinions of the 13 scholars who comprised the Commission on Freedom of the Press regarding the duties and the shortcomings of the mass media. Commission chairman was Dr. Robert M. Hutchins of the University of Chicago.

Wilbur Schramm's *Responsibility in Mass Communication* (New York: Harper, 1957) is the best treatment of communication ethics. It discusses the role of the mass communicator in developing the political, social, and economic fabrics of a democratic society, and the development of modern mass communications.

Several books of readings deal with the role of mass communications in society. Listed in order according to the increasing complexity of their materials they are: *The Press and Society*, edited by George L. Bird and Frederic E. Merwin (New York: Prentice-Hall, 1951), organized for textbook use; *Interpretations of Journalism*, edited by Frank Luther Mott and Ralph D. Casey (New York: Crofts, 1937), a collection of 64 of the "chief utterances of the past 300 years on the subject of newspapers and the press"; *Communications in Modern Society,* edited by Wilbur Schramm (Urbana: University of Illinois Press, 1948), 15 essays on communications problems and research trends; *Mass Communications,* edited by Wilbur Schramm (Urbana: University of Illinois Press, 1960), selected readings on mass communications "through the windows of the social sciences"; *Reader in Public Opinion and Communication,* edited by Bernard Berelson and Morris Janowitz (Glencoe, Ill.: The Free Press, 1953), dealing with public opinion theory, media content, audiences, and effects (1965 revision scheduled); and *People, Society, and Mass Communication,* edited by Lewis A. Dexter and David M. White (New York: Free Press of Glencoe, 1964), dealing with communication research with a sociological emphasis.

The effects of the mass media on the social fabric are discussed in various articles in *Mass Culture: The Popular Arts in America,* edited by Bernard Rosenberg and David M. White (Glencoe, Ill.: The Free Press, 1957). There are sections on the mass literature, motion pictures, radio, and television. One of the important articles is "Mass Communication, Popular Taste and Organized Social Action" by Paul Lazarsfeld and Robert K. Merton.

More complex studies of effects are Joseph T. Klapper's *The Effects of Mass Communication* (Glencoe, Ill.: The Free Press, 1960), and *The Process and Effects of Mass Communication,* edited by Wilbur Schramm (Urbana: University of Illinois Press, 1954). New directions and new findings in communication research are offered by Schramm in *The Science of Human Communication* (New York: Basic Books, 1963), which contains articles by Leon Festinger, Charles E. Osgood, Klapper, Elihu Katz, Paul Lazarsfeld, Ithiel de Sola Pool, and others, on subjects ranging from cognitive dissonance to voting behavior.

The communication process is analyzed most completely in David K. Berlo's *The Process of Communication* (New York: Holt, 1960), and most simply by Chilton R. Bush in the first chapter of *The Art of News Communication* (New York: Appleton-Century-Crofts, 1954). Wilbur Schramm describes "How Communication Works" in the opening chapter of *The Process and Effects of Mass Communication.* Harold D. Lasswell's "The Structure and Function of Communication in Society" (in which he posed the question "Who, says what, in which channel, to whom, with what effect?") appears both in Schramm's *Mass Communications* reader and in *The Communication of Ideas,* edited by Lyman Bryson (New York: Harper, 1948).

Among the leading books on public opinion are William Albig, *Modern Public Opinion* (New York: McGraw-Hill, 1956); V. O. Key Jr., *Public Opinion and American Democracy* (New York: Knopf, 1961); Leonard W. Doob, *Public Opinion and Propaganda* (New York: Holt, 1948); Norman Powell, *Anatomy of Public Opinion* (New York: Prentice-Hall, 1951), which treats the mass media more extensively than most books on public opinion; and Curtis D. MacDougall, *Understanding Public Opinion: A Guide for*

Newspapermen and Newspaper Readers (New York: Macmillan, 1952), with a focus as indicated in the subtitle.

The impact of public opinion and the mass media upon politics is analyzed by Walter Lippmann in his classic *Public Opinion* (New York: Harcourt, Brace, 1922); by Douglass Cater in *The Fourth Branch of Government* (Boston: Houghton Mifflin, 1959), a study of the key role of the Washington press corps; and by Bernard C. Cohen in *The Press and Foreign Policy* (Princeton, N.J.: Princeton University Press, 1963), a study of Washington diplomatic reporting.

Books dealing with the mass media and the voting process include Angus Campbell and others, *The American Voter* (New York: Wiley, 1960); Bernard Berelson, Hazel Gaudet, and Paul F. Lazarsfeld, *The People's Choice* (New York: Duell, Sloan and Pearce, 1944), analyzing 1940 presidential voting in Erie county, Ohio; and Bernard Berelson, Paul F. Lazarsfeld, and William N. McPhee, *Voting: A Study of Opinion Formation in a Presidential Campaign* (Chicago: University of Chicago Press, 1954), case analyses of 1948 presidential election voters in Elmira, New York. Elihu Katz and Paul Lazarsfeld, *Personal Influence: The Part Played by People in the Flow of Mass Communications* (Glencoe, Ill.: The Free Press, 1955), develops a new aspect of the problem.

Part Two

THE HISTORICAL PERSPECTIVE

The most widely ranging of the histories of American journalism is Edwin Emery's *The Press and America: An Interpretative History of Journalism* (Englewood Cliffs, N.J.: Prentice-Hall, 1962). It correlates journalism history with social, political, and economic trends and is especially comprehensive in its treatment of twentieth century journalism—newspapers, magazines, radio and television, press associations, and the relationship of the mass media to government and society.

Frank Luther Mott's *American Journalism: A History, 1690–1960* (New York: Macmillan, 1962) is designed for both classroom and reference shelf, contains much rich detail in its comprehensive treatment of newspapers, but puts little emphasis on other media. Alfred McClung Lee's *The Daily Newspaper in America* (New York: Macmillan, 1937) offers a sociological approach and much valuable data in its topical treatment of such subjects as newsprint, printing presses, labor, ownership and management, news, advertising, and circulation. Willard G. Bleyer's *Main Currents in the History of American Journalism* (Boston: Houghton Mifflin, 1927) remains an excellent account of American journalism until the early twentieth century, with emphasis upon leading editors. Kenneth Stewart and John Tebbel, in *Makers of Modern Journalism* (New York: Prentice-Hall, 1952), sketch early American journalism history and concentrate on twentieth century journalistic personalities. Tebbel, in his *Compact History of the American Newspaper* (New York: Hawthorn Books, 1963), does the reverse, sketching twentieth century journalism in only the broadest terms.

Many excellent articles about twentieth century journalists first published in the *Saturday Evening Post* are found in *Post Biographies of Famous Journalists,* edited by John E. Drewry (Athens: University of Georgia Press, 1942), and its sequel, *More Post Biographies* (1947). A collection of the best magazine articles about leading American newspaper editors and publishers of all periods is found in *Highlights in the History of the American Press,* edited by Edwin H. Ford and Edwin Emery (Minneapolis: University of Minnesota Press, 1954).

The best historical accounts of specific areas of mass communications are found in the following:

Radio and television: Llewellyn White, *The American Radio* (Chicago: University of Chicago Press, 1947); Sydney W. Head, *Broadcasting in America: A Survey of Television and Radio* (Boston: Houghton Mifflin, 1956).

Magazines: Frank Luther Mott's monumental *A History of American Magazines,* in four volumes with a fifth and final volume forthcoming (Vol. 1, New York: Appleton, 1930 and Vols. 2–4, Cambridge, Mass.: Harvard University Press, 1938–57); James Playsted Wood, *Magazines in the United States* (New York: Ronald, 1956); Theodore Peterson, *Magazines in the Twentieth Century* (Urbana: University of Illinois Press, 1964).

Book publishing: Hellmut Lehmann-Haupt and others, *The Book in America: History of the Making and Selling of Books in the United States* (New York: Bowker, 1951); Frank A. Mumby, *Publishing and Bookselling: A History from the Earliest Times to the Present* (London: Jonathan Cape, 1956).

Films: Paul Rotha and Richard Griffith, *The Film Till Now* (New York: Funk and Wagnalls, 1949), world cinema survey; Richard Griffith and Arthur Mayer, *The Movies* (New York: Simon and Schuster, 1957), American film history.

Photography: Helmut and Alison Gernsheim, *The History of Photography* (London: Oxford, 1955); Beaumont Newhall, *The History of Photography* (New York: Museum of Modern Art, 1964); William Morgan, *The Encyclopedia of Photography* (New York: Greystone, 1963).

Press associations and syndicates: Victor Rosewater, *History of Co-operative News-Gathering in the United States* (New York: Appleton, 1930); Elmo Scott Watson, *A History of Newspaper Syndicates in the United States, 1865–1935* (Chicago: Publishers' Auxiliary, 1936).

Advertising: Frank Presbrey, *The History and Development of Advertising* (New York: Doubleday, Doran, 1930), the standard account; James Playsted Wood, *The Story of Advertising* (New York: Ronald, 1958), more readable and up-to-date.

Additional references, by chapter topic, follow:

Chapter 3

Theories and Realities of Press Freedom

Lucy M. Salmon's *The Newspaper and Authority* (New York: Oxford, 1923) is an extensive historical survey of restrictions placed on newspapers. Important periods of the history of press freedom struggles are covered in Fred S. Siebert, *Freedom of the Press in England, 1472–1776* (Urbana: University of Illinois Press, 1952); Leonard W. Levy, *Legacy of Suppression: Freedom of Speech and Press in Early American History* (Cambridge, Mass.: Harvard University Press, 1960); Clyde A. Duniway, *The Development of Freedom of the Press in Massachusetts* (New York: Longmans, Green, 1906); John C. Miller, *Crisis in Freedom: The Alien and Sedition Acts* (Boston: Little, Brown, 1951) and Frank Luther Mott, *Jefferson and the Press* (Baton Rouge: Louisiana State University Press, 1943); and Zechariah Chafee Jr., *Free Speech in the United States* (Cambridge, Mass.: Harvard University Press, 1941), a study emphasizing the effects of modern wartime conditions. James E. Pollard, *The Presidents and the Press* (New York: Macmillan, 1947), covers presidential press relations from Washington to Truman, and has been supplemented by his *The Presidents and the Press: Truman to Johnson* (Washington: Public Affairs Press, 1964).

Excellent discussions by newspaper editors of current problems in protecting freedom of information and access to news are found in James Russell Wiggins, *Freedom or Secrecy* (New York: Oxford, 1964), and Herbert Brucker, *Freedom of Information* (New York: Macmillan, 1949). More detailed studies are Harold L. Cross, *The People's Right to Know* (New York: Columbia University Press, 1953), and Zechariah Chafee Jr.'s two-volume *Government and Mass Communications* (Chicago: University of Chicago Press, 1947).

Supreme Court trends are traced in Edward G. Hudon's *Freedom of Speech and Press in America* (Washington: Public Affairs Press, 1963). J. Edward Gerald's *The Press and the Constitution* (Minneapolis: University of Minnesota Press, 1948) analyzes constitutional law cases involving press freedom from 1931 to 1947. Among the several general works on press law, Frank Thayer's *Legal Control of the Press* (Brooklyn: Foundation Press, 1962) is strongest in its treatment of historical background. Walter A. Steigleman, *The Newspaperman and the Law* (Dubuque, Iowa: William C. Brown, 1950), treats historical and social aspects.

Philosophical problems of press freedom are analyzed by the Commission on Freedom of the Press in *A Free and Responsible Press*, by William E. Hocking in *Freedom of the Press: A Framework of Principle* (Chicago: University of Chicago Press, 1947), and by Fred S. Siebert, Theodore Peterson, and Wilbur Schramm in *Four Theories of the Press* (Urbana: University of Illinois Press, 1956). Among discussions of press freedom by newsmen are Walter Lippmann, *Liberty and the News* (New York: Harcourt, Brace,

1920); Elmer Davis, *But We Were Born Free* (New York: Bobbs-Merrill, 1954); and Alan Barth, *The Loyalty of Free Men* (New York: Viking, 1951).

A selection of historically important writings on press freedom is found in Frank Luther Mott and Ralph D. Casey, *Interpretations of Journalism.*

The film area is covered by Ruth A. Inglis, *Freedom of the Movies* (Chicago: University of Chicago Press, 1947); the book area by Richard McKeon, Robert K. Merton, and Walter Gellhorn, *The Freedom to Read: Perspective and Program* (New York: Bowker, 1957); and the radio and television area by Sydney W. Head, *Broadcasting in America,* and Walter B. Emery, *Broadcasting and Government* (East Lansing: Michigan State University Press, 1961). Movie and television censorship is decried in Murray Schumach's *The Face on the Cutting Room Floor* (New York: Morrow, 1964).

Chapter 4

Technological Growth

The development of printing processes is described in the standard histories of journalism, particularly in A. M. Lee, *The Daily Newspaper in America,* and under various subject headings in the *Encyclopaedia Britannica* and the *Encyclopaedia of the Social Sciences.* Kenneth E. Olson's *Typography and Mechanics of the Newspaper* (New York: Appleton, 1930) contains a clear and brief history of printing. Albert A. Sutton's *Design and Makeup of the Newspaper* (New York: Prentice-Hall, 1948) has excellent factual material on printing processes.

The early history of printing in America is told by pioneer publisher Isaiah Thomas in *The History of Printing in America,* first published in 1810 and republished in 1874 (Albany, N.Y.: Joel Munsell), and by Lawrence C. Wroth in *The Colonial Printer* (Portland, Me.: Southworth-Anthoensen Press, 1938). Daniel B. Updyke's two-volume *Printing Types: Their History, Forms and Use* (Cambridge, Mass.: Harvard University Press, 1937) is the standard work in that field. S. H. Steinberg's *Five Hundred Years of Printing* (New York: Criterion, 1959) is a briefer survey.

The graphic processes are admirably described by Edmund C. Arnold in *Ink on Paper* (New York: Harper & Row, 1963). Among books on the use of type, the best include Arnold's *Functional Newspaper Design* (New York: Harper, 1956); Arthur T. Turnbull and Russell N. Baird, *The Graphics of Communication: Typography, Layout and Design* (New York: Holt, Rinehart and Winston, 1964); Thomas F. Barnhart, *Weekly Newspaper Makeup and Typography* (Minneapolis: University of Minnesota Press, 1949); and Sutton.

The best single discussion of radio's growth is in Llewellyn White, *The American Radio;* Sydney W. Head, *Broadcasting in America,* covers both radio and television. Motion picture technology is conveniently surveyed in the *Encyclopaedia Britannica* and late technological developments in all fields are reviewed in the annual *Britannica Book of the Year*. News of developments in space satellites is found in that publication, in current magazines, and in the pamphlet *Space Communication and the Mass Media* (New York: UNESCO, 1963).

Chapter 5

Growth of the Print Media

The best book-length discussion of the news function is Frank Luther Mott's *The News in America* (Cambridge, Mass.: Harvard University Press, 1952), a survey of the concepts, forms, and problems of news, with historical backgrounds. No one interested in newspapers should miss reading it.

The best books on the opinion function and editorial page writing are Hillier Krieghbaum's *Facts in Perspective* (New York: Prentice-Hall, 1956) and A. Gayle Waldrop's *Editor and Editorial Writer* (New York: Rinehart, 1955). Krieghbaum also covers news interpretation and news magazines. The brief essays written by Allan Nevins as introductions for sections to his collection of editorials, *American Press Opinion: Washington to Coolidge* (New York: Heath, 1928), constitute an excellent history of the opinion function.

Arthur M. Schlesinger, *Prelude to Independence: The Newspaper War on Britain, 1764–1776* (New York: Knopf, 1958), analyzes one period of major press influence. Nevins, *American Press Opinion,* has an excellent section on the partisan journalism of the 1790's. C. C. Regier, *The Era of the Muck-rakers* (Chapel Hill: University of North Carolina Press, 1932), examines magazines during the Progressive era; Louis Filler, *Crusaders for American Liberalism* (New York: Harcourt, Brace, 1939), also covers newspapermen. Writings of the muckrakers are edited by Arthur and Lila Weinberg in *The Muckrakers* (New York: Simon and Schuster, 1961).

The best anthology of news stories is *A Treasury of Great Reporting,* edited by Louis L. Snyder and Richard B. Morris (New York: Simon and Schuster, 1962), covering stories written under pressure since the sixteenth century. Current collections are Bryce W. Rucker's *Twentieth Century Reporting at Its Best* (Ames: Iowa State University Press, 1964) and John Hohenberg's *The Pulitzer Prize Story* (New York: Columbia University Press, 1959).

Biographical essays about leading journalistic figures from Benjamin Franklin to Robert R. McCormick are found in Ford and Emery, *Highlights in the History of the American Press.* Twentieth century figures are subjects of articles in Drewry, *Post Biographies* and *More Post Biographies.* Charles Fisher, *The Columnists* (New York: Howell, Soskin, 1944), has sketches of 20 columnists of the period; *Molders of Opinion,* edited by David Bulman (Milwaukee: Bruce, 1945) offers biographies of 14 newspaper and radio commentators. The histories of journalism and the *Dictionary of American Biography* are other sources.

Top-flight biographies of key figures in the development of the news function include: Carl Van Doren, *Benjamin Franklin* (New York: Viking, 1938); Oliver Carlson, *The Man Who Made News: James Gordon Bennett* (New York: Duell, Sloan and Pearce, 1942); Francis Brown, *Raymond of the Times* (New York: Norton, 1951); Fayette Copeland, *Kendall of the Picayune* (Norman: University of Oklahoma Press, 1943); Candace Stone, *Dana and the Sun* (New York: Dodd, Mead, 1938); Raymond B. Nixon, *Henry W. Grady: Spokesman of the New South* (New York: Knopf, 1943); Don C. Seitz, *Joseph Pulitzer* (New York: Simon and Schuster, 1924); Negley D. Cochran, *E. W. Scripps* (New York: Harcourt, Brace, 1933); W. A. Swanberg, *Citizen Hearst* (New York: Scribner's, 1961); John Tebbel, *The Life and Good Times of William Randolph Hearst* (New York: Dutton, 1952); Gerald W. Johnson, *An Honorable Titan: A Biographical Study of Adolph S. Ochs* (New York: Harper, 1946); James W. Markham, *Bovard of the Post-Dispatch* (Baton Rouge: Louisiana State University Press, 1954); and Homer W. King, *Pulitzer's Prize Editor: A Biography of John A. Cockerill* (Durham, N.C.: Duke University Press, 1965).

Leading biographies of opinion makers include John C. Miller, *Sam Adams: Pioneer in Propaganda* (Boston: Little, Brown, 1936); Mary A. Best, *Thomas Paine* (New York: Harcourt, Brace, 1927); Glyndon G. Van Deusen, *Horace Greeley: Nineteenth Century Crusader* (Philadelphia: University of Pennsylvania Press, 1953); George S. Merriam, *The Life and Times of Samuel Bowles* (New York: Century, 1885); Joseph F. Wall, *Henry Watterson* (New York: Oxford, 1956); and Joseph L. Morrison, *Josephus Daniels Says* (Chapel Hill: University of North Carolina Press, 1963). William Cullen Bryant and Edwin Lawrence Godkin are most easily read about in Allan Nevins, *The Evening Post: A Century of Journalism* (New York: Boni and Liveright, 1922). The McCormick and Patterson families and their Chicago *Tribune* and New York *Daily News* are analyzed by John Tebbel in *An American Dynasty* (New York: Doubleday, 1947).

The best autobiographies are Benjamin Franklin, *Autobiography* (New York: Putnam, 1909); *The Autobiography of William Allen White* (New York: Macmillan, 1946); *The Autobiography of Lincoln Steffens* (New York: Harcourt, Brace, 1931); *Damned Old Crank: A Self-Portrait of E. W. Scripps* (New York: Harper, 1951), edited from Scripps' writings by Charles R. McCabe; Horace Greeley, *Recollections of a Busy Life* (New York: Ford, 1868); Fremont Older, *My Own Story* (New York: Macmillan, 1926), the memoirs of a crusading San Francisco editor; Josephus Daniels, *Tar Heel Editor* (Chapel Hill: University of North Carolina Press, 1939), volume one of a five-volume series; and E. W. Howe, *Plain People* (New York: Dodd, Mead, 1929), the story of a Kansas editor and his readers.

Excellent reminiscences of newsmen include Melville E. Stone, *Fifty Years a Journalist* (New York: Doubleday, Page, 1921); Will Irwin, *The Making of a Reporter* (New York: Putnam, 1942); Webb Miller, *I Found No Peace*

(New York: Simon and Schuster, 1936); and Vincent Sheean, *Personal History* (New York: Doubleday, Doran, 1935).

Lee G. Miller, *The Story of Ernie Pyle* (New York: Viking, 1950), is very readable. Ishbel Ross, *Ladies of the Press* (New York: Harper, 1936), tells the story of dozens of women journalists. Three good accounts of Civil War reporting are Louis M. Starr, *Bohemian Brigade* (New York: Knopf, 1954); J. Cutler Andrews, *The North Reports the Civil War* (Pittsburgh: University of Pittsburgh Press, 1955); and Emmet Crozier, *Yankee Reporters, 1861–65* (New York: Oxford, 1956). Crozier also wrote *American Reporters on the Western Front, 1914–18* (New York: Oxford, 1959).

Among important histories of individual newspapers are Frank M. O'Brien's *The Story of the Sun* (New York: Appleton, 1928), covering the New York *Sun* from 1833 to 1928; Gerald W. Johnson and others, *The Sunpapers of Baltimore, 1837–1937* (New York: Knopf, 1937); Meyer Berger, *The Story of the New York Times* (New York: Simon and Schuster, 1951); Erwin D. Canham, *Commitment to Freedom: The Story of the Christian Science Monitor* (Boston: Houghton Mifflin, 1958); Will C. Conrad, Kathleen F. Wilson, and Dale Wilson, *The Milwaukee Journal: The First Eighty Years* (Madison: University of Wisconsin Press, 1964); and Jim A. Hart, *A History of the St. Louis Globe-Democrat* (Columbia: University of Missouri Press, 1961).

Magazine editors and publishers are the subjects of books by Oswald Garrison Villard, *Fighting Years* (New York: Harcourt, Brace, 1939), the memoirs of the editor of the *Nation;* Peter Lyon, *Success Story: The Life and Times of S. S. McClure* (New York: Scribner's, 1963); S. S. McClure, *My Autobiography* (New York: Stokes, 1914); John Tebbel, *George Horace Lorimer and the Saturday Evening Post* (New York: Doubleday, 1949); Edward W. Bok, *The Americanization of Edward Bok* (New York: Scribner, 1921), autobiography of the *Ladies' Home Journal* editor; George Britt, *Forty Years—Forty Millions: The Career of Frank A. Munsey* (New York: Farrar and Rinehart, 1935); and James Thurber, *The Years with Ross* (Boston: Little, Brown, 1957), the story of editor Harold Ross and the *New Yorker.*

Sensationalism in the news is treated by Simon M. Bessie in *Jazz Journalism: The Story of the Tabloid Newspapers* (New York: Dutton, 1938) and by Helen M. Hughes in *News and the Human Interest Story* (Chicago: University of Chicago Press, 1940), a sociological study of news. Specialized reporting has been treated in monograph form only for the field of science, by Hillier Krieghbaum in his *American Newspaper Reporting of Science News* (Manhattan: Kansas State College, 1941), *When Doctors Meet Reporters* (New York: New York University Press, 1957), and *Science, the News, and the Public* (New York: New York University Press, 1958). Chapter 25 of Emery, *The Press and America,* treats the growth of specialized reporting in several fields, as do several chapters in Phillip H. Ault and Edwin Emery, *Reporting the News* (New York: Dodd, Mead, 1959).

News magazines are discussed in James Playsted Wood, *Magazines in the United States;* Theodore Peterson, *Magazines in the Twentieth Century;* and Stewart and Tebbel, *Makers of Modern Journalism.* Victor Rosewater's *History of Co-operative News-Gathering in the United States* is supplemented by two histories sponsored by the press associations: Oliver Gramling, *AP: The Story of News* (New York: Farrar and Rinehart, 1940), and Joe Alex Morris, *Deadline Every Minute: The Story of the United Press* (New York: Doubleday, 1957).

Chapter 6

Radio, Television, and Film

The best historical accounts are found in Sydney W. Head, *Broadcasting in America,* and Llewellyn White, *The American Radio.* Chapter 1 of Mitchell V. Charnley's *News by Radio* (New York: Macmillan, 1948) traces the history of radio news. Francis Chase Jr., *Sound and Fury* (New York: Harper, 1942), is an informal history of radio.

Biographies include John Tebbel, *Putting Electrons to Work: David Sarnoff* (New York: Encyclopaedia Britannica Press, 1963); Roger Burlingame, *Don't Let Them Scare You: The Life and Times of Elmer Davis* (Philadelphia: Lippincott, 1961); and chapters on H. V. Kaltenborn, Gabriel Heatter, Fulton Lewis Jr., and Raymond Gram Swing in David Bulman's *Molders of Opinion* (Milwaukee: Bruce, 1945). Autobiographies are *Father of Radio: The Autobiography of Lee De Forest* (Chicago: Wilcox & Follett, 1950) and H. V. Kaltenborn, *Fifty Fabulous Years, 1900–1950: A Personal Review* (New York: Putnam's, 1950).

Relationships with government are analyzed in Walter B. Emery, *Broadcasting and Government* (East Lansing: Michigan State University Press, 1961), the best source; John E. Coons, editor, *Freedom and Responsibility in Broadcasting* (Evanston, Ill.: Northwestern University Press, 1962); Harvey J. Levin, *Broadcast Regulation and Joint Ownership of Media* (New York: New York University Press, 1960); and by Head and White.

Educational uses of television are examined in Wilbur Schramm, editor, *The Impact of Educational Television* (Urbana: University of Illinois Press, 1960); Wilbur Schramm, Jack Lyle, and Ithiel de Sola Pool, *The People Look at Educational Television* (Stanford, Calif.: Stanford University Press, 1963); and Charles A. Siepmann, *TV and Our School Crisis* (New York: Dodd, Mead, 1958), a report on uses of television as a teaching instrument.

Rosenberg and White, *Mass Culture: The Popular Arts in America,* examines radio and television, motion pictures, and the mass literature (books, detective fiction, comic books, cartoon strips, and magazines). Wilbur Schramm, *Mass Communications,* offers readings on the entertainment media.

Motion pictures: *Film: An Anthology,* edited by Daniel Talbot (New York: Simon and Schuster, 1959), contains readings on aesthetics, social commentary, and analysis; theory and technique of film making; and history and personal reminiscences. Roger Manvell, *The Film and the Public* (London: Penguin, 1955), is critical in tone. Rotha and Griffith, *The Film Till Now,* and Griffith and Mayer, *The Movies,* are the leading historical surveys.

The history of documentary films is told by Paul Rotha, Sinclair Road, and Richard Griffith in *Documentary Film* (New York: Hastings House, 1964). Newsreels are the subject of one chapter in Drewry, *More Post Biographies.*

Part Three

CURRENT PROBLEMS AND CRITICISMS

An excellent basis for any discussion of the duties and the performance record of the mass media is the summary report of the Commission on Freedom of the Press, *A Free and Responsible Press* (see bibliographical note for Part I). The commission sponsored publication of four studies already cited, Chafee's *Government and Mass Communications,* Hocking's *Freedom of the Press,* White's *The American Radio,* and Ruth Inglis' *Freedom of the Movies,* as well as *Peoples Speaking to Peoples,* by Llewellyn White and Robert D. Leigh (Chicago: University of Chicago Press, 1946), an analysis of international news channels.

Wilbur Schramm's *Responsibility in Mass Communications* is the best general study of media ethics. J. Edward Gerald's *The Social Responsibility of the Press* (Minneapolis: University of Minnesota Press, 1963) examines the press as a commercial as well as a professional agency and argues for a higher degree of professionalization. Curtis D. MacDougall, *The Press and Its Problems* (Dubuque, Iowa: Wm. C. Brown, 1964) is an up-dated version of his *Newsroom Problems and Policies.* Lucy M. Salmon's *The Newspaper and the Historian* (New York: Oxford, 1923) is a classical historical study which analyzes the position of editors, critics, and advertisers, and the authenticity and authoritativeness of the press.

Criticisms of press performance are found in *The Press in Perspective,* edited by Ralph D. Casey (Baton Rouge: Louisiana State University Press, 1963), a series of 17 lectures by leading journalists at University of Minnesota over 16 years; *Social Responsibility of the Newspress* (Milwaukee: Marquette University Press, 1962), a group of talks by leading newsmen and educators; and Dan Lacy, *Freedom and Communications* (Urbana: University of Illinois Press, 1961), an analysis and forecast. Bird and Merwin, *The Press and Society,* and Wilbur Schramm, *Mass Communications,* offer selected readings of wide variety on media performance. A book of essays edited by Wesley C. Clark, *Journalism Tomorrow* (Syracuse, N.Y.: Syracuse University Press, 1958), discusses the futures of newspapers, radio, television, magazines, advertising, press associations and syndicates, photojournalism, and mass communications research.

The Continuing Study of Newspaper Reading, sponsored by the American Newspaper Publishers Association and the Advertising Research Foundation from 1939 to 1952 and covering readership studies of 142 newspapers, offers evidence of readership trends. The results were analyzed by Charles E. Swanson in "What They Read in 130 Daily Newspapers," Fall 1955 *Journalism Quarterly*.

Historical trends in concentration of newspaper ownership are reported in chapters 22 and 27 of Emery, *The Press and America,* and by Raymond B. Nixon in the Winter 1961 *Journalism Quarterly*. The subject of competitive vs. non-competitive dailies is analyzed by Nixon in the Fall 1954 *Journalism Quarterly* and by Nixon and Robert L. Jones in the Summer 1956 issue.

Two interesting studies of press performance during political campaigns are Nathan B. Blumberg's *One Party Press?* (Lincoln: University of Nebraska Press, 1954), a report on how 35 metropolitan dailies covered 1952 presidential campaign news, and Arthur E. Rowse's *Slanted News: A Case Study of the Nixon and Stevenson Fund Stories* (Boston: Beacon Press, 1957), an analysis of how 31 metropolitan dailies reported an episode in the 1956 campaign. News coverage of the 1960 election is analyzed by Wayne A. Danielson and John B. Adams in "Completeness of Press Coverage of the 1960 Campaign," Autumn 1961 *Journalism Quarterly,* and by Guido H. Stempel III in "The Prestige Press Covers the 1960 Presidential Campaign," Spring 1961 *Journalism Quarterly*. The shift in editorial page support in the 1964 election is reported in Edwin Emery, "Press Support for Johnson and Goldwater," Autumn 1964 *Journalism Quarterly,* together with a historical summary. Stempel re-examines "The Prestige Press" in the 1964 campaign in the Winter 1965 *Journalism Quarterly*.

Among professionals' criticisms, Herbert Brucker's *Freedom of Information* is an enlightened defense and analysis of the newspaper press. By contrast Carl E. Lindstrom uses for the title of his book *The Fading American Newspaper* (New York: Doubleday, 1960). Stanley Walker explains the problems facing editors in *City Editor* (New York: Stokes, 1934); he held that post on the New York *Herald Tribune*. A. J. Liebling brought together his satirical articles on press shortcomings written for the *New Yorker* in *The Wayward Pressman* (New York: Doubleday, 1948), devoted heavily to New York papers. Silas Bent, *Ballyhoo* (New York: Liveright, 1927), is strongly critical of the newspaper press of its day, as are Upton Sinclair's *The Brass Check* (Pasadena, Calif.: Published by the author, 1920) and George Seldes' *Freedom of the Press* (Indianapolis, Ind.: Bobbs-Merrill, 1935). Oswald Garrison Villard, *The Disappearing Daily* (New York: Knopf, 1944), and Morris L. Ernst, *The First Freedom* (New York: Macmillan, 1946), exhibit a critical concern over newspaper ownership concentration trends but are not statistically accurate.

Advertising: Neil H. Borden, *The Economic Effects of Advertising* (Chicago: Irwin, 1942) is a lengthy study of the role advertising plays in the national economy; a portion is reprinted in Wilbur Schramm, *Mass Communications*. E. S. Turner, *The Shocking History of Advertising* (New York: Dutton, 1953), is constructively critical; so is Martin Mayer, *Madison Avenue, U.S.A.* (New York: Harper, 1958), primarily a study of advertising agencies. Vance Packard assigned almost unlimited powers to advertising men in *The Hidden Persuaders* (New York: McKay, 1957). Both the Mayer and Packard books are available in pocket book editions.

Radio and television: Gary Steiner, *The People Look at Television: A Study of Audience Attitudes* (New York: Knopf, 1963), is based on extensive research. Leo Bogart, *The Age of Television* (New York: Frederick Ungar, 1956), objectively analyzes scores of research studies seeking to determine the impact of television on American society. Charles A. Siepmann, *Radio, Television, and Society* (New York: Oxford, 1950), analyzes the influence of radio and television on tastes, opinions, and values. Sydney Head, *Broadcasting in America,* also offers criticism of the two media.

Newspapers: Helen M. Hughes, *News and the Human Interest Story,* is the best analysis of the entertainment role of news. Coulton Waugh, *The Comics* (New York: Macmillan, 1947), is an entertaining history of newspaper comic strips. Stephen Becker, *Comic Art in America* (New York: Simon and Schuster, 1959), surveys comic strips, political cartoons, magazine humor, and animated cartoons. David M. White and Robert H. Abel, *The Funnies: An American Idiom* (New York: Free Press of Glencoe, 1963), reports on a major research project.

The only book-length critical study of a newspaper trade association or organization is Edwin Emery's *History of the American Newspaper Publishers Association* (Minneapolis: University of Minnesota Press, 1950). Discussions involving press criticism are to be found in the American Society of Newspaper Editors' *Bulletin* and *Problems of Journalism* series, in the Associated Press Managing Editors Association's *APME Red Book* series, and in the periodicals *Journalism Quarterly, Columbia Journalism Review, Nieman Reports, Masthead, Guild Reporter, Quill,* and *Editor & Publisher.* The Nieman Fellows, newsmen studying at Harvard University, have produced *Newsmen's Holiday* (Cambridge, Mass.: Harvard University Press, 1942) and *Your Newspaper,* edited by Leon Svirsky (New York: Macmillan, 1947), two series of essays on journalistic practices.

Part Four

THE MASS COMMUNICATIONS INDUSTRIES AND PROFESSIONS

The listings in this section are confined to books dealing with the operations of the mass communications industries and professions, and books describing professional techniques and qualifications. For histories of the various media see the bibliography for Part II; for books dealing with the role of the mass media in society and with media performance see the bibliographies for Part I and Part III. Research journals, professional journals, trade publications, and directories for the various fields of mass communications are listed at the opening of the bibliography.

Chapter 9

Newspapers

Textbooks on reporting and newswriting: Phillip H. Ault and Edwin Emery, *Reporting the News* (New York: Dodd, Mead, 1959), offers a strong emphasis on newsgathering and reporting techniques and descriptions of newspaper work. Curtis D. MacDougall, *Interpretative Reporting* (New York: Macmillan, 1963), and Carl N. Warren, *Modern News Reporting* (New York: Harper, 1959), have been widely used since they first appeared in the early 1930's. Other current leading texts are Mitchell V. Charnley, *Reporting* (New York: Holt, 1959); John Hohenberg, *The Professional Journalist* (New York: Holt, 1960); Laurence R. Campbell and Roland E. Wolseley, *How to Report and Write the News* (Englewood Cliffs, N.J.: Prentice-Hall, 1961); Charles H. Brown, *Informing the People* (New York: Holt, 1957); Chilton R. Bush, *The Art of News Communication* (New York: Appleton-Century-Crofts, 1954), restricted to the area of newswriting; Charles C. Clayton, *Newspaper Reporting Today* (New York: Odyssey, 1947); Grant M. Hyde, *Newspaper Reporting* (New York: Prentice-Hall, 1952); and John Paul Jones, *The Modern Reporter's Handbook* (New York: Rinehart, 1949). A valuable adjunct to the reporting texts is E. L. Callihan, *Grammar for Journalists* (New York: Ronald, 1957).

Special fields of reporting and writing: William L. Rivers, *The Mass Media: Reporting, Writing, Editing* (New York: Harper & Row, 1964), covers newspapers, magazines, radio; Neal Copple, *Depth Reporting* (Englewood Cliffs, N.J.: Prentice-Hall, 1964); Robert D. Murphy, *Reporting Public Problems* (Philadelphia: Chilton, 1960); Chilton R. Bush, *Newspaper Reporting of Public Affairs* (New York: Appleton-Century-Crofts, 1951); Victor J. Danilov, *Public Affairs Reporting* (New York: Macmillan, 1955); Curtis D. MacDougall, *Covering the Courts* (New York: Prentice-Hall, 1946); Harry Heath and Lou Gelfand, *How to Cover, Write and Edit Sports* (Ames: Iowa State University Press, 1957); Rodney Fox, *Agricultural and Technical Journalism* (New York: Prentice-Hall, 1952); Roland E. Wolseley, *Critical Writing for the Journalist* (Philadelphia: Chilton, 1959).

News editing and copyreading: Bruce Westley, *News Editing* (Boston: Houghton Mifflin, 1953); Howard B. Taylor and Jacob Scher, *Copy Reading and News Editing* (New York: Prentice-Hall, 1951); George C. Bastian, Leland D. Case, and Floyd Baskette, *Editing the Day's News* (New York: Macmillan, 1956); Charles H. Brown, *News Editing and Display* (New York: Harper, 1952); Robert E. Garst and Theodore M. Bernstein, *Headlines and Deadlines* (New York: Columbia University Press, 1961); Norman Radder and John E. Stempel, *Newspaper Editing, Makeup and Headlines* (New York: McGraw-Hill, 1942).

Photojournalism: Robert B. Rhode and Floyd H. McCall, *Press Photography* (New York: Macmillan, 1961); Rodney Fox and Robert Kerns,

Creative News Photography (Ames: Iowa State University Press, 1961); Joseph Costa, editor, *The Complete Book of Press Photography* (New York: National Press Photographers Association, 1950); Wilson Hicks, *Words and Pictures* (New York: Harper, 1952); Stanley E. Kalish and Clifton C. Edom, *Picture Editing* (New York: Rinehart, 1951).

Community journalism: Kenneth R. Byerly, *Community Journalism* (Philadelphia: Chilton, 1961); Thomas F. Barnhart, *Weekly Newspaper Writing and Editing* (New York: Dryden, 1949) and *Weekly Newspaper Management* (New York: Appleton-Century-Crofts, 1952); Morris Janowitz, *The Community Press in an Urban Setting* (Glencoe, Ill.: The Free Press, 1952).

Production: Allan Woods, *Modern Newspaper Production* (New York: Harper & Row, 1963).

Advertising and management: Frank Thayer, *Newspaper Business Management* (New York: Prentice-Hall, 1954); Frank W. Rucker and Herbert Lee Williams, *Newspaper Organization and Management* (Ames: Iowa State College Press, 1955); Frank W. Rucker, *Newspaper Circulation* (Ames: Iowa State College Press, 1958); John V. Lund, *Newspaper Advertising* (New York: Prentice-Hall, 1947); Leslie W. McClure, *Newspaper Advertising and Promotion* (New York: Macmillan, 1950); Stewart Harral, *Profitable Public Relations for Newspapers* (Ann Arbor, Mich.: J. W. Edwards, 1957); Ralph E. Dyar, *Newspaper Promotion and Research* (New York: Harper, 1942).

Books by professionals: Joseph and Stewart Alsop, *The Reporter's Trade* (New York: Reynal, 1958), a discussion of reporting and a compilation of Alsop columns; Joseph G. Herzberg, *Late City Edition* (New York: Holt, 1947), describing reportorial work on the New York *Herald Tribune;* and *The Newspaper: Its Making and Its Meaning* (New York: Scribner's, 1945), by staff members of the New York *Times.*

Chapter 10

Television and Radio

Introductory books for the broadcasting field include Giraud Chester, Garnet R. Garrison, and Edgar Willis, *Television and Radio* (New York: Appleton-Century-Crofts, 1963); Robert L. Hilliard, editor, *Understanding Television: An Introduction to Broadcasting* (New York: Hastings House, 1964); and Waldo Abbot and Richard L. Rider, *Handbook of Broadcasting* (New York: McGraw-Hill, 1957).

Books which deal with television news are *Television News Reporting* (New York: McGraw-Hill, 1958), an excellent survey by the CBS News staff; Bob Siller, Ted White, and Hal Terkel, *Television and Radio News* (New York: Macmillan, 1960); Baskett Mosse and Fred Whiting, editors, *Television News Handbook* (Evanston, Ill.: Medill School of Journalism,

Northwestern University, 1953), with articles by professionals; and Donald E. Brown and John Paul Jones, *Radio and Television News* (New York: Rinehart, 1954), a classroom exercise book with how-to-do-it chapters by professionals.

Books dealing only with radio news include William F. Brooks, *Radio News Writing* (New York: McGraw-Hill, 1948); Mitchell V. Charnley, *News by Radio* (New York: Macmillan, 1948); Baskett Mosse, *Radio News Handbook* (Evanston, Ill.: Medill School of Journalism, Northwestern University, 1947); Carl N. Warren, *Radio News Writing and Editing* (New York: Harper, 1947); and Paul W. White, *News on the Air* (New York: Harcourt, Brace, 1947).

The production area is treated in Rudy Bretz, *The Techniques of Television Production* (New York: McGraw-Hill, 1962); Edward Stasheff and Rudy Bretz, *The Television Program: Its Direction and Production* (New York: Hill & Wang, 1962); Samuel L. Becker and H. Clay Harshbarger, *Television: Techniques for Planning and Performance* (New York: Holt, 1958); and Carroll O'Meara, *Television Program Production* (New York: Ronald, 1955). Arthur L. Gaskill and David A. Englander cover newsfilm production in *How to Shoot a Movie Story* (New York: Morgan and Morgan, 1959).

The advertising area is described in Eugene F. Seehafer and Jack W. Laemmar, *Successful Television and Radio Advertising* (New York: McGraw-Hill, 1959); Clark M. Agnew and Neil O'Brien, *Television Advertising* (New York: McGraw-Hill, 1958); Irving Settel, Norman Glenn, and associates, *Television Advertising and Production Handbook* (New York: Crowell, 1953); and Harry W. McMahan, *The Television Commercial* (New York: Hastings House, 1957).

Chapter 11

Magazines

An introduction to the magazine field is provided by Roland E. Wolseley's *The Magazine World* (New York: Prentice-Hall, 1951), which treats editorial and business operations of consumer, business, and specialized periodicals. It is out-dated in some aspects.

Views of specialized magazine work can be obtained from Rowena Ferguson, *Editing the Small Magazine* (New York: Columbia University Press, 1958, paperback 1963); DeWitt C. Reddick and Alfred A. Crowell, *Industrial Editing: Creative Communication through Company Publications* (New York: Bender, 1962); Bernard Smith, *Industrial Editing* (New York: Pitman, 1961); William C. Halley, *Employee Publications* (Philadelphia: Chilton, 1959); Garth Bentley, *Editing the Company Publication* (New York: Harper, 1953); Julien Elfenbein, *Business Journalism* (New York: Harper, 1960); Russell N. Baird and Arthur T. Turnbull, *Industrial and Business Journalism* (Philadelphia: Chilton, 1961); James McCloskey, *Industrial Journalism Today* (New York: Harper, 1959); and Delbert McGuire, *Technical and Industrial Journalism* (Harrisburg, Pa.: Stackpole, 1956).

Textbooks on magazine writing include Clarence A. Schoenfeld, *Effective Feature Writing* (New York: Harper, 1960); Helen M. Patterson, *Writing and Selling Feature Articles* (New York: Prentice-Hall, 1956); DeWitt C. Reddick, *Modern Feature Writing* (New York: Harper, 1949); and George L. Bird, *Article Writing and Marketing* (New York: Rinehart, 1956). Richard Gehman, *How to Write and Sell Magazine Articles* (New York: Harper, 1959), tells the story of a successful free lancer. Glenn Gundell, editor, *Writing—From Idea to Printed Page* (New York: Doubleday, 1949), contains case histories of three stories and three articles which appeared in the *Saturday Evening Post.* Arthur C. Wimer, *Writing for the Business Press* (Dubuque, Iowa: William C. Brown, 1950), contains contributions from 100 editors and publishers.

Chapter 12

Book Publishing

A well-rounded picture of the trade or general side of the book publishing industry is given by a score of specialists in *What Happens in Book Publishing,* edited by Chandler B. Grannis (New York: Columbia University Press, 1957). Two stimulating collections of articles have been edited by Gerald Gross in *Editors on Editing* (New York: Grosset and Dunlap, 1962) and *Publishers on Publishing* (New York: Bowker, 1961).

The *Bowker Lectures on Book Publishing* (New York: Bowker, 1957) surveys American publishing over the past quarter century. O. H. Cheney, *Economic Survey of the Book Industry, 1930–1931, as Prepared for the National Association of Book Publishers,* with 1960 Introduction by Robert W. Frase, gives comparative statistics for 1930–1959.

Sir Stanley Unwin, *The Truth About Publishing* (New York: Bowker, 1950), is basic, brief, and highly readable. Julie Eidesheim, *Editor at Work* (New York: Rinehart, 1939), describes what book editing really is like. William Jovanovich, *Now, Barabbas* (New York: Harper, 1964) presents thoughtful essays on his field by a publishing executive.

Roger Smith, ed., *The American Reading Public: A Symposium* (New York: Bowker, 1964), is a particularly succinct and useful collection of authoritative essays by a number of publishing executives.

Chapter 13

The Film

Joseph and Harry Feldman, *Dynamics of the Film* (New York: Hermitage House, 1952), provides a popular explanation of the art of the film and of entertainment film making. The standard work on the history, principles, and technique of the documentary motion picture is Paul Rotha, Sinclair Road, and Richard Griffith, *The Documentary Film* (New York: Hastings House, 1964).

Gloria Waldon, *The Information Film* (New York: Columbia University Press, 1949), is one of the best books on that topic and has an extensive bibliography. *The Dollars and Sense of Business Films* (New York: Association of National Advertisers, 1954) is based upon a survey of makers of 157 sponsored films, and reports in detail on production, distribution, and audiences.

Readings on both entertainment films and documentaries are found in *Film: An Anthology,* edited by Daniel Talbot.

Chapter 14

Press Associations and Feature Syndicates

There is no book as yet describing the press associations. Frank Luther Mott paints a picture of the Associated Press operation in a chapter of *The News in America.* Ault and Emery discuss reporting for press associations in a chapter of *Reporting the News;* Emery traces their history in *The Press and America;* and Ault tells youthful readers how big stories are covered in *News Around the Clock* (New York: Dodd, Mead, 1960).

Oliver Gramling, *AP: The Story of News,* and Joe Alex Morris, *Deadline Every Minute: The Story of the United Press,* capture a good deal of the reportorial excitement of the press associations. Hugh Baillie, *High Tension* (New York: Harper, 1959), is the readable autobiography of a former president of UP. *Kent Cooper and the Associated Press* (New York: Random House, 1959) is the second personal account by the most famous general manager of AP; the first, *Barriers Down* (New York: Farrar and Rinehart, 1942), is Cooper's story of his effort to break up international news monopolies. Melville E. Stone, *Fifty Years a Journalist,* is the autobiography of the first AP general manager.

A UNESCO publication, *News Agencies: Their Structure and Operation* (New York: Columbia University Press, 1953), gives summary accounts of AP, UP, and INS and analyzes other world news agencies. John C. Merrill, Marvin Alisky, and Carter R. Bryan, *The Foreign Press* (Baton Rouge: Louisiana State University Press, 1963), includes world news agencies in its over-all picture. UNESCO's *World Communications: Press, Radio, Television, Film* (New York: UNESCO, 1964) is a reference work for international communications. John C. Merrill, *A Handbook of the Foreign Press* (Baton Rouge: Louisiana State University Press, 1959), deals chiefly with newspapers with some emphasis on magazines, and is illustrated with front pages. John Hohenberg covers foreign correspondence generally in *Foreign Correspondents—The Great Reporters and Their Times* (New York: Columbia University Press, 1964).

A good picture of the variety of the feature syndicates can be obtained by scanning the annual *Syndicate Directory* issued by *Editor & Publisher* as a supplement to a July issue.

Chapter 15

Advertising

Among the general text and reference books on advertising are Charles H. Sandage and Vernon Fryburger, *Advertising Theory and Practice* (Homewood, Ill.: Irwin, 1963); Harry W. Hepner, *Advertising: Creative Communication with Consumers* (New York: McGraw-Hill, 1964); John S. Wright and Daniel S. Warner, *Advertising* (New York: McGraw-Hill, 1962); C. A. Kirkpatrick, *Advertising* (Boston: Houghton Mifflin, 1964); S. Watson Dunn, *Advertising: Its Role in Modern Marketing* (New York: Holt, Rinehart and Winston, 1961); Albert W. Frey, *Advertising* (New York: Ronald, 1961); Woodrow Wirsig, editor, *Principles of Advertising* (New York: Pitman, 1964). An older widely used reference is Otto Kleppner, *Advertising Procedure* (New York: Prentice-Hall, 1950).

Two collections of readings are Wright and Warner, *Speaking of Advertising* (New York: McGraw-Hill, 1963), and Sandage and Fryburger, *The Role of Advertising: A Book of Readings* (Homewood, Ill.: Irwin, 1960). *Printers' Ink* issued a 474-page supplement to its June 14, 1963, issue called *Advertising Today, Yesterday, Tomorrow,* an excellent survey. *Advertising Age* issued a 340-page special issue January 15, 1963, entitled *The World of Advertising,* a comprehensive survey.

Media is the topic of Roger Barton, *Media in Advertising* (New York: McGraw-Hill, 1964); Leslie McClure and Paul C. Fulton, *Advertising in the Printed Media* (New York: Macmillan, 1964); and Ben Duffy, *Advertising Media and Markets* (New York: Prentice-Hall, 1951).

Copy writing is described by John W. Crawford in *Advertising: Communications for Management* (Boston: Allyn and Bacon, 1960); Philip Ward Burton and G. Bowman Kreer, *Advertising Copywriting* (Englewood Cliffs, N.J.: Prentice-Hall, 1962); Clyde Bedell, *How to Write Advertising That Sells* (New York: McGraw-Hill, 1952), and S. Watson Dunn, *Advertising Copy and Communication* (New York: McGraw-Hill, 1956). Advertising production is explained in Thomas B. Stanley, *The Technique of Advertising Production* (New York: Prentice-Hall, 1954), and David Hymes, *Production in Advertising and the Graphic Arts* (New York: Holt, 1958). Both fields are covered in Hugh G. Wales, Dwight L. Gentry, and Max Wales, *Advertising Copy, Layout and Typography* (New York: Ronald, 1958).

Martin Mayer, *Madison Avenue, U.S.A.,* provides a good current picture of advertising agencies. Ralph M. Hower, *The History of an Advertising Agency: N. W. Ayer & Son at Work, 1869–1939* (Cambridge, Mass.: Harvard University Press, 1939), is a documented history of one. David Ogilvy tells a fascinating story about life in an agency in *Confessions of an Advertising Man* (New York: Atheneum, 1963; paperback, Dell, 1964). The story of the pioneering Albert Lasker is told by John Gunther in *Taken at the Flood* (New York: Harper, 1960).

For books about newspaper advertising and television and radio advertising, see the bibliographies for chapters 9 and 10, respectively. The industrial advertising field is described in Fred R. Messner, *Industrial Advertising* (New York: McGraw-Hill, 1961); Roland B. Smith, *Advertising to Business* (Homewood, Ill.: Irwin, 1957); Julian Boone, editor, *Industrial Advertising Handbook* (New York: McGraw-Hill, 1953); and Warren R. Dix, *Industrial Advertising for Profit and Prestige* (Pleasantville, N.Y.: Printers' Ink Books, 1956).

Chapter 16

Public Relations and Information Writing

The best book to read in exploring the public relations field is Scott M. Cutlip and Allen H. Center, *Effective Public Relations* (Englewood Cliffs, N.J.: Prentice-Hall, 1964). It surveys the history, theory, and contemporary practices of public relations.

Other general books include Bertrand R. Canfield, *Public Relations: Principles, Cases, and Problems* (Homewood, Ill.: Irwin, 1964); John Marston, *The Nature of Public Relations* (New York: McGraw-Hill, 1963); Gene Harlan and Alan Scott, *Contemporary Public Relations: Principles and Cases* (New York: Prentice-Hall, 1955); William A. Nielander and Raymond W. Miller, *Public Relations* (New York: Ronald, 1951); Charles S. Steinberg, *The Mass Communicators: Public Relations, Public Opinion, and Mass Media* (New York: Harper, 1958); J. Handly Wright and Byron H. Christian, *Public Relations in Management* (New York: McGraw-Hill, 1949); Louis B. Lundborg, *Public Relations in the Local Community* (New York: Harper, 1950); and Allen H. Center, *Public Relations Ideas in Action* (New York: McGraw-Hill, 1957), which describes some 50 successful public relations projects.

Groups of public relations professionals contributed chapters for *Public Relations Handbook*, edited by Philip Lesly (Englewood Cliffs, N.J.: Prentice-Hall, 1962), and *Handbook of Public Relations*, edited by Howard Stephenson (Englewood Cliffs, N.J.: Prentice-Hall, 1960). A leading counselor, John W. Hill, tells his story in *The Making of a Public Relations Man* (New York: McKay, 1963). New York's practitioners are described by Irwin Ross in *The Image Merchants* (New York: Doubleday, 1959). Edward L. Bernays, in *Public Relations* (Norman: University of Oklahoma Press, 1952), presents a case-history type of discussion by a longtime practitioner. His memoirs are in *Biography of an Idea* (New York: Simon and Schuster, 1965).

Publicity practices are described in Clarence A. Schoenfeld, *Publicity Media and Methods* (New York: Macmillan, 1963); Stewart Harral, *Patterns of Publicity Copy* (Norman: University of Oklahoma Press, 1950); Herbert M. Baus, *Publicity in Action* (New York: Harper, 1954); and Howard Stephenson and Wesley F. Pratzner, *Publicity for Prestige and Profit* (New York: McGraw-Hill, 1953). Among books on specialized subjects are James

L. McCamy, *Government Publicity* (Chicago: University of Chicago Press, 1939); Benjamin Fine, *Educational Publicity* (New York: Harper, 1951); and Harold P. Levy, *Public Relations for Social Agencies* (New York: Harper, 1956). References for other areas may be found in Scott M. Cutlip, *A Public Relations Bibliography* (Madison: University of Wisconsin Press, 1957).

Chapter 17

Mass Communications Research

The reader interested in this field can gain an impression of its scope and methods by examining *Introduction to Mass Communications Research,* edited by Ralph O. Nafziger and David M. White (Baton Rouge: Louisiana State University Press, 1963). It has eight chapters by leading research specialists in journalism and mass communications.

A book which describes more varied types of journalism research is *An Introduction to Journalism Research,* edited by Ralph O. Nafziger and Marcus M. Wilkerson (Baton Rouge: Louisiana State University Press, 1949). Wilbur Schramm surveyed "Twenty Years of Journalism Research" in the Spring 1957 *Public Opinion Quarterly* while Allan Nevins discussed "American Journalism and Its Historical Treatment" in the Fall 1959 *Journalism Quarterly.*

Three elementary books which introduce the reader to research methods are David M. White and Seymour Levine, *Elementary Statistics for Journalists* (New York: Macmillan, 1954); Charles H. Backstrom and Gerald D. Hursh, *Survey Research* (Evanston, Ill.: Northwestern University Press, 1963); and Richard W. Budd and Robert K. Thorp, *An Introduction to Content Analysis* (Iowa City: University of Iowa School of Journalism, 1963).

Examples of mass communications research studies involving the media, which illustrate the range of the field, can be found in the *Journalism Quarterly* as follows: Bruce H. Westley and Werner J. Severin, "A Profile of the Daily Newspaper Non-Reader," Winter 1964; Eugene J. Rosi, "How 50 Periodicals and the *Times* Interpreted the Test Ban Controversy," Autumn 1964; Paul J. Deutschmann, "The Mass Media in an Underdeveloped Village," Winter 1963; Walter Wilcox, "Numbers and the News: Graph, Table or Text?," Winter 1964; John T. McNelly, "Meaning Intensity and Interest in Foreign News Topics," Spring 1962; Bradley Greenberg, "Person-to-Person Communication in the Diffusion of News Events," Autumn 1964; Herbert A. Otto, "Sex and Violence on the American Newsstand," Winter 1963; Roy E. Carter Jr. and Peter Clarke, "Why Suburban News Attracts Reader Interest," Autumn 1962; Jack Lyle, "Audience Impact of a Double Newspaper Merger," Spring 1962; Alex Edelstein and J. Blaine Schulz, "The Weekly Newspaper's Leadership Role as Seen by Community Leaders," Autumn 1963.

Many of the references listed for Part I of this bibliography also are pertinent to this chapter, especially those dealing with effects, the communication process, and public opinion.

Part Five

EDUCATION FOR MASS COMMUNICATIONS

The growth of journalism education is reviewed in Albert A. Sutton, *Education for Journalism in the United States from Its Beginning to 1940* (Evanston, Ill.: Northwestern University, 1945).

The Training of Journalists (Paris: UNESCO, 1958) is a world-wide survey on the training of personnel for the mass media. Three American journalism educators wrote chapters: Norval Neil Luxon on recent curricular trends, Burton W. Marvin on education for journalism in the United States, and Harry Heath on radio and television journalism education. Walter Wilcox, *Liberal Education and Professional Journalism Education: A Study in Curriculum Structure* (Iowa City: University of Iowa School of Journalism, 1959), was summarized in the Fall 1958 *Journalism Quarterly.*

Books about career opportunities include Herbert Brucker, *Journalist: Eyewitness to History* (New York: Macmillan, 1962); Edward W. Barrett, editor, *Journalists in Action* (New York: Channel Press, 1963), stories of 63 Columbia University journalism graduates; Leonard E. Ryan and Bernard Ryan Jr., *So You Want to Go into Journalism* (New York: Harper & Row, 1963); Bernard Ryan Jr., *So You Want to Go into Advertising* (New York: Harper, 1961).

Available in paperback are Arville Schaleben's *Your Future in Journalism,* Edward L. Bernays' *Your Future in Public Relations,* and *Your Future in Advertising* (New York: Popular Library, Inc., 355 Lexington Avenue, New York 10017; price 50 cents each).

A 32-page booklet, *Choosing a Career in Journalism,* is available from the American Council on Education for Journalism, Ernie Pyle Hall, Bloomington, Indiana 47405. It outlines the broad scope of the field of journalism, working conditions, pay, personal qualities, and qualifications.

Other pamphlets available are *Finding a Successful Career in the Daily Newspaper Business* (American Newspaper Publishers Association), *Broadcasting the News, Careers in Television,* and *Careers in Radio* (National Association of Broadcasters), *Magazines in America* (Magazine Publishers Association), *Careers in the Business Press* (American Business Press, Inc.), and *Let's Consider Public Relations* (Public Relations Society of America).

Quill & Scroll, University of Iowa, publishes annually *Careers in Journalism,* in magazine form. The Newspaper Fund, Inc., issues a *Journalism Scholarship Guide* annually.

Catalogues describing the curricular offerings of individual schools and departments of journalism are available upon request to the school or department concerned or to the registrar of the institution.

INDEX